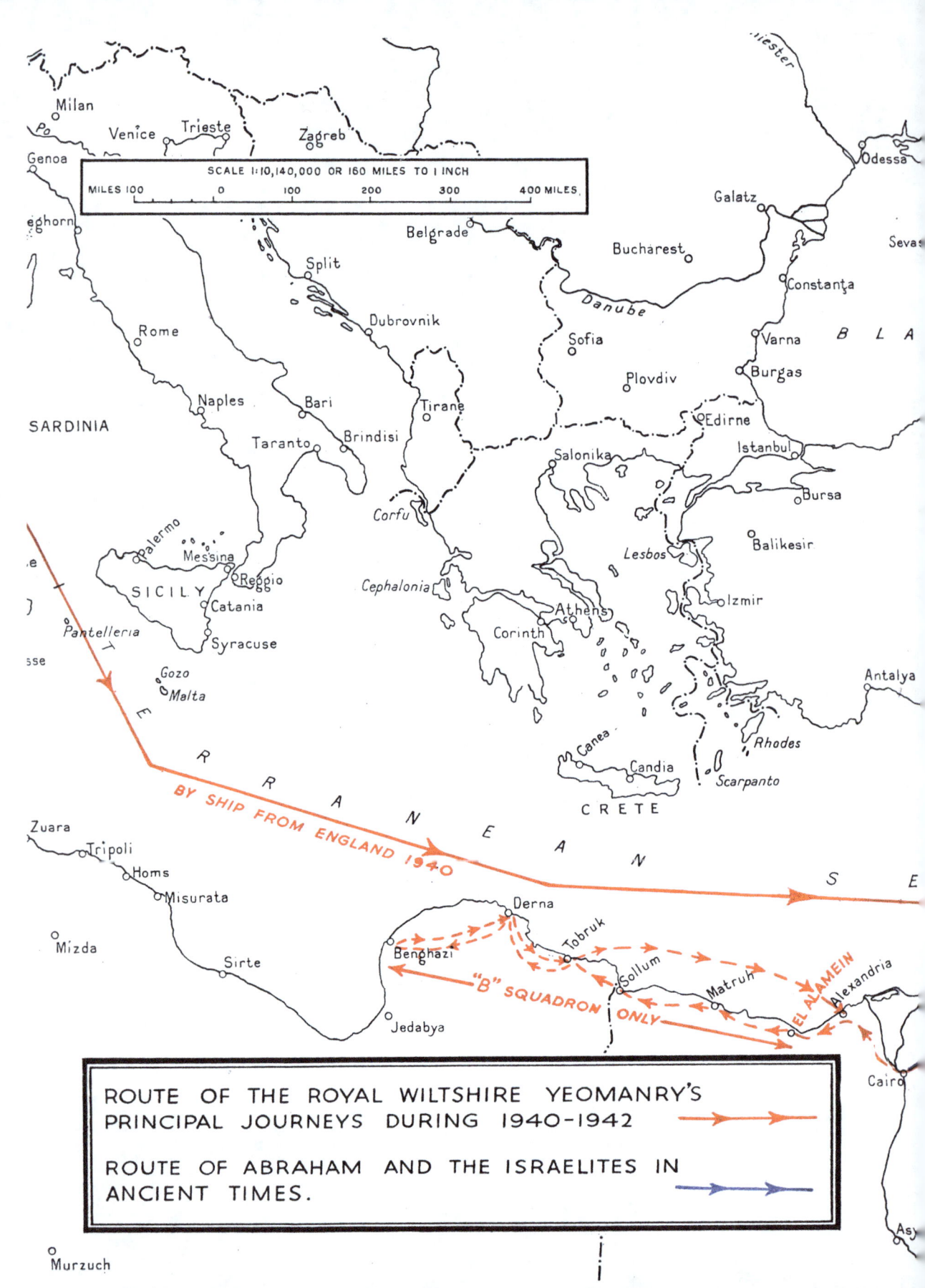

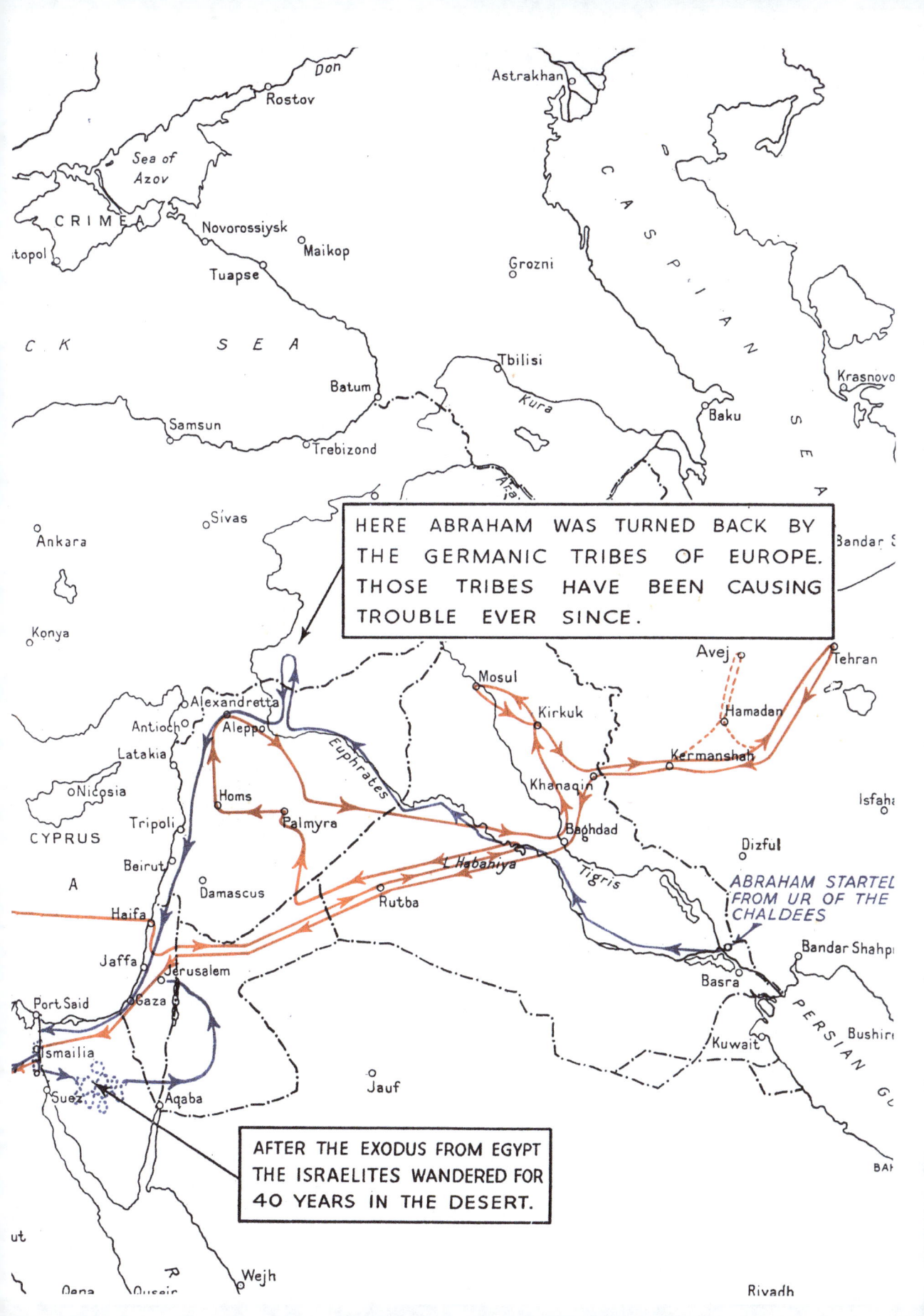

·ROYAL WILTS·

The History of the Royal Wiltshire Yeomanry, 1920-1945

by

Lieut.-Col. P. W. Pitt, T.D.

For
the people of Wiltshire
in the present and the future.

*" Because we forgot our history
we have had to re-live it."*

*Arthur Bryant
in " Years of Victory."*

ROYAL WILTS

by

Lieut.-Colonel P. W. Pitt, T.D.

The Naval & Military Press Ltd

Published by

The Naval & Military Press Ltd
Unit 10 Ridgewood Industrial Park,
Uckfield, East Sussex,
TN22 5QE England

Tel: +44 (0) 1825 749494
Fax: +44 (0) 1825 765701

www.naval-military-press.com
www.military-genealogy.com
www.militarymaproom.com

In reprinting in facsimile from the original, any imperfections are inevitably reproduced and the quality may fall short of modern type and cartographic standards.

· *Foreword* ·

By Lieutenant-General Sir BERNARD FREYBERG, V.C., K.C.B., K.B.E., C.I.A.G., D.S.O.

I am glad that I have been asked to write this Foreword to the History of the Royal Wiltshire Yeomanry. I know, and would like to tell the people of Wiltshire, of the deeds of their men in the battle of El Alamein. I want also to emphasise the friendship which existed in the Western Desert between the men from New Zealand and Wiltshire.

When the Wiltshire Yeomanry were posted to the New Zealand Division in September, 1942, it was for the battle to break through and destroy Rommel's armies. We absorbed these Yeomanry Regiments into our Division. We looked on them, for the time being, as New Zealanders. They shared our common lot in the line, used our Clubs in the rear areas and wore our Fernleaf sign. Of the many regiments which have found their way into the New Zealand circle, there are none with whom we have more in common than the Wiltshire and Warwickshire Yeomanry.

El Alamein was a great victory. History will record its verdict, but it will be a lengthy process. In the meantime, Colonel Pitt's history of the part played by the Royal Wiltshire Yeomanry in the battle of El Alamein fills an immediate need, and I trust it will have a wide circulation.

Although the battle of El Alamein never looked like failing, it did have its critical periods. Colonel Pitt describes how the Wiltshire Yeomanry moved up the axis of the New Zealand Division's attack, supporting our Infantry and guarding them against any possible enemy counter-stroke. This they did with great gallantry, and the first objective of the battle was permanently held.

There is no doubt that the most distinguished action of the Wiltshire Yeomanry was in "Supercharge," the attack of the New Zealand Corps which smashed the line and enabled the British armour to break out. The part they played in this action, although costly, was decisive; in fact it was the action that finally smashed Rommel's armies in the Western Desert.

I am glad to have this opportunity of paying my tribute to the gallantry of Wiltshire men. The farmers from Wiltshire and New Zealand had much in common, and will, I trust, always remember the days when they fought side by side in the Western Desert.

B. C. F.

Headquarters, 2 New Zealand Division,
Florence ——— *Dec. 4th, 1945.*

· *Preface* ·

THIS book contains the story of the Royal Wiltshire Yeomanry from the time when the Regiment was re-formed after the 1914–18 war, until its retirement into " suspended animation " in 1946.

It has been said that general history has no place in a Regimental record. In spite of this, I have included in " Royal Wilts " what seemed to me to be the minimum of historical background necessary for a true appreciation, without reference to other books, of the main and simple story.

I have done this in the hope that the book may be of interest in the future. If we of our generation " forgot our history," it is fair to assume that those who come after us will do the same. In any case the historical sequences can be ignored without the gist of the story being lost.

I have also, when dealing with the important episodes in that story, adopted a similar treatment. Out of the whole vast tapestry of the war, I have tried to sketch in those small portions in which each separate episode took place. I have then, as it were, focussed a magnifying glass upon the particular thread which was followed by the Royal Wilts.

Such a method of handling the story naturally throws considerable emphasis upon the part played by the regiment about which it is written: but that is as it should be in a book of this description. Should it come before the eyes of readers unconnected with Wiltshire, I am confident that it will not be criticised on that account.

All profit from the sale of " Royal Wilts " will go to Service charities.

Apart from those within the Regiment whose assistance has been invaluable during the production of this book, I wish to offer my most sincere thanks to a number of others who have so generously helped me: to those senior officers who have allowed me to quote from their despatches, particularly to Lieutenant-General Sir Bernard Freyberg and Major-General George Clark: to Lieutenant-General Sir Hastings Ismay for his valuable help in connection with the story of El Alamein: to Colonel Walter Elliot for the use of his article: to Sir Alan Herbert for his verses and to the *Sunday Graphic* for allowing me to re-publish them: to Lieutenant-Colonel Palmer Cook for his advice on the general lay-out and printing: and to Major David Duff, who sub-edited the manuscript and read the proofs.

Other contributions are acknowledged in the appropriate places where the subject matter appears.

P. W. PITT.

October, 1946.

ROYAL WILTS

CONTENTS

CHAP.		PAGE
	Foreword by Lieutenant-General Sir Bernard Freyberg, V.C., K.C.B., K.B.E., C.I.A.G., D.S.O.	3
	Preface	5

PART ONE

CHAP.		PAGE
I.	The Long Armistice 1920–1939	11
II.	The Flickering of the Lights	23
III.	The Lights Go Out	25
IV.	The Move to Wincanton	28
V.	Palestine ? But Why ?	33
VI.	The First Move Overseas	44
VII.	Nathanya and Karkur	48
VIII.	Searchlights over the Western Desert	53
IX.	Mechanisation	58
X.	Action at Last	65
XI.	Guarding the Lines of Communication	74
XII.	The War of the Little Columns	79
XIII.	"Round Two" and the Royal Wilts	93
XIV.	The Fall of Palmyra	102
XV.	The Persian Campaign	110

PART TWO

CHAP.		PAGE
XVI.	Back in the "Home from Home"	119
XVII.	The Battle of El Alamein	125
XVIII.	The Part Played by the Royal Wilts	133
XIX.	The Spearhead Thrust	145
XX.	In the Heat of Battle	154
XXI.	"The Rest is History . . ."	163
XXII.	In Egypt—after the Storm	166

PART THREE

CHAP.		PAGE
XXIII.	Interlude	175
XXIV.	Boxing Day in the Lebanon	180

PART FOUR

CHAP.		PAGE
XXV.	Arrival in Italy	187
XXVI.	78th Division—River Melfa to Cortona	191
XXVII.	10th and 4th Indian Divisions	199
XXVIII.	Home Again	207

APPENDICES

	PAGE
Pre-War Camps	211
Personnel Embodied, 1939	213
Personnel Embarked, February, 1940	221
Reinforcements, Autumn, 1940	227
Honours and Awards	229
Casualties	230
Congratulatory	232

ROYAL WILTS

ILLUSTRATIONS

	Facing page
THE REGIMENTAL BAND	18
MOUNTED DRILL ON WEYMOUTH SANDS	18
THE LAST PHOTOGRAPH OF THE REGIMENT HORSED	19
THE MARQUESS OF BATH TAKING THE SALUTE	19
HAIFA FROM MOUNT CARMEL	46
A FAMILIAR SCENE IN A NEW SETTING	46
GLUBB'S GIRLS	70
"DEAR MOTHER, THE FLIES HERE ARE . . ."	70
WRECKED AEROPLANE, PALMYRA AERODROME	71
OIL PIPE LINES—DIAGRAM	76
"DISPERSION"	94
"WHEN IN DOUBT, BREW UP"	94
PALMYRA	106
THE CHATEAU NEAR PALMYRA	106-107
JUFFA AS HABFORCE LEFT IT	107
RESPITE AT PALMYRA	107
DISTINGUISHED VISITORS IN THE DESERT	122
DESERT BATTLEFIELD	122-123
NEW SHERMAN TANK ON CRANE	123
"CLEARING THE GAP"—DIAGRAM	124
EL ALAMEIN SIGNPOST	125
BRITISH AND GERMAN POSITIONS, 23RD OCTOBER, 1942	128
"GAP CLEARED"—DIAGRAM	129
GUNNERS OPEN UP	130
NIGHT—AND DAY	130
OPERATION LIGHTFOOT—DIAGRAM	131
2 N.Z. DIVISION SECTION—DIAGRAM	131
R.W.Y. ROUTE IN SUPERCHARGE—DIAGRAM	146
MINISTRY OF INFORMATION PLAN OF OPERATIONS AT EL ALAMEIN	146-147
TANKS	147
THE DESERT AFTER THE BATTLE	162
SUPERCHARGE OPERATION—DIAGRAMS	162-163
BATTLEFIELD PHOTOGRAPHS	163
CRAK DES CHEVALIERS	178
ITALY—DIAGRAM OF ALLIED CAMPAIGN	187
SCENES FROM ITALY	202, 203

Part One

CHAPTER ONE

THE LONG ARMISTICE · 1920-1939

THE First World War left the Royal Wiltshire Yeomanry considerably disintegrated and, after the Peace Settlement, the Regiment was re-formed. From that time onwards its activities fell into a rhythm which, except upon a very few occasions, remained undisturbed until the autumn of 1939.

By far the most important function in the life of the Royal Wilts was the Annual Training, commonly known as "Camp," but apart from this there were weekly "drills" throughout the winter, rifle practices on the Ranges during the early summer, and a few tactical exercises for the officers and N.C.O.s just before Camp came round. There were a number of social engagements and reunions such as Squadron and Troop Dinners in the towns and villages for the men, and a really grand Regimental Ball, for everybody connected with the Royal Wilts, once a year. There was also a Regimental Dinner in London for the officers past and present, and this also took place annually—except when the Prince of Wales, who was our Colonel-in-Chief, attended it. Whenever that happened, it invariably took the Dinner Fund two years to recover its strength sufficiently to provide us with another dinner!

All these functions were very pleasant, the drills not being excepted, although the latter entailed a great deal of hard work in draughty drill halls, to say nothing of many a night journey through wintry weather from farms which were in most cases a considerable distance away. Nevertheless, by and large, the general standard of attendance throughout the Regiment during all those years was extremely high. Furthermore, many of the officers put in a matter of twenty nights or so during the winter from their places of residence a long way from Wiltshire. For not all of them were fortunate enough to be able to live in the county.

As conditions changed, over that period of twenty odd years, more and more of the officers found it necessary to follow their professions wherever those professions might lead. Eventually they led them far and wide and it is an historical fact that, on one occasion, there assembled at Camp on Salisbury Plain, officers from such far flung places as California, New York, Kenya, Paris and Montreal! But they had one and all dropped whatever business they had in hand and made off at the appointed time to keep this sacred engagement in the County of Wiltshire.

Because the majority of the yeomen were farmers, Camp had to take place in the spring or the autumn and, with only two or three exceptions, the former was chosen. So, by the beginning of May in every year the Regiment, like some hibernating animal, began to stir from the comparative slumber of its winter duties : then it was galvanised into feverish activity. This activity, almost from the first Annual Training after the re-forming of the Regiment, settled down into a regular routine from which it hardly ever varied.

There was, however, one notable exception to this rule. In 1936 the Commanding Officer was invited to bring the Royal Wiltshire Yeomanry to take part in the Regular Army manoeuvres on Salisbury Plain. With alacrity and fortitude, but possibly some misgivings, he accepted. In consequence and in due course the Regiment turned out in full force that autumn and assembled, with considerable excitement and anticipation, on Salisbury Plain. The ardour of most of us was a trifle subdued, however, when we learned that a terse, decisive but apparently rather cross Brigadier had given instructions that the Royal Wilts, being cavalry, were to be placed where they wouldn't get in the way. Anywhere, he said, would do as long as they did not interfere with his plans.

But we had to admit that those plans were good, in spite of the natural disapproval which this Brigadier's antipathy to cavalry called forth. So good were they, in fact, that they defeated both his enemy and the object of the exercise at the same time and thereby brought the proceedings to an unexpectedly early close. His problem was to take three dumps, one to the east and two to the west of the River Avon. Those who set the exercise were trying to find out which of the recognised crossings, " A," " B " or " C," he would use to reach the other side of the river. But this unorthodox Brigadier would have none of them. By a forced march he did a rapid " left hook " down south through Amesbury, after capturing the first " dump " almost before the " kick off " of the exercise. He thus outwitted his opponents and was by many considered rather to have spoilt the fun by his ruthless efficiency and unusual methods.

His conduct of the subsequent " pow wow " was scarcely less vigorous. Having first asked whether we desired a real criticism, and having been answered in the affirmative, he told everyone exactly what he thought of them in plain language and then remarked, abruptly, " there will be no questions."

The name of that Brigadier was Bernard Montgomery.

This adventure, however, did the Royal Wilts a world of good. They acquired a most useful experience of working in the dark and going without sleep in inclement weather and had a real taste of what active service conditions might be like. It should also be recorded that they acquitted themselves well. With the possible exception of one Troop Leader's unfortunate indiscretion (which provided an opportunity for a first class mock funeral to the inevitable " John Brown " refrain) they did all that was required of them in their allotted role. On more than one occasion they were saddled up and on parade in the dark before the regular units ; but this, it must be admitted, was chiefly because they were so keen and excited that, apart from remaining awake all night themselves, they scarcely unsaddled their horses and were therefore practically at a minute's call for the whole of the exercise. They were, in consequence, a very tired and weary band of men when it was finished, and little did they realise that the next occasion upon which they would come under Montgomery's command would be the Battle of El Alamein.

There is one further incident which is worthy of record in connection with those Autumn manoeuvres. " B " Squadron was allotted the task of guarding the river-crossing at Amesbury through which village, as has been mentioned above, Brigadier Montgomery's troops passed during their successful " left hook." The noise occasioned by these events disturbed the guests in a certain hotel and thereby infuriated the proprietor. This individual appeared in the middle of the night and cursed the Military, officers included, for their unwarrantable intrusion upon the peace and quiet of his surroundings. He was going to "have the law on them" and goodness knows what he wasn't going to do to punish them for the inconvenience occasioned to the guests in his hotel by all this damn silly nonsense.

It would be interesting to know whether this particular incident ever occurred to his mind during the subsequent war!

And so, since all the normal Annual Training periods were very much alike, let us imagine that we are at any Camp anywhere from the 15th to the 29th May in any one of those years. In that way, perhaps, we may recapture some of the charm of those delightful weeks which, whatever may happen now, can never quite be repeated in the future.

* * * * * *

There is about our camp life something of the glamour of the circus. At least we can understand to some extent how circus people live. For year by year, during our Annual Training, we pass a small portion of our lives in surroundings which, although the essentials are constant, are on each occasion cast in a different setting. Those essentials are very simple. The bell tents in which we devote the minimum of our time to sleep, the mess tents, the ante-rooms and the horse lines. There are, of course, other and very important places in the camp: the Orderly Room, the Quartermaster's Stores and even the Blacksmith's Shop which consists of an anvil and a primitive forge beneath a tree. But with all this most of us are not much concerned although we know the part it has to play.

And so we always find things much the same, although the site may vary year by year. Sometimes, in fact as often as it can be conveniently managed, we camp beside the sea. This gives the men a holiday and, since many of us devote our annual leisure to the Regiment, this has to be considered. Often we camp on Salisbury Plain. This is good for training but gives less varied recreation. Sometimes we find ourselves in Savernake Forest, where even now a man may lose himself for days on end.

But it is at night that all camps seem to merge into one identity. Then our world is bounded by the interior of one tent or another. The hours of darkness are spent in surroundings which, by lamplight, remain constant throughout the years. The Officers' Mess Tent with its long table and shining silver cups. Each year we read again the inscriptions on these cups and recall their history and the happy incidents of which they are such constant reminders. The canvas passage to the Ante-room where the red and blue striped lining has remained for as many years as we can remember, although we none of us know who chose the colours of the Brigade of Guards. The clock which fits so snugly on one of the tent poles and was designed, made and presented, with its regimental crest, by an officer of days gone by. It is a sturdy clock, as it should be to withstand the rough treatment it receives from young men who annually swarm over it when racing up the tent poles. Perhaps its donor knew a thing or two from practical experience. The pigeon-holed letter rack which retreats discreetly into a corner at the first suspicion of a rowdy evening. The wicker armchairs which are so comfortable in spite of the floppiness of their backs, caused by the onslaughts of generations of subalterns who have somersaulted over them. These are the simple furnishings of the canvas bubbles in which the officers find so much pleasure during the nocturnal hours of camp.

To the men also night gives a sameness wherever the camp may happen to be. Year after year similar silhouettes give a shadow show upon the canvas walls of their bell tents. Men playing cards on upturned boxes or disrobing or cleaning kit by the light of a candle stuck in a bottle. Outside, all is darkness and darkness is very much the same whether it be on Salisbury Plain or on the Downs of Sussex.

But now let us start out upon the exciting adventure of our imaginary camp.

* * * * * *

For the past few weeks we have been busily preparing ourselves for the great event. Amidst a smell of moth balls we have been rummaging about with old uniforms, flea-bags, bits and pieces of harness and all kinds of equipment. At last we have got ourselves sorted out and the great day has arrived. We are on our way to camp from all directions. Some of us are riding in a column which is as yet a trifle ragged. The horses, fresh from their civilian occupations, have not yet settled down. The equipment has not all been properly adjusted. Neither has the skin on those portions of the men which touch the saddle and this becomes more apparent as the day wears on. We know of at least one troop whose officer, in an access of zeal, has decided to make a night march to camp. We also know that the men concerned will arrive quite exhausted and that it will take them probably until half way through camp to recover from the results of this possibly unnecessary ordeal. But it is all in the right spirit

Most of us, however, have travelled to the camp site by road or rail. Our horses have been sent on and we find everything ready for us when we arrive. We have no idea how it all got there but we never bother to enquire. We know that the Quartermaster has been installed, with a few chaps to help him, for the past fortnight and, indeed, he looks very well on it and sunburned into the bargain. But if you asked us about the " Q Branch " we should probably have no earthly idea of what you meant.

Then, having arrived, the officers in particular make a leisurely inspection of the camp. Like a cat which prowls slowly around any new place of abode with its tail straight up in the air, we visit all the familiar tents and generally get an idea of the layout. Are the Officers' Lines too close to the horse lines? They seem to be fairly well sited. Will the noise from the Ante-room keep us awake if we happen to go to bed a trifle earlier than the rest? It will. Is the dining-room tent on a level keel? It is not. It is on the side of a hill and one row of officers will have to sit about a foot below the other row. We shall have to put forks under our soup plates to keep them level and the top row will be able to roll apples down on to the bottom row. Are the men's lines down wind of the latrines? We hope they are not, because this will entail our having an argument with the Quartermaster and he is bound to win. Noting these and many other details we complete our inspection of the camp.

Meanwhile yeomen are assembling from far and near. In one place they are struggling to entrain horses which have never been entrained before and are making the fact known. The doctor's horse as usual is creating hell. In another they are rattling along in buses, exchanging greetings with all and sundry and especially the girls as they drive along. This cordiality they seem to adopt with the uniform, because they surely would not behave like this in their normal clothes. Then there are the ones who have already arrived and are busy getting their horses on to the lines. This always provides plenty of excitement and sooner or later the cry of " loose horse " goes up. We have a few tense moments as a wild-eyed horse goes galloping by with an iron-shod picket swinging from one of its hind legs. There is plenty of entertainment on the first day of camp!

Then come the delightful moments when we greet old friends whom we haven't seen for some time. The brief exchange of chat and reminiscence and the news of how others are faring. Are all the yeomen turning up? Yes they are. They nearly always do. And who would wonder at that? Over everything there is a faint suspicion of the " first day of the term " atmosphere which we remember so well from our school days. It is all rather exciting and what fun it is to be starting a new camp.

Almost our first activity is the "Horse Board." This, if we are part of it, becomes a bore. But if we are not included, it is fun to watch. Our old friends Messrs. Hetherington and Rich, the hardy annual horse dealers, turn up with the contract horses some of which have been to camp before. But many of them have not and therein lies the problem. "Is that horse sound?" "Could we turn that one into a trooper?" "Just a second; trot that horse back again—no that won't do he's dead lame. Cast him." And so it goes on. Unfortunately each year the number of contract horses seems to become greater because less and less of the yeomen are mounted on their own animals. Those of us who have been long with the Regiment can recall the time when many a troop was mounted entirely on owner's horses. In those days a troop leader could send out thirty telegrams and expect thirty mounted men to answer his summons. But that was long ago. Latterly the majority of the horses required for camp are hired in one big contract.

On this first night we all are very tired. The men, especially, feel the burden of the day. They do not therefore burn much midnight oil. As soon as they have managed to get something to eat, find their quarters and shake out their bedding, most of them turn in and sleep the sleep of the weary.

In the Sergeants' Mess, however, things are livelier and renewed acquaintances have led to a round of drinks here and there. In consequence they may some of them sit up quite late and reminiscences will flow the one from another.

In the Officers' Mess things are a trifle stilted to begin with. At dinner the atmosphere is rather frigid. We have not yet got into our stride and the conversation makes little sallies which frequently do not lead very far. But as the wine begins to circulate we get together rather more and, by the end of dinner, it is obvious that we are well on the way to the usual camp atmosphere.

In the Ante-room we stand about in batches gossiping over the somewhat inadequate oil stoves. We frankly feel the cold because the tent in the middle of May is a big change from the warm houses to which we have been accustomed. We wonder why it is that, when men feel cold, they have a tendency to stand rather than to sit down, yet this always happens.

The officer who usually provides our music strolls over to the piano and strikes a tinny note. He shudders slightly and then strikes another. This establishes the fact, which he already knew beforehand, that the piano is out of tune. But so are all our camp pianos and their expectation of life is very short. The Quartermaster purchases these pianos entirely for their "break up" value and that is a wise precaution because seldom has one been known to survive the end of camp. For young men in wine there is a fatal fascination about the disembowelling of a piano; camp pianos usually end in very small pieces. This one will be adequate, however, because the quality of our music will not be very high although its quantity will be unrestrained.

On this first night a few of the older members settle down to a game of bridge, well knowing that this will be their last opportunity before the camp breaks up. For on all other nights, although an uproarious game of poker is usually to be found in one corner of the ante-room, it will be no place for any more serious card game. Finally we drift off to bed in small groups and everybody seems pleased with the prospect of getting at least one early night.

Next morning there is our first parade. This is not a very imposing spectacle but nobody expects it to be one. The Regimental band also makes its first appearance. It is obviously out of practice and the big drummer is the only performer who seems to be inspired with any great confidence. "Ta-ra-ra-boom" they play on their first attempt. "Ta-ra-ra-*boom*." Look out ! Catch that loose horse. There you are. They've ta-ra-ra-boomed the Second in Command off his horse again. It happens nearly every year, but it never fails to amuse us.

The origin of our "Inspection Tune" is most obscure, but somehow it forms a background to all our memories of camp. Nobody seems to know why it was adopted. We are not even sure whence it came. Some of the older officers tell us that its name is "Birds of the Desert." The suggestion, even, of such a name turns out to be prophetic. But we of course are unaware of that.

And so these first few days are devoted to settling in. Equipment has to be sorted out and horses have to be handled carefully. They are not yet accustomed to their shackles and the whole of this new existence must seem strange. But we do not worry over this; we know that by the end of the week it will be hard to tell them from normal troop horses. The rapidity with which they fall into their new rôle is an annual source of astonishment.

Next there comes horse mastership and the riding school makes its appearance. Some of our troopers, especially those from the towns, have hardly ever ridden. To begin with, as they circle round, they assume the appearance of the White Knight in "Alice," and we marvel at the manner in which Sir John Tenniel was able to pass down to posterity such an excellent picture of the awkward horseman. But, strange to tell, we find that horses will go well for a man who has never ridden before. Perhaps it is because the tyro has no fear. He rides his horse like a bicycle and probably that is the way in which it should be ridden. Only when experience tells us what *may* happen do we acquire that sneaking sense of fear: and horses seem to sense this very soon.

After a few days of this we are getting into our stride. Troop leaders have had their troops to themselves for a while and are licking them into shape. We shall shortly be doing squadron drill and the first appearance of the Squadron on parade as a unit will give us that never failing thrill. Then we shall be able to make abortive attempts at such difficult manœuvres as forming "line of troop column"; but it is doubtful whether we shall ever be able to do it correctly. This doubt, however, has never yet prevented the Squadron Leader from having a jolly good try.

"Stables," too, are acquiring a steady routine. Horses are already beginning to show the effect of a few days' grooming. They are also settling down well and we seldom now have any trouble in the lines. Trouble, that is, from the horses: because we shall be lucky if we avoid a certain amount of human frailty. Odd items of grooming kit are bound to "walk" from one squadron lines to another and assuredly a number of nosebags will disappear. We know that, no matter how many nosebags we start with, an extraordinary proportion will have been spirited away by the time the camp is over. We wonder where on earth those nosebags end up!

Meanwhile our after-duty life has already been quietly taking shape. We have sought out the local town and shown off our uniforms and more than one officer, in his blue overalls and chain epaulettes, has been taken for a member of the band. The men, as usual, have been seen about more than the officers, because the latter have been inclined to make a bee-line for the hotels which have the best bathing facilities.

In camp, of an evening, you will not find the majority of the men. They are sampling the unfamiliar attractions of the town, but the officers will nearly all be found in their Mess. There, after dinner, the rowdier elements have started a certain amount of restrained ragging in the ante-room, where the ridge pole has already been tried out to test its powers of supporting the human body. We often wonder what primitive urge induces young men to clamber to the tops of tents under the slightest influence of conviviality. A poker game is also well under way and the poker chips, decorated with such strange devices, have once more made their appearance. During this first week the poker game makes the most of its innings because the players know that, during the second week, there will be little opportunity of finding even the comparative serenity which they require. The fun will be too fast and furious and already the poker school has degenerated into a noisy but good natured bear-garden which renders bridge impossible in the same ante-room.

Then, almost as if by rite, the traditional forms of horse play have had to be performed. "Over the chairs," a race over the wicker armchairs placed back to back to form jumps, which have to be negotiated by means of somersaults, and "Cockfighting" are the most important of these.

But here let us describe what we mean by "Cockfighting." First of all, two contestants lie on their backs on the floor, their shoulders touching but their legs pointing in opposite directions. Then they link arms and each raises the leg nearest to the other. The object, now, is to turn your opponent over until his foot touches the ground behind his head; this each tries to achieve by hooking the other's heel with his own and pressing down his leg with all his might. It is a considerable trial of strength and, if the contest lasts for many minutes, a most exhausting pastime. As usual, last year's champion has to be challenged and a number of contests take place which include the reappearance in the ring of a few old timers. This ill-advised but strenuous exercise at a comparatively advanced age is apt to call attention to the latter's physically weak spots and often it reminds them painfully of a muscular blemish which, in all probability, originated under these identical circumstances a score of years previously. But this by no means induces them to interfere with the young men's fun. It rather seems to encourage them to foster it.

The piano, of course, has not been idle during the first week, but whatever attempts have been made to encourage a musical evening have been somewhat half-hearted. There has been about them an air of expectancy, an "until ready" atmosphere. Old songs have been recalled and possibly a few new ones added. But we are very conservative in our music, if music it can be called. Old favourites are the order of the day. During this first week we know that, sooner or later, a musical evening will develop—and develop with considerable violence—but probably it will not arrive until the second week. These things cannot be organised. If forced, they invariably "flop." They just happen and are all the more enjoyable because of this quality of unexpectedness.

There has, of course, been a "Brass Hat" around. This always happens fairly early on in camp. There are usually several inspections in which we are "discovered at work" but for which most of us make no unusual preparation. There is always, however, the type of officer who shares with the bull the failing of becoming intensely excited by the appearance of red material. But, on the whole, we are quite unmoved by such visitations and scarcely even know the functions of the high ranking officers who make them.

Then, almost before we have time to realise it, the first week of camp is over. That always happens. The Middle Sunday catches us, as it were, a trifle breathless, and enables us to sit down quietly and think things over. It is warm and the weather has changed, as it usually seems to do at this period in our training. The first week is almost always chilly and the second delightfully warm. This gives rise to an annual discussion about Mr. Buchan's famous "Cold Spells" but his invariable accuracy in this matter has never induced the authorities to take advantage of his gift, to the extent of considering his forecast when the date of our camp is fixed.

So here we are, taking our ease in the warm sunshine after a good lunch, and there is an air of lassitude throughout the camp. For the first time, since we arrived it is quiet enough to hear the drone of bumble bees: the horses blink sleepily on the lines, and some of them sway slightly from side to side in their drowsiness. They, too, are well fed, and their coats are already showing that gloss which comes from constant grooming. One or two of the keener of the officers are drifting about amongst the horses, showing them off, and discussing their points with visitors who are probably ex-officers of the Regiment. Many a memory of bygone days is thus recaptured. The men are mostly out of camp, but some are resting. The sergeants, also, are taking it easy, although many of them have sought the pleasures of the local town in their cars. But the Sergeants' Mess is so comfortably furnished that there is little enough inducement for them to leave it.

Nearly all the officers are about and several have asked relations to lunch. This has set a problem for the unattached. Must they stay and make polite conversation or would it be rude to give way to that sleepy feeling which follows a good meal on a summer's day—especially if you have gone short of sleep for several nights previously ! One by one these give way to nature and, with mumbled excuses, they make off to their tents.

Those remaining sprawl in basket chairs outside the Officers' Mess Tent, and gossip quietly with the ladies. Even the marquee itself has the appearance of having " taken down its hair and loosened its stays," for one side has been removed, and within can be seen the dining table, loaded with silver cups and trophies which sparkle in the sun which now can reach them.

The clear voices of the ladies strike an unusual note in the camp, and contrast with the husky speech of the officers. For by this time most of us are suffering from that hoarseness which always assails us when under canvas. Some think it is caused by the damp nights, or the shouting on parade, or even our annual rendering of " Through the Night of Doubt and Sorrow " and " Onward Christian Soldiers," on church parade (as well it might be). Others, less charitable, would give you other reasons. But hoarse we are, and sunburnt into the bargain, as we contemplate, from the slight eminence of our camp site, the spring-clad country around us. Drowsily we take in the peaceful scene of tents and horse-lines, amidst fresh green fields which are splashed with patches of bright yellow buttercups, and we feel that all is well with the world. Camp has, as usual, begun with ample promise.

* * * * * *

The story of the latter half of camp will not take long in the telling. It all passes so quickly, and that is true to form. Somehow the tempo seems to quicken as the precious days go by, to end in a crescendo which leaves us feeling very tired and rather flat.

During this week our time is less taken up with routine matters, because everything runs with less attention. Every man has a better idea of what he has to do, and even the horses have begun to settle down in a surprising fashion. After ten days at camp, almost any horse will behave as though he were a trooper of some years standing. So we are able to devote our time to training of a more advanced sort. Squadron drill, for example, takes the place of troop drill and before two or three days have elapsed, we are doing it at the trot, and making—or so it seems to us—a very creditable showing. We know that it takes a regular cavalry regiment several months to achieve squadron drill at the trot, but we dash in where angels fear to tread. The result, as a matter of fact, has often surprised the regular cavalry officer. But even he would gasp, not without some reason, to see us doing regimental drill at the end of twelve days.

This regimental drill is an experience to which every man and every officer has been looking forward, in secret, ever since the first day of camp. It is, in many ways, a most hussar-like performance. To anybody watching from the outside, it would probably appear most terrifying because, however slowly we do it, there are invariably a number of horses at full gallop on the outer flanks of the wheeling squadrons, there is a good deal of bunching, and occasionally a man or two has been known to fall off. But then there hardly ever *is* anybody watching from the outside, because we are all of us on the inside taking part. But to us it is all-absorbing. We do not take

THE REGIMENTAL BAND.

MOUNTED DRILL ON WEYMOUTH SANDS.

THE LAST PHOTOGRAPH OF THE REGIMENT HORSED.

THE MARQUESS OF BATH TAKING THE SALUTE BETWEEN THE WARS.

it too seriously, are fully alive to our shortcomings, and have almost as much fun talking about it afterwards as we enjoyed in its execution. But the least that one can say of our regimental drill is that it calls for a certain amount of horsemanship and teaches the troops to ride.

Towards the end of camp we also manage to get out into the country a good deal more, and so to stretch our horses' legs. There are field days and exciting schemes which give us all a chance to show what we are made of. If, as sometimes happens, we are " brigaded " with one or two other Yeomanry regiments, we may end up in a full-scale battle, and that is most thrilling. Occasionally it is a trifle too thrilling, because an " incident " may occur which will be remembered and cause a minor feud between two regiments for quite a while to come.

Apart from this, we see little of the regiments with which we are brigaded. There are exchanges of courtesies, of course, and nearly always a midnight " raid " or two, with all the merry consequences, but otherwise our horizon is very much bounded by the Regiment during our annual training. The Commanding Officer is the man who counts. There are " Brass Hats " who come and inspect us, of course, but they are a thing apart. They are vaguely " The Army." Even when we march past them and go through our paces, they are almost the least important item on that most important occasion. What matters to us is the rehearsing for the show, and, indeed, the show itself. Like most amateur actors, we are, to be perfectly honest, very little interested in our audience. No wonder that the Yeoman answers so fearlessly (and often so tactlessly truthfully) to the stereotyped questions of the General. And no wonder that we get such a good report. Incidentally, we always expect to be well spoken of because, after all, we have worked very hard and done our best. This was proved on one rare occasion when we failed to achieve the good report to which we had grown accustomed. Every member of the Regiment was highly indignant about it, and for some time afterwards the tactless General concerned was thought very little of and treated very coldly, at any rate by the more senior officers of the Regiment. Nevertheless, that bad report did us a world of good.

One of the most outstanding events in the last few days, as far as the officers and N.C.O.s are concerned, is the Sergeants' Mess " do." The officers are invited to this, and wish they were able to return one tenth of the hospitality which they receive on that occasion. For the Regimental Sergeants' Mess is a great institution. Their ante-room is far more comfortably appointed than that of the officers', and gathered round it you will invariably find a great many motorcars and motor bicycles. In this respect, the sergeants always seem to be far better off than the officers, a peculiarity of the Yeomanry which speaks for itself. Furthermore, the sergeants do not show the same tendency to break up their mess furniture as do the officers. We don't know why this is, but it is just one of those things and we must leave it at that. Also it is well known that the sergeants do themselves jolly well, and, as far as the exigencies of the service will permit, they have the best of everything, including beer. Since most of the local breweries are well represented amongst the members, this latter is not to be wondered at. In any case, beer there is, plenty of it, and of an excellent quality.

So no wonder the officers look forward to this annual evening, in these pleasant surroundings where, in addition, they are certain of seeing a first-class show. Don't imagine that a lot of professionals will be trotted out for our amusement! There is no need of that. Somehow there always seems to be plenty of talent amongst the sergeants, and the time and trouble they put in shows this off to the best advantage. There will be games as well, in which the officers take part. These games, which by now are almost traditional, are many of them simple enough : almost of the nursery variety, but very few men really grow up, and because of that, we enjoy them. Some are rough indeed, but never are they rowdy. In fact, the way in which order is preserved, and the disciplined manner in which this evening's amusement is unfolded, is quite remarkable. There is no curb on the fun and games whatsoever, but if, as sometimes happens, a member steps ever so slightly over the bounds of what should be, he somehow disappears mysteriously, before he has time to interfere with the pleasure of those about him. Very little misses the stern eye of the R.S.M. and the enjoyment of the evening benefits accordingly.

So, as the officers wander back in the moonlight to their lines, the strains of the not too tuneful rendering of well-worn songs grows fainter as the stragglers around the piano are left behind. Perhaps a pair or two of overalls have suffered from the horseplay, but that is nothing to what will happen to them before the week is over. In any case it has been a splendid evening—and one of the type which could not still be found in many places. There has, for a long time, been a saying in the Royal Wilts that "if the Sergeants' Mess is all right, there is nothing wrong with the Regiment." These officers reflect, as they lay them down for a few brief hours of sleep, that they needn't worry. There is not much wrong with the Regiment!

It must not be supposed, however, that the officers and sergeants have a monopoly of merrymaking on this moonlit night. Coming from the men's canteen, as the officers pull off their Wellingtons, are sounds which bear out the opposite. There, too, a sing-song is in progress and the order which decrees that lights must be out by ten o'clock does not seem to have stilled the vocal chords. Of course, there *may* be a light or two still burning, but that's the Orderly Officer's affair, and nobody else is interested. For the men this fortnight is meant to come as a relaxation although a great deal of hard work is required of them. Nobody bothers much about when they go to bed as long as they are up at six in the morning and manage to get through their work.

As far as the officers are concerned, life goes on much the same in their mess, but during the second week the pace seems to quicken. There are usually a few "guest nights," and what happens on those occasions had better be left to the imagination. The fun is fast and furious, and it may appear to some to be foolish, but we all enjoy ourselves immensely, and the training which we receive in the art of doing without sleep is going to be of inestimable value in the future. But at the time, of course, we do not know this.

Then there are the Regimental Sports. These follow the pattern of the local fêtes and gymkhanas, so favoured in the country during the years when England is said to have "slumbered on her lawns." The mounted tug-o'-war is probably the feature to which we most look forward. It calls for considerable skill, and has, during the past few years, been very popular. But our teams are by no means tyros. They have pulled in many a contest, on the bare backs of these same patient animals, whilst touring the fairs and similar functions in the County. We have here, as a matter of fact, two crack teams, and there is a great deal of interest in the final "pull." There might well be a bit of money on it, too, but that is another matter.

Here again, in these sports, the Yeoman shows his peculiar willingness (and often ability) to perform, at a moment's notice, feats which a regular soldier would take years to perfect. Tent-pegging, for example, requires great skill and practice. Nevertheless we have seen, on more than one occasion, three Yeomen in perfect line take three pegs in the most professional manner. We have also seen some very funny performances, but we need not go into all that. What really matters is that everybody has a go at everything and therefore the sports are a success.

And so that second week of camp rolls swiftly by until we find ourselves, on the last day, holding saddlery inspections and judging troops and individuals for the numerous cups which have been presented from time to time to the Regiment by members who have left it. These cups are awarded for the best turn out, skill in various directions, horsemanship, and whatever other merit is considered suitable.

The men contest for them with great enthusiasm, and the officers take a great deal of trouble in allotting them justly. For it is with great pride that a trooper finds a place for one of them on his sideboard for the period between two camps.

Then, almost as a shock, we find that camp has ended. Always there is the same complaint. If only camp could last for three weeks instead of two! It invariably seems to be over just as it has got into its stride and an extra week, with everybody knowing his job and things running smoothly, would be such an excellent idea. Little do we know that many of us will eventually take part in a camp which lasts for over four and a half years!

At last we sadly hand back the hired horses to the contractor and the men who rode them so proudly return in the humble train. Others, who are fortunate enough to own or have borrowed horses, can ride them home. So little columns set off towards the various towns of Wiltshire, diminishing as they go along as men and horses fall out at the wayside villages. They do not travel swiftly, these little columns. All of us are tired and there is a sort of reluctance to ring down the final curtain. We are apt to dawdle as we ride along, and our minds are full of recent memories. The idea of returning to our normal humdrum existence seems somehow to be unreal.

But real it is and soon we are back in the everyday rut once more. Then our memories of camp seem to merge from year to year. They do much to brighten our darker hours and we turn to them from time to time as one does to a family album. There, as we turn the pages, some pictures stand out as vividly as upon the day when they were taken. Others have faded and look old-fashioned by the light of time.

Such recollections will remain with all of us for very many years, no matter what our rank. Our first day in camp and the strange feel of the rough uniform: learning to ride and the delight in making progress: the way that girl looked at us as we strutted past her on the sea front and the tang of the salt air on our tongues: the cafés and the dances: doing galloper to the squadron leader on a field day: learning to groom and to polish saddles: the day we got our sergeant's stripes—and the wetting of them afterwards in the mess: songs round the piano: the feeling of good fellowship: yarns and beer: the patter of rain on canvas: serving out feeds in a tin jerry: the long table and shining cups in the Officers' Mess: the band struggling with popular tunes and the bandmaster drinking his port: ragging: cock-fighting: climbing over the tents: cheese and Worcestershire sauce on biscuits: stables in pyjamas under greatcoat and gumboots: bonfires in the ante-room: the regimental march on morning parade: that sore behind after three days camp: guest nights and their consequences: " taking wine " at dinner: Bible stories in Wiltshire dialect: David and Goliath: the way the horses improved in a fortnight and, above all, what fun we had.

All this may give the impression that too much of our time at camp was given over to amusement, but that would be a very wrong impression. The Yeomanry, in peacetime, was very much of a club for the men and quite naturally their memories, as time moves on, turn to pleasant things and much of the sterner aspect is forgotten. But they did work hard and showed great keenness in their training: and this meant that the lazy ones were forced to learn for fear of being laughed at by the others. There was therefore very little slacking as far as work was concerned.

Besides, for those whose lot in life it is to live within a small circumference, such an annual change is more than welcome. Mr. Belloc has told us that " There is no fun in doing nothing when there is nothing to do," and that is a very true statement. But at camp the men have a great deal to do and their holiday is thereby the richer. Also, in the local town, especially when we are camping by the seaside, there is much to broaden their minds and give them a change of outlook. Their leisure hours are not often spent in the camp. They prefer to polish up their buttons and go out to see the sights.

The Regiment is made up of all sorts, of course, and those who come from towns may be sophisticated. But for the majority, who are country folk, there is a certain attraction about strutting up and down the front, and what if an odd girl or two does flash a glance in their direction ? The benefit of all this is noticed mostly when camp is over. That long standing quarrel we had with our neighbour, about certain disputed rights, seems somehow trivial after moving in a larger circle. And when we return, our village friends compare favourably with those people we met outside. It is as though a breath of fresh air had blown through our minds and swept away the cobwebs. Most of the men feel the better for it, and look forward to the time when camp will come round again. It has all been worth the drudgery of drills, and the winter's work is not regretted.

In any case, the spirit of jovial good fellowship throughout the Regiment was something well worth while and, after all, the proof of the pudding is in the eating. Anybody who troubles to read to the end of this story will see that, whether or not we took our military duties with sufficient seriousness, the result was not too bad.

CHAPTER TWO

THE FLICKERING OF THE LIGHTS

IN 1937 and 1938 the Royal Wiltshire Yeomanry thought about war in much the same way as did most of the other inhabitants of the United Kingdom. Neither the officers nor the men really believed that it could happen. Undoubtedly the Munich crisis had fused an air of reality into the annual training at camp in 1938 but generally speaking that camp was much the same as any of its predecessors. " Peace in our time " was the predominant note.

It was not until the summer of 1939 that most of us began seriously to consider the probability of war : but even then the idea seemed somehow fantastic. This attitude was particularly noticeable in the atmosphere of a certain Squadron Leaders' Conference which was held in the Cavalry Club during the month of June in that year. Whilst the subject of a possible war was being discussed, with a great deal of natural anxiety, the officers who lived in the country asked those who lived in London for an opinion. The latter, by virtue of their being closer to the hub of events, might be supposed to be better informed in such matters. Their opinion was that those in the best position to know the truth considered war to be " 90 per cent. certain."

Such a statement was indeed hard to believe at that time and in those surroundings. The club was full of cheerful, sunburnt and healthy looking members whose gossip was all of racing, polo and cricket. The smell of warm tarmac was floating through the open windows and, outside, Piccadilly at the height of the London season seemed infinitely remote from the very thought of war. Pretty girls in Ascot dresses, escorted by men in grey top hats, drove past in expensive cars and open taxis. There was a gaiety in the atmosphere which seemed even to have infected the tramps who lounged in the sunshine on the benches across the road. The air was full of busy noises, to which a coaching horn added its strident " twang" as a coach and four came spanking past, its occupants, in their enthusiasm, being blissfully oblivious of how incongruous it appeared amidst the modern traffic.

A flock of rather sooty looking sheep were grazing in Green Park around the slit trenches which had been so feverishly hacked out nine months previously. But the Munich crisis had become somehow remote by now and already those trenches were falling in. It seemed to be nobody's business to keep them in repair and old gentlemen were writing letters to *The Times* about them. They wanted them filled in because they were ugly and they even suggested growing flowers around them !

Gazing through the Cavalry Club windows upon this very pleasant scene, it was hard to believe that another war was likely. There seemed to be no place for war in all this. Surely it could not happen here! Those officers who had fought in France shook their heads doubtfully, as there passed through their minds the scenes of horror which time had robbed of their reality. Not again? Surely we were beyond all that! Somehow a way would be found to spare us from a second war in twenty years! But nobody quite knew how. And several of those officers were far from happy in their minds as they drove back to Wiltshire on that glorious June afternoon.

No active steps were taken at that conference, but it was a very pleasant reunion and the lunch was quite excellent.

But, from that time onward, the situation deteriorated rapidly until the nations of Europe, bewildered and incredulous, were herded by the nemesis of incompetence into the abyss of a second World War.

CHAPTER THREE

THE LIGHTS GO OUT

AS far as the Regiment was concerned, the first to feel the impact of these tragic events were the Commanding Officer, Lieut.-Col. Humphrey Nicholson, and his Adjutant (Capt. Ferris St. George). The latter was at that time an officer in the Regiment, having been seconded from the Life Guards. For him, during those anxious days, life was indeed full. Although he was officially available for " light duty only " as a result of a broken pelvis, he moved his bed into the Orderly Room at Trowbridge and there he remained, day and night, with scarcely an hour's relaxation until the mobilisation of the Regiment had been completed. That Orderly Room, even in its normal and comfortable surroundings, would have been no haven of rest at such a time, but further difficulties were created by the necessity of moving into temporary quarters. A tin roofed hut, with all its attendant inconvenience, was all that could be found to house the Commanding Officer and his Staff during the whole of the mobilisation period.

In that hut the majority of the spade work was tackled successfully by the Adjutant and the Orderly Room Sergeant-Major (S.S.M. Slatford) and no record of the Regiment would be complete without a mention of the part which they played in those activities. The latter, imperturbable under all provocation and possessing a vast knowledge of army procedure, was a tower of strength to all concerned. He had served in the Regiment for years and there were very few details about it of which he was unaware. He also had a rare ability for handling army correspondence which was invaluable at the time (for " General Bumph " was one of the first to come back from the retired list to active service during this war). One piece of advice which he handed out very freely was extremely valuable. " When you get an army form or document," he used to say, " read it through from top to bottom before you do anything else. Then, without attempting to understand it, read it right through again. After that it will probably begin to make sense." Many an officer of the Regiment was subsequently saved hours of work by following this admirable advice.

In the Orderly Room the trend of events was chiefly manifested in what might be termed the " Resurrection of the Mobilisation Scheme." This document had been in existence since the Regiment had been re-formed in 1922, but in all those years it had scarcely excited any interest. It had been " handed over " to each successive adjutant, after which it had been relegated once more to a pigeon hole and oblivion. It was regarded in much the same fashion as a lifeboat on a crack liner—a useful thing to have in case of emergency, but one which was extremely unlikely ever to be brought into action.

But towards the end of 1939 this " Mob Scheme " as it soon became familiarly known acquired a new significance. Letters arrived from the War Office to stir it from its slumber and it was taken from its pigeon hole, blown upon to remove the dust and regarded with an entirely new interest. Soon " amendments " began to flutter into the Orderly Room like the first swallows that herald a change. These were followed by more and more amendments, which indicated that in many quarters the " Mob Scheme " was a source of activity. Meanwhile the Adjutant and the Orderly Room staff struggled heroically with this complicated document until finally it was distributed amongst the senior officers. As delivered to them, each copy was a masterpiece of patchwork in which the amendments were held together by the yellowing paper of the originals. The Squadron Leaders looked at their mob schemes dubiously but took them very seriously. They also admired the detail with which everything had been finally worked out. Each single item had been dealt with, even down to the provision of progress signals, written out for despatch on the successive days of the mobilisation. Certainly this " Mob Scheme " was thorough. But the question was, would it work if the call ever came.

But the call *did* come and the " Mob Scheme " *did* work. It worked perfectly and turned out to be a shining example of efficiency and a lasting tribute to the diligence and perseverance of the Adjutant and the Orderly Room staff in that little hut at Trowbridge.

First of all, a telegram from the War Office embodied the " Key Parties " on the 24th August in that memorable year of 1939. These officers and men had been detailed, under the scheme, to be called up should a sufficient state of emergency arise to render the complete mobilisation of the Regiment a practical certainty. Their duties were to be to implement the preliminary arrangements made at Headquarters and to set " the machinery " in motion should the final call arrive. So the drama had begun !

The next act opened with the calling up of half the strength of "A" Squadron on the 28th, and on the last day of August these bewildered Wiltshiremen were sent to Netheravon under the command of Lt. H. G. Awdry. There they entered upon the unfamiliar task of guarding the aerodrome.

Then, on the 1st September, the dreaded signal arrived from the War Office. It contained but one fateful word ; " Embody." The clutch of the " Mob Scheme " was let in with a jerk and early next morning the officers and men of the Royal Wilts were tumbled out of their beds, wherever they happened to be, by urgent telegrams from Regimental H.Q. at Trowbridge.

By this time the seriousness of the situation was appreciated by everybody. The blow had fallen at last. Nothing but a miracle could stop the British Empire from going to war. But that miracle did not happen and the general mobilisation of the Territorial Army was declared.

It has been implied that the " Mob Scheme " was a praiseworthy example of efficiency and so it was. But unfortunately it turned out to be the last we were to see of efficiency for many a day to come. As soon as the Regiment was fully mobilised things seemed to get into a muddle which went from bad to worse. Confusion reigned everywhere, but nowhere more crazily than in those branches of the army which deal with equipment. There was very little of anything in the various depots and nobody seemed to know how to deal with even that which existed. Quartermasters of the " old soldier " type, who knew the ropes from the last war, came off best because they went and helped themselves. As a result the less fortunate, or more scrupulous, fared very badly indeed.

But, considering the general state of unpreparedness in which the outbreak of war found Britain, it was surprising on the whole how soon the Regiment settled down into a wartime body.

Squadrons formed to begin with on their local headquarters and the names of the officers and men who answered the call to arms are given in a separate appendix.

CHAPTER FOUR

THE MOVE TO WINCANTON

WE first came together as a regiment at Wincanton, where we moved by squadrons during September. This move was an exciting business but nevertheless the old " camp " atmosphere was hard to shake off, in spite of the alarms and excursions which prevailed on every side. Somehow it *did* seem as though this was just one more annual training, especially as the squadrons had formed in their respective districts and were all to join up at Wincanton.

The very name of that little town, made famous by its racecourse, was so soaked in peacetime associations for many of us. It had been the scene of such a host of happy memories. Especially those meetings which were the essence of the sport of horse racing without all the fashionable and money-ridden trimmings which have done so much to spoil the larger and more popular fixtures. Many a Wiltshire yeoman had steered a horse around the tricky bends of that small but well proportioned course, and there had even been a Yeomanry Race for quite a number of years.

But, as one squadron after another arrived, these illusions were quickly dispelled. Wincanton Racecourse in war time was a very different matter. The village had also undergone a considerable change. Normally it had seemed quite a big market town, but the billeting of a regiment of cavalry upon it presented a considerable problem. By the time we had finished there was not a room to be had in the whole place, and it appeared to be literally stuffed with troops and horses. All the hotels and " pubs " were requisitioned for the officers and N.C.O.s and, although Wincanton is blessed with more of these establishments to the square mile than almost any market town in the South of England, there was the greatest difficulty in fitting them all in. Schools, churches, saloon bars and skittle alleys were occupied to capacity by the troops. They slept on wooden floors and even, in the weighing room of the racecourse, on bare concrete. Many were for quite a long time without palliasses and three army blankets are a poor protection against concrete on a chilly autumn night. Those who had been clever enough had borrowed a few mattresses but maintaining possession of them was almost a whole time job which many gave up in despair. As can be well imagined, the washing and sanitary arrangements were altogether inadequate. Being in the centre of a town, however, they managed somehow to accommodate themselves and the local inhabitants went out of their way to provide them with baths and other facilities. There was, indeed, an official bath-house provided in the cooling tank of the Cow & Gate factory, but as the water was cold, there was a definite "September morn" hesitancy on the part of the troops as regards the use of it.

Those were hard conditions for men who, for the most part, had recently left comfortable homes in well-found farm houses. An additional complication was provided by the very closeness of those homes. Leave, even week-end leave, was impossible because, had it been granted, the Regiment would have disappeared and there was so much work to do. But, not unnaturally, the men found it hard to understand this. Officers hated having to refuse to allow them to go back for so short a distance even for a few hours, but it had to be done. It was a constant problem. Some of the smaller farmers had left at a moment's notice without so much as the time to put up the black-out which the law demanded, or to find someone who would help their wives with the farm whilst they were away. Some there were whose cows had nobody to milk them. Could they go back and attend to them? They could not. Probably they did not go back for five years. But that is war.

Meanwhile the Regiment was gradually taking shape. The men were a first-class lot with a good hard core of Yeoman stock. There were also quite a number of townsfolk who had joined the Regiment during peacetime, largely in order to be able to get away from their machinery and into the country for their holidays, and it was remarkable how soon these latter settled down to their new surroundings. Discipline, of course, had to be tightened up and in this respect the Regimental Sergeant Major did valiant work. He had, in fact, to re-educate most of the men, whose idea of discipline was not the sort which would carry you through a war, although it was quite workable for our annual camp in peacetime. For example, normally all the troopers called their N.C.O.s by their Christian names and this was quite natural because, in nearly all cases, they were great personal friends outside the Regiment. It did therefore seem quite a hardship to be forced to use the official title of Corporal and Sergeant and so on.

After a week or two the horses began to arrive. This, as can be well imagined, was a big event and one which was awaited with a great deal of interest. Those "in the know," who had particularly horsey connections, looked very wise about it all and rumours flew in all directions. Some said that the Remounts were buying rubbish and others assured us that Grand National winners were being bought at knock-down prices. As usual, none of these rumours was completely accurate and when they did arrive the horses were a fairly good all round lot. There were quite a few really good hunters (some of them had won point-to-points and prizes in the show rings) and a majority of good business-like animals : but there were also a few that never should have been bought for troop horses.

These latter were chiefly of the cast thoroughbred type, which would never have seen a racecourse in normal times. In days gone by they might have been used as galloping hacks, but they were utterly useless to us. We wanted something that would carry a trooper with full equipment and rain sodden clothes in mud up to its hocks after many days of forced marches and very little food and sleep. Besides, apart from their not being up to weight, many of them had hardly been backed and we wished we had some of the trainers who had received £80 apiece for them on the spot to introduce those animals to a shackle. That in itself was a brave man's job. Some of us were much amused nevertheless to see how the more ignorant of the men were taken in by the flashy appearance of these flat-catching horses and to witness their efforts to get hold of them—also their disillusionment when they found out their mistake ! The wiser ones went for something a little less showy but with more substance and they were subsequently well rewarded.

Having received our horses, our next job was to train them for their war-time duties and to teach the troops to ride them. The first problem was not so difficult as it had at first appeared. In fact we were all much surprised at the way the majority of the horses (which were sensible and well trained in their peacetime avocations) settled down into good solid troopers. The unsuitable ones, which have already been mentioned, were, however, a different matter. They were the very devil to cope with. Fortunately there were in the Regiment a certain number of really first-class horsemen who were prepared to break in anything on four legs. " Murder Squads " were formed from these gallant fellows and they set to work with a will to deal with the incorrigibles, with which, in spite of a number of attempts to have them cast, we were eventually inflicted. Several of these men were of the " gentleman ranker " type and had been used to this sort of thing in the Colonies. They were by no means the sort of characters about which Kipling used to write, but rather were they young men of spirit and horsey inclinations who had joined the ranks of their local yeomanry regiment because that appeared to them to be the simplest and quickest method of getting close to the business end of the war. They all of them did well and they gave a splendid example to all with whom they came in contact.

The next job was to train the men to ride. This was tackled conscientiously by all concerned and very soon the racecourse was decorated daily with strings of horses circling patiently whilst their awkward and unaccustomed burdens went through the routine of the good old-fashioned Army riding school. Here one or two ex-regular Cavalry men were invaluable and very soon they had even the rawest recruits putting up quite a creditable show of horsemanship.

Meanwhile, for the Troop Leaders, there was much to do. They had been told to " get hold of their troops " and were wisely left alone by their superior officers. A Troop Leader must do this job on his own and nobody on earth can help him, except in so far as material necessities are concerned. As a result these young officers, and the men under them, were considerably overworked at this time. But the healthy life made them fit and they were consequently in good spirits. Also there was plenty of beer and a jovial comradeship soon grew up. This helped a great deal.

For the Squadron Leaders, who had less active work for the moment, life was easier, especially up there in the sunshine on that very pleasant racecourse. Some of them had a weird feeling that it was all a dream and the idea of war with all its horrors began to recede to some extent.

After a few weeks of this, the Regiment had settled down into a routine out of which it was rudely shattered when Brigadier J. J. Kingstone, D.S.O., arrived one morning to inspect the Regiment. We had heard that he was to be our Brigadier (there had also been rumours that he was to command the new Cavalry Division) and this, his first visit, was typical. He toured around the racecourse at the gallop, pursued at some considerable distance (and at a crippling handicap in weight) by the R.S.M. whose elephantine horse appeared never to stop sweating throughout the morning. During his hurricane inspection he noticed a great many things, asked a number of awkward questions, talked to all the officers and many of the men and, incidentally, rode for a quarter of an hour unnoticed in the rear rank of a troop which was being drilled by the latest joined subaltern. By lunch time he had departed as vigorously as he had arrived, leaving everybody concerned a trifle breathless.

About this time, Lieut.-Col. Williams assumed command of the Royal Wilts in place of Lieut.-Col. Nicholson who went on the Retired List.

There followed a brief period of intense activity. We threw away our 1912 Manuals of Sword Drill and modernised our training in all directions. Things really got moving in an encouraging manner and we were in consequence all the more disappointed when our activities were curtailed by an outbreak of strangles amongst the horses. The epidemic spread and within a few weeks this filthy disease, with its running sores and disastrous effects upon its victims, brought all training to a standstill. Many of our horses had to be put down as a result and these were, in fact, our first casualties. It was very depressing for a man who had taken a lot of trouble over his horse—and become fond of it—to lose it in this unhappy fashion. We wondered why it had not been possible to check such a scourge, because there had been a similar outbreak at the beginning of the last war when cavalry regiments were being formed. We felt that some benefit might have been gained from past experience, but apparently when horses are brought together in large numbers from all parts of the country, an epidemic of strangles is more than likely and there seems to be little that can be done about it.

Then it began to rain. Steady daily downpours soon reduced the training grounds to slippery and dangerous conditions and the horse lines to an indescribable mess. Those horses stabled in the open had by far the worst of this experience, even though their lines were shifted almost daily. They were almost permanently up to their hocks in mud and filth and their rugs never seemed to get properly dry. Those in the boxes were at least fairly comfortable at night, but the ground outside became a sea of mud into which the wretched animals had to plunge every time they emerged. For the men this period was a nightmare of wet clothes, mud, greasy shackle ropes and pins that wouldn't hold, harness that seemed as though it would never look respectable again and floundering animals.

These conditions, coupled with the steadily increasing sick lines, reduced our spirits to zero. The glamour had gone out of our war and we were glad when we heard that we were to be moved. We did not much care where we were likely to find ourselves in the future because we felt that we could not be very much worse off wherever we went. In that, of course, we were mistaken. But it is not until he is fairly full-fledged that a soldier acquires the ability to appreciate being well off. For us, in our inexperience, the last few weeks at Wincanton had wiped out all the pleasant memories associated with the start of our exciting adventure on that sunny little racecourse in the late summer of 1939.

According to general rumour (which in this case was not far wrong) the Regiment was about to go North, where it was to take its place as part of the 1st Cavalry Division which was then being formed. That was exciting news because we had only just got used to thinking of ourselves as part of a brigade, although we had no idea as to the identity of the other regiments with whom we were to be brigaded. A brigade is three regiments and that was a fairly big idea to us. But a division! That seemed astronomical! We began to add up on our fingers: three brigades each of three regiments—that would be nine regiments of cavalry. Twenty-seven squadrons was what it appeared like to us at first. But of course it was ever so much more than that in reality. To many of us it had not occurred, at that juncture, that there were all sorts of other troops required to make up a division: gunners, supply services, doctors, vets, signals, police, and a host of other odds and ends.

It was quite true, as rumour had informed us, that the 1st Cavalry Division was being formed. It was all happening during those miserable last weeks which we spent at Wincanton. It was happening, as things do at the beginning of a war, in a somewhat disintegrated and haphazard fashion. Somebody had decided that the " Olde Belle " Hotel at Barnby Moor should be the Divisional Headquarters and the padre or " Senior Chaplain of the Forces, 1st Cavalry Division " as he was officially posted, seems to have been the first member of the Division to arrive at the H.Q. Then the " Q " Branch got busy, Major General Clark, M.C., was recalled from France to command, and around this nucleus the Division was built up.

Meanwhile, let us return to the Regiment as we left it—about to depart for the North.

A host of friends had been made during our stay at Wincanton and there were many fond farewells when the troops, after their first experience of entraining as a regiment, pulled out of the station. There was also very nearly a serious accident. Half a dozen thoughtless men had hitched their horses to the rear truck of the first portion of the train, presumably in order that they might grab a quick cup of tea before boxing them in the second portion. There was great consternation, therefore, when this first portion started to move and the wretched animals were forced to try and keep up with the train. Fortunately the driver's attention was called to the situation before it was too late. Otherwise these horses would have been forced to beat Black Bess' record for the journey North or else perish on the railway track.

However, the whole Regiment was packed up and on the move by the evening and, on the whole, the men were in good spirits. They were making their first major move and it was all very exciting, especially under the influence of the issue of beer which had been presented to them by the officers before the start.

But it takes a lot of beer to sustain a man through a journey such as was made that night. It was bitterly cold and seeing that the horses were watered and fed was a dreary business. The horses, too, seemed most unhappy and there were a number of minor accidents, including the loss of an ear by one horse which subsequently came to be known by the nickname of "Earoff."

After a miserable night they arrived at a comfortless northern station and unboxed their stiff and weary horses in the bitter cold. Tea and sandwiches did something to dispel the gloom, but the subsequent ride through the strangely unfamiliar country to the widely dispersed troop billets cheered up both the horses and the men. The Regiment was then split up all over the county and in many respects the horses fared better than the men, who had most of them to start all over again in indifferent billets with no beds, concrete floors, only three blankets and no proper latrines or washing centres. As before, private arrangements were eventually made, but in this part of the world the local inhabitants seemed less forthcoming with amenities, although they were more than generous with food.

It very soon became evident that, in their new location, life was to become an even sterner proposition. Wincanton had at least been close to home, but here these Wiltshiremen were amongst people who, although they were very hospitable, were of quite a different mentality. Besides, with its H.Q. at Lowdham, the Regiment was split up into squadrons, with troops all over the county, and all ranks were thrown back much more upon their own resources. "B" Squadron was once more located on a racecourse (this time in the cathedral city of Southwell) in which respect it was less disintegrated than the others, especially when the snow and ice made it almost impossible to move the horses on the roads.

But during that exceptionally hard winter any form of training was out of the question. All our energies were directed towards making up our equipment and getting the horses as fit as possible after their physical setback in the south. Lectures on horse-mastership were useful, but it was difficult to nurse the animals back to health in a temperature which necessitated breaking the ice on the horse trough every time they were watered.

But our trials and tribulations were considerably alleviated by exciting rumours which were going the rounds about another impending development.

CHAPTER FIVE

PALESTINE ? BUT WHY ?

EVEN before the Regiment had left for the North it had become generally known, by means of those subterranean channels through which news almost invariably seems to travel in the army, that it was destined to leave for Palestine as soon as it was sufficiently trained to make the move.

This news was greeted, on the whole, with favour. Several of the officers had visited that country in connection with their civil affairs in peacetime and they were eagerly consulted. They looked very wise and one of them actually produced a map which made an immediate impression on account of its almost complete lack of detail. Maps of deserts, at that time, were very unfamiliar and few of those present probably realised how well they would get to know them before many years were past. Few also of the officers who had been to the Levant could have appreciated how infinitesimal was their then knowledge of that part of the world, compared with what it would be before they were finished with it. Within four years the majority of them were destined to have a more detailed knowledge of Egypt, Syria, Palestine, and even Iraq and Persia, than they had, possibly, of the British Isles.

General Clark, who already had an extensive experience of Palestine from the military point of view, was the first to enlighten the squadron leaders on this subject, at a meeting which he called at Southwell. He told them of the advantages, and limitations, of that country as far as horses were concerned, gave them a number of tips on health, and advised them to take with them some of those large and gaudy umbrellas which are sometimes used by golfers. None of the officers present seems to have taken the last piece of advice, but many of them subsequently wished that they had, when the terrific downpours of the rainy season in Palestine were upon them. The General also mentioned such pursuits as fishing, shooting and bathing and even, like Ferdinand the Bull, forgot the belligerent nature of his calling to the extent of discussing the wonderful flowers which were to be found in the Promised Land. An air of unreality still somehow clung to our war activities at that time, and, with the " phoney war " in France dragging out its weary existence, we still felt vaguely that something would happen to stop the hostilities before the killing should begin in earnest. We did so desperately long for peace. But peace was far away.

In the whole Regiment there were probably only a handful of people at that time who had any definite idea of the strategic importance of Palestine. Generally speaking, there was a hazy notion that British troops always did go to Palestine, either opposed or unopposed, when there was a war on in Europe, and that, on this occasion, the Royal Wilts were to form part of those troops. Nearly everybody got as far as knowing that it was " something to do with the canal," but detailed knowledge was sadly lacking in those days. It is not to be concluded that the Regiment were more ignorant than most. With the exception of professional soldiers and those whose affairs brought them into contact with that part of the world, few people in peacetime England had definite knowledge on this subject. The French are usually well versed in politics, but they, also, were sadly ignorant. The author discussed it with an eminent Paris business man who was not only more than usually intelligent, but had an English wife and did most of his trade with Britain. " Why," said this Frenchman, " are you sending so many troops to Palestine of all places ? " Why were we ? Bitter experience was to teach us.

As a result of that experience nearly everybody now understands why Palestine was important to the British Empire in this war. It is interesting, however, to know that it always has been, ever since that Empire was founded. It is not just " something to do with the canal." So let us digress, for a few minutes, from our story whilst we dip into our history books and examine this interesting question.

Britain, over a hundred years ago, had to deny Palestine to her enemies in order to safeguard her Eastern Empire, long before the Suez Canal had ever been thought of. Napoleon was the villain of the piece in those days, and when we study our history we are able to appreciate why Hitler eventually hated the sound of that gentleman's name. The comparison between the two would-be world conquerors, their aims, plans and final disappointments is very close and extremely interesting.

Ever since Queen Elizabeth sent her sailors to further her interests across the sea, one of the favourite employments of our enemies has been to devise plans whereby they may deprive us of the empire which has been built up on that foundation. As a consequence, the British people have, up to the time of writing this book, taken the liberty of retaining the bulk of their overseas possessions. Those possessions, in conformity with proper progress, are now more generally known as the British Commonwealth of Nations.

The French, for many years, had designs upon the British Empire. More recently the Germans have made plan after plan to destroy it. From time to time there arises a man who believes that it is his destiny to lead his people to the fulfilment of these ambitions. Such a man was Napoleon, and such a man was Hitler.

Let us take Napoleon first.

Napoleon was convinced that it was his destiny to create a French Empire. But to men like Napoleon an empire is not much good unless it can be completed in their own lifetime. Hitler had the same trouble. Such men are in reality only seeking self aggrandizement and therefore they cannot wait. They are not content to lay the foundations of something which will grow to a magnificent maturity in the fullness of time. The man who designed the Temple of Baalbeck knew that it would take over two hundred years for the buildings to be completed. He designed it that way and was fully aware that he could never live to see it completed. Therein lies true greatness, but that is different. There is only one way to create a large empire in the lifetime of one man. That is to steal great chunks of it at a time from somebody who already has an empire, and this Napoleon decided to do. He can be forgiven for imagining that such enormous tasks were within his power, because he was in the habit of doing things in a very big way. A celebrated historian says of him, " In the short span of twenty years he fought more wars and gained more victories and marched more miles and conquered more square kilometres and killed more people and brought about more reforms and generally upset Europe to a greater extent than anybody (including Alexander the Great and Jenghis Khan) had ever managed to do." If a man can do all that in twenty years, surely he is entitled to consider himself capable of building up an empire in his whole lifetime!

So Napoleon cast about in his mind as to where to begin, and, as it was part of his nature to "play only with the purple chips," he decided to collect the biggest parts of his proposed empire first. That decision naturally led his imagination towards the wealthy Orient. India was the obvious nucleus. Besides, on the way to India he could pick up some very useful material.

The next thing to do was to consider the best route by which the French Army could reach India.

Those who have made a great study of the habits of ants tell us that these tiny insects have an intelligence which is almost akin to that of human beings. Nevertheless, if you watch an ants' nest for long enough you will probably be struck by one thing which does not seem to bear out this theory. The majority of the ants cover a great deal of ground in getting from A to B. They hurry along by tortuous routes which they, being so close to the ground, probably consider to be the shortest. You, however, with your wider view, can see what a lot of time they waste. If you are patient, however, there is almost sure to come along, sooner or later, one ant which goes direct, or almost direct, from place to place. That ant appears to have an instinct which puts it a long way ahead of its fellows. It seems as though this ability to stand back and see things in their true perspective is also given to a few, but very few, human beings. This quality which they possess is called genius.

Napoleon was a genius. He thought straight. In consequence, when he had made up his mind to conquer India he decided to go straight for it. The following map shows how extraordinarily straight his planned route turned out to be. The date was 1798.

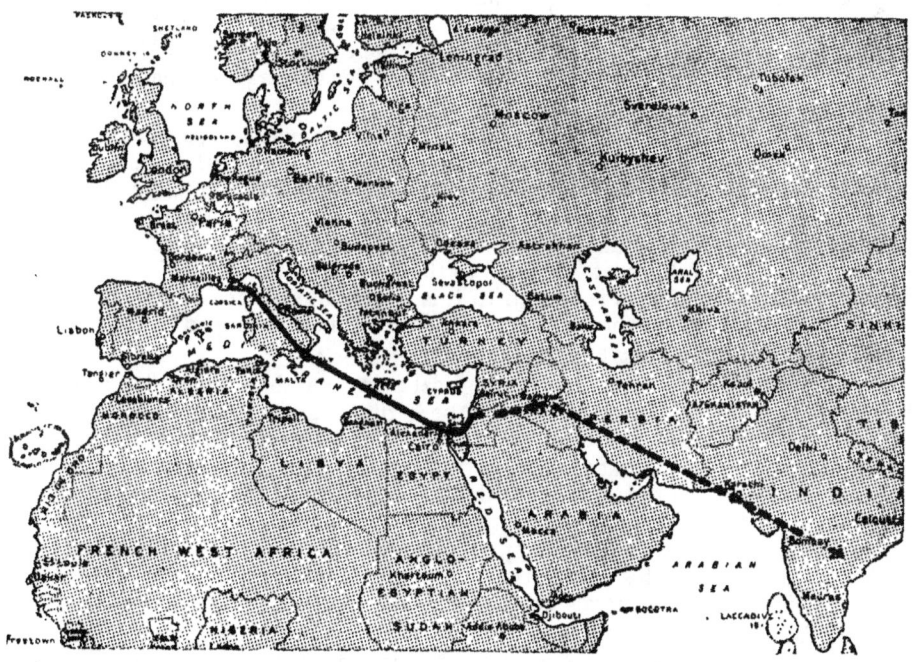

———————— Route actually covered by Napoleon's Armies.

- - - - - - - - Route planned for Napoleon's Armies.

As his next step Napoleon worked out an alliance with a gentleman called Tippoo Sahib, who was a thorn in the flesh of the British as far as Southern India was concerned, and plans were made in the greatest detail whereby the French Army, on its arrival in India, should co-operate with the Indians to drive the British out. This was to be called " Liberating the Indians from the yoke of the British."

But, in spite of his " destiny," Napoleon was not to reach India. He started out in great style and conquered Egypt with a big army which included nearly all the requisites to found a cultured empire (even scientists and " savants " were amongst their number), but British sea power brought his more ambitious plans to nought. He succeeded only in " Liberating the Egyptians from the yoke of the Turkish Mamelukes." Sir Sidney Smith, with two British ships of the line, supported the Turks to such good purpose at Acre that, after sixteen assaults, the French Army had to give up their attempts to take the town and return, plague stricken and half starving, to Egypt. That ended Napoleon's attempt to found a big Eastern Empire. After he had struggled back to Cairo with the remnants of his desert-weary and disease-ridden army he slunk off, almost in the dead of night, without even informing his faithful soldiers that he was leaving them. He was needed back in Europe. His " destiny " had called him. Some historians even claim that the critical nature of events in France, at that time, were responsible for his decision to abandon his Eastern ambitions. But most of us prefer to think that the instrument used by Fate to dissuade him was that jovial, gallant and sometimes even crack-brained sailor, Sir Sidney Smith.

Now what was Adolf Hitler's approach to this problem ?

Hitler was a genius of another sort, but he did not think straight. To call him a " twister " would be to use a slang phrase which nevertheless is very descriptive of his whole character from many points of view. He did not favour the direct approach. There was, to judge from his own book, very little that could be said to be " straight " about his outlook. Even the cross which he chose for his emblem has crooked arms. In spite of this, however, there was more than Hitler's natural aversion to straightforward measures behind his decision against marching straight to India.

The Nazi Party had at its disposal the accumulated experience of past efforts against the British. Planning to destroy the British Empire has, as we have already seen, been a favourite occupation for a long time amongst the more enlightened of the German people. For them it assumed a status comparable almost to the pursuit of sport and games in Britain. There was, therefore, in existence when Hitler came into power a host of different " plans " to that end. In the light of events it seems doubtful whether Hitler added much to this storehouse of ideas. He seems rather to have helped himself freely to what he thought was best as judged by the knowledge gained from his experience as a corporal in the last war.

Judging by the relations between the Nazi Party and the German Corps of Officers it would appear that Hitler had always been quite autocratic in the choice of his course of action. Results seem to indicate that he eventually chose those plans which lent themselves rather to party expediency than to strategic soundness. Even then there was a flavour of impatience about the execution of those plans : an apparent tendency to abandon them before they had time to mature, in favour of others with a more immediate appeal. The Party was always working under the whip of opportunism. Undoubtedly this was at the root of the trouble which grew up so steadily between Hitler and his generals.

One is tempted to the impertinence of trying to picture the inception of one of those major strategic plans. It would have happened, of course, some years before the war, because the necessary machinery was set in motion by the Germans long before actual hostilities broke out.

We can picture Hitler in conference with the leading officers in his various services. He is probably feeling a trifle overdressed in one of the new uniforms to which he has yielded by gradual stages as his power has grown. He would be much more at home in his greasy old trench coat of former days. Besides, these officers make him feel uncomfortable. They are studiously "correct," but they have an air of superiority and a veiled sneer which maddens him, although he cannot pin it down.

But they must be impressed, these officers, and he is going to impress them to no mean tune. He has put a lot of work into his preparations. He has been delving about amongst innumerable " plans " for days beforehand, and now has a considerable superficial knowledge which he is going to display to the best advantage.

" Gentlemen, I am going to take Egypt first."

This is meant to be a Napoleonic opening. However much he may have hated being compared to Napoleon in the light of subsequent events, there is no doubt about the Corsican being his idol and model at that time.

The officers are not, in fact, impressed, but they show a tactful interest and surprise. Then Hitler produces a map and they crowd respectfully round his chair. He turns the map ostentatiously, first one way then another. Finally he tears it up with a magnificent gesture.

" These maps are out of date, gentlemen." He glances round the circle with the rare twinkle in his eye which denotes an impending joke and gives permission for the appropriate laughter when it arrives. " Let us make our own maps, not study those made by other people ! "

The joke being over, he takes a piece of paper on which he rapidly draws an outline map. He has practised this assiduously beforehand and does it with some skill. The outline looks like this :—

The reader may possibly have recognised this outline. It is more probable, however, that he feels like the schoolboy who wrote, in reply to an exam question, "The answer is familiar, but at the moment it escapes me."

But the Fuhrer is putting in some names now, so we shall see what the map is really about. These are the names he fills in :—

The reader will now recognise the map quite definitely, but it may still appear rather odd. The reason for its strange appearance is that he has never seen it this way up. The atlases invariably print maps with the north on the top, but Hitler prefers his map the way he has drawn it. That is the German point of view. Now he is drawing in a huge pair of pincers, like this :—

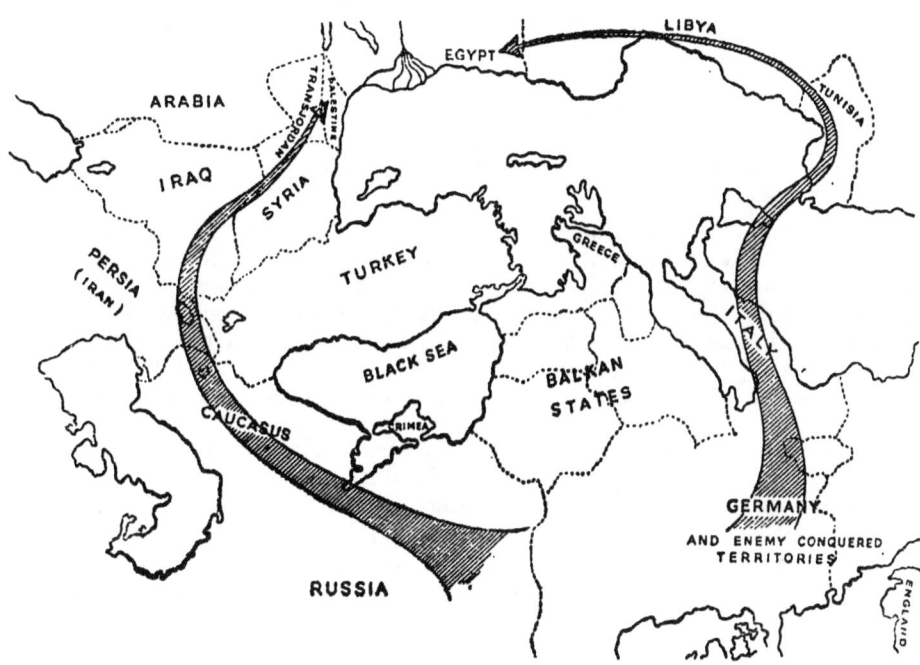

Now that the map is finished the plan becomes clear as crystal. Hitler beams. The officers fawn. Everybody is happy. As a matter of fact the officers learnt all this stuff at their kindergartens. But it pays to be tactful with the Fuhrer.

Then the Great Man explains. "I will show you how easy it will be." His tone implies that only for HIM, of course, will it be easy. Napoleon attempted to destroy the British Empire and so did the Kaiser. But HE will succeed where they failed. HE rapidly outlines HIS method.

"In the West Italy is the key. Mussolini will do as I tell him." There is scorn in his voice for the man who at one time was his inspiration. "In the East Russia will be a problem. That you must leave to me." He puffs himself up impressively. "Turkey we can ignore. The Turks are not essential. . . . But if they are reasonable . . ." he shrugs his shoulders expressively.

"Persia is already prepared." He rubs his right thumb over the crook of his forefinger in the universal sign for "baksheesh!" "Already," he says with satisfaction in his voice, "Imperial Airways have been thrown out of Persia. In Iraq I have my agents. Syria and Palestine will be dealt with in due course. It will all be very simple." He looks round pompously as though about to announce a fact which he alone has discovered. "Simplicity, gentlemen, is the key to success in every plan."

An Admiral with a hard-bitten face clears his throat. He is about to make some tactless remarks about the British Navy. Hitler cuts him short

"I am fully aware, my dear Admiral, that our naval strength lies in under-water craft. That is good. But it will be our armies that will conquer the British Navy." This is a big moment. This will impress them immensely. He pauses for effect. "Look."

The officers bow over him as he runs a finger round the shores of the Mediterranean. Then his finger comes to rest above the port of Alexandria.

"When our armies have captured the ports of our enemies, their navies will be useless. They will perish!"

The finger is raised and hovers indecisively over the Black Sea and Sevastopol. He shrugs slightly, as though dismissing a thought. Then, with a flashing smile, he looks up for approval. The approval is there. Expressions of awed surprise are his reward. This is all the more extraordinary when we consider that all these officers were brought up on the theory of "the march round the oceans." They were smacked by their nannies for babbling about it in their prams when they were supposed to be asleep. The "Geopolitical" enthusiasts in Germany had been preaching it for years. The Kaiser probably lost the last war through building a large navy instead of listening to Haushofer. But the Kaiser was vain. He wanted a big navy because King Edward had one. He'd far better have stuck to his armies. But vanity always seems to bring down these Germans.

And so this momentous conference breaks up amidst protestations of admiration for the genius of the Fuhrer. Lip-service, quite possibly, but vanity makes it palatable. He will not last long, this Hitler, but it pays to keep in with him whilst he has power!

As the door closes behind the resplendent officers the "genius" slumps in his chair, his chin upon his chest, his hands stretched out before him on the table. His fingers beat a nervous tattoo. He has impressed these sneery officers. Or hasn't he? Sometimes big men feel very empty inside. He glowers beneath his ridiculous lock of hair. Anyhow, he'll teach them a lesson one day, the frozen faced stuffed tunics! He'll teach them. Heil Hitler!

Now Hitler's maps have been very useful in showing us the strategic importance of Palestine but there is more to its key position than that. There is the vital question of oil. Modern wars depend to a very large extent upon oil. Armies and navies and, above all, air forces cannot exist without it. This has brought about a very considerable change in warfare generally. In the old days an army could live for a long time on the land and the resources of the conquered enemy. Wars of attrition were therefore possible. It took a long time to starve out a defended country. Starvation is a slow process. But if you fail to put oil in your car it will stop as soon as its existing supply has run out. And it will stop dead. There is no slow process here. The same applies to nearly all fighting machines to-day. Oil, and good mineral oil to boot, is essential to keep them going. Petrol can be made from all sorts of substitutes, but you can only use one material for lubricating engines. Oil which comes out of the ground! If Germany's war machine were to run out of oil it would stop dead, just like your car.

Therefore Hitler was bound to look for oil because he had precious little for his enormous needs. So let us glance once more at the map, but this time we can have it the usual way round. It will be easier for *us* that way, and the time has not yet come when the Germans can reverse all the atlases. This map shows the principal oil fields in the Middle East:—

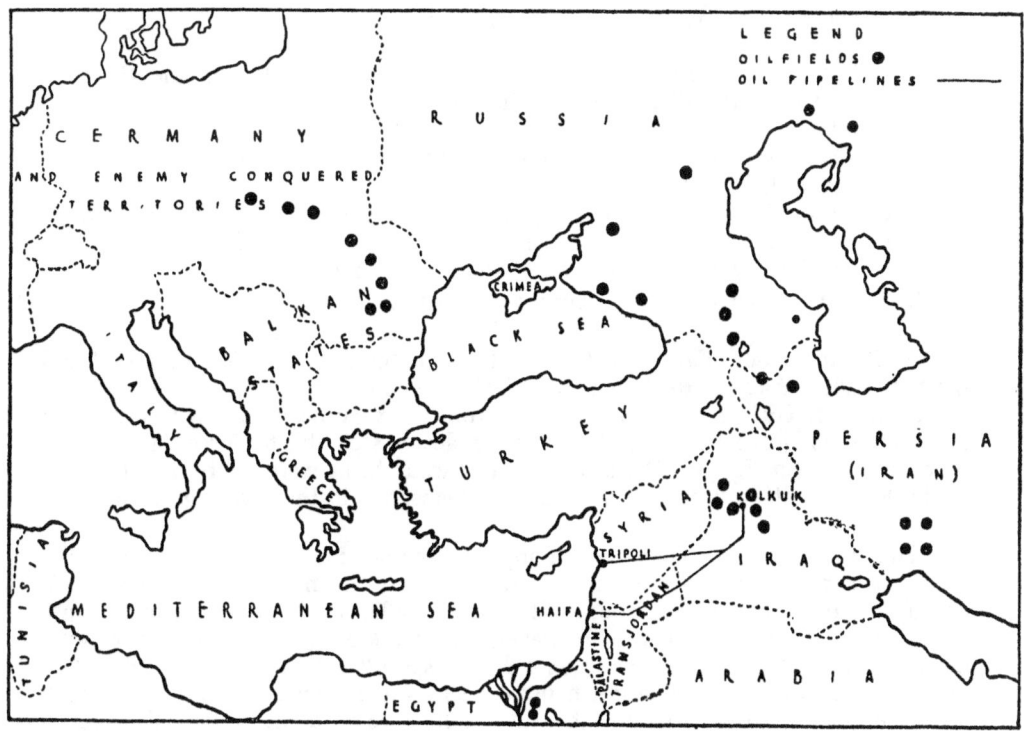

This oil map also introduces us to the oil pipe-lines which run across the Syrian desert from Kirkuk to the Mediterranean. The men of the Royal Wilts were to see a great deal of these pipe-lines before they were finished with the Middle East. That is a figure of speech, really, because you cannot see the actual pipes. They are buried under the sand. But telephone wires run above them, hung on beautiful silver poles, all of which are numbered and equally spaced. These poles are a godsend to travellers in this desert because, as long as you remember whether you are north or south of them it is almost impossible to get permanently lost. Also, by noting the numbers on them and doing a rapid calculation you can nearly always find out exactly where you are on the map. There is, indeed, precious little else in that vast expanse to give you any indication.

So oil was one of the primary reasons why Hitler wanted to capture this part of the world.

Then Palestine was an ideal place for Britain to keep a strategic reserve. By that is meant a suitable country for training large bodies of troops where they will be available for and as nearly as possible equidistant from the principal theatres of operations. In Palestine you can train for almost any kind of warfare and a German general once said, before the war, " We envy you Palestine because it is the finest training ground in the world."

This latter aspect had become more important since the Anglo-Egyptian treaty, which was signed just before the war. There is no need to go into details of that treaty here, but, broadly speaking, Britain agreed thereby to take all her troops out of Egypt, with the exception of those required to guard the Suez Canal.

It should now be clear why Palestine, apart from its having always been the cross roads of civilisation, was of tremendous importance to us at the beginning of

and throughout the progress of this war. To sum up, here are the principal reasons :—
    1. It is essential to hold Palestine in order to guard Egypt and the Suez Canal, the lifeline of the British Empire.
    2. Oil.
    3. The suitability of Palestine for keeping strategic reserves.
    4. The Anglo-Egyptian Treaty.

Because of all this, British troops, in as great a number as could be afforded, had to be sent to Palestine. As that country is particularly suited to cavalry operations, the 1st Cavalry Division was an obvious choice for this duty.

That is why the Royal Wiltshire Yeomanry sailed for Palestine in January, 1940.

As it turned out, Fate had decreed, through the media of Mr. Churchill and the War Office, that the Regiment was to play some part in the cutting off of each of the claws of Hitler's " pincers " which, from the very beginning of the war and even before hostilities had ever started, were closing steadily, by force, bribery and propaganda, upon Egypt. We shall see later what tasks were allotted to the men of the Royal Wilts and how they acquitted themselves in the carrying out of those tasks.

The reader will by now have, we hope, a very fair idea as to the reasons why the 1st Cavalry Division was sent to Palestine. But to the majority of the Regiment, during those bitter months round Christmas, 1939, in Nottinghamshire, those reasons were still most obscure. However, once we knew for certain that we were destined for the Holy Land, there was a deal of speculation as to exactly what part of it we were likely to settle down in to begin with. Therefore we were much intrigued when we were told to label all our luggage to a mysterious place called " Port Q." There was a real " thriller " atmosphere about that and the secret was so well kept that very few of us guessed the answer until we were well away from England.

" Port Q " turned out to be Haifa.

There is no need to dwell much further upon our sojourn in Nottinghamshire. It was, indeed, a dreary time altogether and very few pleasant memories of it remain in our thoughts. Split up over the county in squadron messes we learnt a deal about how to look after ourselves in small units and, as the whole Cavalry Division was in the neighbourhood, we got to know a bit about our fellow units. We were also initiated into the mysteries of how a division is run as opposed to a regiment.

It was bitterly cold, however, the horses were in a poor way because they had not recovered from their sickness at Wincanton, and very soon we began to get a great deal of trouble in connection with the health of the men themselves. 'Flu claimed its victims and a virulent form of sore throat afflicted many. Apart from this, training came almost to a standstill on account of the frost and the snow during that exceptionally hard winter. The Regiment had its last " white Christmas" for five years, but it is to be doubted whether they enjoyed it very much. One cannot help thinking that when, in 1943, they were wont to sing about the joys of a " white Christmas," time must have dulled their memory of the last one which had fallen to their lot.

So it was with mingled feelings of excitement, interest and a slight trepidation that the Regiment packed up for the journey abroad. There were scenes of great excitement everywhere, much discussion about suitable kit and speculation of every sort. As the day of departure drew near the sound of the hammer on packing cases was everywhere to be heard and a flutter of gratitude ran through the ranks when it became known that a few days of embarkation leave would be squeezed in if possible. During this period many a tyro yeoman was very glad of the advice and help of the reinforcements who had joined us during our stay in Nottinghamshire. Several hundred of these men, who had spent the first part of their war in France, had been drafted into the Regiment to bring it up to strength. They were mostly ex-cavalry soldiers who had joined up again with their regiments at the beginning of the War. These " old sweats " were well versed in all that is necessary to make a good cavalry soldier, but it is to be feared that, after the nature of their kind, they also taught the yeoman a number of things without which the latter could have got along very well. As a result there were many " old soldiers " in the Regiment (both reservist and yeoman) by the time we left for Palestine. Nevertheless this infusion of regular soldiers into the Regiment did a lot to stiffen it up and it was quite surprising how well the two different types got along together.

CHAPTER SIX

THE FIRST MOVE OVERSEAS

AT last the day arrived for the first " flight " to leave, sometime during January. The horses were boxed and the trains filled with what probably was, and certainly appeared to be, a great deal more kit than was allowed by the regulations. However, somehow or another it was all bundled in and eventually turned up on the quay from which the troopship was to depart. New and appalling complications arose when it was realised that, instead of going round by sea, we were to go across France and that the first journey by boat would be a short one across the Channel. To many of us the difficulties associated with getting the Regiment (in its small peacetime form) as far as such a place as Weymouth, had seemed fairly considerable. It can be imagined with what fears and hopes we set out, in our very much enlarged form, to travel from Nottinghamshire across the Channel and France, and finally to spend five or six days in crossing the Mediterranean.

However, it all went much more smoothly than had been anticipated and, as one flight set off after another, the 1st Cavalry Division gradually disappeared from England and reappeared at Haifa. The chief difficulties encountered during that eventful journey were the result of the intense cold in, of all places, the South of France. This was to be the first shattering of the illusion that it is always cold in England and warm on the southern shores of the Continent. These men of Wiltshire, before returning to their native land, were to be subjected to intense cold, in places like Italy and the Egyptian desert, such as they had never even dreamt of in their own homes. Marseilles, on this particular occasion, provided their worst experience and at a very inadequate rest camp outside that town quite a few of the horses actually died as the result of exposure. Sea sickness, as might have been expected, had seriously to be reckoned with, and the Mediterranean took the opportunity, with at least one flight, of showing that it is not always the calm and serenely beautiful blue lake which the railway advertisements would have us believe. So rough was it, on one occasion, in the harbour at Haifa, that one " flight " had to stand out to sea for fear of being wrecked inside the harbour itself by the huge waves which were in danger of pounding the ships to pieces against the quay.

During this journey across the Mediterranean, which was for the most part calm and sunny, many of us wondered what Palestine would look like. As the convoys zigzagged to avoid possible submarines and we watched the fussy little destroyers running rings around us like faithful sheepdogs, we tried from our Bible recollections to form a mental picture of the Holy Land. But few of us, nevertheless, were prepared for what we eventually found, especially as regards those who had no knowledge of the country bordering the other side of the Mediterranean, which is in many respects similar. Haifa itself is quite a large town of solid dwellings, straggling up the slopes of Mount Carmel which rises almost out of the sea to a height of some 2,000 feet. Although the town itself has grown up around a fishing village of great antiquity, the buildings are mostly of a very modern flat-roofed concrete uniformity. Our padre expressed it well when he described Haifa as a cross between Hollywood and the Ideal Home Exhibition. This criticism is undoubtedly harsh, but it conveys quite a good impression. In any case, vile as may be what man has done to this range of hills, its natural beauty is such that it still remains a very lovely place.

This " massif " of the Carmel Range runs down the centre of Palestine like a spine from north to south, with plains of varying sizes each side of it, these plains being bordered on the west by the Mediterranean and on the east by the deep cleft of the Jordan Valley. Consequently, in this tiny country which is not much larger than Wales, you have a great variety of scenery. The hills are mostly wild, rocky and rugged and the fertile plains are thick with vines, olive groves and citrus. There are great contrasts in a small compass.

The wild unearthly wilderness of Judaea, with the Dead Sea sunk in its depths some 600 feet below sea level, might be in another hemisphere from the valleys round Zichron Yakov which, with their neat vineyards and green hills, remind one strongly of the French " Midi." Lake Hule, where the duck and snipe are abundant, is entirely different in character from the orange growing country round Rehovoth which reminds one so much of California. Jerusalem, of course, is probably unique. Perched up high in the boulder strewn hills which goats have cropped almost bare over the centuries, it sets one wondering how such an inaccessible place can have become so large and historical a city.

But all this the men of the Royal Wilts were to find out later. Their first impression of Palestine was one of efficiency. They were astonished at the speed with which the port authorities at Haifa cleared this very unusual and exceptionally large consignment of men and horses, which was suddenly thrown upon their hands. To disembark a whole cavalry division with all its men, horses and heavy baggage, is no inconsiderable task. But Haifa, as it turned out, was one of the most modern ports in the world at that time because it had just been equipped, before the war started, with the finest American mechanised dock services and machinery. Very probably the handling of the 1st Cavalry Division was the only time that these facilities had been tried out to their full extent since they had been installed. The surprise was indeed pleasant because many had speculated, during the voyage, as to how on earth, considering their experiences during the journey across France, all the impedimenta of the Division was going to be landed safely at the other end.

The Regiment did not stay long at Haifa, as it turned out. They were really only staging there until a suitable camp had been got ready for them. But during that time they were extremely comfortable. Peninsula Barracks, where they were stationed, is a peacetime cantonment, and has therefore, every convenience both for officers and men. It is not quite so well found for horses though, as normally it is not a cavalry barracks. Horse lines were laid out on the beach, however, and this added a new complication to the Regiment's horsemastership. Sand, in quite considerable quantities, was apt to get into the horses' feed and thence into their stomachs with the most unhappy results. Consequently the horses had to wear heavy leather sand muzzles to which they did not take by any means kindly. In other respects the stay at Peninsular Barracks was quite a pleasant experience.

During that time those who were curious enough to do so were able to study the first piece of the Holy Land to which they were introduced. Mount Carmel and the Carmel Range was the most handy place from which to do this and provided a magnificent grand-stand from which to view the surrounding country which abounds in interest. It was on Mount Carmel that Elijah confounded the prophets of Baal, and to-day it is the home of the Carmelite Monks, who have built upon its crest a vast and modern monastery. The view from the top is really magnificent as the Plain of Sharon stretches out between the foothills and the sea for some 20 miles to the south. In the middle distance, and making a beautifully composed picture, there are the ruins of Athlit Castle, the last stronghold of the old Crusaders before they were driven from the shores of Palestine.

Over the other shoulder of Mount Carmel lies the Plain of Esdraelon of classic memory. Mighty battles have been fought here throughout the ages. Egyptian Pharaohs, Israelites, Canaanites, Greeks, Romans, Crusaders, and, in modern times, Napoleon and Allenby, have all tried their strength in that arena. This connecting plain leads through a narrow gap to the coastal plain on the north of Mount Carmel and that gap was once known as " Harosheth of the Gentiles," through which the Brook Kishon runs in a stream which is at first somewhat disappointing. Somehow the Bible gives us an impression of a mighty river, whereas in reality it is, as it is properly described, nothing more than a brook which swells up to a moderate size when the rains come down in winter. Here it was that Sisera kept his " Nine hundred chariots of iron " and, when you come to look into it, you can reason why he did so. They were kept there to guard the entrance to the Plain of Esdraelon and even to-day this gap is still a key position.

There are many other interesting things to be seen from the top of Mount Carmel for those who care to seek them, but to those of us knowing our History (and face it, how few of us did) the jewel of this whole scene is undoubtedly Acre. It lies straight across the Bay of Haifa, jutting out into the sea on a peninsula and looking very much like one of the eastern cities which we are accustomed to see in old fashioned paintings and prints. Its ancient sea walls stand right up from the water and somehow the sun always seems to be shining through a hole in the clouds to light up its white and beautiful minarets. As has already been mentioned, Acre was the final stumbling block in the way of Napoleon's Eastern ambitions. There the Mamelukes, with the assistance of Sir Sidney Smith and two British " ships of the line " barred his passage on his projected triumphal march to Damascus and India. After those ancient battlements had withstood his resolute attacks, Napoleon was forced to return to Egypt by way of that very Plain of Sharon which we have mentioned, and the Sinai desert. Had the Wiltshire yeomen been able to look into the future they would have viewed the ancient town of Acre with greater curiosity, but they did not know that later on they would take part in a battle of equal importance, which was destined to turn back Hitler, just as surely as Napoleon had been forced to return to the place from whence he came.

Perhaps, for most members of the Regiment, Haifa will be chiefly remembered because of their activities there in connection with the Jewish riots which took place in the March of 1940. To go into political detail here would serve no purpose, but it did happen that the Jews in Palestine went on strike and created a great deal of disturbance in one way and another. This necessitated the calling out of British troops to maintain order and so the Royal Wiltshire Yeomanry found itself once more in the position of those who restrain the rioter. We say once more because it will be recalled that the Regiment, strangely enough, although originally formed in the year 1794 with the express object of dealing with the threat of invasion by Napoleon, was called out in 1820 to quell the Bristol Riots.

History was repeating itself but this time the Wiltshire yeomen found themselves dealing with rioters of a very different type. Here they were trying to keep order

HAIFA FROM MOUNT CARMEL.

A FAMILIAR SCENE IN A NEW SETTING.

under very difficult circumstances amongst a community of cosmopolitan Jews from all parts of Europe, a large number of whom spoke German. Furthermore these Jews were quite unlike, in appearance, the popular British conception of a Jew. For example, you practically never saw one of them talking with his hands wagging palm upwards behind his ears. To the Wiltshiremen it was all very confusing and no wonder; especially in view of the fact that these men had very little idea of what the riots were all about, and the predominant ambition in their minds was to kill German soldiers. Nevertheless, they carried out their job well and this brief experience did them no harm. It gave them a taste of danger, tested out their organisation, and improved their self reliance.

CHAPTER SEVEN

NATHANYA AND KARKUR

IN March the Regiment moved to Nathanya, but not before many of its members had had an opportunity of seeing the wild flowers which cover Mount Carmel each Spring. At that time of the year the quite considerable Carmel range of hills is a truly beautiful place in which to wander. The whole country is carpeted with masses of these wild flowers, including many species of orchid, and in places it is impossible to put your foot down without crushing them. Words cannot convey the beauty of this scene, but one of the Carmelite Monks once expressed the whole thing to the author in a single gesture. " Ah," said that monk, looking around him with glowing eyes, " Palestine in March ! " and with that he kissed the tips of his fingers and wafted that kiss up to heaven, thereby expressing most emphatically all the infinite beauty of the countryside.

Nathanya was originally a little tiny village on the coast, much the same as many other villages along the Levant. Recently, however, the Jews have tried to convert it into a watering place for the inhabitants of Palestine and Egypt. To read the advertisements which they publish, you would imagine Nathanya to be a near approach to the Riviera, but of that it falls far short. It is, however, a pleasant enough place and the Regiment was situated in quite a comfortable camp not far from the half-a-dozen hotels and few shops which, together with a concrete esplanade, go to make up this somewhat ambitious attempt to convert a fishing village into a seaside resort. Here, at the bottom of the tall cliffs and on the sand below, the men enjoyed their first experience of bathing in the Middle East. Very few of them could ever before have experienced such warm and delightful conditions for swimming, although Nathanya shares with the whole of the Levant coast the dangers which a bather must face in those parts. The coast shelves very rapidly and therefore you are out of your depth before you know it and, the currents being very swift, even a strong swimmer is liable to be carried away before he has time to realise his danger. It was difficult to make the troops realise how much care should be taken and as a result the Division lost several men in the first summer from drowning, but fortunately the Regiment was lucky in this respect.

This period of early Spring did much to acclimatise both the men and the horses, both of whom benefited from the sea bathing. For the horses also were taken into the water and on more than one occasion a whole squadron could have been seen, entirely in the nude, riding into the sea like so many Centaurs.

Under these conditions the Regiment was fairly ready for serious training by May. Meanwhile the machinery of the Division had been getting under way and accustoming itself to the new surroundings. The Regiment at that time was brigaded with the North Somerset Yeomanry and the Household Cavalry Regiment in the 4th Cavalry Brigade which was commanded by Brigadier Kingstone. The 1st Cavalry Division, as a whole, was fairly well distributed throughout Palestine, with Divisional Headquarters at Haifa.

May and June were spent in this training area of sand and orange groves and on the whole things went fairly smoothly. Smoothly, that is, as far as the training was concerned because the clouds were gathering in earnest over Europe. During this first part of the Regiment's stay in Palestine the "phoney war" had been going on and even then, after nearly nine months, there were many who still felt that the whole affair was most unreal. There, in the lovely Spring sunshine of the Middle East, it seemed somehow impossible that war, as we had known it from 1914 to 1918, could really take place again. Something would happen to stop it before the real butchery began. Could anybody take the tremendous responsibility of starting that butchery? But somebody did take the responsibility and that man was Hitler. Having marched up and down the frontiers until, like the men of Joshua at Jericho, their enemies were becoming accustomed to these manœuvres and consequently incautious, he struck.

From that time onwards life took on a new meaning to the troops in Palestine. Until June their minds had been more or less at ease. But now it was different. The enormity of what had happened did not strike them at first. It took some time to sink in. Paris captured and most of France in the hands of the Huns? What next? There was much serious wagging of heads and the training went on with a new purpose. It was not to be a "phoney war" after all and the results of this training were going to be tested out in action. It had to be seen to, therefore, that nothing was left to chance. So the 1st Cavalry Division tightened up its girths and got down to it in earnest.

Then, on the 8th June, Italy entered the War and this made a deal of difference to Palestine. The Middle East became an operational area, total black-out was enforced, there were air raids on Haifa and the Western Desert sprang into life. Hitherto those people who knew anything about the Western Desert had been very mysterious regarding it and even in Palestine a very few knew really what it was all about. But now the British troops took open steps to defend that area. Things were warming up.

But still there was bathing for the troops at Nathanya and there, on the beach in the hot sunshine by the lovely blue sea, it required much imagination to picture what was happening in Europe. It was pleasant, that bathing. It cannot be denied. But how can a man enjoy such things when his mind is dwelling upon the blood and sweat and tears of his folks at home? Almost every time a group of men went down to the sea to bathe the remark was heard that "somehow this felt all wrong"—as though it was wicked to indulge in the pleasures that offered with all that misery at home. It was not wicked, of course, but the thought drove away all real enjoyment and anxiety poisoned all pleasure. It was about that time that Lady Astor was alleged tactlessly to have remarked in the House of Commons that nobody need bother about the Cavalry Division because it was "basking in the sun on the shores of the Mediterranean." If Lady Astor really was guilty of such a statement she would have been a sad judge of character!

It was in this atmosphere of bewildered apprehension that the Regiment moved in July to Karkur, a small township composed mostly of Jewish settlements. There they found a different sort of country which was quite suitable for cavalry training because round about the immediate neighbourhood of Karkur there are a number of woods set in sandy soil; but a mile or so farther out the country becomes rocky. Here it was that the horses had their first taste of the hard going for which Palestine is so well known. This was a matter of grave concern to men who had been accustomed to conditions in England and at first it looked as though nearly all the horses would be lame in a very short time. Many of them in fact did get lamed, but the surprising thing about it all was that, after a week or two, the horses began to take more care where they put their feet and lameness gradually disappeared.

After a short while horses in Palestine, even though they may have been brought up all their lives in England, manage to learn how to move over the country without hurting their feet to any great extent. Being farther from the sea there was less bathing at that station, although it was still possible to send the men on bathing parties occasionally. But somehow there was, during the stay at Karkur, little thought or inclination for pleasure. Things were going badly all over Europe and everybody was anxious to get on with the work necessary to turn the Cavalry Division into a really efficient unit. There was, in consequence, all the greater disappointment when the news arrived that the Regiment was to be transformed into a searchlight unit.

The consternation caused by such a prospect can well be imagined. It was true that there appeared to be no immediate need for cavalry in the Middle East, and, owing to enemy air activity, every possible means of competing with the Luftwaffe had to be exploited; but after all the trouble entailed in taking the horses from England to Palestine and the amount of training that had been put in since the arrival of the Cavalry Division there, the proposed step seemed madness to the men whose fate it dealt with. Nevertheless, the order had been given and in consequence the Regiment had to obey. It reflects great credit on all ranks of the Regiment that, after a quite natural explosion of indignation to begin with, they turned, reluctantly it must be admitted, to the idea of their new duties with a determination to carry them out to the best of their ability.

As a matter of fact, the Regiment was not, as it happened, destined to be turned into a searchlight unit at all. " C " Squadron, however, was sent to Cairo to be trained in these new duties and subsequently it was moved into the Western Desert to man searchlights there, with the result that the Regiment, or at any rate a portion of it, came into action sooner than it would have done had it remained mounted. The plan was that, after " C " Squadron was fitted to go into action with the searchlights, "A" and " B " Squadrons, in rotation, were to be trained in Cairo, whilst that portion of the Regiment left in Cairo was to move to Hadera where it would continue its cavalry training until after Christmas.

Just before we leave the subject of Karkur, let us take a glimpse into the life of one who was very closely associated with that part of the world. " George of England " was not, as a matter of fact, of English birth. Although he is our Patron Saint, he was born in Palestine, in the year A.D.270, at Lydda, which is about ten miles from Jaffa (called Joppa in Biblical days) and he spent a great deal of his time at Karkur. He came of a noble and distinguished family and was a Roman soldier. How, then, did he come to be adopted as the Patron Saint of England? The story can be told quite briefly and it is interesting.

George's father and grandfather were both the Roman equivalent of highly placed Civil Servants in Asia Minor. George therefore joined the Roman Army under high auspices and, being one of its smartest young officers at the early age of twenty, he came to the notice of the Emperor Diocletian, who sent him on a mission to England.

There he is reputed to have influenced the Empress Helena, mother of Constantine the Great, towards her conversion to Christianity. Constantine later became King of Britain and Emperor of Rome and the whole course of Christianity may therefore be traced to George's visit to Britain.

Later, whilst George was at his home in Lydda, Diocletian turned against the Christians and decreed that all professing the Christian faith should be destroyed. So George set out, against the advice of his friends, to try and dissuade the Emperor from his evil ways. That was a dangerous undertaking because Diocletian was a most aggressive tyrant. But George was determined to make his attempt and arranged to take ship from Berytus (which is now known to us as Beirut) in Syria.

The people of Berytus, at that time, were having trouble with what they considered to be a dreadful monster. It was, in all probability, a crocodile which had drifted in from Egypt (or even from India) but to these people, who had never seen anything like it before, it was a dreadful problem. Owing, possibly, to its predilection for human flesh, they credited it with divine powers. It also occurred to them that, by offering the creature human sacrifices, they might cut down its foraging problems and thus appease it. So the King of Berytus, who was a fair minded man, decreed that lots should be drawn as to who should play the leading part in the first of these rites. He was most upset when the lot was drawn by his daughter, the beautiful Princess Sadra.

This was the state of affairs in Berytus when George arrived to sail upon his dangerous mission. It was whilst the Princess was awaiting her fate in a sand pit, near a lake which was haunted by the monster, that George rode by. Seeing this lovely maiden weeping in the wedding robes with which she had been decked for the occasion, he enquired as to the cause of her trouble But she would not tell him, being afraid for his safety, and, had he been a less earnest young man, he might well have passed on and left her. Had that happened, for centuries Englishmen would have used coins inscribed with some device other than the now familiar " George and the Dragon."

But as they were talking, the " Dragon " appeared. George, being a Christian and having no fear of heathen gods, was probably not much impressed. Making the Sign of the Cross, he settled down in the saddle of his gallant white war horse, charged with his spear, and slew the evil brute. Judging by most of the pictures which deal with this encounter, he probably had to finish the crocodile off with his Roman broad sword but this is of small importance.

Again, had George yielded to the prayers of the King and populace of Berytus to " marry the Princess and live happily ever after," history might have been different. But he had a job to do and he was determined to do it. He pushed on to Rome where he was brutally put to death by Diocletian for defending his fellow Christians.

So, because he died for his faith, at the age of thirty-three, he was " numbered with the saints in glory everlasting " and has ever since been known as St. George. Three years afterwards Constantine became the first Christian Emperor of Rome and the persecution of the Christians ceased. He made St. George the Patron Saint of England and we have called the 23rd of April, the day of his death, " St. George's Day," ever since. The " Rose of England " was originally the " Rose of Sharon " which still grows on the Plain of Sharon to this day. These roses were St. George's favourite flower and his cross, as every Englishman knows, now forms part of the Union Jack.

Yet how many Englishmen know these simple facts about Saint George ?

* * * * * *

An anecdote in connection with these associations is worthy of record.

The peace time adjutant of the Regiment, Major Ferris St. George, was put in charge of a Driving and Maintenance School at Karkur. The aptness of the names did not escape attention, but a stranger coincidence was to follow. Early one morning, a travel-stained R.A.S.C. officer wandered into the School, having obviously spent the night on the road.

" Is this place run by a man called St. George ? " he asked of the first person he met.

" Yes," came the answer.

"Well, believe it or not," said the weary R.A.S.C. officer, "but I've got thirteen dragons to deliver to him ! "

And so he had. A " dragon " was the name of the type of tracked vehicle which was used at that time for hauling guns and heavy limbers. These particular " dragons " were to be used by the students for practice purposes in connection with the Driving and Maintenance course !

CHAPTER EIGHT

SEARCHLIGHTS OVER THE WESTERN DESERT

TO return to our main story, during the August of 1940, " C " Squadron had moved to Cairo where they were trained in the handling of searchlights. Then they were moved into the Western Desert and " B " Squadron took their place under instruction in Cairo. Meanwhile what remained of the Regiment was moved to another and slightly larger township in Palestine called Hadera. There they once more enjoyed the amenities of the seaside, although by that time none but the hardy cared to brave the bathing after their first summer in the comparatively hot climate of Palestine. This first Christmas abroad, therefore, was spent by those in Hadera under conditions which might indeed have been far worse. Before passing on, however, we must mention " Gracie."

No account of the Regiment's stay in Hadera would be complete without a word or two about her. " Gracie " was an institution in that small township, and nobody seems to have known how she got there. The moment she spoke to the first Yeoman who called at her café she was christened " Gracie " because of the way she spoke and her resemblance to Gracie Fields. It can well be imagined that the last thing anybody expected to hear from an inhabitant of Hadera was a Manchester accent. In those surroundings you might hear the " argot " from almost any mid-European city, but " -ee " and " ba-goom " fell strangely, yet refreshingly, upon the ears.

" Gracie's " tiny establishment quickly became a centre and meeting place for the Yeomanry, for there they were always sure of getting the very best food and cooking without being overcharged. That, it must sadly be admitted, was a rarity in the Middle East. Over and above that, Gracie took a motherly interest in the men, and did them a host of real good turns. She was a fine type, was Gracie, and after leaving Hadera there was many a Yeoman who went back to spend his leave under the care and ministrations of that capable and good-natured woman. She was a very good friend to the Regiment.

" B " Squadron, in the meantime, was being sucked into active operations in Egypt. They were, in fact, the first men of the Regiment to come into action, for things were warming up in the desert. The British had opened their attack on the 7th December and appeared to be sweeping on to victory. Within two days the Mersa Matruh—Sidi Barani area and the Italians under General Graziani had received a good drubbing into the bargain. Then the pursuit began and by Christmas we were pressing hard upon Bardia.

In the wake of this triumphal progress went " B " Squadron manning searchlights at important points along the lines of communication. It was all very exciting. On the 26th November they took over from " C " Squadron eight lights at Mersa Matruh and very soon got into the hang of things because by that time " C " Squadron knew the ropes thoroughly.

" B " Squadron had their first experience of aerial bombardment, as a matter of fact, that very first night. It was not much ; just a few bombs but most of us by now are familiar with that exciting and none too pleasant feeling which comes with one's first experience of bombing. Nobody was hurt and after that there was little offensive action, most of the time being spent in settling in and the finding of desert legs.

Then on the 23rd December they started off for a two days journey across the desert to Sollum during which they met with many minor adventures. As yet they were by no means accustomed to this desert running, although they were subsequently to become experts at this type of travelling. So they arrived late on Christmas Eve far too tired to enjoy any Christmas festivities even had there been any ; but naturally there were none. Father Christmas did not forget them, however, and in place of a stocking full of gifts he presented them with a nice salvo of bombs as dawn was breaking. This unpropitious beginning heralded a thoroughly unpleasant Christmas Day, during which a sandstorm blew its hardest whilst they struggled to get into their new positions in order to go into action on Christmas night against enemy aircraft which were not only expected but turned up in fairly good form.

After that there was fairly frequent air activity, generally around dusk and dawn, occasionally during the night and regularly at midday. The men were delighted with the few successes which they scored in picking up aircraft with their searchlights, especially when one of the German machines retaliated by machine-gunning one of the projectors and scoring a couple of hits without doing much other damage. This period will live in the men's minds chiefly on account of the tremendous anti-aircraft fire which was put up by a Monitor named " Terror " in the bay and the swarms of Italian prisoners who walked ceaselessly across the desert and clambered down the hillside to await removal further east. Living was rough and ready, but most people managed to knock up some sort of a shelter to keep out the sand during the day. It was quite unnecessary to have any kind of dwelling during the night because they were all at a moment's notice, ready to turn out and man the lights.

Early in January Bardia fell and the squadron assumed possession of some brand new Italian searchlights which the enemy had left behind. They took over permanently two of these and had a packet of fun working out by trial and error the best methods of operating them. There was, it must be admitted, a book of instructions, but this was written in Italian and that is a tongue of which the average Wiltshireman has very little knowledge. Their own searchlights, incidentally, gave them a great deal of trouble at this time. They had taken them over from " C " Squadron at Mersa Matruh and although they were British machines they had been sold second-hand to the Egyptians some years before the war. Owing to their previous owners' preference for external paint instead of internal lubrication they were not in the best of condition and it required a great deal of work to keep them running.

The next move was to a charming little port on the Cirenaican coast where the water was a marvellous blue, the fine sand on the beach was a brilliant white and the bathing was the finest that they had ever known. But there again they had little time for bathing. Things were pretty lively in that little port and they were kept busy by frequent raids at night and the multifarious tasks of maintaining their antiquated or tricky foreign searchlights during the day. The place had a name that sounded odd at first and there seemed to be various ways of pronouncing it.

Some called it "Tobb-Rukk" and some "Toe-Brooche" but not for quite a while did it come to be known as "Toe-Brook": later the name of "Tobruk" was to be famous the whole world over. "B" Squadron who were then under command of Major C. E. Awdry, moved into Tobruk on the very day that it was originally captured by the British and there they brought into action four lights during the night which ensued. The remainder of the lights turned up during the next three days, after the usual assortment of minor difficulties which were only to be expected by untried troops in the desert when working with out-of-date and ancient equipment.

Finally all the lights were spread out around the harbour and Squadron H.Q. took up its abode in two comfortable but small villas on the north edge of the town. Unfortunately these villas were too close, for real comfort, to the small landing ground and its workshops and towards the end of February the enemy located this target and made things pretty lively for the people living near it. In fact a single bomb fell early one morning on the road outside the walls of one of the villas which was being used as a canteen. The bag was one tame pigeon in a cage. By a lucky chance everybody else escaped unhurt. There was no warning on that occasion and nobody had time to get out of bed; not even Lieut.-Col. Williams, who awoke after the explosion to find himself richly decorated by a cascade of almost powdered glass. This was too much for Squadron H.Q., especially as three large bombs had fallen on the other side of the villas the day before. So on the 28th they decided to move.

Meanwhile orders had come in on the 13th February to send four lights to Benghazi and a small convoy had been sent off. It made remarkably good time, arriving at its destination on the eve of the 15th. That was a fine performance for the colossal old vehicles which the Australians had christened "the houses on wheels." This journey was justified, although the venture only lasted a fortnight, as the convoy returned on 28th February. Owing to the successful manner in which the lights were handled during that brief period, they managed to pick up several machines and this warned off the enemy aircraft very successfully from that time onwards.

These events started a difficult period for the men of "B" Squadron. They found themselves hundreds of miles from the rest of the Regiment in a very cheerless spot. Soon dive-bombing, which started with an attack on the hospital, was in full swing, and thirty to forty Ju 87's and 88's made regular raids twice daily on the ships in the harbour, the jetties, gun positions and the town. On moonlight nights the sky was full of the drone of enemy planes and nobody knew when a salvo of bombs would descend, for these machines flew so high that the searchlights had the greatest difficulty in picking them up. There was little sleep in consequence for the men who were off duty, because they were continually bombed out of bed. Things improved slightly when the gunners took a hand with some mysterious instruments upon which they were experimenting and this kept the Boche at a respectful distance.

Nevertheless life was seldom dull and the worn out equipment allowed of little spare time because it required such a deal of maintenance. Even travelling from one searchlight position to another was full of thrills with one eye on the road and one on the heavens. Many of these positions had very narrow escapes during the daylight raids, especially those which were close to the targets. One for example was only 200 yards from the distillery which provided the only supply of drinking water and had to be removed after ten bombs had fallen within a hundred yards of it. This was a nasty experience for the men concerned although fortunately enough little damage was done and there were no casualties.

March for "B" Squadron was a quiet month—the calm, as it were, before the storm. The British troops, after capturing Benghazi on the 6th February, were operating on the Tripolitanian frontier and many believed that they would carry on the pursuit to Tripoli itself. But those early days in the desert were anxious ones for the men in high command on either side. Lines of communication were the governing factor in that type of warfare. Like two springs facing each other, whilst one army was fully extended and at the end of its power, the other was coiled back and recuperating its strength on a short line of communication. Then the strong spring would push back the weaker until it, in turn, was at its limit and vulnerable once more. Many there were who thought that this process would continue throughout the whole of the war and we should be grateful to those who saw to it that events turned out otherwise.

As it happened, El Agheila was the limit of the British advance on that occasion. Great was our disappointment when, during the first two weeks of April, we had to fall back. All sorts of rumours went flying round the garrison of Tobruk as the British troops came pouring past them in their retreat to the East. Anxiety was all the more acute because nobody could quite see the reason behind this sudden reversal in fortune. At that time we were not very well versed in the intricacies of desert warfare. Extraordinary stories were heard of captures and escapes, isolated desert battles and deeds of amazing bravery. Unbelievable as those stories seemed, a surprising percentage of them turned out to be true.

The immediate concern, however, of the garrison was quite naturally its own position. Were the men of that garrison to be swept back to Egypt or were they to stand firm? As the little port, with its perimeter manned by determined men, was surrounded the answer was provided. Tobruk was to hold out and hold out it did for many months, a thorn in the side of Field Marshal Rommel which was destined to play a very big part in the final defeat of that capable German commander.

On the whole, however, the most anxious times were when great battles were raging round the perimeter in the great desert outside. There, especially at night, strange things were happening: things which were of great moment to the men of the garrison. Nobody quite knew what the morning would bring forth or what changes of fortune might have taken place during each eventful night. About this time the expression " in the bag " was coined and many soldiers of both sides ended " in the bag." That little band of men in Tobruk knew that they had only a few strands of wire and their own determination between them and another sort of wire—the wire of a Prisoner-of-War cage.

It was little to be wondered at that the handful of Wiltshiremen with whom we are concerned were wont to listen to the sounds of battle with some anxiety throughout the night. There was indeed little rest, even for those who were manning the lights or watching at Squadron H.Q. which was tucked away near the place where the tank reserve was concealed. Out in the moonlight beyond the wire, guns flickered and thundered in the darkness until the " stand to " at dawn brought every man to his allotted place in the defences.

It was an eerie business that " standing to " at dawn. Night leaves the desert as a rule in a very beautiful setting. The colours of sea and sand mingle magnificently as the sun approaches behind the horizon. But to those weary men manning their defences against the possibility of a dawn attack, much of this beauty was lost. What mattered most to them was that another night had passed and the war was that much older. They did not know how long they would have to stay there or what their fate would be. But every dawn was one day nearer and that was comfort, even though it was cold comfort indeed.

As a result and quite naturally the men became despondent. They hated their rôle, useful and essential though it was, because it was not active. But what worried them most was not knowing how long it was to last. Everybody in the garrison seemed too busy to bother about them and they could only correspond with the rest of the Regiment, thousands of miles away in Palestine, by the slowest means. Indeed during the last three months they were practically cut off altogether from the Royal Wilts who were fighting another battle elsewhere. But we shall come to that later.

Consequently, as sometimes happens on such occasions, " B " Squadron began to think that they had been forgotten. But they were not forgotten. The exigencies of the service alone prevented them from being relieved sooner. Every man was wanted in those days and few enough there were who were trained to do the specialised job of manning searchlights. Shipping was being sunk by the Germans at an alarming rate and the " milk run " (as the Royal Navy called the journey from Alexandria to Tobruk) was one of the most dangerous routes of all. Scarce could the garrison be kept supplied with food and ammunition, let alone with bodies to replace the men who worked the searchlights. So, as they listened to the pi-dogs making the night hideous with their unearthly and weird calls as they scavenged about the town, the men of " B " Squadron felt neglected. Those dogs could and did pass freely through the wire to roam at will in the desert. But humans could not pass from one side to the other. Pent up, tired and with a gloomy future, the Wiltshiremen remained there in that beleaguered port until the 17th June. On that day the first relief of 24 men was taken away and this first party to be relieved was watched by the others with a great deal of envy as they left Squadron H.Q. to sail away in a destroyer in the dead of night.

But by the end of June the whole squadron had been relieved and was enjoying a well earned period of leave in Cairo. We will not refer to it as " rest " because, after seven months of being besieged in Tobruk, the tendency was to make free with the amenities of the town which can in themselves be very exhausting.

Jerusalem was the next call, but only for three days, before the squadron went to equip itself as motorised infantry at Hadera, in Palestine, before a long trek north to Aleppo, in Syria, where they joined the rest of the Regiment on the 4th August.

Their searchlight episode in such heroic circumstances was a great adventure for " B " Squadron and one during which they did great service and suffered considerably. Looking back on it, as so often happens, it did not seem so bad. Probably, apart from the moments of intense anxiety which time knows so well how to dull in memory, the incidents most easily recalled would be connected with such trifles as learning to use Italian weapons and the joy of potting back at the enemy with his own guns. Happy associations with the 16th Heavy A.A. Battery at Mersah Matruh and Sollum and later on the 4th A.A. Brigade in Tobruk. Scratch games of cricket and football which were frequently interrupted by flight to cover as the bombers came over. Swimming—not only for pleasure, but in preparation for stern necessity should the unwelcome occasion arise. The Squadron distillery of which they were inordinately proud and which they had constructed themselves from 40-gallon drums to supply quite drinkable water from the sea. The fun of improvising grossly unorthodox repairs to a heterogeneous mixture of out-of-date vehicles, acquired by all sorts of improbable means. Motor cycling under difficulties on the twenty odd machines (and some of them were very odd) which in strange ways had accrued to the squadron.

But behind all that was a ceaseless anxiety and a background of hard work with danger and little sleep. It did, however, prepare " B " Squadron in large measure for the trials which lay before them. Few if any would have gone without that experience had they been given the benefit of the choice. It must be admitted all the same that many of them would probably have preferred the other form of initiation into battle which, almost simultaneously, was falling to the lot of the remainder of the Royal Wilts in another part of the Middle East.

CHAPTER NINE

MECHANISATION

MEANWHILE, let us see what was happening to the rest of the Royal Wilts whom " B " Squadron had left behind in Palestine.

After spending Christmas at Hadera as a horsed unit, they had moved, during the first week in January, 1940, to a hutted camp at Jenin, which is situated at the head of the plain of Esdraelon. This, incidentally was the first time that the men had been given the opportunity of living in huts since they landed in Palestine. Up till that time they had always had tented camps, and the feeling of a roof over their heads after so many months in the open was very welcome indeed. Then, when " B " Squadron left the Regiment to go and relieve " C " Squadron with the searchlights in the Western Desert, the first signs of mechanisation appeared. " C " Squadron, on their return, were issued with 15-cwt. trucks instead of horses.

In a regiment which had always prided itself upon being cavalry this incipient switch-over to mechanisation was, quite naturally, greeted with a great deal of apprehension. Few of the Regiment were mechanically minded and all were concerned at the prospect of losing their horses. There was, therefore, much slapping of riding boots and wagging of heads when the news got round about " C " Squadron and their new, or rather we should say old, because they were very old, trucks. All the familiar and well tried arguments were trotted out again, although we had heard them so many times before, when the regular cavalry regiments had originally been mechanised. " There will always be a job for the cavalry " said the champions of the horse. " Oh no there won't " replied the mechanically minded, " Everything that can be done from a horse can now be done from armoured cars or motor bicycles." " But," countered the die-hards, " a man on a horse can see over miles more country than a man on his feet: there is nothing like cavalry for getting information." But the modernists would have none of it. " All that's done by aeroplanes nowadays," they said and this last argument annoyed the lovers of horses most of all, for they hated aeroplanes. What a noise the beastly things made and, besides, they wouldn't be any use in war because their engines would be stopped by rays from enemy aircraft ! And so it went on, and it must be admitted that there were a number of the old brigade who never really took to mechanisation.

But mechanisation had come, and come to stay. There, on the Plain of Esdraelon, " C " Squadron learned to drive its trucks and was initiated into the mysteries of "maintenance." Strangely enough that spot had been the scene of one of Napoleon's most personal victories, and one in which his cavalry were heavily involved. Kleber had got into difficulties not far from Jenin whilst Napoleon was attending to the Siege of Acre. The Corsican, when told of the situation, went immediately to the aid of his general and extricated him and his troops from imminent defeat by the Mamelukes. This he is reported to have accomplished by the sheer force of his personality and the never failing confidence which he was able to inspire in his soldiers.

What would Napoleon have said if, as he rode back to Acre aglow with his personal triumph, it had been suggested that one day cavalry soldiers would be discarding their horses, on the Plain of Esdraelon, in favour of vehicles which moved of their own accord ? Would he have been incredulous and poured scorn on the idea ? It is much more likely that he would have sent for his Chief Engineer, and told him to look into the possibilities of mechanised warfare !

The Royal Wilts, after their first natural reaction, accepted the inevitable and got down to work in a practical fashion. The Divisional Commander had decided that each horsed regiment in " 1 Cav. Div." should have one mechanised squadron mounted in trucks. So " C " Squadron was chosen at the beginning of November and every man in it trained assiduously until mid-March. Then they took over the job of training " A " Squadron and " H.Q." in their turn. But they were never to have the time to carry out this mission to its full, because, from the end of May onwards, the Royal Wilts (less " B " Squadron) were to learn about mechanised warfare in the hard but trusty school of practical experience. After their mechanised training had started, a nine months programme had been laid down. Before this programme could be anything like completed, however, they made a further move, this time to Nablus, which is full of historical associations. This town, which was known in the Bible as Shechem, has for centuries been the home of the Samaritans.

These Samaritans, a small community of whom still exist in Nablus, were brought to Palestine by the King of Assyria who "came up through all the land and went up to Samaria and carried Israel away to Assyria. And the King of Assyria brought men from Babylon and Cutha and placed them in the cities of Samaria instead of the children of Israel and they possessed Samaria and dwelt in the cities thereof." These imported tribes were a great trouble to the Jews for many years, after which they flourished throughout the whole of the Middle Ages in their adopted country. There are very few of them left now, however, but they still carry out their ancient rites in Nablus. In particular, they are wont to celebrate the Passover by climbing to the summit of Mount Gerizim and once every year all the remaining Samaritan families climb up to the top of this mountain to spend a week there in feasting and worshipping precisely as did their ancestors thousands of years ago. The view from Mount Gerizim is magnificent. In company with its twin, Mount Ebal, which is even higher, it guards the entrance to Nablus. "And when the Lord will bring you onto the land which you are come to inherit, you shall offer up a blessing on Mount Gerizim, and a curse on Mount Ebal."

These and many other interesting historical facts were to be learnt at Nablus, but the Regiment had little time in which to study ancient history. They were, as a matter of fact, probably more interested in the "Valley of Death," a precipitous road which leads through a valley north of Mount Ebal and in which, during the last war, a whole Turkish column was flung to death and disaster in a deep gully. There the Turks suffered what must have been one of the first bombing attacks from the air which has ever been recorded. The Royal Flying Corps, as the R.A.F. was then known, used on this occasion, to stampede the Turkish horse transport on the mountain road, Mills bombs which were wrapped up in tape, so that they did not explode until they had fallen some thousands of feet through the air.

It was in these historical surroundings, at Nablus, that the Regiment (that is to say "A" Squadron, " C " Squadron and " H.Q." Squadron) learnt that it was at last to go into action.

"WAVELL'S THIRTY THOUSAND."

> "The frontiers of States are either great rivers, or chains of mountains or a desert. Of all these obstacles opposing the progress of any army the most difficult to surmount is the desert: next come the mountains and third only, the large rivers."
>
> *Military Maxims of Napoleon.*

Whilst "B" Squadron was incarcerated in Tobruk, the rest of the Regiment was being initiated into desert warfare in Iraq, Syria and Persia. Before we deal with those campaigns, however, we must review the wider Middle East picture and see how Hitler's plans to capture Egypt were progressing.

The war, during the early summer of 1940, went badly for us. Shipping was scarce and the "U" boats were making it difficult to reinforce our armies in the Middle East with those few troops which could be spared from other hard-pressed fronts. "Wavell's Thirty Thousand" had to fight it out on their own and, when Italy's entry into the war ranged the "Italian Empire" against them and the capitulation of France deprived them of all French assistance, they had their hands full. The following map gives an idea of General Wavell's difficulties on the 10th June, 1940. It shows how dangerously outnumbered were the British troops whose task it was, with very little hope of reinforcement, to defend our interests in the Middle East.

This map gives a good idea of how useful Italy was to Germany at that time, and it is well to remember this aspect of the situation, as well as the fact that Italy "stabbed France in the back" just before Pétain surrendered. Memories are, unfortunately, very short in Britain, especially as regards the misdeeds of our enemies.

We must now, for the purposes of this particular story, make sure that we are quite clear as to where Iraq, Syria and Persia fit into this picture.

The first two countries, before World War I, had belonged to Turkey. The Treaty of Versailles handed them over to the League of Nations in 1919, and the League, by a Mandate, decreed that Syria should be governed by the French and Iraq by the British until such time as it was considered that they were capable of governing themselves. Shortly afterwards the Iraquis were given their own government by the British, to whom they were still bound by a treaty, but France retained the control of Syria.

So, at the outbreak of World War II, Syria was, broadly speaking, French, and Iraq was self-governed but friendly to Britain.

Persia was an independent State. Now we must consider how Hitler attempted to get control of these three countries to enable him to push the eastern claw of his pincers through them.

First of all Syria fell into his lap on the day that he finally conquered France.

Secondly, his agents stirred up a revolution in Iraq against the ruling government, which was friendly towards Britain and bound to us by treaty.

Thirdly, Persia, never very friendly to us, was bribed into subservience by Axis gold.

These plans, and many other subsidiary ones, were timed to come to a head simultaneously in the spring of 1941. By this time the Balkans had also fallen sufficiently under the German sway to open up an alternative eastern route to Egypt, the only missing link in which was Turkey.

So, by the end of March, 1941, Hitler found himself with one claw well round the west of Egypt and two alternative claws forming nicely in the east. These maps give a good idea of how the position developed :—

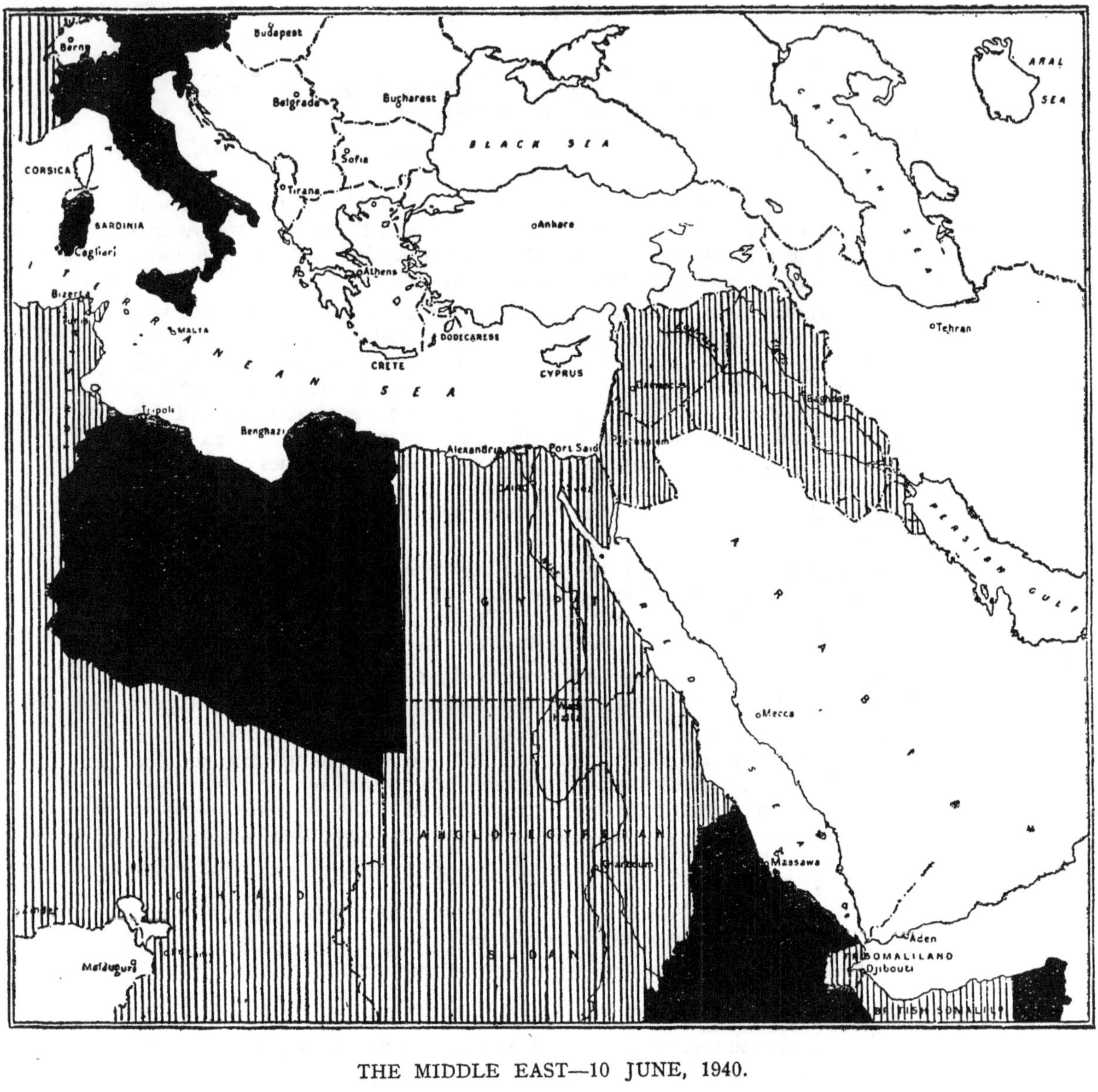

THE MIDDLE EAST—10 JUNE, 1940.

Axis Occupation   Allied Occupation

When Italy declared War France had not capitulated: hence Syria and the French possession in Africa as well as France itself are shown as allied bases. Pétain surrendered on 17th June, and the Empire laid down arms at his behest with the exception of parts of equatorial Africa, leaving the British garrisons to defend the Middle East against numerically superior Italian forces in E. Africa and Libya.

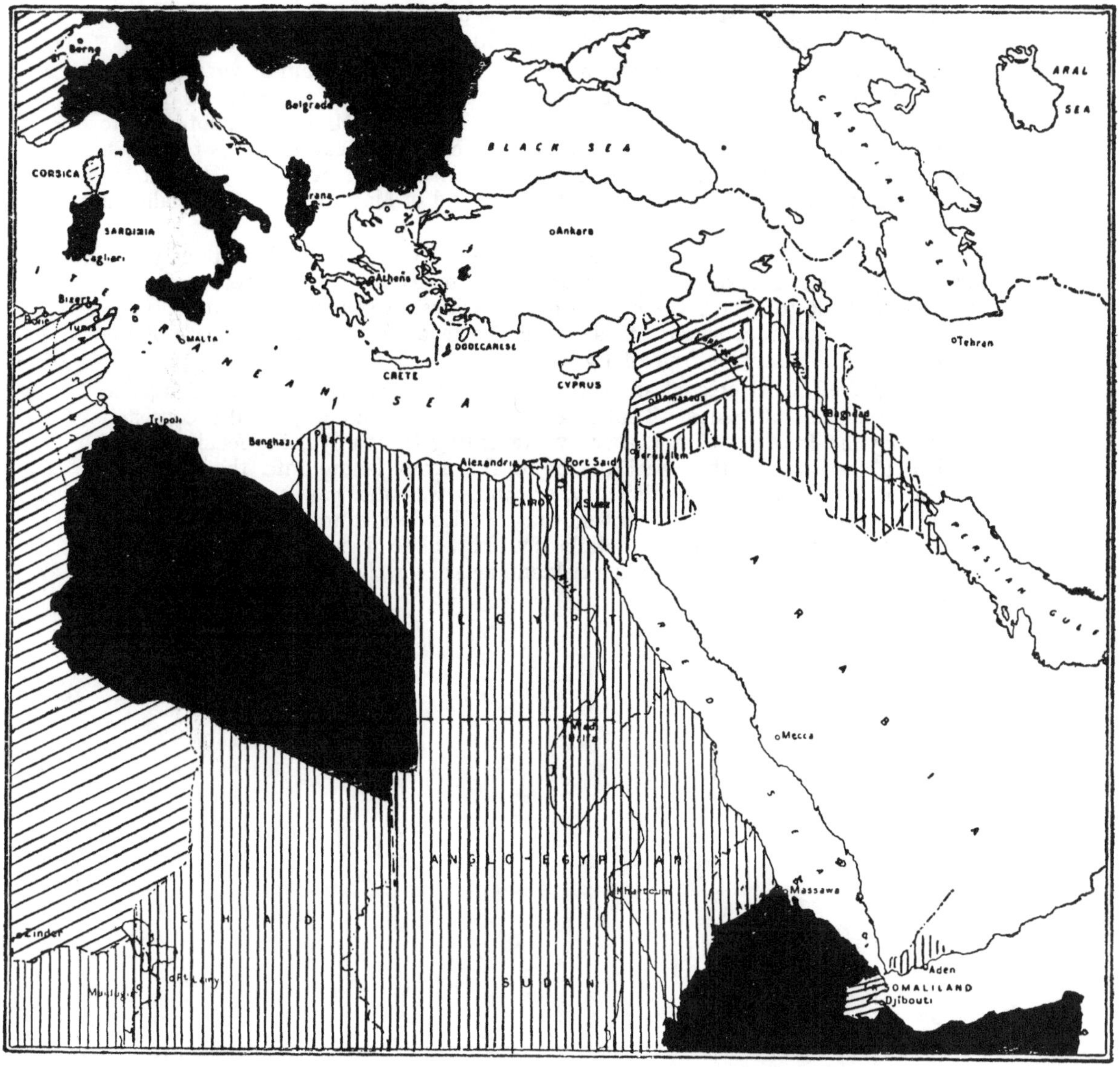

MECHANISATION 63

THE MIDDLE EAST—21 MARCH, 1941.

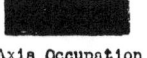 Axis Occupation    Allied Occupation   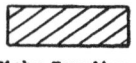 Vichy Territory

This Map illustrates the maximum extent of the territorial gains which accrued from the first Libyan offensive. On 21st March Jarabub was captured, the last gain in Cyrenaica before the commencement of Rommel's first come-back. Greece had been fighting in Albania since October '40 and was more than holding her own. But Germany had entered the Balkans through Hungary, Roumania and Bulgaria, thereby encircling Yugo-Slavia and endangering Greece. In East Africa, Keren had been captured, and Addis Ababa was threatened from the south.

Note that, in his first Libyan Campaign, General Wavell had pushed the western claw back to Benghazi by this time and that Russia was not yet in the war.

All these plans of Hitler's prospered exceedingly and the main blow came when his attack on Greece was intensified. Then Britain had to choose between holding her gains in Libya or going to the aid of Greece. The Prime Minister did not hesitate He sent our troops to Greece, Wavell had one more urgent call upon his resources, and the British had to return to the Egyptian frontier from Benghazi. In spite of this, it was too late to save Greece, and by the end of May Crete had also fallen a prey to the Nazi hordes.

This was the cue for Iraq to take the stage. The revolt in that country was very neatly timed to take place just after the Germans had taken Greece and when they were about to attack Crete. With the British driven out of Iraq, Syria in Vichy hands, and Iran bought off, all would be ready for the final squeeze of the pincers to nip off the ripe fruit of Egypt!

But Wavell, hard pressed as he was, decided to make a desperate attempt to thwart these elaborate plans. That attempt was successful and part of it consisted in quelling the Iraqi revolt and thereby preventing Habbaniya, the focal point of all R.A.F. activity in that part of the world, from falling into the hands of the Germans. Wavell's chief difficulty, of course, was man power. Where was he to find the troops to carry out this difficult task? He decided to send the 4th Cavalry Brigade, assisted by other troops (details of which will be given later), from Palestine to the relief of Habbaniya. It was a risk and he knew it, but risks have to be taken in war-time.

CHAPTER TEN

ACTION AT LAST

WAR consists of long periods of boredom punctuated by moments of intense fear. That is how somebody described World War I and World War II was exactly the same. Furthermore, it is most surprising how suddenly the transition from the one condition to the other can take place.

The spring of 1941 ended, for the Royal Wilts, one of these boring periods. A very long and very boring period. But even then it seemed highly improbable that those men who were not in " B " Squadron would do any fighting for some time to come. And they did so long for a scrap of some sort, even if only to have the satisfaction of feeling that they were in danger equally with their relatives and friends who were being bombed and in fear of invasion at home. But they had only just embarked upon a nine months' training programme and it did not seem possible that they could do any fighting before that period was ended. So they plugged along, their bodies in Palestine but their thoughts in the Western Mediterranean, where, on the shores and amongst the islands, such exciting and frightening things were happening. How lucky " B " Squadron were, to be down there in the thick of it!

But then, towards the end of May, strange rumours began to float around. Their source was, quite naturally, the N.A.A.F.I. That institute was even more prolific of gossip in Palestine than it had been at home. No move in that country could be initiated without telling somebody in the N.A.A.F.I. that food had to be sent to a certain place, and then the cat was out of the bag. No matter what security measures were taken at Headquarters the civilians, whose services were essential because of the lack of man power at that time, would get to know and then the rumours would start.

The rumour on this occasion was that the Regiment was about to embark upon some form of operations. But how? Their horses had been taken from the yeomen and they were far from being fully trained upon their trucks. And where? The N.A.A.F.I. winked a knowing eye in the direction of the Syrian Desert. Incredible! And what went on in the Syrian Desert anyhow? There was a wild rush for maps of that part of the world, but they did not convey very much. They were, in fact, very confusing because the average man (and that goes for officers too) at that time had a very obscure idea about the Middle East strategic situation.

Now that we have examined Hitler's plans in detail and in the searching light of subsequent events, it all seems very clear and obvious. At that time, however, it was a great deal more difficult, especially as most of the people concerned were very moderate amateur strategists, even supposing that they had ever, before the war started, considered such matters at all. It was most confusing, therefore, to try and pick up the threads as the war proceeded, because the pattern developed in such isolated little patches and incidents which did not seem to be related at the time. An atmosphere of "ours not to reason why, ours but to do or die" preponderated in consequence, and the chief anxiety of nearly all ranks was to get into some sort of a battle at any price. The Syrian Desert did not look like leading towards any Germans at that moment, but it would be better to put down a "revolt" of the locals than nothing at all. How vital a part that "revolt" played in Hitler's plans was known to very few in those days.

Once the plans have been studied, of course, it is easy to see where it all fitted in. Beyond the Syrian Desert lay Iraq and Persia.* Those two countries were part of Hitler's left "pincer." Therefore they had to be rendered pro-Nazi. A certain evil gentleman named Herr Grobba had been attending to that for some time past. By promising German assistance (of a material and military type) he had organised the "bad hats" in Iraq into a revolt against the Iraqi Government. Rashid Ali was the ringleader of these revolutionaries and their council went by the flamboyant name of the "Golden Square." But more will be heard of all this later on. The important point, at this juncture, was that the revolt had broken out and General Wavell, on top of all his other troubles, had to deal with it. He had to send troops to the aid of the garrison at Habbaniya before it was too late, and, as has already been mentioned, the Regiment was to be included in their number. The Royal Wilts were on the eve

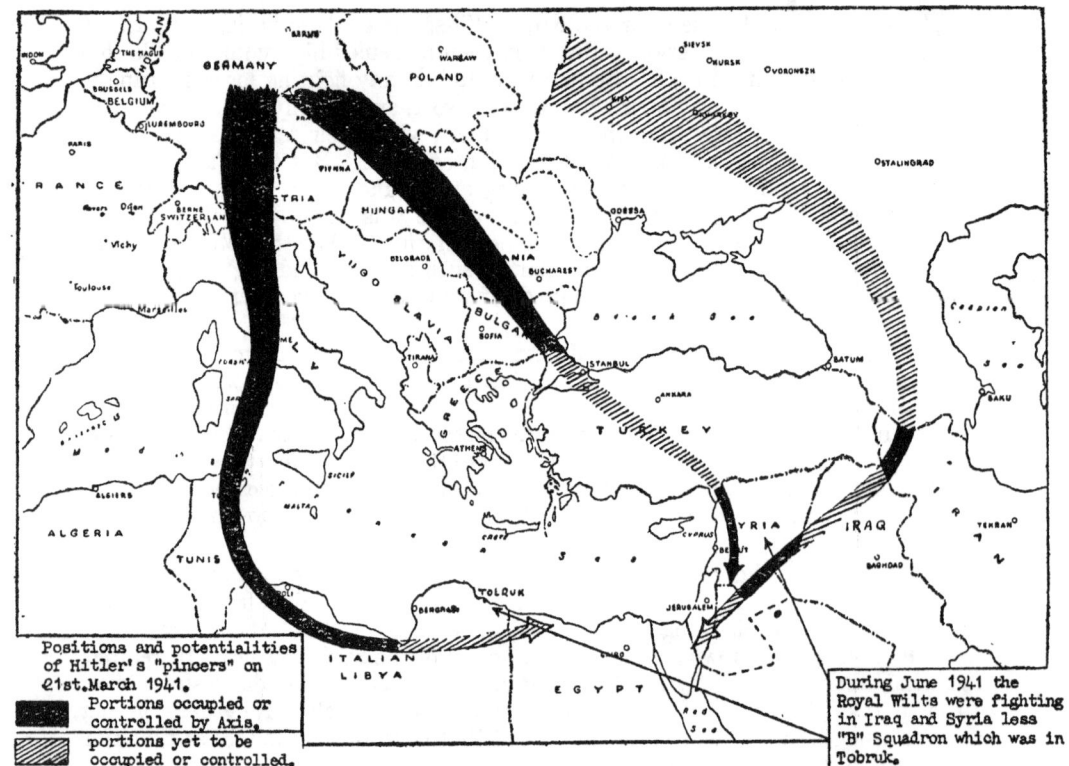

Positions and potentialities of Hitler's "pincers" on 21st March 1941.
■ Portions occupied or controlled by Axis.
▨ portions yet to be occupied or controlled.

During June 1941 the Royal Wilts were fighting in Iraq and Syria less "B" Squadron which was in Tobruk.

*Persia is marked as "Iran" on the above diagram, which explains how Hitler's three "pincers" were developed.

of a great adventure which was to carry them over 8,000 miles of desert in the next three months, during which time they were destined to see some very interesting country as well as to come under fire for the first time.

Here it must be pointed out once more that when " the Regiment " is referred to in describing the Iraqi and Syrian campaigns, " B " Squadron is excluded because they were busy, at that time, in the Western Desert. It should also be noted that, in consequence, men of the Royal Wilts were simultaneously engaged in operations directed at both the claws of those " pincers " with which Hitler was trying to bite off Egypt.

In order to put the reader into the wider picture, before dealing with the detail as it affected the Regiment, we will quote an extract from a report which was written by the author at the time, and has, in consequence, the virtue of being " hot news." It was fairly widely read by a number of people who took part, and, as nobody has as yet objected to any of the statements made, it can be considered to be an accurate description. It was originally written for consumption by the general public over the radio, and its style, for that reason, differs slightly from that of the rest of this story. But here it is.

"THE RELIEF OF HABBANIYA."

On the morning of the 30th April the garrison of Habbaniya awoke to find that they were beleaguered by the Iraqi Army. This Station and Aerodrome, upon which the British Government have spent millions, is the focal point of all air activity in Iraq and the neighbouring countries. On the shores of Lake Habbaniya, out in the desert about fifty miles west of Baghdad, it has been raised from an unhealthy little village to a magnificent cantonment and aerodrome which, on the day it was invested, contained about 14,000 souls.

The siege of Habbaniya was the culmination of a series of indignities which had been heaped upon British subjects ever since Rashid Ali, the German-paid Quisling equivalent in Iraq, had seized power in that country whilst the Regent's back was turned. This man and his henchmen, known by the glamorous name of " The Golden Square," had studied well the gospel of Nazi technique. By propaganda on the most modern lines this evil gang had worked up the passions of the Iraqis to a pitch of frenzy against the British and won over the Army ; then, closely following Nazi methods, they had spun out diplomatic parleys whilst they disposed their troops to the best advantage around the cantonment. Similarly, in Baghdad, they had virtually imprisoned the British Ambassador, Sir Kinahan Cornwallis, in his Embassy, where he had given sanctuary to some hundreds of British subjects.

The position was serious indeed when Colonel Roberts, in command of the British Forces, took stock of the situation. By cutting dykes the rebels had surrounded Habbaniya with flood water from the Euphrates, on all but one quarter of its perimeter. On this quarter a high plain overlooked the aerodrome, the only exits from which were through two deep gullies which led up to the high ground. On this plain the Iraqi Army had taken up its position. In numbers they were a strong mixed brigade group complete with artillery and it is said that they had something like thirty field guns trained upon the cantonment.

The accompanying sketch, drawn from an air-photo of the actual Iraqi dispositions, gives a good idea of the situation on the 1st May.

As Habbaniya was primarily a training centre for pilots, the aircraft at Colonel Roberts' disposal were nearly all training machines, such as Audax and Oxfords, the pilots available being either instructors or pupils. Apart from this he had approximately 1,200 Assyrian Levies, 350 men of the King's Own who had recently landed by air, and 18 armoured cars. His only other military personnel consisted of technicians, air mechanics and men of that description.

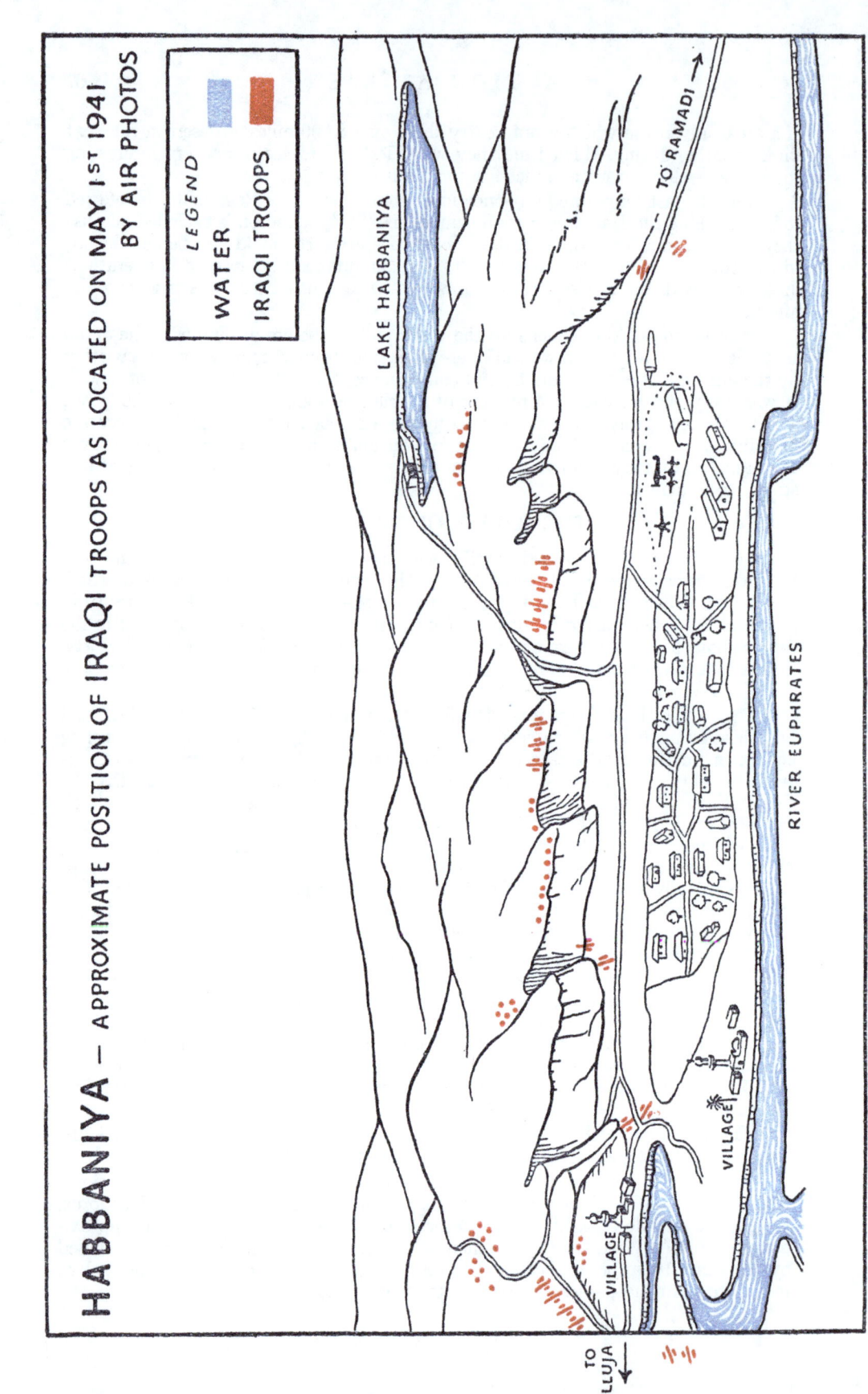

Colonel Roberts, seeing that an attack was imminent, sent out a call for help, estimated that his supplies would last, with care, for about a month, and then got busy with the meagre forces at his disposal in an attempt to clear up what was a very unpleasant situation. He took the initiative and on the morning of May 2nd struck, and struck hard. But there we will leave him for the moment to describe what steps were taken for his relief.

General Wavell, who was then in command of the British Forces in the Middle East, received this call for help at a time when he could least afford to spare troops. On the west the Greek adventure had just ended unhappily and the struggle for Crete was looming. In the Western Desert the situation was critical. The Germans were even now filtering into Syria, where their advance guards of tourists, aircraft maintenance personnel and so forth had already appeared like the few harmless-looking locusts which presage an all-devouring swarm. Rashid Ali's revolt had indeed been timed by the Germans to take place at just such an embarrassing moment.

But help had to be sent to Habbaniya, and quickly. So General Wavell turned to Palestine, 700 miles away from the beleaguered garrison across an arid and waterless desert, where the 1st Cavalry Division had been training since the beginning of the war. Horsed cavalry, indeed, would be of no use for such a task, but recently the regiments in one brigade of this Division had been mechanised ; but they were, as yet, novices in the art of modern mechanical warfare. Nevertheless the need was great, and General Wavell took his decision. So a force, dubbed " Habforce " after the first syllable of Habbaniya, was formed, the nucleus of which was the 4th Cavalry Brigade. Under command of Major-General J. G. W. Clark, M.C., it consisted of the Household Cavalry Regiment, the Royal Wiltshire Yeomanry and the Warwickshire Yeomanry. To this Brigade was added a battalion of the Essex Regiment, and plans were made to supply the force with all the innumerable adjuncts required by modern warfare. This was a difficult task because the Cavalry Division had been stripped bare over the past six months, during which it had given up, to those whose need was greater, most of its services, its vehicles and even a large proportion of its Signals, the Middlesex Yeomanry.

A period of intense activity then took place ; the Middlesex Yeomanry were summoned from the Western Desert, Bofors guns from Suez, vehicles, mostly old ones, from Cairo, and quickly the force took shape. So great was the necessity for secrecy that not until four days before they concentrated on the Plain of Sharon did the actual regiments of Habforce itself know what lay before them. They were swept up during the difficult period of the changeover from horsed cavalry to mechanisation. Finally, on the 11th May, parched by the scorching winds of a most unwelcome " khamsin," this very scratch team set out to the relief of Habbaniya. Habforce, untrained in mechanics and untried in war, was embarking upon a major adventure in mechanical warfare.

The fighting troops went first, a force known as " Kingcol," named after Brigadier Joseph Kingstone, who was in command, and composed of H.Q. 4th Cavalry Brigade, the Household Cavalry Regiment, two Companies of the Essex Regiment, detachments of Gunners and Sappers, eight R.A.F. Armoured Cars and the necessary Medical and R.A.S.C. services. So great had been the emergency and such the shortage of vehicles available that the two companies of the Essex Regiment were mounted in ordinary commercial buses which had been commandeered only a few days before from the local Palestine bus company. These buses were, as a matter of fact, quite a feature of the subsequent events ; many a time during the next few months the men of this Regiment were to be seen driving across the desert in them, reading yellow out-of-date copies of the London press, for all the world as though they were going to their daily job of work in the City.

Across the plain of Esdraelon they travelled and down into the Jordan Valley, below sea level in unbelievable heat, with the Sea of Galilee on their left. Then over the famous river and a stiff climb up the steep gorge to the high plateau which is Transjordan. Many an engine boiled and thumped as it dragged its truck-load of huge guardsmen up these punishing hills. Trundling along, coiled up on kitbags, it was difficult to recognise beneath the topees, open shirts and shorts, the big men who, clad in plumed helmets, cuirasses and topboots, had so often clattered down Whitehall beside His Majesty's State Coach.

After a night on the edge of the desert at Mafraq they set out at dawn along the Haifa-Baghdad Road. This carves a narrow passage through the otherwise impenetrable belt of lava which stretches for miles in every direction and resembles one's idea of the floor of hell. They were now travelling over the 6-in. pipe which carries the oil 700 miles to Haifa from the rich oil fields of Kirkuk and Mosul: that succulent morsel upon which the predatory and somewhat dyspeptic eye of the bloated Nazi monster had already been cast.

After a day in the neighbourhood of H.4, one of the five pumping stations which boost the oil along this pipe line and provide tiny civilised oases in the desert, they set out by night on an eerie journey over country in which it is easy to get lost, even by day, for the famous Rutbah Wells. This was their last watering place before Habbaniya over 200 miles away, and from now on water became more precious than gold. Thirsty men and boiling radiators had to be supplied from water lorries and containers, sometimes for days on end. Many a fastidious officer, who before the war would probably have thought twice about drinking the water from the taps in the Ritz Hotel, Paris, was now only too thankful to take whatever he could get—at the most a gallon per man per day was the ration, for all purposes. They had black water and purple water: water which had to be left five minutes for the sediment to settle, muddy Euphrates water, water from irrigation ditches and even water brought from Egypt. Such was their varied drinking during this campaign.

They found Rutbah Wells eventually after a few anxious moments. Just before they arrived it had been retaken by the Arab Legion from the enemy who had occupied it at the beginning of hostilities. This was the first time our men had seen the Arab Legion and at first they could hardly believe their eyes.

These warriors are picturesque to a degree, with their long curly hair and flowing robes in strange feminine contrast to the warlike array of daggers, cartridge belts and lethal weapons with which they are bedecked. They are all picked men, being mostly the sons of Sheikhs who send them to this Regiment in much the same spirit as young men in England are sent to a university. They have a hero worship for their leader, Glubb Pasha, which is seldom met with except in fiction. This unobtrusive, soft-voiced, scholarly little Cornishman has achieved a reputation which is almost legendary. The name of Abu Haneik (" The Father of the Little Chin "), as he is called on account of an old war wound, already ranks with that of Lawrence wherever dusky tribesmen squat round the tents of Arab chieftains. " Glubb's Girls," as they soon became known to the troops, on account of the feminine appearance of their raiment, were a familiar object of the landscape for the rest of the campaign. Dashing about the desert in huge Ford trucks in a most dangerous manner, they acted as guides and chaperoned our troops, in which capacity they were invaluable. Perhaps they were most appreciated when their picturesque silhouettes could be seen against the moonlight, sitting impassively on spurs of rock keeping a keen look-out across the desert. Very little escaped their eyes and they gave a feeling of quiet security. There were other times at which they danced around madly in their trucks, refusing to disperse properly, and were an infernal nuisance; but for that they were forgiven, as it was only part of their make-up. In battle they were superb.

As Kingcol left Rutbah at dawn on their 200-mile waterless journey, it looked, as do all these islands in the desert, singularly like the fort in the film of " Beau

GLUBB'S GIRLS.

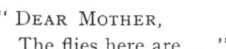
"Dear Mother,
  The flies here are..."

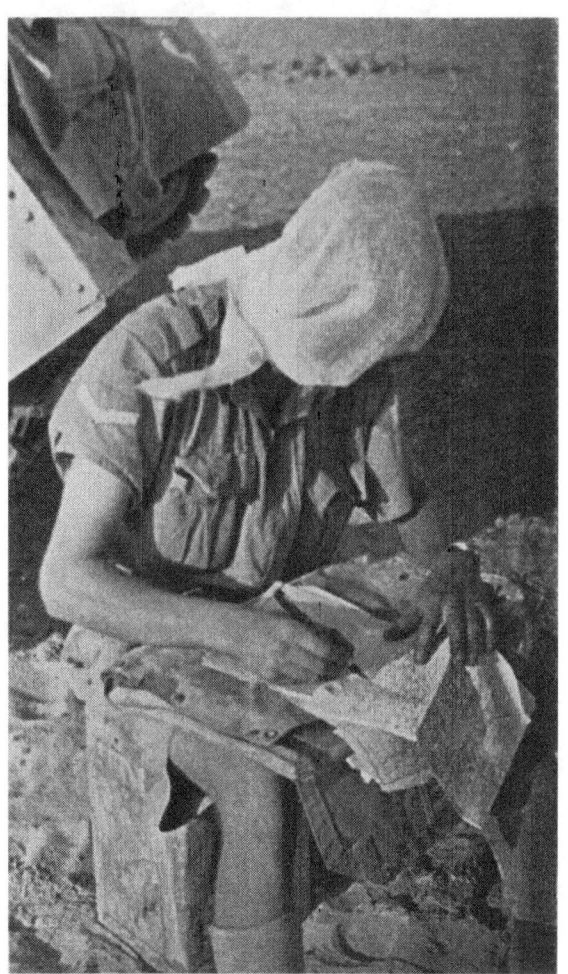

THE WRECKED AEROPLANE FOUND ON PALMYRA AERODROME.

Although Vichy colours had been painted over the German markings, the swastika was still visible beneath the triangle amidships. It can be faintly seen if the photograph is held at arm's length.

Geste." Later they received their baptism of fire, but it was an easy initiation, in the form of a feeble machine-gunning from the air at a great height. Many of them took it to be the knocking of their engines. However, they were bombed again that evening somewhat more effectively, and ran into real trouble when they branched off from the main track on account of a blown bridge and a broken dam by means of which the Iraqis had barred their way. They now had to face a 60-mile detour over uncharted desert round the southern shores of Lake Habbaniya. Boldly they pulled out into the desert, but it soon became apparent that they had met more than they bargained for. The desert is often very deceptive and what looks like good going is only a crust above and a quite impassable surface beneath.

Before the disaster could be averted many of the big three-tonners had plunged up to their axles in the soft sand. An immediate halt was called, but not before sufficient trouble had been caused to delay the column for the rest of the day. Then began the painful process of digging out the trucks in the appalling heat, a task which anyone who has undertaken it will tell you is one to be avoided. This was indeed a terrible day, but nevertheless the men enjoyed it. At last they felt that they were pulling their weight. They were in the war. Many a time during the long cavalry training period in Palestine, when life had been fairly easy, these troopers, busy grooming the big shiny black horses on which they had sat for so many hours outside the Horse Guards, had wished that they might take a more active part against the man who was now destroying the buildings which it had once been their duty to guard.

While this arduous work was proceeding the rest of the column retired back to the beaten track and prepared to spend the night while reconnaissances were made for a better route. At last a passable track round the south of Lake Habbaniya was found.

Meanwhile, the main body had clattered along in their wake on the 12th May, reaching H.4 at nightfall. There they formed a Rear Headquarters, with the Royal Wiltshire Yeomanry and the Warwickshire Yeomanry guarding the lines of communication. By the night of 15th May the whole of Habforce, comprising over 1,000 vehicles and 5,000 men, had passed through the narrow gap in the lava belt made by the Haifa-Baghdad Road, and into the desert beyond.

To those who were apprised of the risks of the situation, the danger in which this force now found itself was very apparent. The Germans were steadily filtering into Syria and had in fact already used Palmyra Aerodrome as a base for attacks upon the British in Iraq. Even as our main body arrived at H.4 they saw our fighters and bombers take off to attack the Nazi air bases. These British airmen, on that very occasion, shot down on the Palmyra Aerodrome in Syria a Heinkel bomber with French markings and a Swastika plainly visible through the paint which had been crudely slapped over it to disguise the true nationality of the machine. This Heinkel remained pinned to the aerodrome for months, an incontrovertible proof of Vichy duplicity and a visible justification for the subsequent British invasion of Syria.

The presence of the Germans in Syria, however, made the position of Habforce most precarious. A very small number of enemy troops could have sealed the bottleneck through the lava belt back into Palestine, and at that time British troops had not made good the eastern exit from the desert *via* Basra. Habforce could, therefore, have been trapped with ease. The " Q " Branch, with an eye to this danger, functioned furiously. They rushed a huge quantity of petrol, stores and provisions through the gap and dumped them down at H.4. There, it must be confessed, they would have been fair game for even a moderately sized force coming from Syria, but risks have to be taken in a campaign of this description. Frankly, there were insufficient troops available adequately to guard either this dump or the long line of communications through the desert.

But let us return to Kingcol, who by now had found a passage round the south of Lake Habbaniya. Their trek round the Lake was a perfect nightmare. The going was so sandy that it was all that the first vehicles could do to get over it, and after a few hundred wheels had pounded it successively it became well-nigh impassable. The column arrived, however, very exhausted, on 18th May. The regiments themselves had travelled 700 miles in six days, but the prize for endurance went to the Middlesex Yeomen, who, having started from the Western Desert, had completed 1,200 miles in nine days.

Meanwhile, in Habbaniya itself, tremendous activity had been taking place. This handful of British people had put up a fight which can be favourably compared to any of the sieges which have so frequently occurred in the history of British arms. By the time Kingcol arrived, women had been evacuated and reinforcements brought in by air; the enemy had been driven from the gates of the cantonment and sent packing down the road to Baghdad. The R.A.F. had grounded the Iraqi Air Force and the few troops available to Colonel Roberts had cleared the plain of Iraqi forces and repaired the bridge on the south of the Lake to enable Habforce to enter the cantonment. This was indeed a tremendous achievement, largely due to the magnificent work of the R.A.F. pilots in the garrison, nearly all of whom were training instructors with little knowledge of aerial offensive weapons or combat flying.

Fortunately there was a large stock of bombs on the aerodrome and these they had stowed into their training machines, to be dropped on the enemy, very often by hand even, from perilously low altitudes. One such attack, in particular, on a convoy of Iraqi artillery reserves of ammunition seems to have turned the day. Every vehicle was knocked out and the wrecked convoy remained there for months afterwards as an object lesson on the necessity for dispersion against aerial attack. The artificers in the cantonment even furbished up two old 4.5 Howitzers, ancient relics from the last war, which had decorated the Officers' Mess. With these they shot back at the Iraqis, who couldn't imagine where these guns had come from.

Courage is the lesson to be drawn from this episode. If Colonel Roberts and his garrison had lacked the courage to attack they would surely have perished. Had the Iraqis had the courage to break their way into Habbaniya, there is little doubt that they would have been successful.

The situation, therefore, when Kingcol arrived was a great deal more hopeful than it had been when they left Palestine. There was, however, much work to be done and they quickly set about doing it. Before Habbaniya could be considered safe, and the German menace removed from Iraq, the rebel army had to be defeated, Rashid Ali removed, and the Regent placed once more on the throne to restore law and order in the land. Baghdad had to be taken before this could be accomplished, and General Maude, during the last war, had discovered that, before Baghdad could be safely held, Fallujah must be taken; otherwise the dykes can be cut and the capital cut off from the west by water. Fallujah was therefore attacked and taken on the 19th May by the King's Own and the Iraqi Levies, with the assistance of the R.A.F. It was nearly lost again, however, on the 22nd, when the Iraqis counter-attacked the town with a full brigade. Reserves of the Household Cavalry Regiment and 1st Essex had to be rushed up, wading to their armpits in the water with their rifles held above their heads, and after some fierce fighting the town was held. Brigadier Kingstone was sent over to Fallujah by motor launch to take command on the spot. After restoring order in the town and suppressing the sniping, which was going on from almost every house, he was able to repulse the counter-attack. For this action he was awarded a bar to his D.S.O. This counter-attack was full of interest to those officers who remembered that a British Military Mission, only a few years previously, had taught that identical brigade how to attack Fallujah, in a peacetime exercise.

During all this time work was proceeding day and night (often interrupted by ground-strafing) to repair the bunds and so enable vehicles to reach

Fallujah Bridge, which remained intact. After several tedious days and nights the attempt had to be abandoned owing to the pressure of water, which increased as the gap was narrowed. It was then decided that the remaining 100-odd feet must be crossed by improvised ferry, and work at once commenced to construct one. When all was prepared the task of conveying some 300 vehicles over the river began. Crossings could only be done at night owing to enemy (German and Italian) aircraft. It was only possible to cross at the rate of four vehicles per hour. A Northern column (Household Cavalry Regiment and attached troops) used an improvised flying ferry north of Fallujah Bridge to cross the River Euphrates itself. Whilst this was going on the remainder of Kingcol was being ferried across the floods to rejoin the road at Fallujah Bridge. These crossings took three whole nights, those who crossed each night lying up the subsequent days in the palm groves waiting for their columns to reform. The tail of Kingcol crept into Fallujah as dawn broke, less than thirty minutes before the advance was timed to start, a tribute to good timing by the staff.

The attack on Baghdad then immediately took place, one column being sent round to the north and another along the main Fallujah-Baghdad Road. By this time matters were reaching a climax. The situation of Habforce was a very dangerous one and, to borrow from the Arab phraseology, "The Wind of Insecurity began to blow through the Shirt of Self-Confidence." Habbaniya itself had been denuded of troops for the attack on Baghdad. The long line of communications was very thinly held. Yeomanry Regiments were stretched across the 700 miles of desert like sparrows on a telegraph wire. Messerschmitts and Heinkels had been heavily attacking Habbaniya and there were rumours of enemy reinforcements to come from this direction. The inveterate bad hat known as Fawzi Quwackchi, who for many years had been a stormy petrel in Palestine, Syria and Iraq, was harrying our transport convoys with his band of 500 cut-throats mounted in well-equipped armoured vehicles. The artificial floods caused by the cutting of the dykes by the enemy were falling, and although their presence had hindered our efforts, their absence would have rendered Habbaniya vulnerable to attack on a far greater perimeter by large numbers of enemy troops at present cut off by the water. Altogether, when the two columns were finally held up outside Baghdad on the night of 1st June, the situation was a grave one.

But just as the darkest hour comes before the dawn, so on this occasion the enemy capitulated when it was least expected to do so. Surrounded by sycophants in the security of Baghdad, the pigmy Hitler, Rashid Ali, and his satellites had pumped themselves up in their own imagination into leaders of an Arab "risorgimento." The mouse, drunk with the exuberance of its own propaganda, had dared to defy the lion; but when it was sobered by the rumbling of the lion's roar at the gates of the city, it saw itself in true perspective. Rashid Ali and "The Golden Square" fled the country and took refuge in Iran.

The enemy then sued for peace and General Clark and Air Vice-Marshal d'Albiac drew up the terms of an armistice with the Iraqis at 4 o'clock in the morning, four miles from the outskirts of Baghdad. There, as the dawn broke over the flood waters on a scene reminiscent of wild fowl shooting on the Norfolk Broads, the Iraqi rebellion came to an end. The gong had sounded for the end of Habforce's first round.

CHAPTER ELEVEN

GUARDING THE LINES OF COMMUNICATION

IT will be gathered from this account that the Royal Wilts did not take a very active part in this " first round " of Habforce's operations in Iraq. Active, that is in a metaphorical sense, because, literally speaking, they were far from inactive. They were one of those yeomanry regiments referred to as being " stretched across the 700 miles of desert like sparrows on a telegraph wire," whilst guarding the thin line of communications between Palestine and Baghdad. They were therefore kept very much on the move, although only a very few of them actually came into action. " Round 2 " was to be their opportunity, when Habforce was switched into the Syrian campaign.

Those first two weeks in the Syrian Desert, between the 12th and 31st May, were of great use to the men in finding their " desert legs." Perhaps, on looking back, one of their most lasting impressions is the sense of freedom a man gets when stripped for action. There, in the desert, they carried the very minimum and their possessions were only those which were for immediate use. Everything else (and one is bound to admit that, after nearly eighteen months in Palestine, there was a great deal else in their possession to clutter up the Regiment) was stored with the heavy baggage, and many of us wondered, as we passed through that lava belt into the Syrian Desert, just *when*, if ever, we should see that heavy baggage again !

Consequently, packed up on their trucks, with no surplus possessions to worry about, and ready to go anywhere at any moment, and, gipsy-like, to camp wherever the end of a day might find them, the Royal Wilts felt a spirit of adventure flow through them. They were going to do something useful at last. Some of them may then have realised, for the first time, the inner meaning of the Bible words " sell all that ye have and give unto the poor. . . . "

It was in this mood that they reached Irbid on the night of 12th May, and there they had their first experience of bivouacking under active service conditions. Dispersal was the order of the day, because it was known that the Germans were building up an air force in Syria and the Vichy French were well provided with aircraft of all descriptions. Until the first bomb dropped it was difficult to make the men realise the necessity of dispersion. Two hundred yards between vehicles, which was then decreed, made a column seem interminable, and when at rest the Regiment appeared to cover the whole of the visible desert. Walking on the hot sand from one vehicle to another was most exhausting, and, generally speaking, " dispersion " was unpopular—until the bombs began to fall !

GUARDING THE LINES OF COMMUNICATION 75

Irbid was only semi-desert, and it was not until the 14th May that the Royal Wilts moved into the desert proper. This they did on the way to H.4, a pumping station which will be described later. But, as this was their first experience of " desert running," let us for a moment talk of deserts. Some of them had crossed the Sinai Desert, but not as a unit, and not in trucks. From the train they had gained a fair impression of what a desert looks like, but it must be remembered that deserts are not all identical. Indeed, they are very different in character. The Sinai Desert, for example, is very much like any bit of country between London and Bristol, except that it is completely devoid of vegetation and water, which two things, of course, really go together. But it is by no means devoid of features. There are hills and valleys, even little ranges of what almost might be called mountains, and the country generally dips and undulates quite considerably. The road from Palestine to Cairo, in consequence, has just as many twists and turns in it as the road from London to Bristol, and nowhere would you find such a straight stretch as you do on, for example, the Hertford Bridge Flats.

The Syrian Desert turned out to be quite different from the one which crosses the Sinai Peninsula. It is flatter and has less features, which makes it more boring to travellers. Also it has less water and, before the oil pipe-line was built, there was only one group of wells between Mafraq and Ramardi, a distance of 440 miles. Those wells were at Rutbah, and there are many human bones bleaching in the sand as a result of people being unable, in the past, to reach this oasis. More than one airman has perished here for the same reason, because, in the early days of flying, it was easy to miss this pinpoint in the desert. After the last war the R.A.F. dug a trench for hundreds of miles across the sand to guide aeroplanes to Rutbah. Then the pipe-line was laid. Above it the telephone wires, on their silver posts, are a godsend both to airmen and travellers on the ground.

The Haifa to Baghdad road has now completely altered the problems of crossing the Syrian Desert. It stretches, like a black ribbon across the gleaming sand, for 700 miles, and is one of the few roads upon which you really " can't go wrong," because there is not a single turning. The accompanying sketch will convey more than words can do the nature of this wonderful feat of engineering.

The Haifa-Baghdad road was not completed when the Royal Wilts clattered on to its western end from Palestine. Fortunately the engineers had dealt with the " lava belt " which had to be crossed on the second day out and had driven a tarmac track of ample proportions right through this weird wilderness. It looks like the bottom of some enormous furnace with pieces of what resembles coal, embedded in its surface, stretching as far as the eye can see. Those of us who took the trouble to think about it viewed this passage through the lava belt with considerable suspicion. We realised that such a bottle-neck into the Syrian Desert could very easily be closed, and, should we be unlucky and even a small force of the enemy get down behind us, they could very easily cut us off altogether from our source of supplies in Palestine.

The sand of the Syrian Desert, after the lava belt is left behind, is very fine and of a yellow-orange appearance. Also it has a faint but rather sickly sweet smell which remains in the nostrils for long periods and is very distinctive. So, as the trucks rolled along, this fine sand was stirred up even on the tarmac and covered everything in the column with dust. It gave a strange appearance to the men. Their hair was powdered like that of the old-fashioned footmen, and their faces were coated with a matt orange layer, similar to the make-up which film stars used when they had to work under the old-fashioned lamps in the studios.

One's first impression of the desert is that it all looks exactly the same. As the troops expressed it, hundreds of square miles of " sweet Fanny Adams." Before long, however, this " sameness " wears off, and very soon you get to recognise features in even the flattest desert. A sapper major, who was acting as our guide, had spent twenty years on this particular stretch in connection with work on the Haifa-Baghdad road and previously with the Nairn Transport Company, which operates between Palestine and Iraq. To him, every mile of the desert was familiar. We were much amused on one occasion when we had to stop because of a boiling engine. Waving his hand around to indicate the horizon, he said : " Isn't this a lovely spot ? This is where we all come from working on the Haifa-Baghdad road, to take our summer holiday." To us, at that time, the idea sounded ludicrous, because that was just one more bit of a limitless desert. But to the major it was a health resort, being a few feet higher than the desert all round, and therefore a place where the breezes were slightly more full of ozone than they would be in the surrounding desert.

Our first stopping place in this desert was H.4, one of the pumping stations along the pipe-line which runs from Haifa to Kirkuk. Here is a sketch map which should fix in the reader's mind the layout of these pipe-lines.

It will be seen that the pumping stations, which are all practically identical in design, are designated by the letters " H " or " T." Those along the Kirkuk to Haifa line are given the initial " H " and those along the Kirkuk to Tripoli line the initial " T." They are then numbered in sequence. Incidentally, it should be remembered that the Tripoli to which the Northern pipe-line runs is the Tripoli in Syria and must not be confused with the Tripoli which later played a very considerable part in the North African campaign, and which is situated on the coast of Tripolitania.

These pumping stations are the most astonishing places : you would scarcely believe them possible unless you happen to have visited them and seen what they are really like. They exist solely for the purpose of " boosting " the oil along the pipe-lines, and, as a considerable amount of pressure is required for this purpose, each of these stations has a large engine house and a great deal of machinery. A considerable staff is required to look after it and therefore small communities have grown up around these oases.

Life under these conditions is far from normal or pleasant. But the oil companies do everything they can to make the Europeans who have to live in them as comfortable as possible. Water, electricity and oil are, of course, available in abundance, and, as you can grow anything in a desert provided that you have enough water, it is possible to lay out the most beautiful gardens and even to grow trees. Full advantage has been taken of these facilities and, in consequence, these " land lighthouses " contain within their circumference nearly all the comforts of a really modern village. They are surrounded by tall wire fences to keep away marauding Arabs, and within this orbit the staff lives out its life for years on end, many of them hardly going outside the wire at all. The manager of H.4, a big, bluff, hearty man who loved a gossip, had not been away from his desert prison for seven years. Originally, he told us, his sole relaxation was to drive his wife around the perimeter, outside the wire, once every evening. But latterly, he admitted, they had rather tired of that, and so he had given it up. That was not surprising.

One further characteristic of these pumping stations should be mentioned. Each of them boasts a small shop, and this, like everything else in the pumping station, is usually very well found. At H.4 a number of old favourite articles, which had run out long ago elsewhere, were still to be seen upon the shelves of this local shop. Good vintage champagne, genuine French liqueurs and Havana cigars were amongst them : but after our troops had passed by it must be admitted that there were very few of these luxuries left. An invading army, whether it be friendly or hostile, bears many resemblances to a horde of locusts.

So, on the 14th May (the day on which the Warwickshire Yeomanry moved on to H.3 accompanied by a detachment of gunners) the Royal Wilts moved on to H.4. Regimental H.Q. and a few of the senior officers took up their abode inside

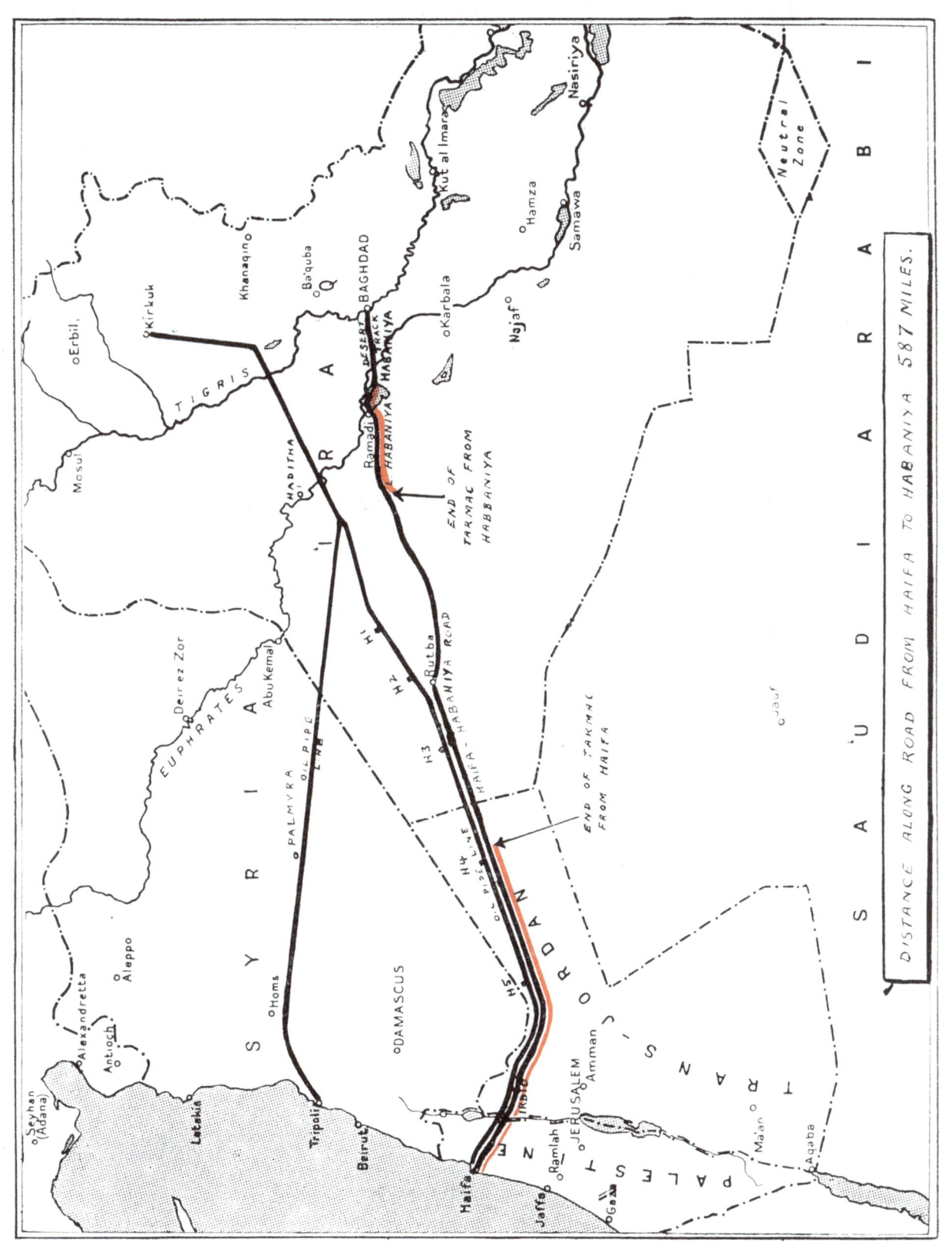

GUARDING THE LINES OF COMMUNICATION

the perimeter, where they were able to find quite comfortable quarters, and the rest of the Regiment camped outside on the aerodrome. It should also be mentioned that each of these pumping stations has an aerodrome marked off, although for the most part the desert is so flat everywhere that aeroplanes can land more or less at will. They have to take great care, however, that they do not land in sand which looks perfectly good from the air but is boggy when tried out in practice. That is why the R.A.F. have marked out proper aerodromes, although at first it looks, to the uninitiated, as though such procedure were rather a waste of time.

This particular aerodrome was very active when the Regiment arrived. A squadron of R.A.F. bombers had just moved in and was busy carrying out a series of raids on the Vichy aerodromes in Syria, particularly the one at Palmyra. This was probably the first occasion on which the members of the Regiment heard the name of Palmyra, and little did they think that within a few weeks they were to experience adventures which would leave its name for ever in their memories. The presence of the R.A.F. in action here was most inspiring, as it was really the first time, with the exception of air-raids on Haifa and other parts of Palestine, that they had had a real taste of war. Incidentally, these bombing activities brought forth the inevitable reprisals, and many a Wiltshire man was attacked directly for the first time by the German planes which came over to bomb H.4 during the short stay of the Regiment there. Nobody was hurt, but R.H.Q. got rather badly shaken up.

It was dull work, this guarding the lines of communication, except for those who were sent out on active patrols, or on escort duties. For them it was full of excitement. Those left behind kept abreast of the news by picking up gossip from the Signals, and from drivers of vehicles who were coming down the pipe-line from Habbaniya and spots which were active further east. It must not be imagined, however, that those who were not thus actively employed had any idle time upon their hands. They were far too new to the game not to be busily occupied every minute of the day. To begin with, coaxing the very rickety old trucks with which they had been equipped was in itself more or less a full-time job. These trucks were a very miscellaneous collection. The fighting portion of the Regiment were issued with standard type 15-cwt. trucks, and the supply columns with three-tonners. But only nine out of the nineteen three-tonners required to do the job were eventually supplied. In consequence, a lot of old crocks had been commandeered from local sources, and even these were always grossly overloaded. It is hardly to be wondered at that the troops very soon nicknamed the force " King Cole's Flying Column."

One particular convoy which passed through H.4 on its way to Habbaniya is worthy of mention here. It was commanded by a major in the Regiment who was at that time doing a staff job on Habforce H.Q., and was escorted by a troop of Wiltshire yeomen. The Messerschmitts had been giving a lot of trouble at Habbaniya and in consequence there was a great need of Bofors guns. A hurried call had been sent out for a Light A.A. battery, but these were hard to come by in those days. However a battery had arrived at Suez from England on the 8th May, but its transport and stores were delayed by bombing. It therefore proceeded to Cairo where it was completely re-equipped from Ordnance and on the 21st May at 0530 hours, four hours after it had received its last lot of stores, it set off for Habbaniya. Its subsequent diary is interesting, and gives a good idea of the sort of thing that was required of the troops in the early days in the Middle East. This is how the battery travelled, with absolutely newly issued transport, 1,100 miles in seven days.

   20th May ... Cairo.
   21st May ... Camped in Sinai Desert.
   22nd May ... Sarafand.
   23rd May ... Irbid.

24th May	...	H.4.
25th May	...	Rutbah (two out of six Bofors guns were left at Rutbah).
26th May	...	L.G.4.
27th May	...	Habbaniya (where four guns were in position for the defence of the aerodrome by nightfall).

That was a really extraordinary performance and those Bofors guns did great service from then onwards. The interesting part of their journey as far as we are concerned is from H.4 to Habbaniya. There the R.W.Y. Major was put in command of their convoy, which had now been joined by a petrol company, R.A.S.C.

The resultant very large and important convoy was a great responsibility for the major concerned, especially as he had up till then had no experience whatever of desert running, and only a few days' experience of deserts themselves. The convoy got through all right, however, in spite of a number of difficulties. Amongst these difficulties were the fact that the lorries pulling the Bofors guns boiled if they went slowly, and the lorries carrying the petrol boiled if they went fast. The escort of armoured cars failed to turn up: so did the escort sent out to take the convoy into Habbaniya, at the other end, the whole convoy going in, in consequence, without any escort other than the one troop of Royal Wilts. Nobody in the whole convoy of 170 vehicles had ever been over the route before, and certainly nobody in the whole convoy had any experience of desert running. Nevertheless the journey to Habbaniya was more or less uneventful except that the two nights spent in "Leager" were full of alarums and excursions. What was more interesting, however, was the return journey which the convoy made empty, again escorted by the troop of Wiltshire Yeomen.

Throughout the whole of the outward journey, great apprehension had been felt because it was known that Fawzi Kuwacqji was on the track of the convoy. That gentleman being an absolute past master in the art of desert fighting, there were innumerable opportunities for him to ambush the column. And this he did when it was returning from Habbaniya to H.4. Fawzi waited behind what he knew to be a dip in the desert, but which looked like ordinary plain sailing to the uninitiated. He cut out about a dozen trucks and neatly bisected the whole convoy. The first portion hurried on and got away, but the second half came into action, ably supported by the troop of Royal Wilts under command of Lieut. The Marquis of Lansdowne, who were thus the first in the Regiment to come into action on this particular campaign. They did very well and eventually drove off Fawzi's gang, but not before several drivers had been killed and about a dozen taken prisoner. Fawzi had already become the bogey man of the troops in the desert, and from that time onwards he became their hated enemy. Later on, when some of the R.A.S.C. drivers' bodies were recovered, it was found that they had been mutilated in the traditional fashion.

The R.A.S.C. drivers in that particular column there and then declared a private war on Fawzi and henceforward each truck carried a handful of 6-inch nails in its tool box and it was understood that any of Fawzi's gang who might fall subsequently into their hands would be crucified on their trucks. As a matter of fact they were never able to avail themselves of that satisfaction.

CHAPTER TWELVE

THE WAR OF THE LITTLE COLUMNS

AFTER Baghdad had fallen and the Armistice with the Iraqis had been signed, the situation in Iraq generally had to be cleared up. Although the Iraqi Army had been defeated, steps still had to be taken to make sure that the Nazi machinations in that country had been brought to an end.

There now began, therefore, what might be described as " The War of the Little Columns." One column of Household Cavalry Regiment was sent to Mosul, where they made good the aerodrome, although not without a certain amount of minor trouble. There they found ample evidence of the care with which the Nazi plan had been prepared. German spares and machinery were aplenty, but unfortunately most of the aircraft had been flown away.

Meanwhile another column of the Household Cavalry Regiment had been sent direct from Baghdad to show the flag at Kirkuk, where many British I.P.C. personnel had been held by the Iraqis. This column did much to restore the confidence of the I.P.C. staff who were required to begin work again on the oil fields.

Other columns were sent out with various missions, mostly reconnaissance, but to one was assigned the task of rounding up Fawzi Quwackchi on the River Euphrates near Abu Kemal. At that time it was thought that these brigands were a comparatively small force, in the neighbourhood of fifty to a hundred men, and the column allotted the job was proportionately weak. When it drew up with Fawzi, however, it discovered that he had no fewer than 500 highly trained men mounted in over seventy well-equipped trucks. It is greatly to the credit of the men of this " little column " that they succeeded in driving his force out of Iraq into Syria before he captured Abu Kemal.

Fawzi Quwackchi was probably one of the finest experts on guerilla warfare alive. His gang always managed to cut out a force of inferior numbers and, by harassing the rear of our columns and attacking transport convoys, he created alarm out of all proportion to the magnitude of his forces. That is the great advantage of guerilla warfare. For one man killed, hundreds may be immobilised and thousands rendered uneasy in their minds. Fawzi, throughout the Iraqi and Syrian campaigns, was definitely the " bogeyman " of Habforce.

True to his glamorous reputation, this colourful bandit, who incidentally was a competent soldier with a first-class European education, played a typical practical joke at this juncture. He rang up a detachment of British armoured cars on the wireless from one of their own vehicles which he had captured, and bade them goodbye as he slid across the border into Syria, assuring them that the British forces would still be flattered by his attentions at a later date in that country. It would seem that even before the allied troops marched into Syria, Master Fawzi had read the programme!

By crushing Rashid Ali's revolt General Wavell had removed the Nazi influence from Iraq and secured the great R.A.F. base of Habbaniya. He was thus once more well placed to attack from the air any German thrust southwards, either through the Caucasus or Turkey, and thence through Syria to Palestine and Egypt.

Another glance at the last map will show at once what the next British move was bound to be. Hitler's pincers must be eliminated from Syria. The Vichy French must be cleared out of that country.

But let us examine the situation in Syria at that time and to do that we must once more switch our minds back to the fall of France in June, 1940. When Petain capitulated there were many Frenchmen in Syria who would have liked to come over to our side. General Clark, who was then commanding all Northern Palestine from his H.Q. in Haifa, received envoys who had crossed the border to tell us that the British could walk into Syria with very little resistance. "I Cav. Div." could have taken the whole country—and, as can be well imagined, was itching to do so.

Why, then, did we fail to take this opportunity? The answer was lack of manpower. That went for most of our difficulties in those early days. We could not spare the troops to occupy Syria, so nothing could be done until reinforcements should arrive in the Middle East. Meanwhile, it was hoped that loyal Frenchmen would garrison Syria until we were strong enough to move in. But that gave the Germans the chance of getting rid of as many loyal Frenchmen from Syria as possible. They took this chance, repatriated many Frenchmen upon whom they could not rely, and replaced them with those of the "Vichy" type. So the German claw got a deadly grip on Syria.

Meanwhile, from the very first day after France had capitulated, there started a trickle of Frenchmen across the Syrian border. This trickle rapidly swelled until it became a steady stream over many weeks. General Clark's H.Q. set up a reception camp at El Mansura, overlooking the Mediterranean, where the wire fence runs between Syria and Palestine.

There, in the shade of an old Roman aqueduct, Yeomanry and Household Cavalry officers welcomed as polyglot and picturesque a host as one could wish to see. There were smart French officers and men (some dressed in sandals and the baggy flowing trousers of the French desert units), Russians, Poles, Greeks, Levantines of every shade, and even a few "coal black mammies." They all had one thing in common—they hated the totalitarian regime and they wanted to get away from its clutches. The exploits of these men as they fled would make many a story in itself. Some units fought their way out complete, making forced marches from the very north of Syria, hiding by day and travelling by night. One artillery unit with mules for transport made such a journey without firing a shot. It was an edifying example of how to travel light across country, for it was a completely equipped unit and ready to go into action when it crossed the border. These men were all that is implied by the word "tough!"

The French Navy also played its part in this exodus and quite a number of ships slipped down the coast from Beirut to Haifa.

The French element of this influx from Syria was the nucleus of the "Forces Francais Libres" in the Middle East. It was much regretted that the famous "Foreign Legion" did not join them and we were all to be sorry later that they remained behind in Syria. But, in view of the unusual composition of these troops, their action on this occasion is not really surprising.

THE WAR OF THE LITTLE COLUMNS

Many in England must have wondered how it came about that the first time the Royal Wilts went into action, on any considerable scale, they were fighting Frenchmen. This seemed all the more mystifying when it was realised that Frenchmen were also fighting on their side. No wonder many of the Yeomen floundered in their letters home when they tried to explain why they were fighting alongside and against the allies of Britain at one and the same time.

It is hoped that the reader will understand this paradox after the above explanation. It was really quite simple. The only Frenchmen left in Syria by the summer of 1941 were pro-Nazi, augmented by a large number of "collaborators" who had been sent over by the Boches from France. All the decent Frenchmen had escaped over the border and now, re-armed and equipped by the Allies, were organised into a considerable force known as the "Free French" and subsequently the "Fighting French."

Whilst the Iraq situation was being finally tidied up by Habforce, General Wavell had decided to invade Syria, and on the 8th June the operation began. Lieut.-General (as he then was) Sir Henry Maitland-Wilson, who was commanding Force Headquarters at Jerusalem, had hoped, quite naturally, that he would be able to spare the Free French from fighting against their fellow countrymen and it was not, at the beginning, expected that their services would be called upon. But the old manpower difficulty arose again and, as will be seen later, the resistance in Syria turned out to be greater than had originally been expected. Every available resource had to be brought to bear and, in consequence, the Free French were called upon to take part.

So that is how the situation arose in which the Free French were fighting against the Vichy French to assist the British in the invasion of Syria.

When it had been finally decided to invade Syria, great secrecy was exercised to prevent the Vichy authorities from getting wind of the British plans. In consequence it was possible to make a surprise attack across the Palestine border in the early hours of the 8th June, 1941. But after that all attempt at secrecy was abandoned and our intentions were loudly proclaimed through amplifiers which were carried with the leading troops. These methods were used to try and persuade the Vichy French, who were garrisoning Syria, that there was no use in their putting up any resistance, and to tell the local inhabitants that they should allow the invading troops to pass and give them every assistance. For some reason or another connected with Military Intelligence, it was thought that this plan would be successful and that very little fighting would have to be done to kick the Axis sympathisers out of Syria. A "walk-over" was expected and throughout the campaign an impression was given to the outside world by the Allied Press that the invasion of Syria was a simple operation conducted with very little bloodshed.

That was misleading because the Syrian campaign, though short, was very fierce. Furthermore, as Frenchmen were fighting against Frenchmen, it contained all those elements of bitterness which have been associated with civil war for centuries. This story, however, mainly concerns the part which was played by the Royal Wilts. But, before that is dealt with in detail, an idea must be conveyed of the campaign as a whole and here the reader can be largely assisted by maps and diagrams.

The plans for the Allied invasion of Syria were rather complicated considering the size of the country, on account of the difficulty of the terrain. Briefly, a three-pronged attack was originally launched, one column along the coastal road, another up through Merdjayoun and a third directed at Damascus. The accompanying map will give an idea of how it was hoped that the plan would work.

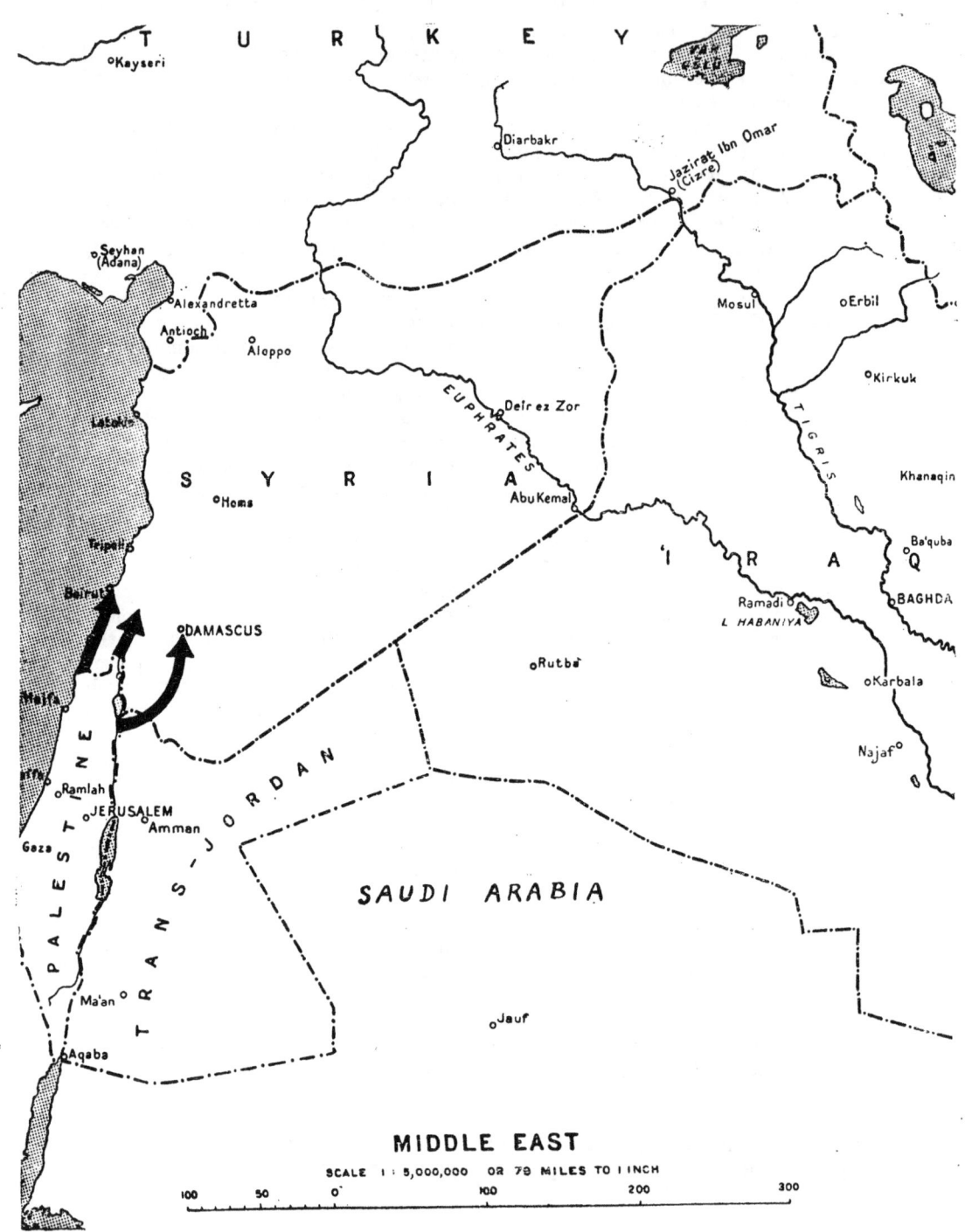

MIDDLE EAST
SCALE 1 : 5,000,000 OR 79 MILES TO 1 INCH

THE WAR OF THE LITTLE COLUMNS

The resistance encountered, however, was far greater than had been anticipated, and to begin with the invasion did not go too well. Therefore, when the Iraqi campaign was finished, it was considered advisable to fling Habforce into the battle against the Vichy French. It was hoped that by bringing a " right hook " round through the desert, the Vichy French communications might be cut. The following map explains how the original plan was varied :—

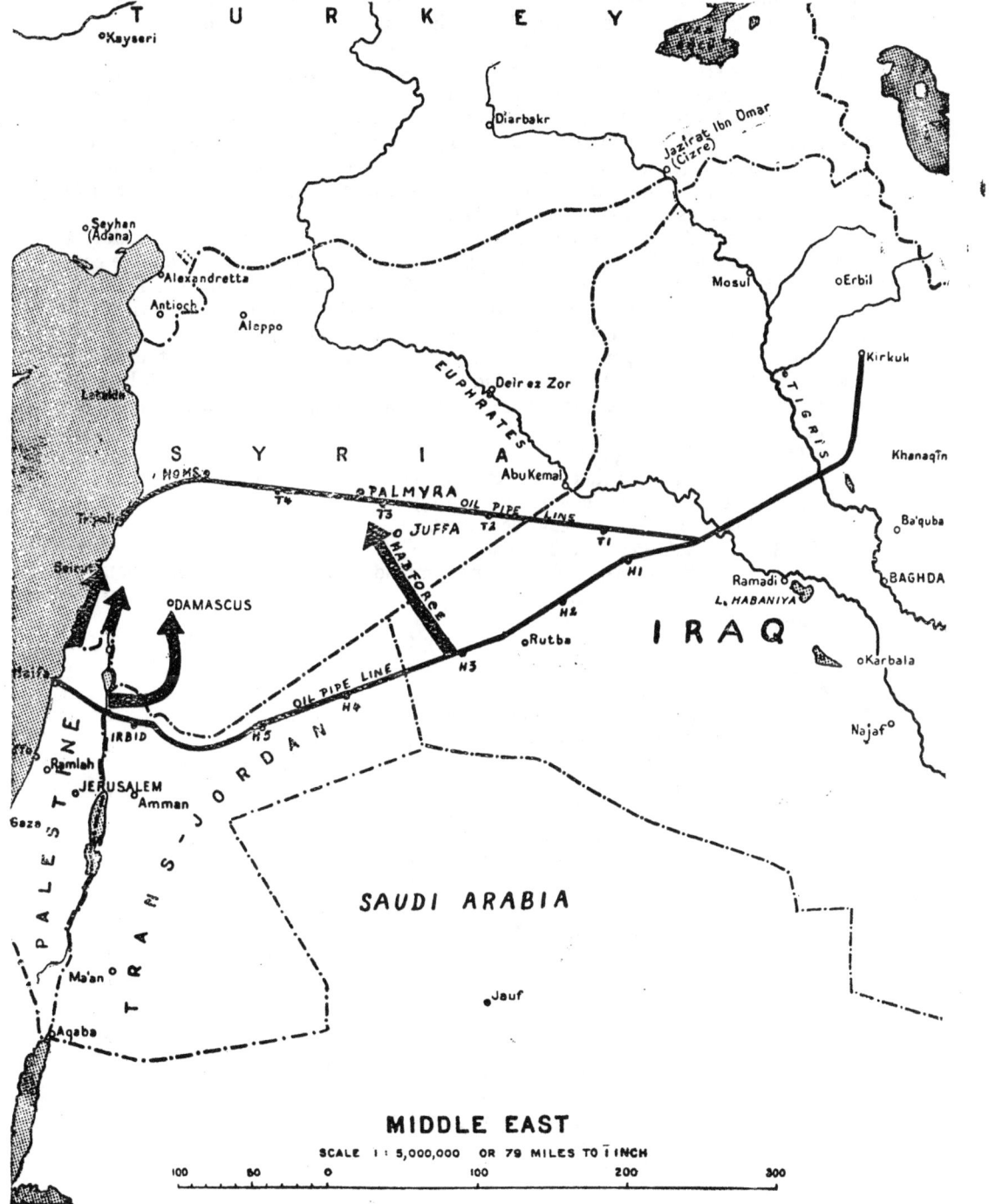

At the close of the campaign in Iraq, Habforce was widely dispersed. One squadron of the Household Cavalry, with some Artillery and Armoured Cars, was at Mosul, another squadron was at Kirkuk, with the remainder in Baghdad. There was also a detachment of that regiment at Haditha. This wide dispersal of units suggested a ruse which turned out to be very successful.

The simplest method of making use of this disposition of his troops appeared, to the Commander of Habforce, to be to give the enemy the impression that his main advance into Syria was to be along the Euphrates Valley. So the remainder of the Household Cavalry was sent up to join the column at Haditha and make a display of force. This stratagem was backed up by a series of bogus wireless messages in clear, all designed with the object of misleading the new enemy into thinking that Habforce intended to reinforce the Euphrates area and advance into Syria from that direction. The B.B.C., whether intentionally or not it is hard to say, gave colour to the illusion by frequent reference to a " large column advancing along the Euphrates Valley." In addition an agent was sent to the Sheik of the Ruwalla tribe near Damascus, giving the same impression.

Meanwhile, H.3 was the obvious jumping off point for an attack on Palmyra from the south and this was the actual plan adopted. Habforce was therefore concentrated over the very wide area, Rutbah—H.3—H.4—Abu Kemal. On Tuesday, 17th June, all the troops which had been operating at Habbaniya, with the exception of the Household Cavalry Regiment, left Habbaniya for H.3.

Then, on the 20th June, after three days at H.3, all was set for the Syrian adventure. " Kingcol " had been disbanded, and the composition of the 4th Brigade Group, which took its place under the command of Brigadier Kingstone, was as follows :—

H.Q. 4th Cavalry Brigade.
Household Cavalry Regiment (under command from 0400 hrs., 20th June).
Royal Wilts Yeomanry (less one Squadron).
Warwickshire Yeomanry (less one Squadron).
237 Battery, R.A. (less two Troops).
One Troop, 239 Battery, R.A. (under command from 0400 hrs., 20th June).
One Anti-Tank Battery (less one Troop).
Three Sections, 2 Field Troop, R.E.
One and a half Sections (9 armoured cars), 2 Armoured Car Coy., R.A.F.
Four Troops, Arab Legion.
Administrative Services as detailed.

The rôle which was given to Brigadier Kingstone was as follows :—
   (a) To seize PALMYRA as early as possible on 21st June.
   (b) To despatch following columns for harassing enemy's L. of C. :—
      (i) *Against HOMS Area.*
         Two Cavalry Regiments.
         One Troop 25-pounders.
         One Troop Anti-Tank Guns.
         Three Troops, 2 Field Troop, R.E.
         One Section, 2 Armoured Car Coy, R.A.F.
         Arab Legion at discretion.
           This column was known as " H " Column, Code Name GELU.
      (ii) *Against QUTEIFE Area.*
         One Cavalry Regiment.
         One Troop 25-pounders.
         One Troop Anti-Tank Guns.
         Half Section, 2 Armoured Car Coy, R.A.F.
         Arab Legion at discretion.
         Administrative Units as detailed.

The plan decided upon by the Commander of the 4th Cavalry Brigade Group, a simple one, was for the Royal Wilts Yeomanry to advance upon Palmyra from the south, and skirting round the salt lake, to seize the Yellow Ridge on the west, and the ruined chateau on the north-west of the town. These appeared to be two excellent positions from which covering fire could be given to the remainder of the Brigade Troops. These latter were to proceed by a route east of Palmyra to the hills round Ouémere, north of the town, from which vantage point they were to capture it.

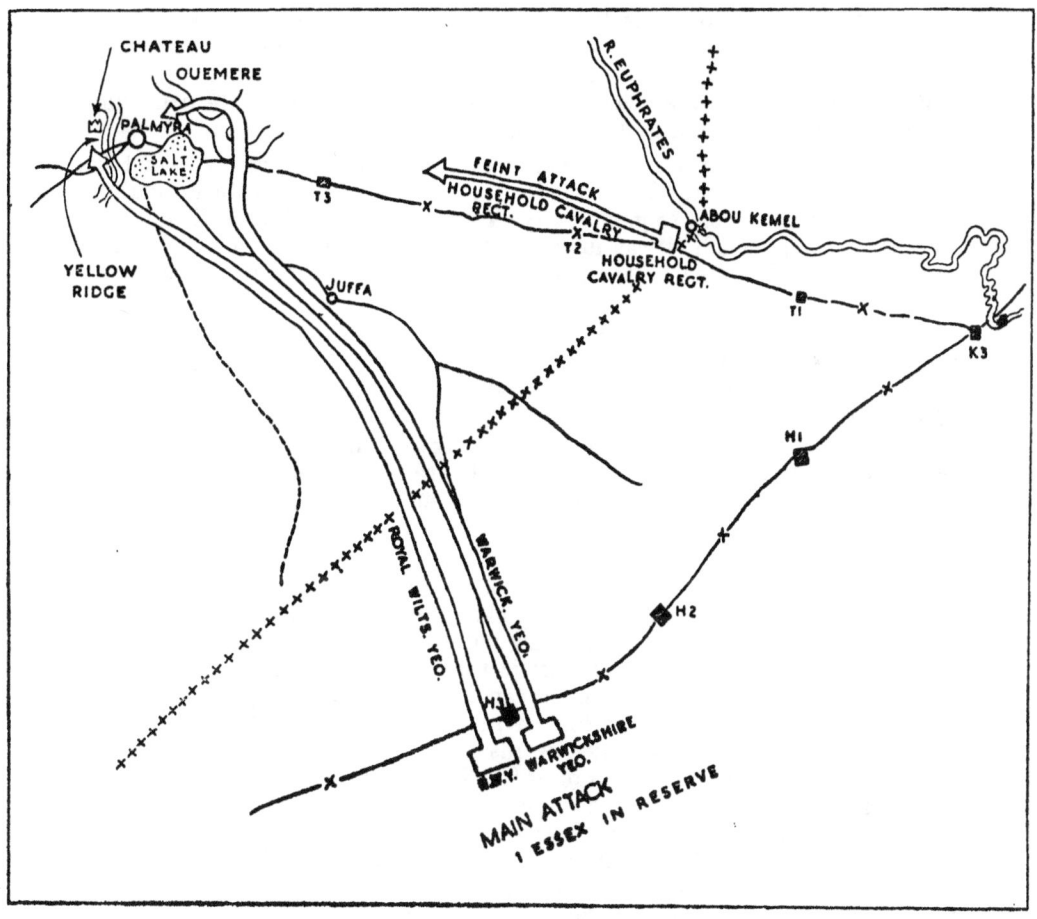

Accordingly, the 4th Brigade Group moved up into position on the frontier on the night of the 20-21st June, the Royal Wilts leading, and at first light on the 21st June the operation began.

Before we describe the actual fighting, however, it would be as well to give the reader a clearer idea of the country round Palmyra and a few details of the ghostly but fascinating ruins which formed the main centre of the Vichy resistance.

The desert north of H.3 and the pipe-line is completely flat as far as a place which came to be known as Juffa. To be strictly accurate, Juffa is a small village to the east of the spot which was always referred to by that name during this campaign. The latter is not very far away, however, and is clearly marked on the map: it consists of a little circle of sugar-loaf hills in the desert. There, owing to its suitability, Habforce Headquarters halted and established a Rear H.Q.

Looking north from Juffa, where this circle of little hills provides a very good grandstand from which to survey the desert round about, T.3 (one of the pumping stations on the northernmost pipe-line, from Kirkuk to Tripoli) can just be seen. Almost directly north-west lies Palmyra, beyond which lies a range of low hills, forming a rim to the basin of the desert. Due south of Palmyra is what the majority had thought, from looking at the map, would turn out to be a lake. It was found to be, however, a salt lake, which contains no water at all. It is, as the name implies, a dried-up basin of salt and quite impassable to motor transport.

Palmyra, or "Tadmor in the Wilderness" as the Bible calls it, is a town of great antiquity. For centuries it was lost in the sands which still surround it. It hardly seems possible that so great a city can originally have been built in the heart of a desert, even though it was undoubtedly the crossing point of the rich trade caravan routes. Presumably the surrounding country must then have been rich and fertile.

In any case, Tadmor was a great and powerful merchant city: this is obvious from its ruins to-day, which are so well described by Mr. H. V. Morton. This is what he says about it: "Everywhere rose the remains of Palmyra, a great arch, temples, broken pavement: a ghostly city lying in a golden desert. Sometimes when you are travelling in the desert, even in these days of motor transport, you come across the skeleton of a camel lying in the sand. Palmyra is like that: a long Hellenistic backbone which is the main Street of Columns and the ribs leading off to right and left; a ruin picked clean by Time and bleached by the sunlight of centuries to the colour of pale honey."

The ruins thus scattered about the sand are essentially monuments to the great Queen Zenobia, who rose to the height of her power in Palmyra towards the end of the Third Century. There, ruling with a firm hand the polyglot merchant princes who had amassed great fortunes in this trade centre, she made a fair bid to become Queen of the East. As the Roman Empire was tottering under the savage invasions of the barbarians, her highly-trained soldiers, the Palmyrini, captured Egypt and were well on their way towards Europe when the Emperor Aurelian put a stop to the ambitious plans of this romantic Queen. He besieged Palmyra, captured Zenobia, and cunningly saw to it that she would cause him no more trouble. Playing up to her vanity and human weakness, this astute Emperor kept the turbulent Queen from further interfering with the convalescent fortunes of the Roman Empire by enmeshing her in the society of his capital. There, in Rome, she spent the rest of her days amongst those social activities which made up the life of a Roman matron.

The rich city of Palmyra, neglected, if not forgotten, by its colourful Queen, then started on the decline which has led it, over the centuries, into oblivion and the ruined condition in which it stands to-day. In 1813 Lady Hester Stanhope set herself, in her eccentric fashion, to attempt the rebuilding of the fame of Palmyra and, probably as a result of this, a small Arab town has grown up around the ruins. But that part of the modern "Tadmor" looks—and smells—very much the same as any other normal Arab village.

The original plan had been to take Palmyra on the evening of the 21st June, and then to push out the Homs and Quteife columns to harass the enemy's lines of communication. This proved to be impossible, however, primarily on account of the stubborn resistance put up by the Foreign Legion in the Vichy forward defences. The operation did proceed according to plan, nevertheless, until the head of the Royal Wilts column reached a point near Juffa. It would seem, therefore, that the feint down the Euphrates Valley was successful and the attack from the south was undoubtedly unexpected until the leading column captured a standing picket at Juffa. This picket, by means of an aeroplane which escaped before the infantry were taken, succeeded in giving warning of the proposed attack upon Palmyra. It therefore saved the town from surprise, although it surrendered without fighting.

Apart from this element of surprise, it must be appreciated that the Vichy French, realising that Palmyra was a strategic point, had gone to considerable pains to see that it was well fortified. The defence plans of the town were found in Deraa when the latter was captured during the first two days of the Syrian campaign, and these were sent to Habforce Headquarters, where they turned out to be extremely helpful. The detailed maps and diagrams of the Palmyra defences made it obvious that the town was not to be taken without a good deal of fighting.

This became more apparent still when the Royal Wilts arrived at their objective, where they met with a hot reception. It soon became obvious that there was no question of their being able to give supporting fire to the troops on the east of Palmyra. It was all that they could do to look after themselves! This will be seen more clearly in the next chapter, when we describe in detail the part which they played in the capture of the town. For the purposes of this general account it will suffice to say that the Wiltshire yeomen, having made a very gallant initial attack, were forced to fall back at nightfall to a most unhealthy position, where they remained, with the exception of the time spent in patrolling and making attacks upon the Yellow Ridge, for the best part of thirteen never to be forgotten and thoroughly unpleasant days.

Further east the Warwickshire Yeomanry was also held up, this time by the Foreign Legion garrison in T.3 and the Vichy air attacks were intensified, in the complete absence of opposition, as the day wore on. The attack on Palmyra had not gone according to plan.

The next day, the 22nd June, was equally unpleasant. Our troops underwent intensive bombardment, machine gunning and cannoning from enemy aircraft whilst an attack was being made on " T.3 " and eventually that small oasis was by-passed. A troop of Warwickshire Yeomanry was left to guard it whilst the rest of that regiment was ordered to push on with the main attack on Palmyra.

The general situation at this stage was as follows : The Royal Wilts had reached Palmyra, which had turned out to be strongly held, and was retaining a somewhat precarious grip on the western outskirts of the town. On the east, " T.2 " had surrendered to the Household Cavalry Regiment. The Warwickshire Yeomanry were between " T.3 " and Juffa, and the Essex Regiment had spent the night half-way between Juffa and " H.3." Enemy armoured fighting vehicles were reported to be approaching Palmyra from the west and, during the previous 24 hours our troops had suffered casualties from air attacks amounting to approximately fifty personnel and thirty vehicles.

The bombing now worked up to a crescendo, as the enemy had complete freedom of the air. His air force was based on Homs (under a hundred miles away) and Aleppo, and the bombers used were about twenty Potez " 630 " and " 63." As soon as they had unloaded their bombs (of which they appeared to have an inexhaustible supply), they flew back to their bases, bombed up again, and reappeared with monotonous regularity. Dewoitine " 520's " were bombing the forward troops and preying unhampered upon staff cars and signal trucks, and their very skilful pilots were showing an uncanny knack of picking out Brigade H.Q. wherever it moved. Brigadier Kingstone himself had some very narrow escapes from near misses.

Air support was again asked for, but it was not forthcoming. It subsequently transpired that the only fighters available were being used on the west coast of Syria, where they were protecting the Royal Navy, whose battleships were doing tremendous work on the coast road, and thoroughly wrecking the morale of the Vichy troops, who simply could not take on their shelling. The officer commanding the Royal Navy detachment realised, as a matter of fact, that he was monopolising all the fighter strength of the Army, and did, at one time, suggest that he should return to Haifa and release the fighters for work on the sorely tried east of the Front. His offer was declined, however, as it was considered that the effect on the Vichy morale of having the Navy in operation offset the net result of the gruelling to which our troops in the east were being subjected. In other words, the desert column had to " take it " and with them the Royal Wilts took their full share.

This lack of air support gave the R.A.S.C. convoys and Light Aid Detachments a very trying time. Compelled to drive about over the desert, they were under almost constant attention from enemy air reconnaissance patrols, which they did their best to dodge, like lizards scuttling for the shelter of the rocks, to escape from the enemy above. One lesson stood out above all else during this period. It was the security afforded by the slit trench against bombing. Taking into account the weight and number of bombs dropped during this period of vicious attacks it is well-nigh incredible that the casualties were so small, although the loss in material, especially serious in the case of water and petrol lorries, was considerable. Neither was the effect on morale to be lightly assessed, although the troops stood up manfully to their ordeal. Officers who had been present at both Dunkirk and Greece said that in neither place was the bombing so intensive as at Palmyra. The target area was so small compared to the number of bombs dropped.

Apart from this heavy bombing which was now taking place on the front-line troops around Palmyra, on Rear H.Q. at Juffa and the Essex transport line, our efforts were very much impeded by the fact that we had no air reconnaissance whatsoever. And air reconnaissance in desert warfare, to give warning of the approach of the enemy ground forces when operating with scattered and therefore individually small parties of troops, is absolutely essential. The uncanny feeling of isolation which assails comparatively small bodies of men in enemy-held desert, where the mirage restricts the visibility sometimes to a matter of yards and distorts objects in an alarming fashion, must be experienced to be realised.

The next two days were full of interest, and provided a very unpleasant experience for the troops concerned. The enemy air activity reached its height and at one time over a hundred bombs, mostly 250-pounders, with an occasional 500-pounder, were dropped on the Brigade's dispersed vehicles within thirty minutes, in spite of the protection of four Bofors guns. The supply situation also was becoming difficult, owing to the destruction of petrol lorries and water carts.

To make matters worse Fawzi now had to be coped with as well and his men were constantly lying in wait for small isolated supply columns near " T.3." His forces augmented by French armoured cars, he more than once attacked our convoys in the rear and his nuisance value was very considerable. In conjunction with the air activities, he had a marked effect, particularly, upon the morale of the R.A.S.C. drivers, to whom by now he had become a veritable bogey-man.

The destruction of vehicles was also becoming a serious matter. " A " Echelon of the Royal Wilts, for example, had been reduced from fourteen vehicles to four in the past thirty-six hours ; recovery had become a very hazardous business.

Enemy fighters had "taped" certain spots through which the L.A.D. cars had to pass, and so constant were their attentions in these particular places that one can only assume that they used to land on the desert, watch for their prey approaching, and then catch them completely unawares from an altitude of under 100 ft. The accuracy of their machine gun and cannon fire was remarkable, and there was one particularly unpleasant spot (where the track turned into the hills to the south-west of Palmyra) which claimed the lives of several of our men.

A very unpleasant incident occurred on the 24th June. One troop of the Warwickshire Yeomanry had been left to watch T.3 (which had been by-passed by the main body) and they were wiped out under the most unsavoury circumstances. After they had been driven into their slit trenches by enemy aircraft, six Chevrolet cars drove up from the west, flying a white flag. Then an Arab in khaki slacks and a long coat, with no hat, dismounted from the leading truck and walked up to a corporal, who left his trench under the protection of what he thought to be a flag of truce. On the Arab asking in broken English to speak to an officer, the Lieutenant in charge of the troop stepped forward and was promptly fired upon by the men in the lorries. The troop was then surrounded and forced to surrender, but the men rushed back again to cover when they were fired upon. After that the trucks drove away and, a quarter of an hour later, a French officer came out of the fort and captured the remaining men who had been disarmed. The enemy's score from this underhand piece of work was eight killed, one officer and nine other ranks captured, two wounded and two missing.

The accompanying sketch map sums up the position in the immediate vicinity of Palmyra on the 24th June.

From the 25th onwards, bombing and fighter attacks increased, and the climax of this unfortunate period was reached when Brigadier Kingstone was evacuated to hospital. This was a severe blow to the Royal Wilts, amongst whom he was held in great respect whilst remaining extremely popular. Major Eric Gooch of the Household Cavalry took over for the time being and subsequently Brigadier J. G. E. Tiarks assumed command of the Brigade.

As has already been pointed out, the defences of Palmyra were very considerable and, apart from this, the natural features and tumbled ruins made an infantry attack very hazardous. On the west side were steep slopes covered with pillboxes and machine gun positions in excellent condition, below which were ruins filled with machine gun and snipers' posts. The fallen pillars and huge solid blocks of masonry formed virtual fortifications of a formidable character. All that was necessary to make machine gun posts was to dig a little trench behind these features which were sited, owing to the way in which they had tumbled down, to cover all directions. Furthermore, they rendered that portion of the ground completely impassable for M.T. or carriers. On the south-west a further protection was given to the town by closely-planted palm groves, and gardens surrounded by walls 18 ft. high which provided the most excellent positions for snipers. On the north and east of the town open desert country extended, over which it would have been extremely difficult to advance. This side of the town was also amply provided with tank traps and very substantial pill boxes, in addition to the well-fortified positions in the barracks and stores which were completely equipped forts in themselves. Finally, the town itself, especially the new village which was laid out in rectangular form, was most admirably adapted for sniping and to comb it thoroughly would have required a comparatively large number of troops.

Although a flight of Gladiators were under command, these were quite unserviceable and the enemy still had complete air superiority. Any attack would therefore have had to be made in the face of the Vichy bombers and fighters, thus rendering the evacuation of casualties a most difficult matter.

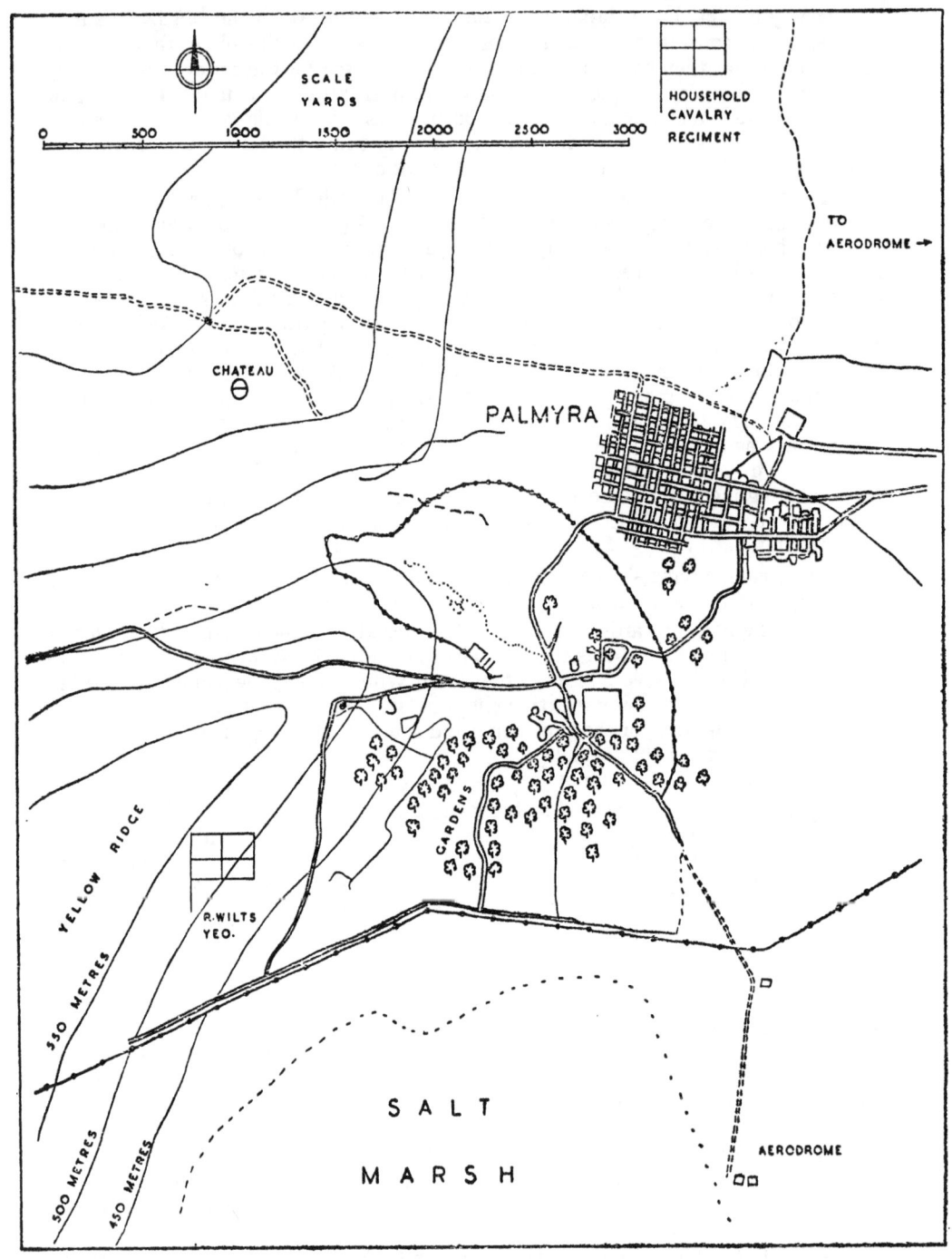

POSITION AT PALMYRA ON 24TH JUNE, 1941.

On the 26th June the village of Sab Biyar was taken by the Arab Legion and the capture of this small post made our lines of communication much safer and paved the way to shortening them quite considerably. This was very helpful because by now the enemy's bombing and fighter attacks had settled down into a regular half-hourly blitz on the three favourite targets, Rear H.Q. at Juffa, the vehicles dispersed in the plain, and the troops surrounding Palmyra. These attacks were usually preceded by an early morning reconnaissance, during which one or other of the targets were favoured with an isolated bomb or two, just to wake them up.

An air attack was also carried out upon the village of Rek, where troops had been spotted at the water point half a mile or so west of the village. As a result, at 6.30 on the morning of the 26th, this water point was ineffectively bombed. Although the enemy failed to cut off the water supply, they spread consternation and alarm throughout this village, which was composed of a number of small dwellings and a thousand or so black Bedouin tents. The appalling shrieking and wailing which went up from the village was blood-curdling, but in actual fact only one Arab woman was killed and one wounded. The result, nevertheless, was electric, and within a few hours the hundreds of native dogs, which had scattered in all directions on the explosion of the bomb, were joined by a mass exodus of the town dwellers with their camel-trains and cattle. By that evening not a single tent remained in the neighbourhood of Rek. An interesting but unpleasant sidelight on this occurrence was the arrival amongst the troops of swarms of flies. These were either borne there on the full blast of the explosion or had sought out an alternative object for their attentions after the Arab village had removed itself.

Then, at long last, bomber support was promised and the first practical results of this were seen on the 28th, when at 10.30 in the morning our planes attacked and set fire to the stores in the fort at Palmyra. This, however, was not a very inspiring performance to our own troops who, blasé from more than a week's spirited performance by the Vichy bombers, had hoped for something more forceful. The R.A.F. appeared flying very high and in admirably tidy formation. They then, with a certain appearance of pomposity, dropped all their bombs at once, turned round and, with the air of a well-dressed man who has buried some unpleasant object, made back immediately to their comfortable bases. They were in the air for a very short time and it is doubtful whether the morale of our troops was much improved by their appearance. However, the R.A.A.F. soon made amends because, by a lucky chance, a number of Tomahawks piloted by Australians brought off a most spectacular coup a short while afterwards. Whilst making a sweep over the area, as protection to our bombers, they had sighted a number of columns of sand sent up by the enemy over our positions in the neighbourhood of Palmyra. They immediately gave chase and shot down, in full view of our delighted troops, no fewer than six of the bombers in as many minutes. The effect of this performance on the morale of our men can well be imagined!

A combined attack was now planned for the night of the 29-30th June, with the intention of finishing off the whole business and finally capturing Palmyra. Unfortunately, however, this operation misfired as far as its main object was concerned, but it did achieve the taking of the Chateau, which fell to a patrol of the Essex Regiment. As the Royal Wilts played a major part in this operation, during which they suffered considerable casualties and passed a very anxious time, it will be described more fully in the next chapter. It need not, therefore, be dealt with further here.

So, on the 1st July, the situation seemed well in hand at Palmyra and our prospects were improved by the taking of Sukhne by the Arab Legion. This was a very gallant little action, led by Glubb Pasha himself, in which six armoured cars, two trucks, twelve machine guns and eighty prisoners, to say nothing of a nondescript collection of antique weapons (which were promptly annexed by "Glubb's Girls") were captured.

The Arab Legion had given a magnificent demonstration of a mechanised cavalry charge, reminiscent in its way of motor polo, during which it put the enemy to flight and chased them at sixty miles an hour back into the desert. It is true that a squadron of the Household Cavalry Regiment, who were in the neighbourhood, eventually joined in the hunt. They were, however, completely outdistanced and one N.C.O. aptly described the situation when he said that "although he was doing sixty he was quite unable to live with hounds." After the battle, large truckloads of "Glubb's Girls," driving round singing songs of victory and giving to all and sundry the "thumbs up" sign, were indeed an inspiring sight.

Meanwhile, the Royal Wilts were having a very unpleasant time indeed. Their ranks had been severely thinned and, short of troops and equipment as they were and with no relief or support, their outlook was gloomy indeed as night fell on the 1st July. But during the usual evening blitz our own gunners, who were hammering away at Palmyra from the east, provided sweet music to accompany the noise of the enemy bombs.

The end of this unpleasant episode came suddenly and, as can be well imagined, the news that the garrison wished to surrender was received with considerable relief on the part of the troops by whom it was surrounded. The desertion of the Camel Corps from the enemy, probably a repercussion of the affair at Sukhne, coupled with the accurate shelling of the enemy positions by our gunners, which had been intensified on the evening of the 2nd-3rd July, were probably largely responsible for the final capitulation. The town was entered on the 3rd July.

CHAPTER THIRTEEN

"ROUND TWO" AND THE ROYAL WILTS

THE fall of Palmyra was virtually the end of the fighting in Syria and, now that the picture as a whole has been sketched, an attempt will be made to examine it more closely. A more intimate view will be taken of the part which the Regiment played.

The end of the Iraqi campaign was followed by a movement order which sent them on their way back to Palestine, but as soon as they had reached H.4, on their return journey, they were halted. Then they were issued, to their disgust as cavalry soldiers, with bayonets and a few mortars which were provided with a paltry two bombs per weapon. Finally, some thirty men, who were left with nothing better than pick helves and shovels with which to defend themselves, were armed with captured Iraqi rifles. A sorry assortment of weapons with which to start out upon a major encounter with the enemy!

After that they continued their journey back to H.3, a hundred miles or so to the east. There, as has been recorded, the Brigade Group (with the exception of the troops making the feint down the Euphrates) was concentrating for the attack upon Palmyra. There also the Wiltshiremen met a romantic and much-bemedalled character in the form of a "last-war" veteran. In the rank of captain, he was commanding a column of armoured cars. Equipped with a formidable array of weapons by the Government and manned by as tough and polyglot a crew as ever sailed the Spanish Main, this little commando bore much the same relation to Fawzi Quwackchi's murderous band as does the "G" man to the American gangster. But what their actual task was, nobody was able to find out. They seemed to spend their time patrolling the pipe-lines and hounding off any unfortunate marauders with whom they might come into contact. But what yarns that captain could tell!

Meanwhile, the rest of the troops concentrating on H.3 were asembling from the various parts of the desert to which the Iraqi Campaign had led them. For the most part they made their journeys without incident, although many of the aged vehicles began to show signs of fatigue, and a fair number of lame ducks straggled in at the finish. They were helped along, however, by the L.A.D. at Rutbah, which worked overtime, and during the next few days this desert-weary collection of motley vehicles was hammered and welded into sufficiently good shape to start off into battle.

Then the plan was revealed and it was known for the first time that the Royal Wilts were to play a leading part in the attack upon Palmyra. The actual nature of that part has already been explained, but the account which follows shows in greater detail the adventures which befell them.

"Round Two" opened in earnest when they left the Syrian border at first light as advance guard to the Brigade, and all went well for several hours. A section of the Arab Legion went ahead, followed by three armoured cars as a screen, and then "C" Squadron, under command of Major Alistair Gibb. Next came Regimental Headquarters, a section of Australian anti-tank gunners and finally "A" Squadron under Major Lord Weymouth; Lieutenant-Colonel D. G. Williams was in command of the Regiment, and it will be remembered that "B" Squadron was still beleaguered in Tobruk.

In this formation the vehicles, well dispersed in all directions, rattled, banged and bumped across the desert, throwing up great plumes of dust behind them and making very good time. There is a queer companionship about this progress of mechanised troops across a desert. It is vaguely reminiscent of a hunt, when hounds are running. The ground slips by beneath, but the relative positions of those on the move change seldom. It becomes exhilarating and there is always a tinge of excitement. At any moment a fall (or a breakdown) may happen. And what is more heartbreaking than a fall when the hunt is up? Sheer bliss one moment and misery the next! A man may be cast from the pinnacle of enjoyment into the midst of a ploughed field, with tight boots which were never meant for walking, no horse and the sounds of the chase receding into the next parish.

The convoy driver may not reach the same heights, but he certainly plumbs equal depths when something goes wrong with his vehicle under circumstances such as those under which the Royal Wilts approached Palmyra. A strange noise in his engine may lead to his being left behind in the silence of the desert, to wrestle with recalcitrant machinery whilst his companions roll on without him. There, too, he may become a prey to enemy aircraft; but we shall hear more of this later.

"Glubb's Girls" had been sent ahead because it was thought that they knew every inch of the desert, but that was a regrettable mistake. As it turned out, this detachment came from an entirely different part of Syria (which is a very big country), and they were less able to find their way about than our own officers, who at least had compasses, even though the greater part of their maps was marked "unsurveyed." But nobody could blame the enthusiastic warriors for this particular error, nor (being human) for their understandable diffidence in admitting their ignorance.

In any case they led the Regiment astray before very long and let the Commanding Officer in for a rare good gallop as he tore across the desert at 60 m.p.h. to catch up the head of the column and redirect it on to its proper bearing. Then he tried to catch the "Girls," but that was too much for his tyres and, after a blowout, he gave it up and left them to find out their own mistake. This they did later, but still they were quite undismayed. They next appeared driving furiously into the head of the column, with their automatic rifles blazing gaily at a herd of gazelle which appeared to be only slightly more scared than the Wiltshire Yeomen themselves.

The next exciting incident occurred when the head of the column bumped into an enemy standing picket at Juffa. This picket consisted of a French Sous Officier, one other white man and about two sections of black troops. Some of Glubb's Girls were swanning as usual about the head of the column, rather like flies buzzing round the head of a weary traveller, and they very soon had this picket "in the bag." Then, having been told to put out of action any wireless sets they found, they proceeded to carry out these instructions with the aid of a sledge hammer, and thus made it impossible for us to tell subsequently whether any message had been got back to Palmyra or not. Whilst the members of the picket were fleeing in disorder

"DISPERSION."

"WHEN IN DOUBT, BREW UP."

without firing a shot, an old French aircraft, parked about a mile behind the picket, was seen to nose into the air. This aircraft seems to have reached Palmyra and given away the approach of our column. So the cat was now out of the bag!

After the victorious Arab warriors had finished paying attention to the material effects of the picket, all that the Sous Officier managed to salvage from the wreck of his tent was a small sponge bag, a large bottle of red-coloured hair restorer (he was as bald as an egg) and a copy of Hitler's "Mein Kampf" which was translated into French and which he explained that he was reading "purely out of curiosity." He was last seen clutching, with loving care, a large blotter inside which were some clothing and ration returns, in strange contrast to the legend which was emblazoned in gold letters on the outside, "Dedicé a Josephine Baker."

The captured prisoners were now sent back to the rear for interrogation and one of the Royal Wilts officers who escorted them was himself captured whilst rejoining the Regiment, so there is little doubt that the enemy soon got busy in sending out patrols to see what was going on*. Their air force was also galvanised into activity and soon a Vichy bi-plane, followed by a squadron of fighters, made their appearance. Although these were obviously reconnaissance machines, it was not long before large numbers of enemy aircraft appeared over Juffa, T.2 and T.3.

Meanwhile, after the delay caused by the capture of the Vichy patrol, a conference was held on a small hill on the edge of the salt marsh south of Palmyra and here began the bombing with which the Regiment was to become all too familiar during the next fortnight. From this vantage point could also be seen another factor with which they were to become unpleasantly associated—the formidable range of hills on the west of Palmyra which was known as Yellow Ridge. A sergeant of the Arab Legion, who claimed to have known the place in his youth, volunteered the information that no car could cross that ridge for twenty miles south of the gorge through which runs the Palmyra to Damascus road. He was readily believed at the time, but later on, in actual fact, a possible and useful passage was found.

Then the column moved on once more until they ran into real trouble just short of their objective. Arriving, around one o'clock in the afternoon, at the half-mile wide strip between Yellow Ridge and the Salt Marsh, the armoured cars and "C" Squadron were held up by a road block where a hot reception awaited them. The armoured cars were forced to withdraw temporarily, but "C" Squadron dismounted and put in a spirited attack. They were held up, however, by machine gun fire from the Yellow Ridge and the garden walls; then, as had previously been arranged, a right flanking attack was put in by "A" Squadron over the marsh in their cars. The going was too soft, however, and an attempt to continue dismounted was also stopped by machine gun and artillery fire.

The armoured cars probed forward on several further occasions, but each time they had their tyres shot through. This became too expensive, as they would soon have been quite immobilised, and therefore a better use was found for them. Later on, when the pass over Yellow Ridge, which followed the pipe-line telegraph, was discovered they were able to patrol up to the Damascus Road, and also link up with the Household Cavalry Regiment, who were coming round from the north.

This operation lasted for about six hours, during which the bombing from the air intensified and one troop managed to advance towards the outskirts of the town by short rushes and gained three hundred yards. It was forced to fall back at

---

* Incidentally, this officer had a very interesting journey after being taken prisoner. He was conveyed back to France by way of Germany, and on the way he passed very close to Berchtesgarten, where, incidentally, there was no blackout. No sooner had he arrived in France than, an armistice having been declared in Syria, he was returned to his regiment by the Vichy French. The whole of that adventure must have seemed like an impossible dream, especially when he found himself back again in Syria, after having travelled half-way across Europe.

nightfall, however, and the Regiment then dug itself into a most unhealthy position where it remained, with the exception of the time spent in making attacks on Yellow Ridge (which are described later) for the best part of thirteen days.

Nobody who took part in that episode will ever forget those thirteen days. The casualties were surprisingly light, admittedly, because the men were well dug in; but the anxiety was intense throughout. The party felt terribly cut off and, as they watched their vehicles being knocked out steadily from the air with no apparent prospect of replacement, there were times when it seemed as though the Vichy French, perched in their commanding positions on Yellow Ridge and behind protecting walls of the gardens and lofty ruins, had only to sit tight and wait for the inevitable end. Movement was difficult by day, even for the most urgent calls of nature, although somehow the rations, limited but adequate, managed to find their way into the slit trenches at night: and all were grateful to those who managed to get them there. Water was scarcer than ever, as over five hundred souls had to share what little there was, down to a minimum of one-third of a gallon per head per day for all purposes. Shaving, of course, was out of the question, and that alone is bad for a man's morale.

As a matter of fact it was only a stroke of luck which made the Regiment's position tenable at all. They could not possibly have held it had they not discovered two wells containing drinkable water, one to the south-west of the Salt Marsh and one in the position held by " C " Squadron. From these the Regiment's sole remaining 200-gallon water-lorry managed to supply the troops during the hours of darkness (although the water had a super-Enos effect), and this partly explains what appeared to the higher command to be a new species of " loaves and fishes " miracle. For Brigade and Divisional Headquarters, deprived of accurate information on account of the wireless interference caused by the conformity of the ground, were unable to make out how the Regiment was being maintained. To them it seemed as though its supply columns had been lost and they did not know about those precious wells. This caused Brigadier Kingstone a great deal of anxiety.

Meanwhile, the bombing and " ground strafing " by aerial machine gun and cannon attacks was taking deadly toll of the vehicles. Fortunately, the Vichy French pilots were foxed by the care with which every vehicle that moved by night was replaced in identically the same position before dawn. This made it impossible for them to tell which ones had been hit and which were still serviceable. They admitted, as a matter of fact, to members of the Regiment who contacted them later in Aleppo, that they had felt certain that the whole of our transport was knocked out in the first few days. This really was true as far as the anti-tank gunners were concerned, because the lorries which carried their guns were so conspicuous on account of their size. They, therefore, suffered badly, those Australians, and their lot was made the harder by the loss of several of their men who were burned to death by the firing, with incendiary bombs, of newly-arrived ammunition which they were burying. The R.A.F. armoured cars also had a bad time from persistent and successful attacks upon their tyres. Eventually they were immobilised completely, as spares were finally used up with no hope of replacement.

And so it went on, day after day, with a relentless monotony which was only broken, for those who took part, by patrols and attacks upon Yellow Ridge. A graphic account is given later, which describes such a fighting patrol and is written by the officer who led it. From that a very good idea can be gained of life in the front line outside Palmyra; but it must not be supposed that those in the front line were the only men who were having a difficult time. Work on the lines of communication was equally dangerous because of the complete air superiority which the enemy had achieved.

So let us try and give an impression of what was going on in the desert behind the men who were pinned down outside Palmyra.

"ROUND TWO" AND THE ROYAL WILTS

When the fighting troops of the Royal Wilts left H.3 at dawn on the 21st June, the " B " Echelon—that is the supply column—followed them twelve hours later. In common with the rest of the Regiment they imagined that Palmyra would fall without much trouble and the Squadron Quartermaster-Sergeant, being a thoughtful fellow, had made sure of having plenty of beer on board to celebrate the occasion. So there was considerable disappointment all round when it became known that the first night out was to be spent in the desert. There was also a slight argument between the S.Q.M.S. and his storeman, as the latter, an old soldier from the last war, wanted to broach the beer before anything happened to it. The S.Q.M.S., remembering that the fighting troops were to have their share, was adamant. The beer was to be drunk in Palmya, and there it should be drunk.

Around twelve o'clock next day the column was spotted from the air. Bombs began to fall and the men of " B " Echelon had their first opportunity of testing the drill which they had practised so assiduously for such occasions. They stopped their trucks, dismounted, dashed to a flank, and hid in whatever cover they could find, which was little enough in the desert. Then, as they cracked off their rifles at the approaching aircraft, they could hear, above the rumble of the engines, a stream of imprecations coming from the storeman. Hiding behind a rock, his face powdered yellow like a circus clown, he was bewailing the fact that the beer, which against his advice had not been drunk the night before, was now going to be blown to blazes before their very eyes. But the beer, and incidentally the men, remained intact although the Vichy aircraft kept coming back every five minutes or so to hold up the procession. Rifles proved very ineffective against the air attacks, the two old Hotchkiss guns jammed after a few rounds each, and it was a decidedly shaken " B " Echelon that went into leaguer as the daylight failed. " What's think on it ? " was a common question in the Wiltshire dialect that night.

Let us hear the rest of this story from the S.Q.M.S. himself. This is what he says :—

" Half an hour before dawn the trucks dispersed from the leaguer and the order was given to dig slit trenches because it was improbable that the Echelon would move from that area.

" I drove my truck to the appropriate distance from the others and issued the necessary instructions. Each man dug for himself, and, after I had been sweating with pick and shovel for about three quarters of an hour, I decided to see how the others were progressing. The remainder of the crew had achieved a depth of approximately five inches—the same as myself and had equally large blisters on their hands. The exception was my driver, who had disappeared from sight.

" I walked over to the spot where I had last seen him—and discovered him watching the sky from a lovely deep trench ! Naturally I asked him how it was that he reached such a depth when the remainder of us had only gone down a few inches. His reply amazed me, but I most certainly agreed that he was correct. ' Oh, this is an Arab grave,' he said, ' but if it is good enough for the dead then its good enough for the living, so I have thrown out the bones to make room for myself '.

" The heat that day was about as unpleasant as the continuous bombing, whilst the haze made it impossible to discern anything over a hundred yards away. Consequently when the cool of the evening came, the Royal Wilts ' B ' Echelon, together with the company of R.A.S.C. attached, discovered that the remainder of the column's Echelon had moved on—where to, nobody knew. The Echelon commander had received no order to move. The one wireless set was put into action in order to get information, but contact could not be made with the Brigade Echelon commander. It was then decided to contact the fighting portion of the Regiment and, this having been successfully achieved, it was decided to join them the following day. Owing to the very poor maps, which were marked all over with the word ' Uncharted,' the trouble soon began and the Echelon commander found it impossible to proceed very far owing to the sea of sand dunes. Therefore he decided to stop until he had reconnoitred a route that would carry the Echelon. Finally, it was decided to remain in that area until Palmyra was taken. From this location the Echelon maintained the Regiment, the necessary trucks travelling by night in order to avoid the fighter aircraft. Through the sand dunes they went, into the hills bordering the desert, guided only by the stars, for prismatic compasses were an almost unknown luxury. The return journey was made the following night, the day being spent in caves in the hills.

" The first journey nearly ended in catastrophe. A small convoy of three trucks left the hills to rejoin the remainder of the Echelon just after sundown. The commander of the convoy had procured an old prismatic compass and decided to use it to march on a bearing. Unfortunately this instrument was badly in need of repair and played tricks with him. Consequently, after travelling all night, daybreak found the three trucks still ploughing their way through masses of sand dunes but heading due north, according to the position of the sun.

" As I had previously observed the position of the sand dunes from the Echelon's location, I knew that we were heading direct into the salt marshes bordering the enemy's eastern flank. I instructed my driver to speed up in order to catch the leading truck but, owing to the heavy sand, it was impossible to decrease the interval.

" To have gone much further in the same direction would certainly have meant being shot up, but luck was with us. The leading truck suddenly stopped. The fan belt had broken. I dismounted and went forward to the Commander to explain that we were going right into trouble, but I found that his confidence in the compass was still unbroken, despite the night's experience. I argued and argued but still he would not admit that the compass was wrong, persisting that the way we were going was correct. A further argument took place about towing the vehicle and it was not until everyone agreed with me that it was decided to run the truck without the fan belt, as it was impossible to tow it with our vehicles in such deep sand.

" I decided that I would go my way, and let the other two trucks go straight on. So I turned right, heading straight into the sun, and in less than a quarter of an hour was on a high ridge of hard stony desert. There I was able to see the Echelon out in the desert, but, a much more satisfying spectacle, I was also able to see the other two trucks following in my tracks at a tremendous speed.

" I waited for the commander in order to point out the short distance he would have had to travel to meet a lot of trouble. He good naturedly agreed with me, showing his appreciation by inviting me to have a cup of tea with him as soon as we arrived back. The tea, incidentally, looked very much like a mixture of red and blue ink as it was made with water brought from H.4 in two-gallon containers. The water would have passed for ink had it been bottled in nice little bottles. It was absolutely filthy stuff, but water was so scarce that no one worried about the colour or taste, so long as it was wet.

" The following night I was ordered to report to Div. H.Q., which had moved up to Juffa—a mere spot in the desert about twenty miles south—to collect supplies and also to act as guide to some urgently required ambulances. I started off with a 15-cwt. truck and a three tonner, trusting to the stars to guide me. After going through practically every bomb hole in the desert I reached my objective at nine o'clock the following morning, with the 15-cwt. on tow. It had broken down after half an hour's travelling.

" I reported to the D.A.Q.M.G. and Staff Captain, who asked me to pin-point the position of the Regiment and its Echelon on my map. When I explained that I had no map they were amazed, and asked how I expected to take back stores and ambulances. My reply that my sense of direction would get me back, as it had got me to Juffa, did not sound very convincing, although I was able to give them a rough estimation on their maps as to where the Regiment was located. As they had no alternative method or guide, I was despatched with the convoy at approximately three o'clock in the afternoon. I reached the Echelon at 8 o'clock the following morning, despite the fact that most of the night was spent digging the trucks out of the salt marshes a few miles from the Fort of Palmyra."

This is the S.Q.M.S.'s story and, to judge by the casual way in which he mentions it, he appears to have been blissfully ignorant of the consternation caused at Division and Brigade H.Q. by the disappearance into the blue—and presumed loss—of the Royal Wilts " B " Echelon.

* * * * * *

Here is another impression of convoy work in the desert. This time the story tells of the adventures of the Technical Adjutant and gives a good idea of what went on behind the lines during the first two or three days of the attack on Palmyra.

" In order to get the events in their correct sequence, I think it would be best if I described the adventures of my little party from the time we left the halting place on the Syrian border until we finally rejoined the Regiment. As you know the Regiment started off from the halting place in the early hours of the morning, the idea being that we reached Palmyra by about breakfast time, or at least in time for lunch ! We had been told that air opposition was unlikely, and I am ashamed to say that at that time of my life I was simple enough to accept the statement. I was soon to be disillusioned.

" All went well for some time, and at about 0800 hrs. I had to deal with my first breakdown. The Corporal and I had our heads in the bonnet when three planes were reported coming from the direction of Palmyra. We were not left long in any doubt as to whether they were friendly or otherwise for they unloaded about a dozen bombs on us, and followed up by a little machine gunning. Fortunately nobody was hit, and the only damage was a few splinters in the store lorry and two punctured tyres on my pick-up. We attempted to engage them with our solitary Hotchkiss, but it gave up the ghost after firing about half a strip. A great pity, as the planes came very low and we stood a good chance of getting a hit. The planes left us and returned in the direction of Palmyra, and a few minutes later we heard them bombing the main body.

" After finishing our repairs, we got under way again, and about five miles farther on saw two vehicles halted in the open. As we approached they took cover behind a low ridge, and through my glasses I could see about half a dozen men take up a position on the ridge, one of them obviously carrying an autometic of some sort. Owing to the haze it was impossible to identify either the men or the vehicles. I was in a quandary for my total armament consisted of one Hotchkiss (*not* very reliable !), two rifles and my own pistol. But the problem was quickly solved for us, for a French plane came over, bombed us, and then repeated the dose on the other people. After he had gone we approached carefully and found that it was the Royal Wilts medical officer, who had stopped to attend to a wounded man—I was very grateful to the French plane for, Geneva Convention or not, I've no doubt that the doctor would have opened up on me.

" Soon after that we caught up with the Regiment and learned that one man had been killed, our first fatal casualty of the Campaign.

" A conference was held and it was decided that I should remain with ' A ' Echelon while the Regiment went on to Palmyra. The vehicles were dispersed and we remained in that position for the remainder of that day and the whole of the next, being frequently bombed and machine gunned.

" During all this time, no word was heard of ' B ' Echelon or the L.A.D. which had accompanied it. This in spite of messages sent back by drivers of vehicles conveying wounded men and prisoners to Juffa. By the evening of the second day we had lost both petrol lorries, and as far as we knew had only 200 gallons of water in reserve. As a result of this it was decided that I should go back to Habforce H.Q. and explain the situation, taking with me any men who could not be accommodated in the remaining vehicles. Meanwhile what was left of the Echelon would move nearer to the Regiment.

"We started off early, and arrived at H.Q. in time for breakfast. The journey was uneventful. The S.O.M.E. (the Major in charge of the Divisional Mechanical and Engineering Branch in those days) after very kindly putting my own vehicle in order, offered to come back with me to see what could be done to salvage the vehicles I had been unable to deal with. Just as we arrived and I was getting out of my P.U. I heard the now familiar hum of a plane. At first I could not see it, as it was in the sun, but by this time we were taking no chances and scattered quickly. After having a go at us the plane flew low over the ridge behind which the other vehicles were coming up, and I heard a few bursts of cannon and machine gun fire. A few minutes later I saw my other vehicle approaching, and assuming that it was O.K., walked over the ridge to find that the S.O.M.E. had 'copped it.'

"Seeing that there was little or nothing to be done for him, I sent him back with his driver, and returned to my own two vehicles. On arriving there, I found that the driver of the 3-tonner was dead, having got a cannon shell straight through the heart. The lorry had been driven in by a trooper, himself so badly riddled by machine gun bullets that it seemed unlikely that he could survive very long. In the back were two other troopers. A fifth man later turned up who had jumped from the lorry and escaped with flesh wounds in the arm. The two troopers in the back of the 3-tonner were badly hit, and it looked as if we should lose the three of them if we did not get medical aid quickly.

"We removed the dead driver, and placed him in a bomb crater for later burial, and made the others as comfortable as could be in the lorry. While we were doing this we were again attacked, fortunately with no further casualties. Then we tried to start up the lorry, and of course the darned thing would not start. Leaving the fitter to attend to this, I went to my own 'pick-up,' to use in case the lorry had died on us completely. That, too, had got temperamental and would not start. But, in the meantime, the 3-tonner had come to life and, after patching up a hole low down in the petrol tank and putting in enough juice to get us back to Juffa, we started off. We went down the first slope at about fifty ! When I cursed the driver for losing his head, he told me the brakes were not working. It was only by a miracle and some very skilful handling that we managed to get on to a level patch without turning over. Thereafter we got into low gear at the slightest sign of an incline, and except for being bothered by the attentions of the planes for the first few miles got back to Juffa without further incident. On the way we passed the S.O.M.E. whose driver had taken him from the truck as he could not stick the travelling. The driver told me he had sent in for an ambulance, so we left him there, and shortly afterwards met an ambulance on its way out.

"We left H.Q. again in the evening and, except that we ran into the Arab Legion in the dark, reached our original position without any scares. I must confess however that when we ran into 'Glubbs Girls' I had a nasty sinking feeling !

"We remained at our position during the night, and after burying the dead driver and getting my 'pick-up' in running order, took a few hours sleep before setting out to rejoin the Regiment at first light. We reached them at about 0730, not at all sorry to be back."

As a matter of interest, the S.Q.M.E. arrived at about 2000 hrs. that evening with all the rations, petrol and water we required. Three hours later, the missing "B" Echelon turned up, also with all the necessary supplies."

* * * * * *

The final act of this drama was set in the sordid surroundings of the Casualty Clearing Station at Juffa. The use of the word sordid is no reflection upon the R.A.M.C. personnel concerned. They did everything they could, but in spite of that the place was sordid. It consisted of two marquees about a cricket pitch apart and joined together by a canvas roof, making a shaded portion in between. There was no means of keeping out the flies and insects, water had to be carried more than a hundred miles from H.3, and water carts and supply vehicles were being bombed out of existence hourly. Sanitary arrangements were, naturally, of the crudest, and washing was confined to the most urgent wounds.

Normally the amenities of a hospital do much to lessen the burden of sickness. The cleanliness, the hygienic atmosphere, the friendly sister within call, the peace and quiet and above all the knowledge that everything humanly possible will be done to protect the patient and coax him back to health. But out there at Juffa, the wounded had none of these comforts. The prospect before them was bleak indeed. Treatment of the most elementary kind was all that they could count on, and before them lay a dreaded journey. They would be lucky if they had an ambulance to take them back to the base, and there was no evacuation of wounded by air at this stage. Their most likely lot was hundreds of miles of jolting in a truck, still at the mercy of enemy aircraft and with a water ration cut to a minimum.

To this already overcrowded C.C.S. were brought the survivors of this little party, and there they were patched up as well as could be managed. There also the S.O.M.E. was brought to spend a few brief hours. Amidst the wounded men he was bandaged from head to foot and dressed once more in his khaki shirt and shorts, for there were no clean sheets and pyjamas at Juffa. A piece of mosquito netting was placed over his face like a grotesque bridal veil to keep off the pestering flies, and his stretcher was raised on two empty packing cases. This was all that could be done for him.

He seemed to recover slightly after a few hours, although he wandered in his mind occasionally because of the morphia which they had given him. Then, praising the Vichy airman's marksmanship, and waving his bandaged limbs in witness, he died.

CHAPTER FOURTEEN

THE FALL OF PALMYRA

To return to those front-line troops of the Royal Wilts who were held up outside Palmyra, we have already mentioned that they were chiefly occupied in patrolling and making attacks upon the Yellow Ridge. The first men to obtain an actual foothold as a matter of fact were one section of Machine Guns and one troop from " C " Squadron, who occupied the ridge for thirty-six hours on the 23rd and 24th June. Their casualties were so heavy, however, from shelling, and their water so scarce on account of the bombing from Vichy aircraft that, in that intense heat, they were forced to retire. Nobody could blame them for this as the position was a heartbreaking one to take and hold, consisting as it did of a double ridge, with a peak at the end which the Vichy French had fortified with a stone redoubt. Towering over the Royal Wilts' slit trenches to a height of 1,500 ft., it was altogether too much for a man to get more than himself and his rifle to the top and carrying parties had to be found for machine guns and extra ammunition, apart from water and rations.

In spite of this, repeated and stubborn attacks were carried out which culminated in the combined operation which was planned for the 29th June. In preparation for this, " C " Squadron of the Royal Wilts was ordered to reconnoitre Yellow Ridge on the night of the 28th. This order, it should be added, was greeted with very little enthusiasm by the men whom it affected, because they had already gained considerable experience of patrolling this very difficult ridge. They knew to a nicety the reaction to be expected from the enemy. He invariably reinforced any point thus reconnoitred, for some days afterwards. But orders were orders and so the patrol was carried out. It succeeded in getting to the very end of the Yellow Ridge where it surprised the Frenchmen who put up very little resistance before running away. Then the patrol established itself in the captured redoubt on the northernmost tip of the ridge and managed to remain there for about twelve hours. The enemy, however, threw in a very strong counter attack, because he realised that it was essential for him to re-capture so commanding a position. So the patrol, after holding on grimly for as long as possible, was eventually forced to fight its way out. But here is the story of that patrol, told in his own words by the officer who led it.

" It has been decided that the Observation Point on the peak overlooking the Roman Ruins and Town of Palmyra must be taken by this Squadron to-night, presumably to secure the right flank of the Essex Regiment if they attack from the Chateau on the ridge north of the Homs Road. There has been an idea in all our heads that the Essex were to have taken this observation point last night but nothing has come of it.

The O.C. "C" Squadron has given orders to get seven other-rank volunteers to join an Officers' fighting patrol of seven men and myself. We are to move up during the early hours to the point and take it so as to be ready to fight off any French counter attack to-morrow morning. . . .

Dusk is approaching as we move rather heavily up on to the ridge, above and to the left of the Squadron position. It is incredibly steep and the heat makes our equipment seem overbearingly heavy. We are armed with rifles, bayonets and hand grenades and, for myself, I am glad to have only a pistol. Two of my volunteers are labouring, in fact staggering, under the weight of our much oiled and checked, but extremely unreliable Hotchkiss gun, while two more carry its equally cumbersome ammunition boxes. There is no need for any formation or alertness, thank goodness, on the way up to Third Troop's position on the top, and we realise that there is a considerable distance between first and last now that we are at the top. . . .

Now it is dark and eerie up here. Our orders run through my mind. Very simple ones—"Take the peak. No success signal. Hold it if you can." We shall be out of touch once we leave here.

Although two or three days ago (time seems very vague in this desert) this Troop had attempted this in daylight, and for two hazardous days had held on to the peak in front of our objective, we had little or no knowledge now of the enemy dispositions. We did not know whether they were between us and the peak, nor did we know in what strength they might be, nor how they were disposed on the objective. . . .

It is time, we must move now. Two men move off in front as silently as possible over the clattering rocks—the old Cavalry eyes. Then, a few moments later, a connecting file; then myself, with the others struggling after under their various burdens. The moon will be coming up soon, but meanwhile it is as dark as pitch. We have been over this ground before but it is incredibly difficult to tell one of these jagged rocks from the other. It seems as if we are making a most abominable noise. Surely they must be able to hear us. Practically every step brings a rolling and rattling of stones. Small avalanches to our anxious ears. Every now and again someone slips and his bayonet raps against his tin hat with a noise like a cracked dinner gong.

Time is getting on. We have been moving for nearly an hour now. There is a growing tenseness amongst the men. We have reached the position the Troop held previously under such uncomfortable circumstances. Under an overhang of rock we close up with our two eyes and connecting file. It is our first stop. We listen for a moment—not a sound. Whispering hoarsely we discuss the next extremely awkward advance. This is as far as we have been before. All we know is that when we creep round this corner and along about a hundred yards we must descend a very steep, completely open slope in full view of the post we must take. It is, as far as we know, a little fort built of stones on the very point of a sharp peak. From it the enemy can look straight at us at a range of about two hundred yards as we creep down this bare slope. The moon is coming out too. It is a nerve racking idea.

Now everyone's mind is clear. We continue as before. Round the corner, slipping and clacking on the rocks. The noises seem louder as we get closer. We are still out of sight of the enemy. Now, in the moonlight, the two eyes approach a corner in the rock, look around it, and stop. One beckons. I move up to him and look round. The rocks drop away steeply in front of me, gleaming white like salt in the moonlight. Only occasional patches of coal-black shadow. Down into pitchy darkness. Then up the other side, and just above eye-level the clear outline of the post, sitting at the very top. It is so clear that it seems impossible that a sentry is not looking along his rifle sights into our eyes.

Everyone is already sweating with the exertion or we should break into the traditional cold sweat of fear. That moonlit slope. About a hundred yards of open, loose shale too ! But there is no other way of getting there. We have no time to make a long detour. We must be in that post in forty-five minutes ; no, forty-three.

" Carry on. Keep to what shadow there is. For God's sake make no noise." Vain hope ! " If they open fire lie still. Don't run back. Hotchkiss gun with me."

The Patrol starts down the slope and we feel better for the movement. The shale is loose and rattles. It seems incredible that the French up there have not opened fire. They must be able to see us. The patches of shadow seem miserably small, and the open moonlit rock endless in length, and devilish in its desire and ability to make noise ; cruel in its denial of any cover.

Now we are at the bottom, in the darkness again. Over us looms the triangular hill, and on its top the little fort. Panting heavily the party pauses to catch its breath. Hand grenades are brought out of pouches and their pins loosened. The quiet click of rifle bolts betrays the examination of weapons.

We start to creep up the dry gully which zig-zags up the face of the hill. It is too dark to see more than a shadowy outline of each other. But although we are moving in the same formation we are now crawling on hands and knees and each can touch the feet of the man in front. There is a certain amount of sand in the gully and the loudest noise is the heavy breathing as we struggle up the steep, rough ground. Now the two in front pause. A shadowy hand is raised, points. There it is. The rough, loose stone wall of the fort, about ten yards away, almost immediately above us. The Patrol bunches, crowds together. Out come grenades. Pins are drawn. Rifles clutched in the left hand. " Now ! " Away go the grenades, one, two, three, sailing up through the dark. A mad panting scramble. Every man for himself. Up, up. Here's the wall. Up again. A crash of exploding grenades almost in our faces. Showers of sparks. A vague shouting form looms over the wall and with arms flung wide, leaps towards us. An awful shriek as it is impaled on the Sergeant's bayonet. Shots ring out. A vague white face in the dark, the pistol explodes in my hand. Now, quiet. " Are we all here ? " Yes, we are all in, everyone alright. Good Lord, we've done it ! The walls are manned, but there are only three of them. Another, facing the town must be built. The moon seems to have disappeared. Nothing much can be seen below. One man is look-out while the wall is built. Work is feverish for soon the sun will be up. A French officer, his blank white face turned, lies on his back watching us. He is dead. The look-out whispers hoarsely that someone is approaching from the way we have come. Is it our carrying party, or is it the enemy ? They must have heard that incredible mad din. It is the carrying party. They come piling in, deposit overcoats, water, ammunition, food and are gone. Lucky people. It is too dark to make any dispositions. The best thing is to rest.

Now the sun is rising over the edge of the endless desert beyond Palmyra and we can see, below the precipitous slope, the Roman ruins, the gardens, the town. Directly under us is the road and the road-block which the R.A.F. armoured cars had investigated to the cost of their tyres. There is also a gloriously blue swimming pool !

There are the other defences. Not a soul in them. A machine gun post, a mortar post, another machine gun, and a man asleep beside it. Two men jump over the parapet, rifles in hand and run down the slope. They prod him awake with a bayonet, and one of them hustles him up the slope again, while the other dismantles the heavy gun and takes out a vital part. It is too heavy to move. The prisoner is a dishevelled little man, extremely frightened. He sits in a corner and smokes a cigarette. Two more of the party go down and spike the mortar and the other machine gun. Their emplacements face the wrong way for us and the weapons are unfortunately too heavy to move. Our men come back with a French light automatic, but it won't work.

At last the enemy are moving. Two armoured cars with open tops drive out of the town, right under us, and stop at the road block. What looks like a company of infantry starts to move, in open order, across the road and up the lower slope of the hill towards us.

Three hundred yards, two hundred yards, a hundred and fifty. Fire! The rifles crack out, the Hotchkiss gun fires and stops. Stops for good. The Foreign Legionaires scatter and drop to cover. One drops in the open and lies still. Fire is directed on the armoured cars. One of them raises a Tricolour flag. Obviously they do not know that their hill is now ours. We fire at anything we can see but, without a machine gun, it is impossible to stop those cars from moving, and now they turn round and drive back to a position near the town and open fire with their machine guns. Their bullets sing close around us and chips start to fly from the stones with vicious whines. They get more accurate and it is impossible to do more than pop up quickly and down again.

Already it is midday and blazing hot. The machine gun fire pins us down. That swimming pool looks inviting!

Suddenly there is a whistling in the air and, with a shattering crash, a mortar shell explodes twenty yards behind us. Good shooting. A minute passes; here comes another. Closer. Then another, ten yards to one side. Then a shriek and a terrific crash as a mortar shell explodes on the loose stone wall. Fragments go whizzing about. There is a cloud of dust, and stones come tumbling down. The machine guns are hard at it. The French infantry are beginning to move. Running quickly between cover. Half are going round the right flank, half round the left under cover of the machine gun and mortar fire. We crane our necks. Up quickly, fire, and down again. Someone claims a hit. The enemy mortars are accurate.

Suddenly there is a crack and a vicious whine and a man rolls over clutching his leg. A nasty gash above the knee. The only thing to do is to send him back before the infantry get behind us. He goes staggering away supported on one side by the prisoner (a friendly little fellow) and on the other side by an armed escort. A message goes with them, " We cannot hold this after dark. Herewith one prisoner."

The afternoon is passing; the sun is going down. The French infantry has disappeared, working round behind us. The mortar shells keep on whining and crashing down. There is another direct hit on the wall.

A decision has to be made. Soon it will be dark. I decide to move back before we are surrounded, if possible. A hole is made in the wall at the back, and, encumbered with the French automatics and the silent Hotchkiss, the depleted party scrambles out, down the slope and up to the next ridge. Just as we reach our places the French infantry make their way up the rear slope which we have just come down, and fling themselves into the now deserted post."

* * * * * *

On the night following this episode, that is on the night of the 29th June, the big attack upon Palmyra was to be launched. Owing to the activities of the fighting patrol, the Yellow Ridge was now held by at least one company of the enemy, but this, it was thought, might possibly prove to be of advantage to the main attack, in that it would have reduced the troops defending Palmyra itself.

The plan was as follows :—

At 10 o'clock on the night of 29th June, " C " Squadron was to attack along Yellow Ridge and capture it.

At midnight " A " Squadron was to launch an attack upon the gardens to the south-west of the town and clear them of enemy as far as the Palace.

At 5 o'clock on the morning of the 30th June the Essex Regiment was to attack the main town of Palmyra from the direction of the Chateau which they were to capture earlier in the night.

It is interesting to note that the total strength of other ranks which the two Royal Wilts' Squadrons were able to muster on this occasion was seventy-six men. Casualties and sickness had reduced them to such an extent that the success of this attack had become vital. They would not have been able to make a second attempt.

The carrying out of the plan started according to schedule. At ten o'clock " C " Squadron attacked and found the whole of the ridge to be crawling with enemy. Progress was therefore slow but by midnight the situation did not look too bad. Although not much headway had been made " A " Squadron launched their attack and this met with more success. They penetrated well into the gardens in spite of most difficult terrain, with high walls every few yards and considerable enemy opposition.

Meanwhile " C " Squadron, by one o'clock in the morning, were well on along the ridge, but they were too heavily outnumbered to push the enemy out completely. It was hoped, however, that as soon as the Essex attack got going the French would have to retire or else be surrounded.

Then, at one-thirty, a message was received which said that the Essex attack had been cancelled because there was no certainty that the Yellow Ridge would be taken by five o'clock in the morning. The Essex had, however, captured the Chateau.

The taking of that Chateau was, incidentally, a magnificent piece of work on the part of a subaltern of the Essex Regiment, who reconnoitred it himself the night before and finally brought off a successful surprise attack. To look at it from the ground the building appeared almost impregnable, perched as it was on the top of a very high mound in a most commanding position, which was somehow reminiscent of those castles in the illustrations to Grimm's Fairy Tales.

After this the Royal Wilts were ordered to withdraw " C " Squadron far enough to enable the artillery to shell the end of Yellow Ridge, and to recall " A " Squadron from the gardens. These orders were easier to give than to carry out. By that time it was daylight and whilst " C " Squadron, in a much exhausted condition, fought its way back to a point half-way along the ridge, where it consolidated, " A " Squadron had become irretrievably mixed up inside the gardens. Later the French mounted a strong counter attack on those gardens and the Squadron, without any support whatever and surrounded by snipers on every side, had to fight a fierce rearguard action. With great skill and courage they battled away until darkness fell and enabled them to extricate themselves. Their casualties were, however, very heavy.

On the 1st July our gunners shelled the enemy on Yellow Ridge throughout the entire day, whilst a fresh plan was being worked out. But the Royal Wilts were not to take part in that plan. They were told, quite rightly, that they had done their share, which indeed they had. Their bolt had been shot and they must now content themselves with holding their position and doing a little patrolling.

So, on the next night, the Essex captured the Yellow Ridge with practically no opposition because the enemy, having no stomach for such intensive shelling, had

PALMYRA.

PALMYRA.

THE CHATEAU NEAR PALMYRA.

JUFFA, AS HABFORCE LEFT IT.

RESPITE AT PALMYRA.

withdrawn. Then, at first light on the 3rd July, as the Essex were pressing their attack through the ruins on the outskirts of the town, they were met by a white flag. The French Commander was offering to surrender if a twenty-four hour truce in the air could be arranged. This latter proviso was easily satisfied because the Commander of Habforce, as has already been stressed, was sadly lacking in aircraft.

Thus Palmya fell and the town was occupied the same day. Quite a fair number of prisoners were taken, together with a large quantity of material. The prisoners, it should be added, were all found to be in a state of glorious intoxication, and this timely assistance from Bacchus was welcomed by our diminished troops because it rendered the evacuation of these prisoners much easier.

On the evening of the surrender of Palmyra, the Royal Wilts joined General Clark's Advanced H.Q. at Rek. Here they were to take over guard and patrol duties, whilst the rest of the 4th Cavalry Brigade and attached troops moved to the spring at El Beida, twenty miles west of Palmyra. Our men were in a pretty bad way by this time, but their spirits very soon rose once the ordeal was over. So closely had they been confined to their slit trenches during that nightmare fortnight that it had been well nigh impossible even to shave, and the washing of any clothes or equipment had been quite out of the question. As a result, most of the officers, as well as the men, had long beards, and they presented a very tattered and torn appearance when they arrived at Rek. Even then they had very little time to smarten up, because there were many duties to be performed.

To begin with, on the 4th July, an ultimatum was issued to the garrison which was holding out in T.3. When it was pointed out to the gallant Foreign Legion detachment which had held it so long that their position was now hopeless, they capitulated and surrendered in the best tradition of that very fine regiment. They turned out as though on church parade, which they were able to do because, unlike our own men, they had not been actually fighting whilst they were beleaguered in the pumping station. In consequence they presented a most unfortunate contrast as our troops had not had time to get rid of their tattered clothing, transport not being yet available to bring them up a new issue. It seemed a great pity that men of the Foreign Legion should have been fighting against us because a year previously they would have been only too willing to come over to our side.

So the position on the morning of the 5th July was as follows:—

4th Cavalry Brigade (less Royal Wiltshire Yeomanry) with one troop of 25-pounders. One troop Anti-Tank (2/1st Aust. Anti-Tank Regiment, 4th Battery) and detachment R.E. One troop 169 Light A.A. Battery.	In El Beida area, approximately 20 miles west of Palmyra.
1st Essex and two troops 25-pounders. One section Anti-Tank. One troop 169 Light A.A. Battery.	At Palmyra.
Royal Wiltshire Yeomanry (less detachment) with 3 armoured cars and section Anti-Tank.	At Rek, guarding Advanced Habforce H.Q.
Detachment Royal Wiltshire Yeomanry. One troop Anti-Tank guns. One troop 169 Light A.A. Battery and 3 armoured cars.	At Juffa, guarding Rear Habforce H.Q.

During the next two days the Regiment began patrolling daily to Sukhne whilst the Essex were settling in at Palmyra. Other patrols reported the road from Palmyra to Hama clear of the enemy until they arrived at Furqlus, which was held by the enemy with armoured cars.

Life at Rek was fairly peaceful for a few days and the Royal Wilts settled into the old Roman aqueduct which was still occupied by the Advanced Habforce H.Q. The aqueduct here was a deep trench leading out of the flat desert below into the hilly country round the edge of the basin, and served the purpose of a hide-out very well. It was shown of course, on the air photographs taken before hostilities had begun, but, since no vehicles were allowed to approach within about a mile of the actual H.Q., no wheel tracks were shown in subsequent air photographs. These precautions were successful and even though they had no interference from our side enemy aircraft failed completely to locate the troops living in the aqueduct.

The 4th Cavalry Brigade H.Q. now moved to El Quaryatein where enemy air activity was slight, except for the spectacular bombing by a fair number of French aircraft of a herd of camels twelve miles west of our forward troops. In their wake, Habforce H.Q. moved into Palmyra and the troops found it a pleasant change from the discomforts of the desert.

This ancient and historic town, with the broken beauty of its classic columns gleaming in the light of the full moon, provided a very romantic experience for the men who captured it. The past fortnight had been a nightmare in which, plagued by flies and unable to put up any sort of cover for fear of attracting attention from the air, all ranks, including Divisional and Brigade H.Q., had grilled in the sun. The best form of shade to be hoped for was that afforded by a hole in the ground, except in the case of the lucky few who had found some caves in the hills. In slit trenches life became almost unbearable from about ten o'clock onwards, when the sun crept over the eastern lip, until the evening when, by shifting across to the western side of the trench, one could hide from the sun as it set.

Perhaps the chief joy of Palmyra was the swimming pool which, surrounded by unexploded hand grenades and bomb splinters, was discovered in the heart of the ancient ruins. Here the troops splashed about in the sulphur water which, in days gone by, was supposed to have done so much for the beauty of the powerful Queen Zenobia. Judging by the beneficial effect which it had upon the desert sores of our troops, the Queen had chosen her spa well. Other centres of attraction were the very few inadequately stocked shops, which were soon sold out, and the local laundry, which was rushed off its feet. But there was one distinct disadvantage to life in Palmyra. The sulphur of the baths, which did so much good to the skin, played havoc with the stomach, and as a result the tortures of some at any rate were not yet finished.

This comparatively peaceful existence was disturbed on the 10th July by the sudden and almost unheralded arrival of nineteen Hurricanes, which used the aerodrome as an advanced base for a raid on Aleppo and the desert aerodromes which were being used by the Vichy French in the neighbourhood of Meskene. Such a large force of fighters raised great enthusiasm and we really felt that help was near at hand. The thrill of their appearance in perfect formation in the desert sky will be remembered by many for the rest of their lives. Their raid on Aleppo appears to have been successful and everybody was more than glad to see this outward and visible sign of what had up till that time appeared to be a somewhat inward and spiritual air power. The Hurricanes refuelled once more at Palmyra on their return journey and the next morning, as might have been expected, the aerodrome was bombed by eight enemy fighters. This resulted in the destruction of one Lysander and two Gladiators, with one Lysander temporarily damaged.

However, the end was very near and, on the night of 11-12th July, just as the Royal Wilts had moved from Rek to a village called El Quariatein, the " Cease Fire " was signalled. For the second time in six weeks " the heat was turned off." Once more the campaign had collapsed and after this a period of suspended animation set in until the armistice was signed.

The relief was very considerable as the Regiment had passed a very unpleasant few weeks which were, nevertheless, an excellent training for what was in store for them later on.

CHAPTER FIFTEEN

THE PERSIAN CAMPAIGN

FOR the remaining adventures of the Royal Wilts on the long journey which was to follow, we will quote again from the article which was written at that time. Here is what it says:—

"Immediately Palmyra fell, the Brigade moved forward a distance of twenty miles and covered the approaches from the direction of Homs. The advance towards that place was continued and the Brigade moved forward in three columns, driving back enemy armoured cars and infantry. During this time they cut the important railway between Baalbek and Homs, blowing up the line at several points.

"When hostilities ceased at midnight 11-12th July, the Brigade was in touch with the Eastern defences of Homs. There is no doubt that the threat to this important place hastened the end of the Syrian campaign. The end of the fighting in Syria did not however mean that the Brigade were to rest, as orders were received for it to move through Homs and Hama to Aleppo.

"Here the Brigade were the only troops in North Syria and were responsible for internal security and the control of the Turkish frontier over a huge area. They were also responsible for the custody of the Vichy Troops, numbering 5,000, who were to await repatriation, and for collecting from them their arms, vehicles and equipment.

"Posts were established at all points where roads and railways crossed the Turkish frontier between the River Euphrates and the Mediterranean, a distance of no less than 200 miles. In addition continuous patrolling of the villages, roads and tracks in the area was carried out.

"After a certain amount of difficulty to begin with, the handing over of the Vichy equipment was carried out smoothly. The attitude of the Vichy officers, although not friendly, was very correct. After less than three weeks the Brigade were once more on the move, and on 6th August it set out again for Iraq, this time accompanied by 'B' Squadron of the Royal Wilts, which had rejoined the Regiment from Tobruk. In six days a desert march of 850 miles was carried out under very hot and trying conditions. The first day's march to Deir-Ez-Zor on the Euphrates was 214 miles and took place in a continuous dust storm.

"Their route then took them down the valley of the Euphrates, past Hit and Ramadi, and on the third day they found themselves once again on the late side at Habbaniya. A bathe in the lake to wash off the dust of the desert was much appreciated, and the next day the Brigade had a short march to Baghdad. Two more marches brought them to the famous oil fields of Kirkuk, where they waited for the opening of the Persian campaign. While at Kirkuk, road patrols were carried out as far as Mosul.

"At last the order came for the Brigade to concentrate at Khaniquin, 120 miles away on the Persian frontier. The Warwickshire Yeomanry were already there guarding the oil refinery. On August 25th before dawn the advance into Persia commenced.

"The Persians were holding a strong position on the Paitak Pass, thirty miles from the frontier. The plan was for a mobile force to enter Persia by another route and to place themselves astride the main road at Shahabad, fifty miles in rear of the enemy position. The advance was led by the Warwickshire Yeomanry and a Squadron of light tanks. Opposition was encountered at a place called Gilan, but this was overcome early on the second day, and the Warwickshire Yeomanry pushed on towards Shahabad followed by the rest of the Brigade. The pace was too hot for the light tanks which had to be left to bring up the rear.

"The route lay through rocky hills with steep winding passes. The Persians had carried out a number of demolitions on the road but did not cover them with fire. With the aid of the Sappers these were all cleared during the night and early on August 27th the Warwickshire Yeomanry entered Shahabad.

"A Squadron of the Household Cavalry Regiment was immediately sent back along the main road in the direction of the Paitak Pass.

"The arrival of a force in their rear had, however, caused the Persians to evacuate their position on the Paitak and the Household Cavalry Regiment joined hands with the infantry that had been facing the Persian position.

"Some opposition was encountered by the Warwickshire Yeomanry east of Shahabad, where they were relieved in the afternoon by the Royal Wiltshire Yeomanry. Patrols were carried out during the night and it became apparent that the enemy were holding a strong position barring the road to Kermanshah.

"But before the arrangements for an attack on the position by two Battalions of Gurkhas had been completed a Persian officer came forward under cover of a white flag and arrangements were made for the cessation of hostilities.

"So ended the third campaign in which the 4th Cavalry Brigade had played a part in the short space of little over three months.

"The Brigade then moved to Kermanshah, with one squadron of the Household Cavalry Regiment at Sultanabad and 'B' Squadron of the Royal Wilts at Avej, under command of the 2nd Indian Armoured Brigade. Later they moved back to Hamadan where the Squadron Leader and his second in command met the Russians for the first time at a dinner party given for the Brigadier of the Indian Armoured Brigade. The chief recollection carried away by the British soldiers present, however, seems to have been the fact that in that part of the world an empty petrol tin would purchase thirty eggs!

"On September 15th the Brigade received orders to move to Teheran, a distance of 400 miles, and to occupy it in conjunction with the Russians. The march was carried out in three days and on September 17th the 4th Cavalry Brigade, less the Warwickshire Yeomanry who were left behind at Kermanshah owing to an outbreak of malaria, and Russian troops under the Command of General Novikov, entered the city.

"During the time spent in Teheran close contact was maintained with the Russians and a combined parade of British and Russian troops was held in the British lines. The following is a description written on the spot :—

"Difficulties, so they say in the Army, are made to be overcome and they were plentiful that day. All units both British and Russian sent detachments, and they varied from Cavalrymen over six feet to Indians under five. We were an assorted collection and so were the Russians.

"At 10.15 a.m. the British detachments were beginning to file slowly from their rooms when suddenly truck loads of Russians arrived sitting smartly to attention. They were thirty minutes early. It had been forgotten that their time was thirty minutes in advance of ours. However, they de-bussed and formed up on the square facing, perhaps luckily, the correct direction. The British markers were formed up and the detachments were marched without difficulty into their correct positions and there they waited for the Generals.

"Meanwhile the spectators were assembling. Many of the British inhabitants of Teheran were there armed with cameras. All British troops in the billet were there, criticising our own troops and examining with curiosity the Russians.

"There were Russian Mechanised troops in their blue overalls and black boots, there were cavalry soldiers and infantry in their green steel helmets of the French pattern; in our ranks there were the Household Cavalrymen, Yeomen and the Ghurkas not forgetting the Gunners and the medical staffs. There was even a party called Brigade details.

"At eleven o'clock the two Generals arrived and the British troops presented arms. The General Salute was sounded which conveyed as can be imagined nothing to the Russian General, who was followed by a bevy of Staff Officers.

"The British toops were inspected first; all Russian officers remaining at the salute during the inspection. Then the British General inspected the Russian troops who as they were inspected first stood at ease and then came swiftly to attention.

"When the inspections were over and the Generals had returned to their saluting base, the British troops on parade gave three cheers for the Russians, but before the Russians did so, for some reason best known to themselves they advanced towards the British troops, halted and made a noise like an air raid siren. When the wailing sound had died down, it was seen that the Russian Commander had placed himself in such a position that he would have the greatest difficulty in forming his men up to march past. By some skilful manoeuvring he eventually arrived past the saluting base in the correct formation and very impressive did the Russians look, stamping their feet and swinging their arms across their bodies.

"The British Troops followed and their slower pace and longer stride was very noticeable and again contrasted with the Gurkhas pace which is so extraordinary to watch.

"The par de was over and the entertaining was to follow. Long tables had been laid for the men, literally covered with beer bottles. The officers dined in a different room where an excellent lunch had been arranged. If you have never catered for the Russians before you too will probably make an error. Here is the menu.

      Caviar
      Trout
      Steak
      New potatoes
      Carrots and beans
      Fruit salad
      Cheese
      Coffee

"Now would you know that a Russian eats cheese with caviar? How would you know that after the meat course they would require fish again? How would you know that they eat bread with fruit salad? How would you know that they prefer beer to wine?

"However they do eat caviar and they do drink vodka. In the end everything was placed on the table and everyone grabbed.

"All were in excellent form when the party adjourned to listen to the Russian band and to watch the dancing. What a wonderful performance they gave. They held 200, let it be admitted, slightly intoxicated troops spellbound for ninety minutes. It was extraordinary to think that every Russian Brigade had a band like this. The Cossack and Ukrainian dances were terrific. Swords flashed.

"Eventually the happy party broke up and all had left except for the Chief Commissar whose hat had been 'lifted.' It was never found."

* * * * * *

Finally orders arrived for the Brigade to return to Palestine and the march of over 1,300 miles was carried out in twelve days, including a day's halt en route. It arrived on the shores of the Mediterranean on 8th October, just five months after it had set out. During this period the average distance covered by the vehicles was 8,000 miles.

There is really very little more to tell as far as the Royal Wilts were concerned. For them the Persian campaign really was a walk-over. Perhaps it would be more accurate to describe it as a "drive-over," because they drove their trucks for many weary miles under the most difficult and interesting conditions. Just how interesting is shown by the map inside the front cover of this book. It gives an idea of how closely the Royal Wilts followed the routes used by Father Abraham and the Jewish tribes, who came from Ur of the Chaldees by way of the Euphrates to Egypt and then, after spending forty years in the desert, to the Land of Promise.

Like them the men of the Royal Wilts "wandered through the desert and the sown, passing from country to country." They hardly "lived the lives of nomad shepherds," but in many respects their mode of living was very similar.

In case the reader is a trifle disappointed to find that the Israelites are not shown as passing through the Red Sea, a word of explanation is necessary. The most modern theory is that they did not go near the Red Sea, which is known to us by that name. The country between Egypt and Palestine, all along the coast especially in the southern portion, is of a most peculiar construction. The sea stretches inland for sometimes a few miles of very shallow water. Where this happens the land has the appearance almost of marshes and tall reeds grow plentifully in those places. That part of the sea has been referred to in the past as the "Reed Sea," and that is the sea through which it is now thought that the Israelites passed. A good storm of wind might well blow back the water to allow them to negotiate this part dry shod. A fall in the wind would have allowed the water to flow back again and overwhelm the Egyptians who were not so fortunate. That would account for what happened. All this becomes very apparent when you fly over this "Reed Sea" because, as usual, you can see many things from the air which are not to be noticed on the ground beneath.

So the Yeomen came to the end of their Desert Journey, the poorer by the loss of comrades, the richer by the wealth of memories and experience. In the thunderstorm of war that rolled on round the world during the time of the Royal Wilts' "sojourn in the wilderness" the particular clap that they contributed may not have been heard as clearly as it deserved by the peoples of the Allied Powers, and by those at home in Britain. Yet their praises did not remain unsung, and from the articles about Habforce the following by Colonel Walter Elliot, M.P., published in *The Spectator*, is reprinted.

* * * * * *

" This is the story of a brigade of Englishmen. I say Englishmen, and I mean Englishmen. I do not mean Britishers. I do not mean Scots, Irish, Welsh, or Australians. The other fighting men have many tales and much glory. These men were English.

" It happened in 1941—the year after Dunkirk—the early summer ; much of it before the Russian war, all of it before the American war. It was an episode in the Six Wars of General Wavell—the two in Libya against Graziani, and then Rommel ; the war against Italian East Africa ; the war in Greece and Crete ; the war against the Iraqi Generals (the Golden Square) and against the old Shah of Persia. He lost the war in Greece and Crete, he drew against Rommel. All these wars he was fighting simultaneously. He had nothing in his favour—nothing but interior lines. Even that was a paradox ; for, though his lines were interior, his whole system hung like a plum from the longest lines of communication—13,000 miles of sea—that any army has had to draw out. Nor were these lines unassailed. When he began, the most vital of them all, the Red Sea line, was flanked by Axis air and Axis sea, from Mogadishu on the Indian Ocean to Massawa next to Port Sudan.

Two Kingdoms, then Syria.

The Brigade, Wavell's very last strategic reserve, was drawn up and sent forward when the Axis had pushed the Iraqi Generals into revolt and had brought a challenge against us from the Persian Gulf to the frontier of Trans-Jordan. The Brigade, as I have said, was pure English. It was for the main part mechanized cavalry—cavalry soldiers travelling in lorries. All soft-skinned vehicles. No tanks. Practically no armour. Practically no air. Go on and go to it. Only the Iraqi Generals and their forces to meet—and the Shah is turning out Persia against you—and, by the way, Vichy France is turning out Syria. You may be wanted there. You can't get round to Syria, of course, till you've mopped up the other two—the other two Kingdoms. When you've done that, let us know. You'll have to take on the French aeroplanes and the Foreign Legion. We can't send very much to help. The aeroplanes and the armour are in the Western Desert trying to shift Rommel.

They mustered at Tel Aviv, in Palestine. Let the regiments be named and remembered. There were the Household Cavalry Regiment, whose cuirasses and white plumes we used to see on sentry duty in Whitehall or jingling across St. James's Park. There was the Wiltshire Yeomanry. There was the Warwickshire Yeomanry. There was, for much of the time, a battalion of the Essex Regiment—foot soldiers in lorries. And there were two batteries of 25-pounders—the Grimsby Territorials, raw off the ships at the Canal. They had to make up transport at Tel Aviv from Civil sources.

Habforce is created.

They were given the unromantic and strictly functional name of Habforce and told to proceed like blazes to the great aerodrome at Habbaniya, almost equidistant from Suez, Aleppo, the Caucasus and the Persian Gulf. The best part of a hostile Iraqi division was there, having posted itself in the high ground above the camp, and was plastering the bungalows and the runways over open sights.

" The Iraqi forces were being bombed and held by trainer aircraft. Also by a battalion of the King's Royal Regiment, come by sea to Basra from India and thence by air. But the need was urgent.

" Blazes was the word. They pushed out into the desert in a May hot wind of 110 degrees Fahrenheit. Too hot even for Glubb's Arabs. A great deal hotter than Grimsby any day. The first clash was at Rutbah Wells, in mid-desert. They brushed aside opposition and hurried on. They reached the aerodrome, drove off its attackers and relieved the forces there. Having got into the aerodrome, the next task was to get out. The defenders had broken down part of the embankment to bring the river to aid the defence. This it had done, but the same flood that shut out the attackers now shut in the relievers. They ferried across the gap through which the flood was pouring, in the round boats of these parts. This was going to take a month. They had to secure the great iron bridge across the next river and make for Baghdad before the revolt could draw breath. So one regiment drove ahead. It arrived outside Baghdad, and Baghdad capitulated in the morning.

"First round over. There was much of the Great March still ahead. Next to Mosul—Mosul of the oil. German aircraft were already beginning to land there. However, that was made secure. Back to Baghdad. The Syrian campaign was going slowly. A new wedge had to be driven in. Up across the desert went Habforce, striking for Palmyra, which was held by the Foreign Legion, the local levies and eighteen Vichy aeroplanes. The Force had three days' march across the desert, throwing up dust like a sandstorm. It had a Lysander, for co-operation. It was bombed and bombed. They sent the Lysander back to base; there didn't seem any reason in getting good men killed to no purpose. At the end of the third day they arrived. They had to fight for Palmyra. They did, and took it. British forces were all round Syria then—right up to the Turkish frontier. Vichy capitulated. Second round over.

No Respite.

"You would think they might have a rest? No—the assault on Russia had just begun. Hitler was pushing the Shah of Persia against us. Persia had to be made good. It meant the Persian Gulf. It meant the railway to the Caspian. It meant touch with the Red Army. Back came the Brigade to the Euphrates, crossed the Great River again, across the plain and up into the Persian plateau by the Paitak Pass, to the high 6,000-8,000 feet plateau that runs to the Caucasus. They went up the Pass. The Shah's men capitulated. Third round over.

"From there they marched to Teheran and linked up with the Red Army. Habforce was pretty shabby by this time—shabby, and ill-clothed for its new surroundings high up in the hills. Ill-clothed for its new neighbours, the perfectly drilled, splendidly-dressed divisions of the Red Army. But the hardest blow of all was that the Russians had horses. This for the Household Cavalry—and almost more perhaps for the Yeomanry—was a comparison very bitter to bear. However, they had gained touch. The junction was made. Fourth round over.

You think they might have rested there? You would be wrong. Divisions were weak and reserves were few in the Middle East. Back they came to Tel Aviv. There they parted with the battered motor trucks with which they had travelled so far. They had marched 8,000 miles, and Habforce was at an end. The regiments were served out at last with armour—armoured cars, tanks. Proper armour with which to seek out Rommel. They marched at length towards him and engaged. They were last heard of from El Alamein, fighting most gallantly in the Battle of Egypt. They are marching still."

Part Two

CHAPTER SIXTEEN

BACK IN THE "HOME FROM HOME"

AT the end of this very long trek, on the 8th October, 1941, the Regiment found itself back once more in Palestine. It was interesting to hear the troops, when they knew that Palestine was to be their destination, telling each other that they were going " home." Already that word had crept in—a home *from* home, undoubtedly—but it sounded strange when one remembered the epithets which had been applied to this " Promised Land " by those same men during the first few weeks of their stay there. Nevertheless, after five months in the deserts surrounding it, they were well able to understand the impression which it must have made on Jews after forty years in those self-same deserts !

This time Gedera was chosen as the Royal Wilts Camp, a place further south than they had been before, in what was once known as the Philistine country. Not very far away was Gaza, where Samson was imprisoned and came by his death when he pulled down the pillars of the Temple. Ascalon was also close by, and the ruins of the old " Ashkelon " are still visible, for on the site of the old Biblical town the Romans built a wonderful city. There the Crusaders fought many a battle and, strangely enough, the place has given its name to the humble vegetable which to-day is known as " Shallot." The Romans called this kind of onion " Ascalonia," which the Norman French translated into " Escallion," and " shallot " is the English version.

The camp itself was just like all the others except that, during that very inclement winter, it was colder, wetter and muddier. The country round about, however, was full of Bible stories. It was a strange experience to read, in those surroundings, the portions of the Bible which refer to them. The reader will appreciate this if he turns up, in particular, Judges XVI, Kings XVIII, and Acts VIII.

At Gedera the Regiment encountered a spell of very cold and wet weather, which they felt the more from having spent the summer in such heat, and they were glad to be issued with battle-dress for the first time. Few who were there will forget the mud in that camp at Christmas time, but Christmas dinners were voted the best yet enjoyed, and there was no lack of good cheer. At last, too, they were beginning to get the tanks which they had been promised for so long, and were able to get down to really serious training as an armoured regiment. There was considerable secrecy about the new type of American tank with which the Royal Wilts were being equipped. They were officially called "Stuarts." But from their first appearance they were always known by the troops as "Honeys." They seemed most formidable in 1941, but before two years had passed, they looked puny and almost ridiculous beside the giant "Shermans" which were to be the Regiment's pride during their greatest battles. Incidentally many a wife or relation in Wiltshire was puzzled at that time by sentences in their letters from Palestine such as " Gee —you should see my new steed—it's a honey ! "

The Regiment could now feel that it was no longer inexperienced; it had undergone all the discomforts entailed by desert warfare, it had seen active service, and it was in the true sense a Regiment, and a team pulling together in the spirit of keenness, co-operation and cheerfulness. All were ready and anxious for the more serious work which lay ahead. At the end of March, Lieut.-Colonel Williams, who had commanded the Regiment since it left England, finished his period of command, and Lieut.-Colonel P. T. W. Sykes, of the Queens Bays, took his place. At the same time the Regiment moved to Hadera Sea Camp, where, between training, it was able to do some bathing. Also at this time, " B " Squadron, which had been in Jerusalem, acting as guard to the High Commissioner, returned and was replaced by " C " Squadron.

The Squadron Leaders, by the middle of May, were: "A" Squadron, Major Hubert Blount; " B " Squadron, Major the Viscount Weymouth; " C " Squadron, Major Charles Awdry; " H.Q." Squadron, Major the Hon. Anthony Herbert. Major Alistair Gibb was Second-in-Command of the Regiment.

REGIMENTAL CHRISTMAS CARD, 1941.

Ever since the successful conclusion of the Iraqi, Syrian and Persian campaigns, the men of the Royal Wilts had been casting envious glances in the direction of the troops who were fighting in Egypt. That is where they wanted to be. There were Germans to be killed down there and that is what these Wiltshiremen had crossed the Mediterranean to do. Libya was the big stage in the Middle East Theatre and for the past eight months they had been waiting in the wings. They felt they had acquitted themselves well " on tour " and now they wanted a part in the big show.

The opportunity came at the beginning of May, 1942. The Regiment was moved from Palestine and trekked across the Sinai Desert to Khatatba where, and this was exciting news indeed, they were to take over a complete new outfit of tanks. Enthusiasm ran high and reached its climax when H.R.H. the Duke of Gloucester inspected them in their new surroundings. It is difficult to describe the feelings which this visit from a member of the Royal Family aroused in men who had been nearly two and a half years in the Middle East. It was a sort of link with home. The very normal inspection by so well known a figure made them feel somehow less cut off. Already the memories of England were beginning to grow misty in the minds of some and this episode did a lot to bring the once familiar scenes back into focus. It was good for morale and it occurred to many that we are fortunate to be ruled by a family which has so great an understanding in these matters.

On the 27th May the Germans attacked the Gazala line and thereby brought one more disappointment to the Wiltshire yeomen who had not had sufficient time to train properly by then: their tanks were taken away as reserves for those whose need was greater. So the Regiment went back to its trucks once more, as a mobile column to assist in the defence of Egypt in case the Germans broke through.

Nothing exciting happened to them in the Delta, however, and by the end of June they were still training at Khatatba. Things were moving now. It had been a terrible month. Disaster after disaster had attended British arms in the Western Desert, ever since Rommel had attacked the Gazala line on the 27th May. For two and a half anxious weeks the Battle of the Cauldron had raged, and in spite of the heroic defence of Bir Hacheim our troops had been driven right back to the Egyptian frontier by the 19th June. Things looked bad, but we still held Tobruk—that thorn in the side of Rommel which had stood us in such good stead for so many months. Things would turn out alright as long as we held Tobruk. It was a magic name.

But then came swift calamity. With sickening suddenness the fall of Tobruk was announced on the 20th June. It did not seem possible. There must have been some mistake. All over the world the United Nations were incredulous. But there *was* no mistake. The Allied troops had withdrawn to Mersa Matruh. Those who knew about these things began to count upon their fingers the defensive positions left between the oncoming German troops and Egypt. El Alamein was a strong position. They comforted themselves with the thought. But El Alamein was only a couple of hours by car from Alexandria and only a handful of people had even heard its name!

Nevertheless El Alamein it was to be and to that line our troops withdrew during the remaining days of that fateful June. There they braced themselves for and withstood the final thrust which exhausted the enemy's strength for the time being. The rot was stopped. The Alamein line held.

Mr. Churchill was in Washington on a visit to President Roosevelt at that time and his speeches gave a sober indication of the humiliation which he must have felt. A victim of one of the chief defects in the social system for which the United Nations were fighting—an abuse of the freedom of speech—he had to listen in patience to the bitter outpourings of the British, and to some extent the American, press. The " Public " raged and stamped in its frustration like a spoilt child. Heads were demanded on chargers, and the armchair critics, in the security of their clubs and pubs, worked themselves up into a state of apoplexy. How fortunate it was that the Prime Minister was in the company of a kindred spirit who understood this outburst. How difficult his task had he been on a visit to the leader of a nation ruled by any other social system than a democracy. But those two great men *did* understand. The President's reaction to the bad news and the clamour was essentially practical. What could America do to help? There *was* something and Mr. Churchill was, as usual, not slow in sizing up the situation and seizing the opportunity. The new Sherman tanks were just then beginning to come off the assembly lines in the workshops of the United States. The first fruits of manufacture had already been issued to the United States Armoured Divisions, who had hitherto been equipped with obsolete types. Mr. Churchill said he wanted some of these tanks for his troops in Egypt. Lots of them. As many and as soon as possible. It is a terrible thing to take the weapons out of a soldier's hand. Nevertheless, the President agreed at once and the matter was put in hand with the usual American promptitude. Thus, whilst the fate of civilisation was swaying precariously on the tight-rope of the El Alamein line, the President of the United States of America and the British Prime Minister set to work and discussed the ways and means of preserving its balance.

Meanwhile throughout the Middle East there was great agitation. Egypt was the centre of the vortex and troops poured in from all directions to the aid of the stricken Eighth Army. From Syria, Iraq, Palestine and even Persia they came, denuding those countries of protection to such an extent that many feared for the consequences should a surprise attack come from the North.

Staff Officers from the various headquarters made feverish plans to defend those countries, even down as far as the Sinai Desert. The final defence plan of Palestine was, as a matter of interest, left in the hands of a G.S.O.II. who belonged to the Royal Wiltshire Yeomanry. Local defence of the " home guard " type was rushed to the environs of Cairo and Alexandria as well as the vital points of the Suez Canal. All sorts of people were co-opted for these duties, and many an officer and other rank found himself in the marshes or desert round one of those places within a few days of his arrival at Suez from England.

Simultaneously the attacks on Malta were at their peak. Convoys from Haifa and Gibraltar were making joint efforts to keep the island supplied—and losing 50 per cent. of their ships in doing it. The Royal Navy had to clear out of Alexandria, abandoning the great floating dock and H.M.S. *Queen Elizabeth* to whatever fate was in store for that port. Great relief was felt later when the capital ship managed to slip away as the moon was down. Haifa became the chief Mediterranean port—and nearly the only one left. Britain had lost control of the Central Mediterranean for the first time in 150 years!

There was a terrific exodus from the threatened towns, and the causeway leading to Alexandria was, in particular, a remarkable sight. A solid mass of cars made movement difficult and, as usual, hampered military activity. The climax to all this excitement came when wisps of acrid smoke were seen to be emanating from the buildings at G.H.Q. in Cairo. " Middle East " was burning its secret files!

But throughout July the stand at El Alamein was maintained. At the beginning of the month the Royal Wilts had moved to Quassassin, near the Bitter Lakes, and there they trained hard for the job which was obviously looming ahead. Their sole relaxation in this desert station was the bathing in the Bitter Lakes which form part of the Suez Canal. But indeed there was little time for amusement and the days passed in quick succession. One was much like another—with a single exception. That exception was the day upon which they received a surprise inspection from the Prime Minister. With his characteristic genius for bobbing up in the right place at the right moment he had decided to visit the spot where such crucial events were

DISTINGUISHED VISITORS IN THE DESERT.

The picture on the opposite page, together with the description and diagrammatic guide below, are reprinted exactly as they appeared at the time in the American publication "Life." They give a vivid impression of the critical nature of the situation and all its implications. The author is greatly indebted to the proprietors of "Life" and to Mr. Norman Bel Geddes for permission to reproduce this valuable material.

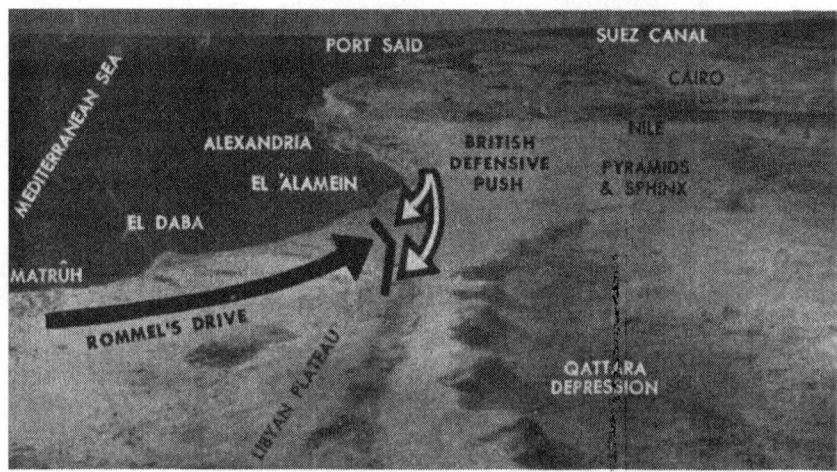

THE DESERT BATTLEFIELD IS THE DOORWAY TO RICH NILE DELTA, SUEZ AND THE EAST

The desert of North Africa is cruel and wide. But at its far end, just beyond Rommel's reach, lies a paradise that holds the key to half of Africa and all the Levant. The airview at left, taken of a terrain model designed by Norman Bel Geddes, shows the gateway to Alexandria and the Nile. A guide to the picture is above. Naturally the towns appear much bigger than they really are. The solid line between the arrows at center left marks the German position on July 11 at El 'Alamein.

What funneled Rommel's drive in toward the coast was the vast, salt Qattara Depression (*right*), rashly called "impassable" because of its cliff wall and the marshes in which run leopard, boar and plover. Often before, the Axis has made a point of going through the "impassable." But at this neck between the Depression and El 'Alamein, British General Auchinleck massed "a forest of guns" and held Rommel with guns rather than tanks. His New Zealanders, called in from Palestine and thrown against Rommel's 90th Light Division, took the battle cry, "Make it heavy for the 90th Light." Two fresh British armies, the Ninth and Tenth, that had been cooling their heels in Palestine and Iraq (*far upper left, over the horizon*) rushed into battle, while British M.P.'s suggested that Britain borrow a general from Soviet Russia. Some ships began to slip out of the great naval base at Alexandria toward escape by way of the Suez Canal and the Red Sea. Cairo still danced and flirted, while dust-covered ambulances rolled silently into the city.

No matter how it turns out, the long-drawn-out Battle of Egypt will be read in the history books of the future as one of the world's decisive battles, a crucial turning point one way or the other.

"... THE NEW SHERMAN TANKS WERE BEGINNING TO ARRIVE."

passing and the ever swelling tide of enemy forces was being dammed up as it threatened to sweep over Egypt. He arrived suddenly in the Western Desert!

Mr. Churchill's tour of the El Alamein line achieved two very concrete objects, whatever else it may have done. It enabled him to see for himself what was going on and it gave the troops great cheer. It was hard to appreciate the seriousness of the situation when they saw his sturdy figure moving amongst them. The puff of his cigar was inspiring and his jaunty delivery of the " V " sign appealed to them in more ways than one. As far as the Royal Wilts were concerned his visit was most important. To begin with, he took the trouble to go slightly out of the normal course of his journey to pay them a call at Quassassin. This gave them confidence. They were beginning to feel a trifle neglected, but he reminded them that he, too, had once been a cavalryman. He even insinuated that the Yeomanry had not so far been given a proper chance in this war. But he had news for them. To make up for any hard luck stories that might have come their way, he had issued orders that they were to be equipped with those very Sherman tanks which were even now on the ocean in fulfilment of President Roosevelt's promise!

The effect of this announcement can well be imagined. The Yeomen were going to be given a part in the big show after all! And Sherman tanks were, at that time, the height of their ambition. The thought of such equipment did, in fact, carry them through the further slight disappointment of the next few weeks. The Regiment was once more split up after being rushed back to the Western Desert during the Battle of Alem Halfa when, from the 30th August to the 6th September, Rommel made his final desperate effort to break through the Alamein line and conquer Egypt. As an earnest of what was to come, however, the Royal Wilts was given a small part, almost a " walking on " part it is true, but nevertheless a part, in this particular show. A composite regiment of tanks was formed, one squadron of which they provided. This armoured column was commanded by Lt.-Col. Sykes, and its role was to deal with any enemy armour which might penetrate the El Alamein line. The rest of the Regiment struggled on with its training in between periods of acting as mobile reserve to protect desert aerodromes against parachute attack. Their problems were many because the tanks with which they were issued had never before been seen by British troops and were not in their first flush of youth. They had been withdrawn from American armoured units and were taken over by the Royal Wilts with considerable mileage to their credit. But the point was that they were tanks of the latest model!

* * * * * *

The Regiment came together again just six weeks before the Battle of El Alamein —that is towards the middle of September. The big news was out by them. The 9th Armoured Brigade had been chosen to form the armour of the famous 2nd New Zealand Division, commanded by Lieut.-General Sir Bernard Freyberg, V.C. Things were looking up!

Those six weeks were very hectic. They were principally devoted to rehearsing the Brigade's role in the coming offensive but, besides this, there was " so much to do and so little time in which to do it." A deal of training had to be rounded off as recent events had sadly hampered training. Then the new Sherman tanks were beginning to arrive and these held a thousand mysteries. New machinery, new types of gun, new gadgets galore. All had to be studied and mastered. But even so those responsible were wise enough to ordain that forty-eight hours leave should be taken by every person. That was a welcome " let up " and probably paid a good dividend in the strenuous times that lay ahead.

To reveal the plan which the Brigade rehearsed might spoil the story, so that risk will not be taken. This is, however, an appropriate place to describe a novelty in that plan which will be mentioned later. Eighth Army had evolved a new method of dealing with enemy minefields. Most people have a hazy notion of what that method was, but few, even now, are quite clear in their minds about exactly how it was carried out. The matter is worth a little study so it will be as well to describe it in detail. Let us imagine that we are in the middle of one of the forthcoming battles.

Across an enemy minefield in the midst of an inferno there proceeds slowly, with great care and difficulty, a sort of Dante-esque edition of the Lord Mayor's Show. In the forefront comes the " Recce Party." This is composed of riflemen. Their job is to smell out pockets of resistance that have been left behind by the infantry who have already passed through. Next come the " Tommy Gunners " and they help the recce party to deal with the enemy thus found. Together these two parties protect the sappers behind them from observed small arms fire. Even so, the dangerous work of clearing a path for the armour will have to be carried out amidst the shelling and random shooting which is going on from all directions.

So much for the local protection of these groups. The next to follow up are the " Bangalore Men." They poke six foot long bangalore torpedoes under the barbed wire and blow it up so that the sappers can get to the mines. And in the rear of this advance party is the Section Leader. The " Tape Party " meanwhile keeps about level with him and tapes out the track to be cleared. Sixteen feet wide is this track and divided in the middle by a third tape, half the track being cleared at a time after the fashion of repairing a tarmac road.

When they have passed, the men with the " Detectors " arrive. These are instruments which look very like a " Hoover " and emit a high pitched buzzing noise when they are immediately over a mine. In later battles the enemy will use a wooden cased mine which will greatly increase the difficulties of clearing tracks, but for the moment he has none of these. So when the two men working the detectors come near a mine, the one with the ear phones directs the one with the " Hoover," on the " hot and cold " principle, until they have spotted exactly where it is. Then the next actor in this weird and eerie drama makes his appearance, the " Mine marker." He it is who marks the mine for the benefit of the next group, the gallant men who, amidst all this danger and confusion, calmly lift the mines, render them harmless and place them on the side of the track.

Finally, at the rear of this procession come the men who put up signs to mark the newly-cleared track : red on one side to denote the presence of mines and white on the other to show where a path has been cleared through them. The diagram shows it all very plainly and the whole process looks very simple. It is, in fact, one of the most dangerous tasks in modern warfare.

At El Alamein the " Scorpion " made its appearance for the first time and it was hoped that this new, rather " Heath Robinson " invention might make the sapper's task both speedier and less dangerous. This " Scorpion " was a tank chassis fitted with a device which flayed the ground some yards ahead of it with chains, as it moved along. These chains exploded any mines in the path of the vehicle before it was close enough to suffer any harm from them. There was also a " Fowler Roller "—a tractor which pushed a heavy spiked roller ahead of it for the same purpose.

CHAPTER SEVENTEEN

THE BATTLE OF EL ALAMEIN

After the last war, two engineers were building a railway across the desert from Alexandria towards Benghazi. When they were about sixty miles out, they planted two flags in the sand to mark a certain place. As there was no other feature in the desert by which to refer to it, they always called that place " The Two Flags." By that name it is still known. The Arabic for " The Two Flags " is "El Alamein."

AND now this story leads up to its great climax. It has been said that Stalingrad and El Alamein will prove to have been the turning points in this war. Certainly they marked the high tide of Nazi conquest. Together they were probably Hitler's " Waterloo." There will therefore be many accounts written about them.

But this is the story of the Royal Wiltshire Yeomanry. It must therefore be confined to the activities with which that Regiment is concerned. Nevertheless. in order fully to appreciate these activities, the broad picture must be understood, An attempt will therefore be made to convey the general outlines of the wide canvas whilst at the same time painting in the details of those portions with which the Regiment is most intimately connected.

Probably the best way of doing this will be to quote certain official accounts of these events and then to try and elaborate the parts which affect the Regiment and explain them in simple language. It must be remembered that this is a story for ordinary people, but the inclusion of portions of the official accounts will also be of interest to those of military experience.

To begin with, then, let us take an extract from the official record prepared by the Ministry of Information. It will re-capitulate part of what has been told but it will also put the whole of the circumstances surrounding the final battle into their proper perspective.

Here is what it says :—

For two years the pendulum had been swinging to and fro on the south-east shores of the Mediterranean until it finally came to rest with a most satisfying click hard over in our favour.

Between December, 1940, and February, 1941, General Wavell swept the Italians out of Cyrenaica. Having reached the Gulf of Sirte, the General and the British Government had to decide whether to pursue the offensive in the hope of clearing everything up to French North Africa, or to send substantial help to the Greeks. Both agreed that the Greeks must come first, and a substantial part of General Wavell's army was therefore shipped across to Greece. In consequence, our positions in North Africa were very thinly held; and before reinforcements could arrive from home or from East Africa, the Germans, who had been forced to come to the rescue of the Italians, attacked with two armoured divisions and swept our men back to the Egyptian frontier. This was held, and so was Tobruk, the defence and supply of which was an eight months' epic. Tobruk was a thorn deep in the enemy's flank; and its possession governed the strategy of the offensive launched on November 18th, 1941, by General Wavell's successor, General Auchinleck.

Once more, after hard fighting, the pursuit swept across Cyrenaica to El Agheila, on the eastern angle of the Gulf of Sirte. Though an unquestionable victory, our attack neither crippled nor disorganised the enemy enough to prevent him standing on the strong position at El Agheila. The forces which we could supply at that time in this region were too weak for attack and too strong for a mere screen. Rommel's counter-attack drove us back as far as the line Gazala-Bir-Hacheim, and restored to him the use of a number of supply ports, notably Benghazi. There, for four months, the two armies glared at each other, both working like beavers to make themselves strong enough to attack and too strong to be attacked. Thanks to his shorter supply lines from Greece and Italy, the enemy was ready first. On June 2nd, 1942, he attacked with his full strength, established a gap in our minefields about half-way down the line, held on to the gap resolutely, and started to enlarge it. For eleven days, the southern bastion of Bir Hacheim, manned by a French garrison, held out against the fiercest attacks, and prevented the enemy from exploiting the gap. So long as it held, the battle generally seemed to be going well; but when it was evacuated under orders, deterioration was rapid. Between June 11th and 13th, tank battles resulted in disproportionate losses to our armour, and the whole army was involved in retreat.

It had been hoped to hold Tobruk once again and counter-attack from the Egyptian frontier. But this time Tobruk succumbed to a powerful attack within 36 hours. General Auchinleck had lost both the lever for a counter-offensive and about 23,000 men made prisoner. The blow was very nearly mortal. The remains of the Eighth Army had to retreat rapidly over the frontier, back past Sidi Barrani, past Mersa Matruh, and back a hundred miles more to El Alamein, where there is a gap of only forty miles between the sea and the generally impassable salty marsh of the Qattara Depression. At El Alamein General Auchinleck, who had himself taken over the tactical direction of the battle, called for a stand.

It was both the last and the best defensive position from which to deny Alexandria and the Nile Delta—only sixty miles away—to the enemy. To the North, the coastal road and railway run over level sandy desert, not far from the salt lagoons which fringe the sea. In the centre are ridges and hillocks on which a film of sand covers underlying rock. In the south, the rock breaks through the sand into outcrops, and then falls away in a sheer cliff to the Qattara Depression. South of the depression again stretch soft sand hills impassable for cars, and the single track from Siwa to the Bahariya Oasis and the Nile Valley can be held with ease against an invader. The El Alamein-Qattara position cannot therefore be turned. It can only be pierced by a frontal attack, and that is what Rommel set himself to do.

On 30th June he launched against it the tanks of the Littorio Division, but they were driven back with heavy loss by the remains of our armour. Next

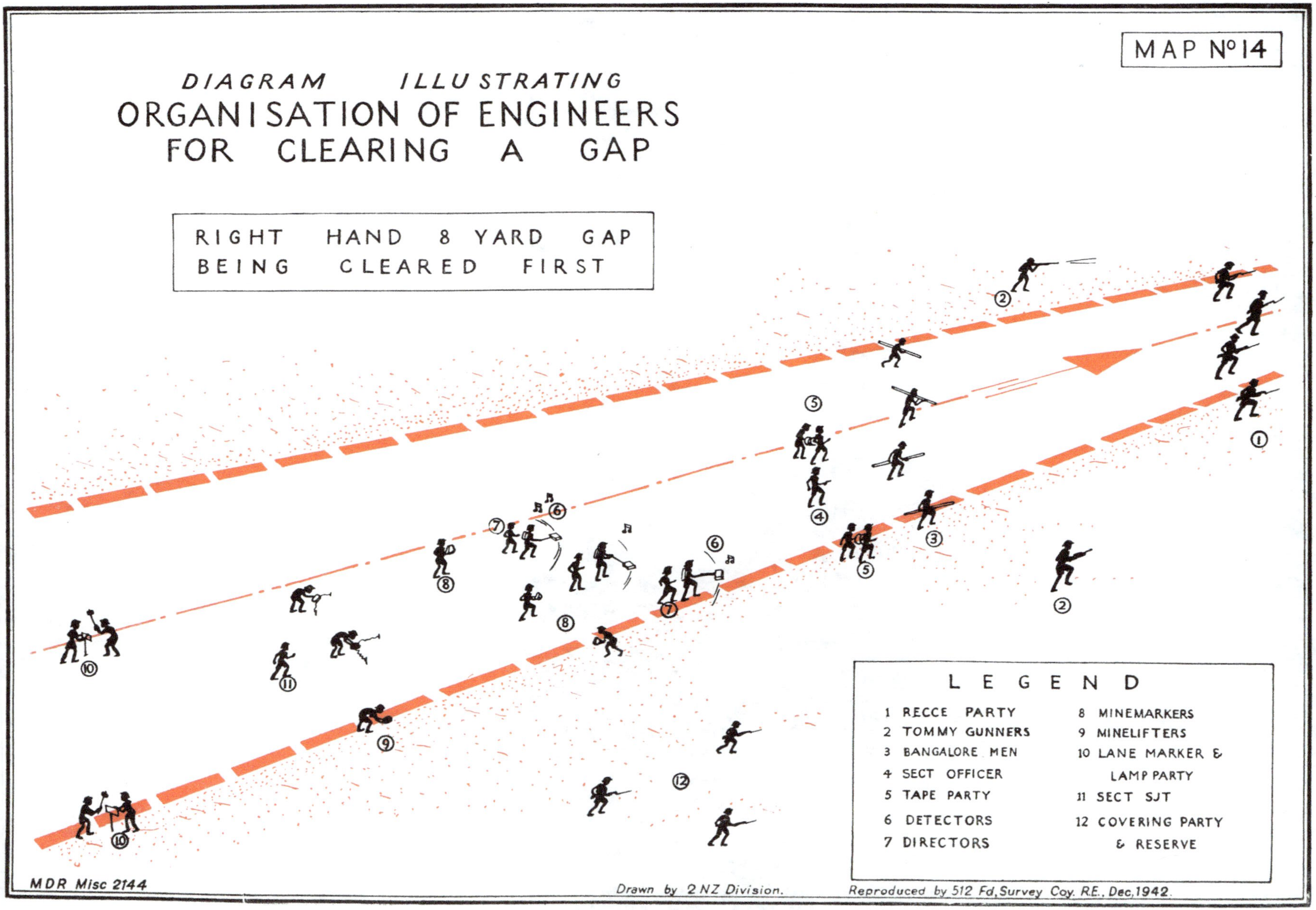

MAP N° 14

DIAGRAM ILLUSTRATING
ORGANISATION OF ENGINEERS FOR CLEARING A GAP

RIGHT HAND 8 YARD GAP BEING CLEARED FIRST

LEGEND

1 RECCE PARTY
2 TOMMY GUNNERS
3 BANGALORE MEN
4 SECT OFFICER
5 TAPE PARTY
6 DETECTORS
7 DIRECTORS
8 MINEMARKERS
9 MINELIFTERS
10 LANE MARKER & LAMP PARTY
11 SECT SJT
12 COVERING PARTY & RESERVE

Reproduced by 512 Fd.Survey Coy RE. Dec.1942.

Drawn by 2 NZ Division.

MDR Misc 2144

day his infantry had come up, and he flung them straight at the South African Division holding the north end of the position. Every attack was bloodily repulsed. Further south, the battle-worn 4th Indian Division dealt faithfully with tanks all day. But when the assault was renewed at night an Indian strong point was over-run. Rommel thought he was through; and on 2nd July the German High Command announced to the world that he was " pursuing the beaten British into the Nile Valley."

But this critical day in fact witnessed his frustration. When he tried to " pursue " he was furiously counter-attacked, and by nightfall had started to withdraw. Renewed attacks on the next two days proved equally futile and costly. Thereafter the 9th Australian Division counter-attacked and took Tel El Eisa hill. For some days longer the battle swayed bloodily to and fro, neither side being able to dislodge the other. But we had held our ground; and the greatest credit is due to General Auchinleck for having robbed Rommel of the fruits of his victory by this successful stand after so long a retreat.

During the following month two considerable attacks by our forces improved our positions, but showed that the enemy was too strongly consolidated to be shifted by anything short of a large-scale offensive. But the door was shut tight against anything less on his part also. General Auchinleck was succeeded as C.-in-C. Middle East by General Alexander, who had been the last man to leave Dunkirk and had so brilliantly brought our small army out of Burma. General Montgomery succeeded General Ritchie in command of the Eighth Army.

This official record of the Ministry of Information gives some description of the type of country round El Alamein, and the accompanying diagram from "Life" shows clearly how all operations are hemmed in between the sea on the one side and the Qattara Depression on the other. For no army can move over the Depression, although during that crucial time our haunting fear was always the possibility of the enemy trying to find some means of bringing this about. Quite a number of rumours spread. One said that he had equipped his vehicles with huge tyres: another claimed that his scouts had found a passage through, and so on. But all of these reports were false, and it was correct to suppose that Rommel would only reach Egypt by penetrating our defences. It was, in fact, the first time since the collapse of the Maginot Line that a static defence had been built up during this war. General Montgomery appreciated that to break through the last war type of defensive position would require last war technique. But Rommel did not. The German final bid for Egypt was conducted on present war lines, and here is the official description:—

These changes had hardly taken effect when Rommel made a serious bid to break through. Our lines to the south, towards the Qattara Depression, had been (probably deliberately) left gappy. If the enemy had tried a headlong rush through he could have been met by a heavy blow from the north against his flank and by a reserve army moving out from the Delta on his front.

On 30th August, in a night attack, the enemy did break through this lightly defended southern sector between the Ruweisat Ridge and Himeimat, and having blocked the southern edge of this gap, he turned north behind our lines and made for the coast with the intention of bringing our armour to battle. The bait was refused. Remaining on the defensive, the Eighth Army, during three days, hit back at the enemy with bombing, artillery fire, and concentric harassing attacks. He dared not leave an unbroken army on his flank; supplies were difficult to come by and petrol was running short. On 3rd September, having been badly mauled, he began to retire. Under cover of three fierce attacks next day, he hauled his men and armour off, with nothing to show for heavy losses except the occupation of the original no-man's land on the southern sector.

* * * * * *

The masterly handling of this final attack by Rommel's forces deserves a word of elaboration. It was probably the first occasion upon which we had put into practice the well-known principle of "accepting penetration." Hitherto we had almost always dashed out with our armour and met such an attack with a head-on collision of tanks. Seldom had we been successful in such an encounter. Rommel was banking upon our using these tactics again. In " refusing the bait " General Montgomery was relying upon one of the principles of war which never change. But it required an iron nerve to " stay put " with Eighth Army on that slight eminence in the desert and to watch the huge German column churn its way through our lines to a point where it was between Eighth Army and Alexandria !

Rommel seems to have been surprised when Eighth Army refused to budge. He was probably frightened too, because he had a great knowledge of tactics. He must have been fully aware that General Montgomery, by remaining on the defensive, was putting him in a dangerous position. So, being frightened, he blustered. He tried a colossal bluff. He contrived to have a message delivered to this commander of Eighth Army, demanding his surrender on the score that he was surrounded. The actual text of the reply has never been published but it would probably make amusing reading. Our map shows, however, that physically speaking the German general was correctly expressing the situation.

But whereas Achilles is reputed to have suffered from a vulnerable heel, Rommel's weak spot was his " tail." This attack was no " reconnaissance in force." It was carried out by a very formidable column of some three hundred tanks. But since those tanks were so far from their base and all supplies had to be brought through the gap which they had forced in our defences, they had to rely upon an enormous number of wheeled vehicles to keep them going. Those vehicles were the " soft tail " which proved to be the column's undoing.

Rommel's failure on this occasion was primarily due to the R.A.F. and General Montgomery's superb tactics. Whilst Eighth Army nursed its depleted armour on that slight ridge in the desert, sortie after sortie flew out from the Delta airfields and played havoc with the mass of soft-skinned transport down below. Meanwhile our anti-tank gunners, profiting by their forty foot advantage in height, found some excellent targets amongst the German tanks. The whole column was " seen off " properly and left behind between eighty and ninety tanks and over one thousand vehicles. Eighth Army had given Rommel a " bloody nose " and that was as close as he and his cohorts ever came to the fleshpots of Egypt.

This battle was the beginning of the end for the Germans in Africa. They never recovered, and it is as well to bear the fact in mind when considering their subsequent rout.

* * * * * *

Let us as we approach the description of the Great Battle of El Alamein, sum up the whole situation as briefly as possible. The essential points are these :—

The El Alamein line, as finally held, was about forty miles of desert which could not be turned because of the sea on the one side and ground impassable to mechanised forces on the other.

The British and enemy lines consisted of discontinuous belts of minefields interspersed with strong points and machine gun and anti-tank gun emplacements.

The only way to penetrate these defences was by a frontal attack.

General Montgomery adopted last war methods slightly modified because of the tank factor. An artillery bombardment was followed up by infantry attacking through the minefields. Sappers then cleared lanes through the minefields for the supporting tanks to come through and take up positions where they could protect the infantry from counter-attack by enemy tanks.

Where Rommel attempted to turn the flank of the 8th Army on August 30 by forcing a way through around Mount Hemeimat, whilst Italian forces in the centre launched an abortive attack in support. The dual attack, and its subsequent repulse, are here indicated.
Drawing by E. G. Lambert.

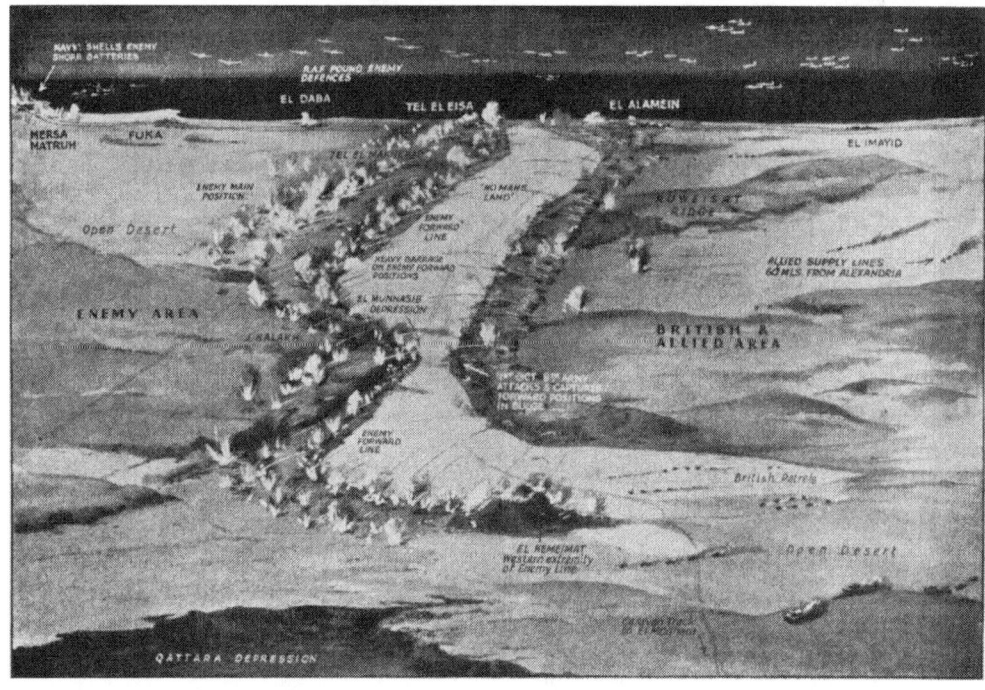

The British and German positions at the opening of the British offensive on October 23, with the wide gap of no man's land from Alamein to El Hemeimat.
Reproduced by permission of the " Sphere."

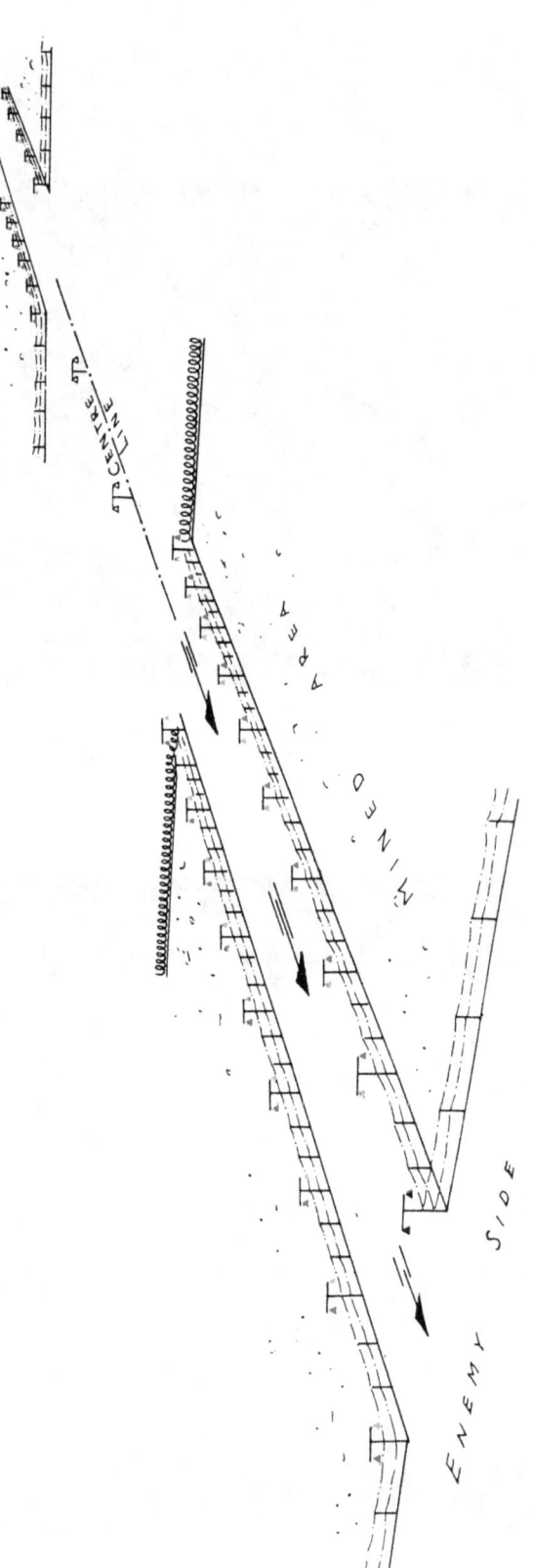

After that the plan was to pass the main body of our armour through the gap thus made. The battle would then be won.

Rommel had disposed half his armour in the north and half in the south. He probably expected Eighth Army to attack his weak spot, the centre. Had it done so he would have tried to crush the attacking force between his Panzer Divisions converging from north and south. But it did not, the Eighth Army attacked not the weakest but the strongest part of Rommel's line, the north.

General Montgomery himself used simple words whilst explaining his plan to the troops. He said that he was going to " break in " to their defences, " worry their guts out " for ten days and then " break out " the other side.

As far as this story is concerned, we are interested in the two main battles in which the Royal Wilts took part. The first of these was during the " break in " on the night of 23rd/24th October and most of the 24th October.

Briefly what happened during this first 24 hours was that in the South the operation was not very successful, but in the north (in which the Royal Wilts were operating) nearly all the infantry objectives were captured. Our armour, which had been meant to pass through the infantry, had been held up, however, by an uncharted minefield ; nevertheless it had followed up close enough to the infantry to prevent them from being counter-attacked by the enemy tanks.

Now, before we go any further, we must understand quite clearly the part which the Regiment played in all this.

To begin with it was in the 9th Armoured Brigade, that Brigade being composed of the Royal Wiltshire Yeomanry, the 3rd Hussars and the Warwickshire Yeomanry.

The 9th Armoured Brigade was under command of the 2nd New Zealand Division. That is, they were at the disposal of Lieut.-General Freyberg, V.C., to assist his New Zealanders in whatever capacity he might think fit.

So now is the time to consider exactly how General Freyberg used them and to gain a clear impression of the role they were to play. But before we do this we must know what part the 2nd New Zealand Division itself took in the operation. It had a threefold mission, its tasks being
    (i) to capture Miteiriya Ridge,
    (ii) to facilitate the passage of the main British armoured force,
    (iii) to exploit success S. and S.E.

A glance at the map will make this clear. The Division had a simple object which was difficult to achieve.

Now for the job allotted to the Royal Wiltshire Yeomanry.

First of all, two troops of " B " Squadron R.W.Y. were told off to support the leading New Zealand infantry. They were to advance immediately behind the men on foot along tracks made by three " Scorpions."

These two detached troops, that is six tanks, were to help the infantry, by machine gun fire, in dealing with any enemy posts holding out. Also they were to be prepared to deal with any enemy tanks which might be encountered.

The remainder of the Regiment were to give the fullest possible assistance to the infantry attack by taking on any enemy tanks encountered and dealing with pockets of resistance which might hold up the advance.

The vital part which pockets of resistance play in such an attack was particularly stressed in the orders issued to the Regiment.

So much for the advance. Now for their role when the infantry objective was captured. Here they had two tasks laid down. Firstly to exploit success to the S. and S.E. and secondly to resist the counter attack. In order to do this they were ordered to pass right through the infantry on the latter's final objective, and to take up a position right ahead of the forward defended localities,

This second task was the most important. On several occasions previous to this the New Zealanders had captured positions after desperate fighting, only to be driven back again subsequently by enemy tanks which had appeared and, by virtue of their superior armour, had robbed them of the fruits of victory. General Freyberg did not want this to happen again. So he ordered his supporting tanks to go as much as one thousand yards in front of his infantry, after the final objective was captured, to prevent any counter attack of this sort. That was the chief task allotted to 9th Armoured Brigade. The Royal Wilts were to be in support of the 5th New Zealand Infantry Brigade, the Warwickshire Yeomanry in support of the 6th New Zealand Infantry Brigade and the 3rd Hussars in reserve.

Next, before we follow the Regiment itself through this first phase of the battle, let us hear what General Freyberg says about the operation up till the evening of the 24th October. His report is as masterly example of how clarity can be combined with brevity and this is how it runs :—

The Operation "Lightfoot."

On the evening of 23rd October four divisions—the 9th Australian Division, 51st Highland Division, 2nd New Zealand Division, and 1st South African Division—forming 30th Corps, were ready for the assault, which it was hoped would " seize a bridgehead in time to pass the armour through by first light."

After dusk all tracks, lit with their distinctive signs—Sun, Moon, Star, Bottle, Boat and Hat—began to fill up with transport in orderly sequence from the rear areas, the heavy tanks of the armoured divisions rumbling in the rear. It was an impressive display of armoured strength. It was a brilliant and calm moonlight night. There was a tense atmosphere as everyone waited.

At 2140 hours all guns, field and medium, opened fire on suspected enemy batteries; it was a twenty-to-one concentration, twenty troops of artillery battering each enemy troop. Assembly forward, which had been proceeding feverishly but silently since dusk, went on even more actively. Noise no longer mattered. The bombardment continued for fifteen minutes, directed against enemy located batteries, and at 2200 hours switched on to the enemy F.D.L.s Meanwhile our infantry, who had assembled on a start line 1,700 yards from the enemy position, went forward to the attack in time to get right up to the bombardment before it started to lift back. Retaliation against our guns was negligible, confirming that we had gained tactical surprise, and demonstrating the efficiency of our counter-battery work.

The Assault on Miteiriya Ridge.

Both our infantry brigades got away to a good start, 5th Brigade on the right and 6th Brigade on the left. 23rd Battalion attacked the first objective on the right, and 24th Battalion the first on the left. 28th (Maori) Battalion had the role of mopping up enemy strong points between the start line and the first objective over the whole Divisional front.

Visibility was extremely bad owing to dust and smoke caused by the barrage, and great difficulty was experienced in keeping touch. The situation remained obscure, and when the barrage paused at midnight we did not know whether the first objective had been captured. 5th Brigade appeared to have succeeded. The situation was still not clear at 0100 hours on the 24th, but work on the gaps in the minefields was being pressed on under fire and 21st and 22nd Battalions on the right and 25th and 26th Battalions on the left had leap-frogged through the attack to the second objective.

Meanwhile optimistic reports came in from 51st Division, whilse 1st South African Division reported strong opposition on the inter-divisional boundary. Visibility was reported to be no greater than twenty to thirty yards owing to

23rd October, 1942, 21.40 hours. The gunners open up, whilst . . .

the infantry wait to advance through the dust and smoke as the great barrage thunders at El Alamein. By morning they were four miles forward.

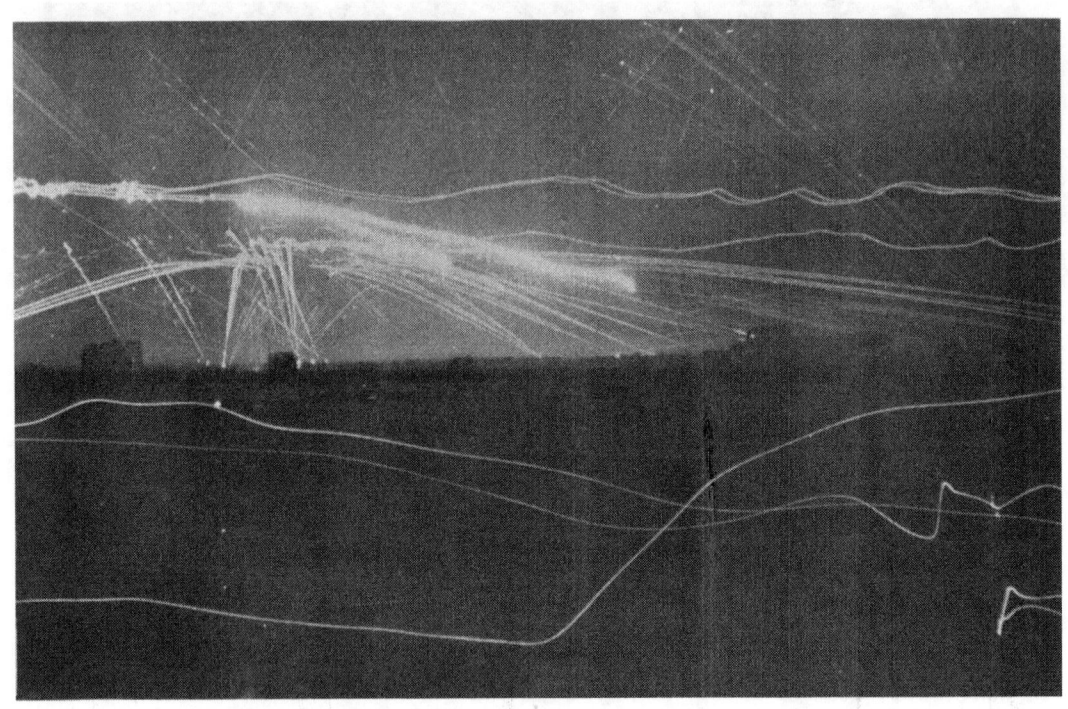

NIGHT . . .

. . . AND DAY.

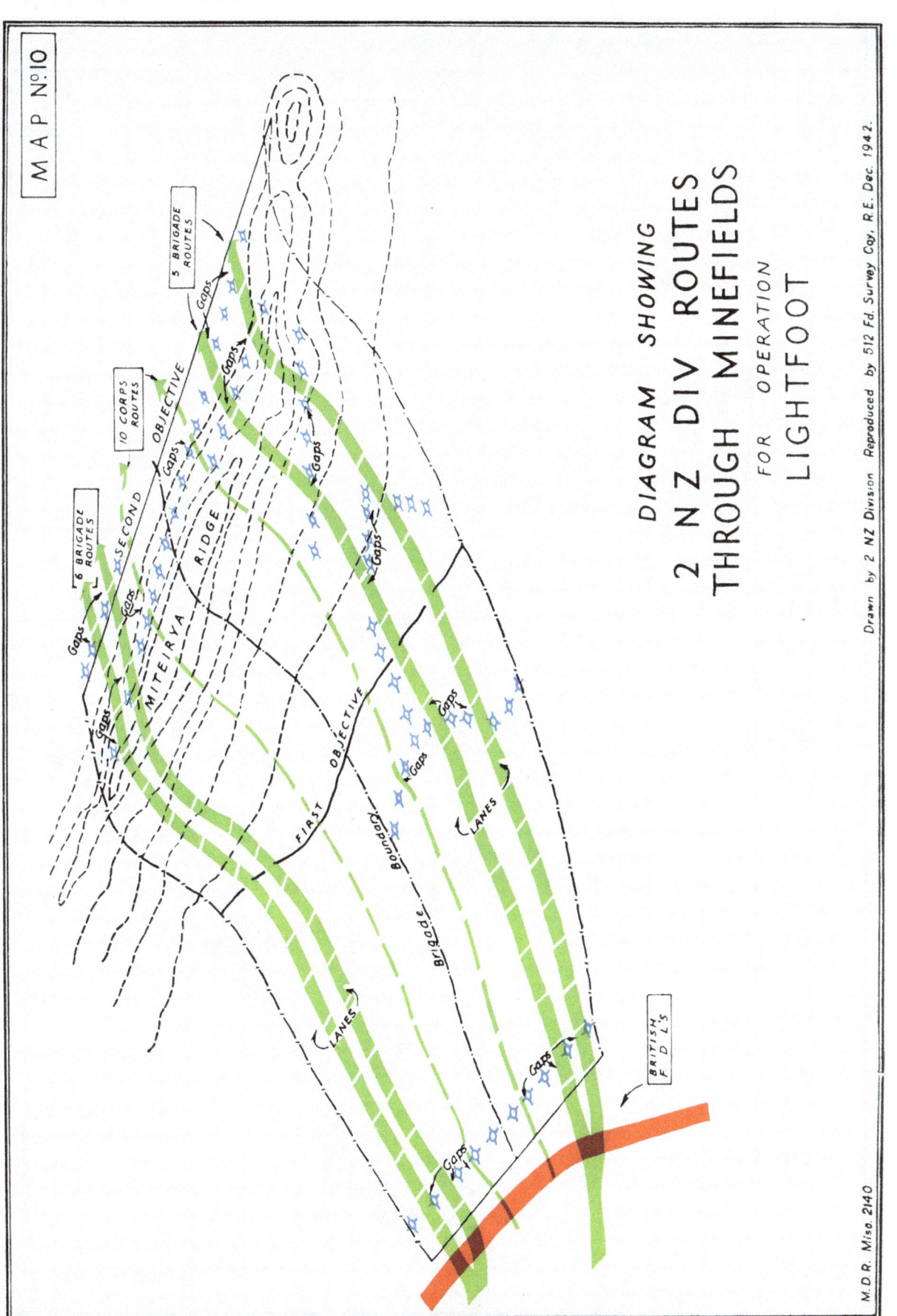

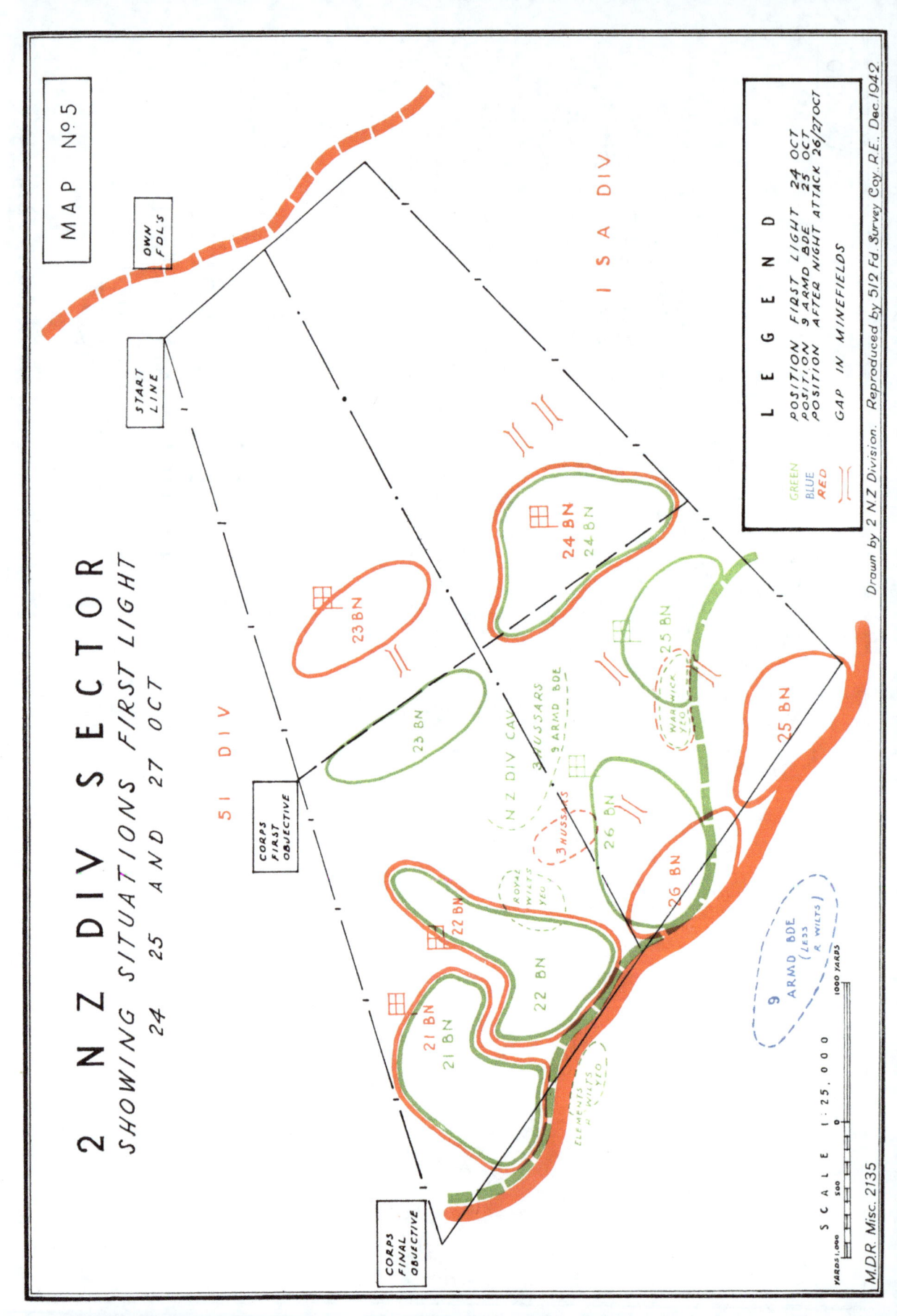

dust and smoke. Under conditions as they existed the type of success signal we had was unsatisfactory. In point of fact both battalions reached their first objectives according to schedule, but no report got through till much later.

When the capture of the first objective was confirmed by both brigades at 0300 hours, I went forward with Tactical Headquarters to Miteiriya Ridge. At this time gaps in the first minefield were through, and leading elements of the Divisional Cavalry and 9th Armoured Brigade were moving forward.

The assault on the final objectives continued against strong opposition. Identifications from prisoners of war indicated the the line was held by elements of the German 164th Division and the Italian Trento Division, the German troops having relieved Italians a few days before. Held up by strong resistance, which caused them to lose the barrage, the infantry pressed on and although in some companies all officers became casualties direction was kept. Shortly after 0400 hours 5th Brigade reached the final objective, but there was no news from 6th Brigade.

Time was getting short, we were behind schedule, and with the approach of dawn the situation gave cause for anxiety. At 0530 hours supporting arms had not come up to the infantry and gaps through the second minefield were not complete. On 6th Brigade front there was no definite information except that 25th Battalion were in touch with 26th Battalion but were held up on the Ridge. Both routes were through but transport was moving slowly while sappers searched for stray mines. Small pockets of enemy missed by the infantry had caused some delay as the sappers had to dispose of these themselves before carrying on with mine lifting.

The Ridge is Captured.

At 0600 hours came better news—the gaps on 5th Brigade front were reported clear. Supporting arms were passing through and the tanks had begun to move also. The appearance of the Sherman tanks of 9th Armoured Brigade with their 75-millimetre guns was a great encouragement to the infantry who, for the first time in the campaign, found tanks with them in the F.D.L.'s. When daylight came, leading tanks of 8th Armoured Brigade of 10th Armoured Division were also passing through on the centre lanes reserved for 10th Corps.

Meanwhile, on 6th Brigade front, 26th Battalion had gained its objective and was slightly forward of it; 25th Battalion had gained the crest of the Ridge after hard fighting, but had been unable to get further forward due to heavy fire from a strong point just outside the Brigade boundary and another between 25th and 26th Battalions. 25th Battalion was in touch with 26th Battalion though there was a gap of some 400 yards between them; but was not in touch with the South Africans. We found later that the latter had been held up short of the Ridge. It was getting light when the transport finally reached units and it was, therefore, not practicable to send anti-tank guns forward of the Ridge.

By 0700 hours on 24th October the Miteiriya Ridge was in our hands but the Armoured Divisions had not got far enough forward before daylight to make a sally possible, especially as other unmarked minefields were found to exist. Tanks of the Royal Wilts Yeomanry had gone forward and ten had become casualties on mines. During the morning the Royal Wilts Yeomanry and a Regiment of 8th Armoured Brigade were heavily engaged with enemy tanks and anti-tank guns. They suffered heavy casualties in tanks knocked out but repulsed all attempts by the enemy armour to make a counter-attack on the 5th Brigade front. The main concentration of tanks of 8th and 9th Armoured Brigades was behind Miteiriya Ridge. It was clear that the bridgehead could not be exploited by our armour at this stage and the day was, therefore, spent in reorganising the position to hold what we had gained. The front was heavily shelled throughout the day but the expected enemy counter-attack did not eventuate. The enemy were no doubt hampered by their own minefields and apart from that the array of big tanks close to our F.D.L.'s was likely to daunt any attacking force.

CHAPTER EIGHTEEN

THE PART PLAYED BY THE ROYAL WILTS

NOW that we have read the official account of the fighting on the night of the 23rd and the morning of the 24th October, let us see, in greater detail, what happened on this memorable occasion. Let us try to gain some human impression of how the battle went for the men of the Royal Wilts. To do this properly we must imagine, for the time being, that we are with them out there in the desert.

The first active steps are taken when the C.O., Lt.-Col. Sykes, calls a Squadron Leaders' Conference at half past eight on the morning of the 23rd. Here he explains the plan, after which he takes them on a reconnaissance of the battle area. So, before we try to follow what is to happen, it is best that we should gain some idea of what the country looks like and the lie of the land.

Most of us, when we left the shores of Britain, had a very false impression of the appearance of a desert. Many of us visualised it as being much akin to Weymouth sands, only on an enormous scale and peopled with the sort of characters we had seen in films of the " Beau Geste " and " Bengal Lancer " type. But this is altogether wrong. To begin with, there are many different kinds of desert and each has its own peculiarities and characteristics. The one with which we are at the moment concerned is very flat and, until the surface is disturbed or crushed, has very little sand upon it. In appearance it somewhat resembles a light dun-coloured baked mud with frequent outcrops of soft greyish stones. In places it is covered sparsely with a dingy green camel scrub, but otherwise there is no vegetation.

And so what they see, this reconnaissance party, as they approach as close as they dare to the scene of the forthcoming battle, is rather like a vast but somewhat bald and burnt up edition of Salisbury Plain. Miteiriya Ridge, which is to be the final objective of the infantry, rises almost imperceptibly and the ground, as seen through their glasses, is a trifle broken and stony at its summit. But unless you are on the summit and can see how it commands the desert which slopes away each side of it, you have the greatest difficulty in realising that it is a ridge at all. You are quite staggered when you notice that the contour of this ridge is only marked as thirty metres on the map. But an advantage in height of only half that measure is worth fighting for in the desert. A trifling eminence sometimes commands vast tracts of country.

Omar Khayam's line " . . . and that inverted bowl men call the sky . . ." may not seem a very apt description to the average Britisher. But standing in that desert with the morning sun blazing in an absolutely cloudless sky, the significance of the simile is very obvious. As you turn slowly through three hundred and sixty degrees, the horizon makes an almost perfect circle and there is not a single feature to be seen except in one place where the Himeimat Ridge, a real ridge this one rising some 150 metres, makes a dent in the rim of the " inverted bowl " which is the empty sky.

In almost all respects the scene is just what the members of the reconnaissance party expected. It is, in fact, very much like the dress rehearsal battlefield with which they are already familiar. It all looks fairly innocent, really, except for a certain amount of wire which is scattered here and there. But they know that between them and their objective there are many obstacles. First of all, at the foot of the ridge, our own minefields, some hundreds of yards in depth. But they will be easy. Then, further on, beyond no-man's land, the enemy minefields. These are very formidable and the air photos show that they are 5,000 to 9,000 feet in depth. But of what there may or may not be beyond all that, our reconnaissance party are completely unaware. There may be other minefields which have not shown up on the photos. There are certainly enemy infantry and anti-tank positions a plenty. These the photos show up only too well. But therein lies the risk of battle. Complete knowledge of the enemy's defences can only come after the fighting, and in all probability it will have to be dearly bought.

So Lt.-Col. Sykes and his Squadron Leaders return to their duties on the whole content. An appreciation has been made, orders have been given, and all that now remains is to find out the answer by the trial of strength which will follow. The die is cast and nothing more can be done about it for the moment. There is quiet consolation in that thought.

But nevertheless these officers have much upon which to ponder as they return to their respective duties. All this may sound like fiction, but they are well aware that it is real. It is actually happening. It is a grim occasion. To few men is it given to experience moments like these, and there will not be many like them in their lives. They are on the eve of one of the decisive battles of the war ; and they are playing a leading part in that battle. Perhaps there may occur to some of them the words which the Prime Minister has recently uttered. " When we consider the magnitude of modern events, compared to the men who have to deal with them and guide them, and the appalling consequences of those events to millions of people throughout the world, the importance of not making avoidable mistakes grows impressively upon the mind."

Finally, a start is made upon this big adventure and, at seven o'clock in the evening, whilst it is still possible to see dimly in the twilight, the Regiment starts to move forward from the Onsol area where it has trained so strenuously for this moment. Along " Bottle Track " and " Star Track " they rumble and, as General Freyberg says in his despatches, the advancing Brigade " is an impressive display of armoured strength." Ahead of them in orderly sequence is the transport of 9th Australian Division, 51st Highland Division, 2nd New Zealand Division and 1st South African Division whose troops are ready for the assault which it is hoped will " seize a bridgehead in time to pass the armour through by first light." The tracks through the minefields, each lit with its distinctive signs—Sun, Moon, Star, Bottle, Boat and Hat, gradually fill up throughout their whole length until, in the brilliant moonlight of a calm night the Royal Wilts reach a point three miles short of the Infantry start line.

Here, in an atmosphere of tense expectancy, the Regiment waits with the rest of the Brigade for the battle to begin. It is an altogether weird experience, this waiting. Under such circumstances a couple of hours can seem like an eternity. The bravest of these men must have some qualms. It is bad enough for those who are more or less ignorant of what is in store for them and only know that it is going to be just one more infernal battle. But for those who know the whole story it is a severe mental strain.

Yet, on the whole, the impression of their deportment is one of unnatural calm. Most of them have climbed out of their tanks and are sitting in small groups chatting or leaning against them. Some betray their feelings by small nervous gestures—the drumming of fingers or the aimless rolling and unrolling of little bits of paper. Some chew sweets. More than one has a good swig at a flask. A few rather forced jokes are cracked and greeted with equally forced laughter. These men are human and under considerable strain. But few there are, undoubtedly, who would willingly yield their places at this moment.

But time must pass, however slowly, and as the over-anxious glance furtively at their wrist watches they see that the longer hands are catching up the shorter on their journey to the appointed hour. Then, a little after half past nine, a searchlight appears behind the British lines. Nothing very remarkable in that, and it is solely for want of anything else to do that some of the waiting men watch it as it idles across the sky. And then another beam flashes on, some distance further down the line. As the minutes tick off, these two fingers of light wander rather aimlessly amongst the stars.

But the gunners are watching those searchlights. Eight hundred gunners are watching them with intense interest. And each gunner is behind a loaded twenty-five pounder with a lanyard in his hand. They see the beams coming closer together . . . four minutes . . . three minutes . . . two minutes . . . one minute ! ! ! Then the two shafts of light clash and it seems as though all hell has has been let loose. As one man the gunners tug their lanyards. The bombardment roars into the night. The party is on.

From where the Royal Wilts are waiting, the effect of this bombardment is beyond description. They are almost in the centre of the arc described by the mass of hurtling shells, and the whistling of their passage overhead is mingled with the staccato bark of the guns behind them and the " crump " of the shells bursting on the enemy positions to their front. Apart from this, the pyrotechnic display alone is awe inspiring. " This is all right," shouts a subaltern through the din. " This is very good, but personally I prefer the Turf Club every time ! " His sally amuses those who hear it. They store it mentally, to be added to the " One of the best remarks " series for use in reminiscences after it is all over. But that subaltern does not know, of course, that it will be a very long time before he will see the Turf Club again, or anything like it. For such establishments form no part of a Prisoners of War Camp in Germany.

For fifteen ear-splitting minutes they thunder on, those guns. Sixty thousand rounds for the twenty-five pounders on our own Divisional front alone have been dumped by the New Zealand A.S.C. and the gunners are helping themselves freely. It is a twenty-to-one concentration and twenty troops of our own artillery are battering away at each enemy troop. No wonder their retaliation against our guns is negligible. Besides, we have gained tactical surprise. The enemy must have known that we were likely to attack. He probably even guessed that General Montgomery would take advantage of the moon. But he didn't know just where or when.

Next comes the turn of the infantry. Theirs is the unpleasant task of following up close under the artillery barrage and putting in the main attack. This is last war technique and it was dangerous enough then, but this time they have the additional hazard of having to pick their way through enemy anti-tank minefields sown with booby traps. The mines are not, possibly, so unhealthy for infantry as you might expect, but on this occasion the Boche is using an extremely unpleasant type of booby trap and these must take their toll. They are trip wires which run along the forward edges of his minefields and are attached to the noses of a number of our own two hundred and fifty pound air bombs, a dump of which he has captured. A formidable obstacle indeed!

But all this has to be risked and at ten o'clock punctually the infantry of the 5th New Zealand Brigade set off to a good start. Behind them, in close support, are the three "Scorpions" to flay out a track through the enemy minefields for the six Crusader tanks of the Royal Wilts which will follow.

From the eminence of the turret of his tank, the advance is an inspiring sight to the Captain who commands this small column of armour. He can see for a considerable distance because, in spite of the lateness of the hour, the moon is so bright, that by its light he can read quite easily the orders in his hand. Besides, the sky is full of every kind of illumination—flashes from bursting shells, flares, great "chandeliers" which cast a yellow glare as they descend slowly from aeroplanes, and a thousand other pin pricks of incandescence. As a background to this, the silver moonlight creates a filmic effect over the whole remarkable scene.

The infantry advance with slow determination, their rifles clutched diagonally in front of their bodies. They might appear just a rabble, for there is no orderly formation in their ranks. They vaguely resemble the crowd at a cricket match as it surges forward to examine the pitch in the interval. But in reality they are all very carefully controlled. They have rehearsed this advance for weeks beforehand and each man knows exactly where to go. In this ragged formation they are less vulnerable as a body.

At first it is all plain sailing and the supporting armour makes a rumbling background of sound as they approach the enemy minefields. And then the fun begins. These minefields are studded with the advanced posts of the enemy and in spite of the terrific bombardment, many of these are still inhabited. Machine guns clatter out, and there, in the midst of this mine strewn sand, the New Zealanders go into action by moonlight whilst the Crusaders, in their turn, bring their machine guns to bear upon the enemy positions.

Meanwhile, as the battle gets well into its stride, the noise becomes terrific. Against the background of stuttering barks from the bombardment the night is rent by all kinds of explosive sounds. The irregular rattle of the machine guns which swing from time to time into a rhythmic cadence as two or more hit a periodic synchrony. Tuttle—uttle—uttle—uttle—tut—tut—tut—tut . . . . They chatter, those machine guns, like monkeys, scolding, answering in different keys as the wind takes their sound. Bop—op—op—op . . . tat—at—at—at . . . Then a sulky one throws in his ill-tempered comment from a distance. Bop . . . op—op—op . . . op . . . op—op. And through it all the infantry walk steadily forward, taking on an occupied enemy post here, passing an abandoned one there but always forging slowly ahead. After an hour and a half of this nightmare progress under the great round moon and the firework infested sky, they arrive at their first objective. Here they lie down and take a well earned hour's rest.

During this time the body of the Royal Wilts has been ploughing with great difficulty through our own minefields to get into position for the final move when the infantry has taken the Miteiriya Ridge. End to end, almost touching, they crawl along the track called "Bottle." These lighted lanes through our own minefields looked gay as could be to begin with. The troops quickly named them "Piccadilly Circus" and so on. Indeed, it looked as though everything was going to be dead easy. Just "follow my leader" with red lights to guide you on your way. But in a short while it becomes obvious that we are in for a most unpleasant time; even before reaching the enemy minefields, the dust begins to make itself felt. Gradually at first, then with increasing intensity, a heavy choking fog builds up as the tracks churn the desert into powder. When all the tanks are on the move this fog is blinding as well as physically unpleasant. Visibility is only a few yards and it is all the drivers can do to keep in touch with the tank ahead of them.

The red lights, as they loom up eerily through the murk from time to time, are barely sufficient to mark the track. The noisy procession lurches and rumbles on for what seems to be hours before even reaching the start line where the infantry kicked off when this frantic struggle began. But we are there now. We are through " Star " track and our next job will be to tackle the enemy minefields.

Meanwhile we must wait until the 5th New Zealand Brigade have captured the Miteiriya Ridge, for which such a bitter struggle is going on in front of us. But there is also something else going on ahead of us which is of vital importance—the clearing of the tracks through the enemy's minefields! And this doesn't appear to be going too well. It seems that the first minefield has been dealt with but the second one is giving trouble. There are a number of enemy posts in it which haven't been mopped up and they are holding up the work. In fact, as the hours drag on it becomes increasingly obvious that the whole operation is behind schedule. And so it is. General Freyberg himself is getting anxious. From his tactical Headquarters on Miteiriya Ridge, where he moved when both his brigades had taken their first objectives, he is watching the battle intensely. Although the enemy is strongly resisting his troops as they struggle to gain their final objective, he is fairly confident that the Ridge will be in his hands by daylight. But will the second minefield be cleared by then? It must be if the tanks of the 9th Armoured Brigade are to come through and stave off that dreaded counter-attack from the enemy's armour! For that counter-attack will surely come—and if it is successful the whole night's effort will be wasted. Probably the whole of General Montgomery's plan will be jeopardised. Even that battle scarred old veteran, General Freyberg, who does not appear to be possessed of human nerves, cannot bear to contemplate the consequences which might ensue from that. The whole fate of Egypt is in the balance . . . and then . . . !

But the situation is serious and there's no gainsaying it. It is nearly four o'clock, with only a bare two hours more before the daylight will bring the whole terrific plan into the enemy's deadly focus, and the second minefield is still an obstacle between our tanks and Miteiriya Ridge. There has been no news from the 6th New Zealand Brigade for some time, although the 5th seem to be doing well. They must nearly have gained their second objective by now although the enemy are fighting like devils. The supporting Crusaders are having a rough time and are now almost too far-behind to be of much help to the infantry. Several of them have been blown up and the others are stuck because the " Scorpions " have overheated and can no longer clear a way for them. But wait a minute! What was that? A new kind of firework has soared into the sky. A rocket. Yes . . . it *is* a rocket . . . and a yellow one too . . . fired from the crest of the Ridge! General Freyberg nods approvingly as it bursts into a cluster of bright yellow stars. It is the success signal from his 5th Brigade. They have taken their final objective. He has one leg in!

But it is not only the infantry who have been watching for that rocket, it has a meaning for the men in the tanks as well. It is the signal for the armour to move forward and, as it explodes, it quickens the pulses of the waiting men of the Royal Wiltshire Yeomanry. This is the moment for which they have been waiting so long. They are about to take their Sherman tanks into action. Nobody has yet fought a Sherman; what will it be like? Will their 75 millimetres be a match for the German guns? It will be a record if they are. Hitherto the Boche has always outranged our tanks and we have had to rely upon our tactics to compete with him. What will it feel like to be in a tank which gets a direct hit?

There has been much speculation about this. Will it stun the men inside, even if the shell doesn't penetrate ? Lots or problems like these are going to be solved in the near future because those tanks have got to be steered right through the enemy's minefields, across the Miteiriya Ridge which the infantry are now holding and then to a point on the forward slope of the ridge—probably at least half a mile further on. And they are not going to do that with impunity ! Somebody's going to find out what it feels like to be hit ! But they've got to get there ; some of them at any rate, because those infantrymen must be protected, when the daylight comes, to give them time to dig themselves in, get their anti-tank guns into position and bring up their supporting weapons before the enemy can put in his counter-attack. They've been caught unprepared before, these New Zealanders, and they know that being over-run by the enemy's tanks is a most unpleasant experience. That is why the task of the Royal Wilts is so important. The 5th New Zealand Brigade is in their care and the tough fighters of which it is composed take comfort in the thought.

But we're off now. Lurch, clank, bump. Up comes the dust again and before we've gone a few yards we're back in the " pea-souper " once more. The two heavy squadrons lead the way, with Regimental Headquarters in between. " A " goes first with its Shermans, " C " with its Grants, and " B " follows with its Crusaders, minus the six that went ahead with the infantry. We're through our own mines now and after two or three hundred yards we shall enter the gap in the enemy's forward minefield. Yes . . . here it comes . . . the green and amber lights blink at us through the murk. Now we're for it, let's hope the sappers have done a good job ! We get a prickly sensation round the napes of our necks and take a stronger grip of our over-taxed nerves. Funny feeling this being in a sort of fantastic slow motion bumping race in the fog, with death caged on each side of you in little round tins and ready to spring out at you like a jack-in-the-box if you make the slightest mistake.

And, now that our tanks have started to go forward in earnest, death begins to leap about in other fresh forms as well. The enemy has spotted what is happening and, as usual, is not going to take it easily. New noises are added to the general uproar as he tries to take on our armour, which appears to him fitfully in the moonlight. The earth-shaking kurr-rumph of the heavy mortars, like the dry cough of some gigantic metal monster, then his 88-millimetre anti-tank and field guns. For some unknown reason you hear their noises backwards ; first the burst of the shell, then its passage through the air, and finally the firing of the gun itself. And our Shermans cracking back chancily at an occasional flash, clang . . . whoosh . . . thud, they go, and let's hope they are making their mark. What a racket it is, even our old friends " crack and thump " are with us as the infantry sporadically let off their rifles. Probably less dust where they are, and they seem to be getting quite a bit of shooting in the moonlight ! Besides, the whole sky is lit up by star shells and a thousand other smaller illuminations. What a firework display ! Through it all the red tracer shells of the Bofors follow each other like the windows of a lighted train, and their smaller brothers from the machine guns remind us of swarms of infuriated, waspish fireflys. What strange signposts, indeed ; but quite effective. They point to our objectives. And those objectives seem a long way off !

For we've still got a long way to go and little time in which to get there. Things have slowed up again ; we move a few jolting places up the queue and then stop. Hour after hour this goes on as the great tanks growl and tear at the sand with their talons, like caged beasts trying to burst out of bondage. What the hell are those sappers doing. Why hasn't the second minefield been cleared ? We shall never make it at this rate ! In an hour or so it will be daylight.

But those sappers are working like madmen. Fighting their way forward almost by inches they clear the enemy out and feverishly tackle the mines. Fine sort of job to do in a hurry! The armour must be through by first light, and it's already half past five!

The sappers have made it, however, and as dawn breaks the two heavy squadrons of the Royal Wilts begin to trickle through the far side of the gaps and move slowly up to the summit of the ridge. All may yet be well.

And, as the dawning day steals the colours from the pyrotechnics in the sky, the strangest of scenes is revealed. A sort of orderly confusion reigns everywhere and the activity is intense. Within the minefields themselves small segregated battles are still raging where enemy pockets of resistance are being mopped up with fierce determination. For those individuals concerned, their immediate struggle is as important as anything else in the whole operation! The gaps in the minefields are cluttered up with mechanical contrivances of all kinds. Shermans, Grants, Valentines and Crusaders take up most of the space, but soft-skinned vehicles jostle for what is left with the anti-tank guns and supporting weapons which are trying to get up to the infantry. Droves of surly prisoners are herded along whilst doctors fuss around in jeeps, and ambulances go quietly about their business. Wounded men are dressed and propped up along the sides of the tracks to be picked up later. Others, less fortunate, are tidied out of the way of the oncoming troops. In one place a stretcher bearer is going through the pockets of a dead British soldier. He comes across some snap-shots. Bathing at Tel-Aviv. A cheerful waving group of healthy looking young men! He covers the dead man's face, places the photographs under the steel helmet on his chest and passes on.

The mine gappers are pressing on as fast as they possibly dare with their steady routine of detecting, marking, lifting and so on. The infantry up forward are fighting grimly to hold the positions they have so dearly won . . . whilst they wait for the armour to come up! But the tanks are not so very far behind now. If only the sappers can clear that last obstacle it won't take them so very long to get to their final objective. Already, although this is their first experience of this kind, the men are settling down to it. The strangest jobs so soon become routine in the army. There is even a military policemen walking about in the minefields asking people for their identity cards! A necessary precaution this, as a matter of fact, ridiculous as it may seem. All kinds of spies and observers might be drifting about. There is also a minefield " traffic cop "—a peculiar job indeed. But routine must go on, even in the waiting tanks where some of the crews are filling in the time with a " spot of maintenance " now that it's light enough to see. What a business it all is!

Meanwhile, how has the battle been going? To General Freyberg in his Tactical Headquarters the news seems better around six o'clock in the morning. The gaps on his 5th Brigade front are reported clear. The supporting arms and the tanks are said to be moving up. And so they are, but all is not well with the Royal Wilts. Those in the rear of the column have been speculating about the origin of a new addition to the carnival of noise which is going on around them. Something different, this one. Deeper and more earth shaking than the rest. Woomph! This is quite unmistakable. A very sinister sound. Big aerial bombs, perhaps? But they really know instinctively what causes those noises, even though they have never heard them before. Mines! But why mines? Something must have gone wrong. The first squadron ought to have been clear of the minefields by now. There are no mines where those noises come from. Or shouldn't be, according to the air photographs. But Woo-umph! There it goes again. And this time there is no mistake. A spurt of flame appears in the distance through a gap in the fog and quickly grows into a flaming mass. Little figures jump out and run for their lives as the sand spurts up around them in the eerie light from the burning tank. For it *is* a tank. They can see that clearly now. What's more its one of their

Shermans and the Boche are turning everything they've got on to the crews as they scurry for safety. Something *has* gone wrong.

And now the fog is thinning out as the tanks ahead slow up. They see clearly what really has happened. "A" Squadron has run into an uncharted minefield! They're in for trouble! And on their first trip, too. Here comes the Intelligence Officer in his scout car. He has been running up and down the line in all this chaos, as cool as could be and apparently quite oblivious of the danger. His job is to shepherd the tanks through the gaps and he really has been behaving like a mechanical sheep dog. He hands a report to the Commanding Officer and then goes roaring back in the dust and muck towards the stricken front of the line. What did he say? He was going to try and find a way through the uncharted minefield? In that scout car! He must be crazy. But he has gone and nobody seems to be stopping him. They see him climb up the ridge to where more and more of our tanks are blowing up. He becomes a tiny speck as he nears the crest. Then that tiny speck bursts into a sheet of flame. One more sickening "woo-umph" and it seems to those watching that there is a momentary silence. But the unholy din carries on, just as it did before.

Yes, that is the tragedy of it. The Colonel has appreciated that he must "chance" this hazard and disaster has overtaken the Royal Wilts. The extent of the calamity becomes increasingly apparent as the daylight grows. The two heavy squadrons are dotted about on the near approach to the ridge in grotesque attitudes which show clearly how they have tried, but failed, to avoid the menace which is hidden in the sand. But some appear to have got through. There they are, just visible and well up to the top of the ridge. Let's get our glasses on to them! One, two, three, four . . . there must be about a dozen of them all told. They're moving about freely so they must be clear of the mines. About fifty-fifty Shermans and Grants, they are . . . all that's left mobile of the two heavy squadrons? Gosh! What'll the next move be?

But the next move is not far off. The chaps in those surviving tanks are opening up. Slowly at first, shot by shot. Then, as they get on to their targets, they let the Boche have it for all they are worth. They're taking on his tanks, soft-skinned supply vehicles and anything they can get at. It's a real battle now and they are blazing away as fast as they can re-load, they are the first men ever to fire a shot in anger from a Sherman! Behind them many of the tanks spatchcocked on the minefields are joining in. Even a tank with its tracks blown off can still fight as a pill-box! The din becomes terrific. Those survivors won't be able to go on long at this rate. The amount of ammunition a tank can carry is strictly limited. But this will put heart into those New Zealanders who are hanging on to that ridge. This is the first time they've had any armour up with them in their forward positions. Its a comforting feeling for a chap that's trying to dig himself in against time. Besides they'll never be able to get their anti-tank guns into position forward of the ridge now. Not in broad daylight, even though their supporting vehicles have managed to get up to them. Yes, 9th Armoured Brigade are going to come in very handy, even in their decimated condition. Those 75 millimetre guns poking out of the turrets give the infantry great encouragement.

So, whilst what is left of the Royal Wilts keeps the enemy at bay (they are fighting furiously with between thirty and forty of the Boche's best tanks by now) more and more armour from 10th Corps rolls up behind, along the lanes reserved for the bulk of the tanks in the centre. By the time that those survivors of the Regiment have run out of ammunition and retired to a hull-down position to await some more, there is a goodly assembly of armour all along the slope on our side of the Miteiriya Ridge. It is too late for them to make the intended sally, deep into the enemy's lines, but, nevertheless, this display of force is bound to have its effect. The Boche will hardly dare to launch a counter attack in the face of it!

In this manner there starts a fantastic day. The battle develops into a long-range duel between the opposing masses of huge modern tanks. Thank Heavens we are able to compete with our " Seventy Fives " on the Shermans and Grants. Or rather thank that meeting between the President and the Prime Minister when it was arranged to send them to the Middle East. They only just arrived in time ! But they can and do compete with the best that the enemy can produce—for the whole of that nightmare day.

But fate still has trouble in store for the Royal Wilts. At a quarter to eight in the morning Lt.-Col. Sykes is hit in the chest by a shell splinter. The Regiment has lost its Commanding Officer who is sent back to the medical services. This is a serious blow, but there are plenty more leaders to take his place. His logical successor is Major Gibb, the Second in Command, but that officer happens to be at 5th New Zealand Brigade Headquarters when Lt.-Col. Sykes is wounded. So Lord Weymouth takes over in the meantime. For fifty hectic minutes he commands the Regiment. He may well say with the poet Mordaunt, " One crowded hour of glorious life is worth an age without a name " !

Major Gibb is actually talking to the Brigade Commander when the signal comes through reporting that Lt.-Col. Sykes has been wounded. The latter tosses the piece of paper across the table to Major Gibb and remarks casually " You'd better go up and take over." Then he goes on with the job he's doing. Take over ! Take over what ? The reports are now in and Major Gibb knows that six Shermans and thirteen Grants were blown up on that hidden minefield alone. That was in the first half-hour and goodness knows what's left of the Regiment now after the furious battle they have been waging all the morning ! But he can't stop to think about that now. He must get going, back to that inferno up forward.

Getting back to that inferno, however, isn't so easy. The gaps are all chock-a-block with tanks, trucks, guns, cars and jeeps and it is nobody's business to get by them. You can't just shout " make way for the Master " and nobody would hear you if you did. It is just a question of nipping your scout car in when you can and shoving your way forward as forcefully as possible. There are what seem to be long waits when you can't get moving at all. It is maddening but can't be helped. During these waits, in spite of his impatience, his eyes wander over his surroundings and take in the details of this grim battlefield. He is right in the centre, now, of what was the enemy's forward positions in their minefields a few hours ago. There is ample evidence of the haste with which they have departed. That one on the right must have been an Italian position, probably a " defended company locality." The empty Chianti flasks give away its nationality. Besides, the shallow dug-outs have a thin cover over the top; the " wops " always do that. It's not even bullet-proof, this roofing, but they like to have something over their heads ; sort of hiding under the eiderdown complex. The Boche never bothers about that sort of thing; rabbit scrapes are good enough for him.

All sorts of discarded articles are lying around these evacuated positions. Topees respirators, boots, socks and the inevitable packs of cards, with their flamboyant continental court cards, are strewed about in the sand. Some of the fugitives have not even had time to put on their underclothes ! That initial barrage must have woken them up in a devil of a hurry ! And peppered over the whole scene is unused ammunition of all sorts and calibres ; masses of it lying in heaps or scattered about. " Red Devils "—(the little Italian hand grenades which look like children's money boxes)—are everywhere, too ; what a scene of waste and confusion ! But the dominant thought in the mind of Lt.-Col. Gibb (for he is promoted now) is the loss of all those tanks.

As he regains his own Sherman, which now becomes Regimental Headquarters, he can see these stricken monsters dotted all over the ridge. Some are whelmed in smoke, others are gutted right out. A few appear more or less normal, but they are tied down by broken tracks. These fight on fiercely, engaging any target within range. One sergeant has even stripped the machine guns from his knocked out Sherman and taken them over to the New Zealanders where he is carrying on alongside the infantry ! In one apparently burnt out tank right up near the enemy there sits a Subaltern doing a valuable job. The only thing that works in that hulk is the wireless which has miraculously escaped. The young man hides there the whole day through, steadily reporting and directing the fire of others behind him from his vantage point. He gets away with it too, although at any moment the Boche may spot that the tank is occupied and blow it to smithereens.

From Lt.-Col. Gibb's Headquarters he can see it all going on but do very little more to direct the battle. Every now and again one more of our tanks goes up in a fount of flame and it is a sickening sight to watch what remains of his new command melting before his eyes. These feelings are in no way mollified by the infuriating remarks of a Boche officer over the wireless. This man has been making caustic comments the whole morning after tuning in to the Regiment's sets. " Allo ! Allo ! " his guttural voice comes over the air, " How nice it is to see all your beautiful new tanks burning ! " Blast the fellow ! But at any rate he seems to have more sense of humour than most of his filthy breed.

Then, as the sun climbs up the " inverted bowl," an amazing day unfolds. On our side of the remaining minefields a host of tanks has gathered all along the line. They are spaced out almost as far as the eye can see on either side. They look just like Halma men squared out on some gargantuan board. On the other side of the ridge the enemy has massed his armour into one large column and now it starts to move. What is he up to ? He seems to be moving down our line towards our left flank. Later the column comes back again, as though undecided. For several hours these massed tanks " swan " up and down as a moving target for our gunners. Are they marching up and down to find our weak spot ? Will they suddenly turn from this apparently useless patrolling and strike swiftly as Marlborough used to do. (Or, as Hitler did in France—or Joshua at Jericho, come to that !). Or are they intimidated by all this array of the armour of the British 10th Corps. It looks as though the latter is the answer. Anyhow they don't come on.

Meanwhile our troops are taking the matter in good part. They seem to find it an exhilarating battle. This type of tank duel seems to appeal to them. They are treating it rather like a point-to-point. The air is thick with missiles but nobody seems to be taking much cover. Those troops who are not furiously serving their guns are watching with admiration and typical comment. The officers have all pulled out their glasses and might well be in the paddock at Sandown. " Good shot, Sir ! " (No ! This isn't cricket, far from it, this is a deadly battle.) But it *was* a good shot. One of our gunners had scored a direct hit on a moving German tank. " Biggest bird *he* ever brought down, I'll bet," says one officer to another in admiration. A Brigadier and a Lieut.-Colonel look up from a map over which they are poring on the back of a Crusader. They train their glasses on the Germans baling out of the stricken tank and add their admiring comments on the shooting. " Phee-e-e-u-u-w-w-clang-thud ! " A shell hits the skirting of the tank by which they are standing. The Brigadier ducks, the Lieut.-Colonel is delighted ; that is the first time he's seen the Brigadier duck all the morning. They move inside the tank after this and carry on the discussion there.

But all this is taking terrific toll of the Royal Wilts, especially after their appallingly unlucky start. Nevertheless, what is left of them still fights back gallantly. But what *is* left of them. Lt.-Col. Gibb takes stock of his position at mid-day There are only one Sherman and three Grants left in the two heavy squadrons, and a few hours ago they went into battle with fifteen Shermans and sixteen Grants.

THE PART PLAYED BY THE ROYAL WILTS

The Regiment's initiation into armoured fighting has been a severe one. But it has done the job alloted to it. It couldn't ask for a better reward than the words used in General Freyberg's own despatches :—" During the morning the Royal Wiltshire Yeomanry and a regiment of 8th Armoured Brigade were heavily engaged with enemy tanks and anti-tank guns. They suffered heavy casualties in tanks knocked out but repulsed all attempts by enemy armour to make a counter attack on 5th Brigade front."

* * * * * *

By the middle of the afternoon all three Brigades of 10th Armoured Corps were in action in one way or another, but the Royal Wilts, having very little left with which to fight, had become largely spectators. Then, at six o'clock in the evening, the Brigade Commander ordered them out of the battle. Lt.-Col. Gibb sent his remaining tanks back to the replenishment area, to be handed over to other units of the Brigade and the men—or what was left of them—clambered disconsolately into the regimental supply vehicles, to be taken back for the night to the Onsol area from which they had originally started.

Next day, as they moved to Hammam to rest and refit, they were a sad and dejected body of men and it seemed to them impossible that they could be the same human beings who had set out from that place only just over twenty-four hours before, keyed up, full of enthusiasm and wondering what their fate would be. They had expected almost anything but that which had actually happened. So this was the end of all they had looked forward to. All those years of waiting and months of training ! Knocked out in the first round like a heavy-weight boxer ! They thought sadly of all those brand new tanks, brought all those thousands of miles from America, through so much toil and danger only to be smashed to bits in the first few hours of combat ; turned into useless iron skeletons which would disfigure the desert till the sand, with the passage of time, should flow over them and gradually cover them up.

But those Wiltshire Yeomen were only half-way through the programme and, had they but known it, the worst was yet to come !

At Hammam the Regiment had a welcome rest—but not for long. There was good news ; they were going to be re-equipped ! Somehow they hadn't thought of this. The loss of all those tanks seemed to have stunned them and, after years during which they had been starved of equipment, it didn't appear possible that they could be supplied immediately with a new outfit of tanks. But things were different now. John Bull and Uncle Sam were pulling together and they were going to see the thing through this time. As General Montgomery had said, Rommel was going to be " hit for six out of Africa."

So the ensuing week was spent in " buying a new set " of tanks. And this entailed a great deal of " shopping." All ranks, in their respective spheres, were kept fully occupied. Crews were despatched to a score of different depots and workshops to collect the tanks and all the mass of equipment that went with them. There were, as always, new gadgets to be coped with and modifications to be understood on the new models. Also they had to accept some old ones which needed a lot of tuning up. For example, the majority of the new tanks were " Crusader III " instead of " Crusader II " because the former were not popular and they were therefore the only ones on the market. The Crusader III has a six pounder gun but, although Crusader II has only a two pounder, it has room for a crew of four. The complications caused by having to distribute the various duties amongst only three people (the limited capacity of the Crusader III) are considered to outweigh the advantage of the more powerful weapon.

Furthermore the tank crews, after the considerably exhausting task of rounding up their respective tanks from the numerous collecting points, had to become familiar with their new vehicles. And, strange as it may seem, these mechanical contrivances are much akin to horses in this respect. They have all sorts of peculiarities and idiosyncrasies which have to be found out before they can be driven to their best advantage. The man who knows his horse is many points ahead of the man who doesn't and the same applies to tanks. Equipment, also, was a difficulty. Tools were extremely scarce and the wireless sets none to good. Guns had to be tested and " shot in " before going into action and a thousand and one other jobs had to be done. But everybody went about it with a will and the thought of having another chance spurred them on.

At the end of the week the Regiment was re-equipped. Not well equipped to be sure, because the time had been too short. In particular, the shooting-in of the guns was far from satisfactory because that is an operation which cannot be done in a hurry. But there wasn't going to be any more time to spare. The Royal Wilts were booked for another job ! After this hasty re-habilitation they were in poor shape to go into a major battle but they didn't care a hoot for that. They were only too glad to get another chance !

CHAPTER NINETEEN

THE SPEARHEAD THRUST

WHILST the Royal Wiltshire Yeomanry had been thus engaged in re-equipping, the battle had continued to rage on the El Alamein line. General Montgomery was busily engaged in " worrying the guts out " of Rommel's troops. But it was a fierce struggle and these guts were proving very tough. The enemy was charging about like a wounded beast, but nowhere was he able to shake us in our newly-won positions. In fact his own situation had grown worse in that first three days of the attack when, as the official account has it, we " drove a great salient into his defences with considerable loss to the enemy in men and material. We also inflicted crippling casualties on his armour in the North."

Probably the Australians and the Rifle Brigade saw the two most outstanding episodes during those crucial days. The former put up a magnificent show when they pressed their attack so hard in the North that they reached the coast behind 125 Panzer Grenadiers. They fought those crack German troops, and themselves, to a standstill, and Rommel's subsequent frantic attempts to free them from the trap were a definite sap to his strength.

The Rifle Brigade, by a stroke of fortune, found themselves quite close to a German tank leaguer and picked off 57 tanks in 36 hours, a very satisfactory bag indeed !

To sum up the battle briefly, thus far, it can be said that the enemy was at a great disadvantage by the 28th October, the day upon which Rommel returned from Germany. He was visiting Hitler when our attack opened. The Germans had been taken by surprise when the original attack went in and they had consistently miscalculated where we should strike next. They had worn out their mobile force by engaging it piecemeal at first and then, when it had been concentrated, by using it purely on local objectives. It had also been severely handled by the R.A.F. wherever it had tried to concentrate. The accompanying map shows clearly the various stages in which this happened.

In spite of this, General Montgomery's attack was in danger of losing momentum—and that would have been disastrous. Besides, our armour was not yet through. So he decided to fool the Boche once more, and changed his plan. Rommel's chief concern on taking over command seems to have been to rescue his precious Panzer Grenadiers and his attention was directed to the North where he thought we were going to attack up the coast road. He was therefore fully extended in that direction and had concentrated all his armour near the coast. So General Montgomery abandoned his original intentions of breaking through the Miteiriya Ridge and decided to attack instead towards Tell-El-Aqqaqir somewhat south of where Rommel expected him to do so, and in a westerly direction.

Once more the New Zealanders and their faithful 9th Armoured Brigade were to be the spear-head, but this time they were to have more assistance. General Freyberg was given, under command of his 2nd New Zealand Division, the followign troops in addition :—

23rd Armoured Brigade (Royal Tank Regiment)
151st Brigade from 30th Division (Durham Light Infantry)
152nd Brigade from the 51st Highland Division (2nd and 5th Battalions of Seaforths and 5th Battallion of Camerons).

North countrymen, Highlanders and New Zealanders. A proper mixture for the Boche to take.

It was planned that this now very strong division should attack on the 31st October. A New Zealand Brigade would take over the forward defended localities, whilst the assault was carried out by 151st (Tyneside) Brigade and 152nd Highland Brigade. The 1st Armoured Division would then come up a centre route and break through the gap made by the assault. The destruction of the German tank forces (by this date estimated at 140 runners), plus the Italians was envisaged, followed by the sallying forth of the mobile 2nd New Zealand Division.

The full official report of this phase of the battle has already been published. Many will wish to study it in detail, but, for the ordinary reader, what it says, bereft of military jargon, is this.

General Montgomery had decided that the time had arrived for Eighth Army to " break out." In order to punch a hole, through which 10th Corps could pass, he was going to fling the whole of the strengthened 2nd New Zealand Division at one point in the enemy's defences in the neighbourhood of Tell-el-Aqqaqir. This battering ram was given a steel tip. The steel tip was to be 9th Armoured Brigade. The point of that tip eventually turned out to be the Royal Wiltshire Yeomanry.

So, on the night of 27th/28th October, 2nd New Zealand Division and the other two regiments of 9th Armoured Brigade left Miteiriya Ridge (where the position had been more or less stabilised since the first hectic encounter), handed over to the South Africans, and retired into reserve. There they were joined by the Royal Wiltshire Yeomanry and the whole Brigade got busy for its part in the new plan.

On the 31st October General Freyberg called his Brigadiers and Staffs together and discussed his plan in detail. To begin with, this operation differed from the one at Miteiriya Ridge in that the exact position of the enemy's defences was not known. So our infantry were to be withdrawn 1,500 yards behind their forward defended localities so that the artillery bombardment could start right on the spot where our original forward positions had been. Then there would be no chance of missing out any of the enemy's defences.

And what a bombardment it was going to be ! Three times as heavy as the one which had opened the original battle, with one gun to every 11 1/3 yards ! A rate of advance of 100 yards every 2½ minutes was fixed and the assault must go forward at all costs. The infantry were ordered to keep up with the barrage and to by-pass pockets of tank resistance rather than lose it. If the pace was too fast, and the barrage *did* slip away, the tanks were to continue to press forward, with the infantry following them.

The 9th Armoured Brigade would go forward as fast as the route was cleared, with the Shermans and Grants ready to support the infantry if they were held up.

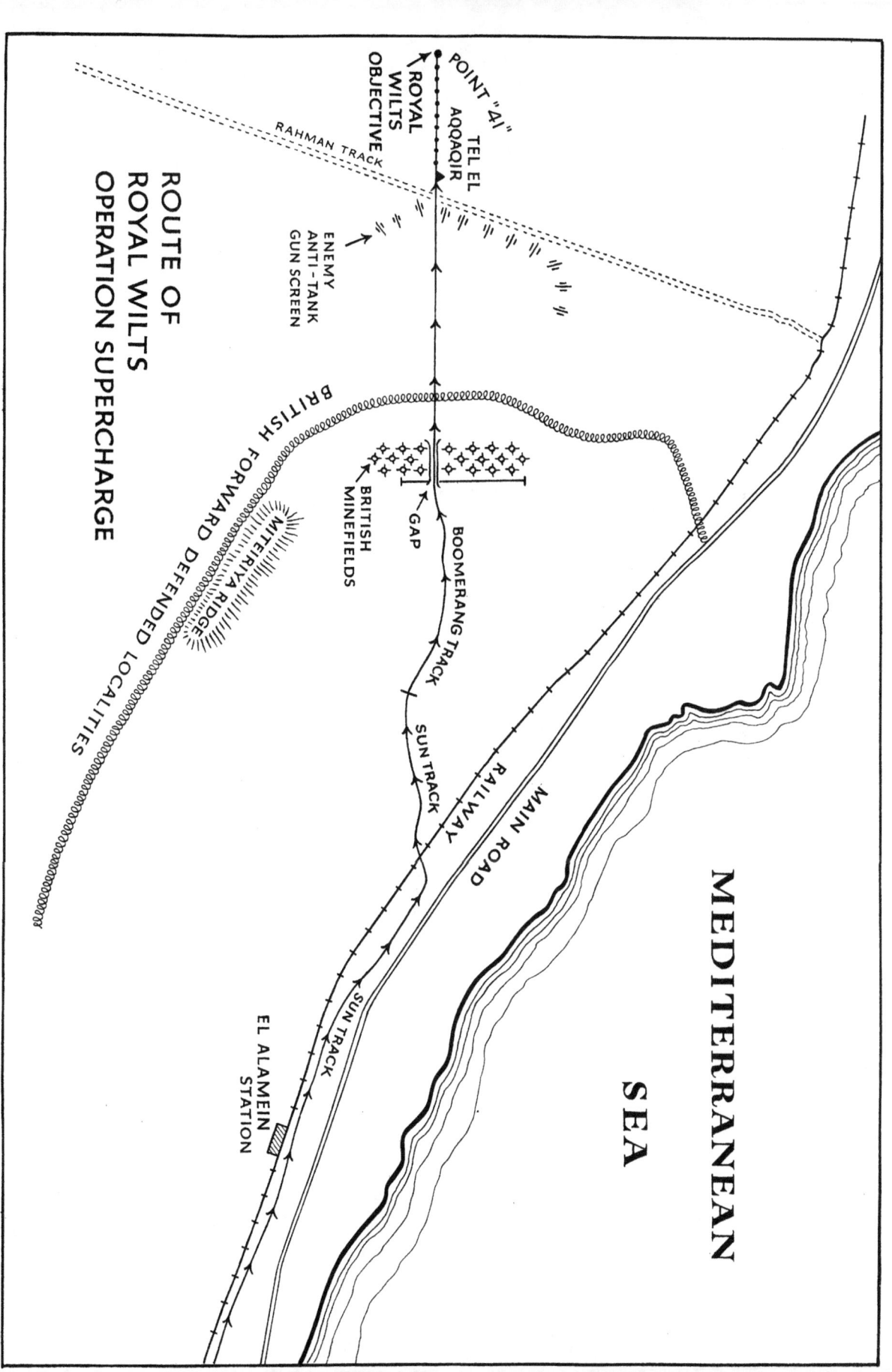

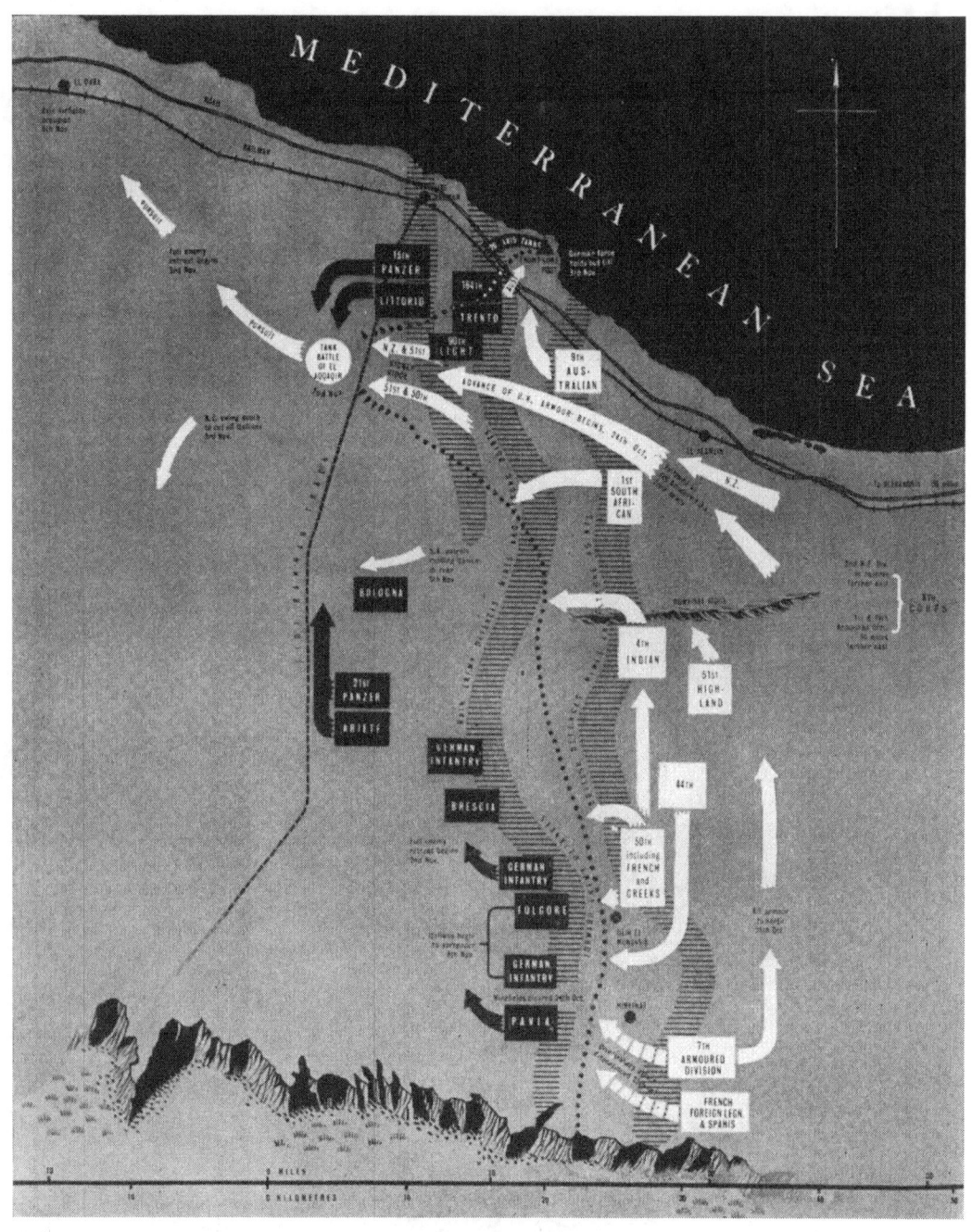

THE BREAK THROUGH AT EL ALAMEIN.
Reproduced from "The Eighth Army (September, 1941, to January, 1943)", by kind permission of the Controller of His Majesty's Stationery Office.

CRUSADERS.

GRANTS.

MAINTAINING A GRANT.

Should the enemy be met on the objective they were to deal with him. (The Intelligence reports said that it was possible that two enemy tank regiments would be found on the objective). General Freyberg said that there were to be no "ifs" nor "buts"—it was an all-in battle, a "Slogging Match." It was made quite clear that the situation after dawn would be difficult, that the salient would be shelled and bombed and would be under machine gun fire from three sides, so that the carriers only could get through with supplies to the men holding the line. It was quite possible that the infantry would be shelled on the start line and trench mortared during the advance, while a counter-attack seemed inevitable.

The role of the armour was further explained. They were to emerge as soon as possible, take up a position on the high ground and engage the enemy armour. In addition, three regiments of armoured cars were detailed to gate-crash enemy defences in the darkness, go right through, and harass the enemy communications in the rear.

The whole plan had, in fact, the makings of a jolly party for all concerned— especially for the armour. It occurred to the Brigadier commanding 9th Armoured Brigade that the role thus allotted to the tanks was, to say the least of it, unorthodox. He said as much, rather diffidently, to his superior officer, but added that he thought the job could be done if he were prepared to accept fifty per cent casualties for 9th Armoured Brigade. The answer came back promptly. He was to be prepared to accept one hundred per cent casualties. So that was that! The Brigade was to be sacrificed if necessary, in order to punch a hole through which the main forces could pour and "hit Rommel for six out of Africa."

General Freyberg's report summarises these preparations very succinctly and his summary of the plan is useful for fixing the timings in the reader's imagination, so hear it is.

The infantry were to leave the start line at 0055 hours on the 2nd November.

Zero was fixed at 0105 hours, which was the time the artillery fire opened on the enemy forward defended localities.

The objective was to be taken by 0345 hours.

A creeping barrage was to open at 0545 hours for one hour, during which 9th Armoured Brigade would advance a further 2,000 yards to its objective.

At 0645 hours 1st Armoured Division were to pass through the 9th Armoured Brigade's objective.

It now remains to be seen how the Royal Wilts were to fit into this picture. The 9th Armoured Brigade plan was a simple one. The three regiments were to divide the front between them, advance behind the infantry as far as the infantry objective, and then pass through them as soon as possible. If they met with no opposition they were to occupy a position well in front of the infantry, to protect them from the counter-attack whilst the main body of the tanks passed through to smash Rommel's armour. If they met opposition, the "Slogging Match" was to begin and they were to blast a hole in that opposition to let our armour through.

The Warwickshire Yeomanry were to be on the left, the Royal Wiltshire Yeomanry in the centre and the 3rd Hussars on the right.

The Royal Wilts' actual objective was given as "Point 41," accompanied by a map reference, but, in reality, this meant dead reckoning on a compass bearing. The best way to fix this in the mind is to look at the map, where it will be found just to the west of the track which runs almost due south from Sidi Abd El Rahman to the Quattara Depression. The Regimental Group (it was a "group" now because the Regiment had been strengthened by having under command one Squadron of 2nd New Zealand Divisional cavalry as well as one company of 14th Battalion Sherwood Foresters and 26th New Zealand Battery, Royal Artillery) was to seize this objective by first light. They were to reach their objective in two phases. The " first phase " was to start at seven thirty on the evening of the 1st November by an advance along " Sun " and " Boomerang " tracks to a position just ahead of the forward defended localities on the infantry's final objective. There they were to remain until a quarter to six on the morning of the 2nd November.

They were to march in double line ahead in this order :—
    " B " Squadron (18 Crusaders)
    Regimental Headquarters (1 Grant, 5 Crusaders)
    " B " Company 14th Foresters (Infantry)
    " C " Squadron (8 Grants, 1 Lee)
    " A " Squadron (8 Shermans, 3 Grants)
    1 Squadron Divisional Cavalry
    Column of 21 supply vehicles.

(The N.Z. Artillery is omitted because it never actually joined up.)

The " Divisional Cavalry " (so called as a relict of the horse-mounted days, because they carry out the jobs the cavalry used to do, such as contacting the enemy, scouting and so on) consisted of light American " Honey " tanks and carriers.

In the " second phase " they were to fan out on reaching the final infantry objective, in this manner :—

            " B " Squadron
            Infantry Company
" A " Squadron   " C " Squadron
           Regimental Headquarters
             Divisional Cavalry
          Column of Supply Vehicles

The vital point was that the Regimental Group should be on the infantry final objective and ready to go forward by a quarter to six in the morning. They had to take the risk, once more, of running into any uncleared minefield in their path. As we have already seen, there were to be no " ifs " and no " buts."

After looking once more at the maps to make sure that we are " in the picture " so far, let us now try and gain some human impression of how the battle went, and of what actually happened that night. In order to do this, we must place ourselves in the most suitable position to see and hear as much as possible of what is going on. To begin with that position would probably be the Regimental Headquarters of the Royal Wilts. So let us imagine, for a little while, that we are the proverbial " fly on the wall " of the Grant tank named " Trowbridge " from which Lt.-Col. Gibb commanded the Regiment during this historic battle.

Throughout the 1st November there has been great activity everywhere. The Royal Air Force has provided almost continuous fighter cover and their formations of bombers, known as the " eighteen imperturbables," have gone over time after time to soften up the enemy by " pattern bombing " him wherever he has concentrated.

At nightfall the tracks known as " Diamond," " Boomerang " and " Square " have begun to fill up, just as they did on the 23rd October. Sapper parties, the supporting arms and the tanks, with us amongst them, have moved forward.

And now the Regiment is assembling near El Alamein Station. Everything must be ready to make a start by half past seven and it is very dark because the moon has not yet risen. There is therefore considerable confusion. Final orders are being given and sometimes not quite understood. Sometimes they are understood, but impossible to carry out. But by and large the situation is under control and the Regiment will be ready by the appointed hour. There is an atmosphere of breathlessness because it has all been such a rush during the last few days. Probably, therefore, few of those present have had much time to consider the implications of the forthcoming battle. Everybody guesses that something big is on, but only those at the very top are aware of the supreme gravity of the situation. It is probably fair to state that the feeling of apprehension diminishes more or less in accordance with the ratio of rank.

And now we are on the move. All along there has been a certain amount of noise as recently acquired tanks have been arriving right up to the last moment. But the comparative lull of the last half-hour is broken by a swelling roar as the Headquarters tanks start up. Men have to shout to make themselves heard outside their tanks, and this noise increases to a crescendo as one by one the great metal monsters are stirred into movement and lumber into their places in two parallel lines.

The first of our difficulties now arises. It becomes immediately apparent to the Colonel (we shall call him " The Colonel " from now on, to simplify the story) that the original plan of advancing in double line ahead will not be practicable. It is far too dark and there is altogether too much dust. So he changes the formation to single line ahead. That takes some time to sort out because a large number of tanks are involved. There appears to be indescribable confusion at first, but eventually things straighten out and the long line seems to be forging slowly ahead. The dust of the desert, pulverised by all these tank tracks, is as much as two feet deep in most places. Like fluffy snow upon the ground, it rises into the air and hangs like a thick fog in the darkness. Eyes, ears and noses are filled with it and it nearly chokes a man whenever he opens his mouth to speak. Each tank, running almost blind, can only see the one in front when so close that it nearly bumps, and so the procession rumbles on in a roar of sound, by slow but jerky movements through the night.

At last, after what seems like ages of this hideous journey, we have reached the infantry start line and, for the time being, there comes a slight respite. Whilst the Colonel contacts the New Zealand sappers we take a deep breath and have a look round. The dust settles almost as quickly as it rose, and the late moon, well up by now, has plenty of light in spite of its diminished size. It is obvious that quite a number of our tanks have already fallen by the wayside from mechanical reasons alone. But the wonder of it is that so many have, in fact, emerged from this ordeal. They were a very " reach-me-down " lot to start with !

Everything is ready for the attack although it is only eleven o'clock. Zero hour is still two hours off, but all ranks are keyed up and a quiet tenseness is apparent everywhere. It isn't quiet really, of course, because a battlefield is never quiet. But somehow we gain the impression of quietness. And, in a way, this period of waiting is the most trying of all. It is the second occasion in ten days upon which these men have had this experience—and the outcome of the first encounter is still fresh in their memories. What will happen now ? Time will give the answer, and time is running out. Zero hour will come soon enough and then the Gunners will get their signal, the bombardment will crash out, more terribly even than before, and the Royal Wilts will be in the thick of it again. The infantry will advance upon their objective and, when they have taken it, 9th Armoured Brigade will start out upon its dangerous mission ; leaving the infantry behind, they will have to brave the unknown, make their way through no-man's land and batter down the enemy's defences. If they are successful they will break the enemy lines, our main armoured force will be able to stream through the gap, and the whole enemy position will be turned. In all probability this will result in Rommel's forces being driven step by step out of Africa. If they fail, the safety of Egypt will be severely jeopardised and with it the whole Allied position in the Middle East. But it is better not to think about all that !

Sentimental people often ask what men *do* think about on such occasions.

What are their feelings? Does their past life come before them? Do they think of home and wife or sweetheart? Perhaps some of them do. But, for the most part, they have other pre-occupations. One is reminded of the famous prayer which Sir John Moore is reputed to have offered up before he went into battle—" To-day, Oh Lord, I shall be verie busie. Perchance at times I may forget thee. But I do pray, Oh Lord, that *thou* wilt not forget *me*."

Generally speaking, a man's thoughts at times like these are on the job in hand. The trooper is concentrating upon his immediate orders. The tank driver is probably engrossed in the behaviour of some little gadget which he fixed last night; he is praying that it will hold out until the battle is over. The officer has a number of worries of a different nature. Yet any one of those present may have almost his whole attention monopolised by one of the fleas which abound in this part of the desert. Such a pest can drive a man nearly mad when he has to suffer without the opportunity to destroy.

There is also the mental aspect of the coming ordeal. The psychologists have already infected the army with their ideas. These " trick cyclists," as they have come to be known among the troops, have a theory that human beings react to danger in accordance with the type of animal predominating in their remote ancestry. The " lion type," for example, fights back fiercely when attacked. The " insect type " keeps perfectly still. The " faun type " runs away. From this it might be argued that the brave man is not necessarily the " lion type," who merely fights instinctively. True bravery consists in fighting on against the almost overwhelming urge to cower or run away.

In any case, whatever they are thinking, the time passes just the same. And the Colonel is back again now. He has confirmed that all arrangements have been made to clear the minefields; he has put the leading squadron in touch with the sappers; he has cleaned up all outstanding points which needed attention. There is therefore nothing more to be done except settle down and wait for the fireworks to begin.

Punctually at five past one the fireworks *do* begin. And with a vengeance! The barrage is an inspiring sight. Every gun on the Corps' front which can reach the target has opened fire. It is a strange fact that explosives work on the " up and up." For instance, a 500 pound bomb does not explode with only twice the blast of a 250 pound bomb. Its force is far greater than that. By the same token this artillery barrage seems a great deal more than three times as powerful as the one which preceded the attack on Miteiriya Ridge. It is devastating in its intensity. We find ourselves comparing it to its predecessor. How odd to be judging artillery barrages of this magnitude as though one has dealt with them all one's life! But it seems to be effective, this barrage, and no wonder! During the next four and a half hours 15,000 rounds will be fired on this Divisional front alone. The infantry move off once more and for about forty minutes we watch this magnificent show. Then it is time for us to move as well.

The first part of our journey should be comparatively easy, but it turns out to be more difficult than we expect. There is a deal of dust about from our own and the enemy's artillery fire and it is none too simple to find the lane through the minefields which is known as " Sun " track. And when we do find it, it is very twisty and difficult to keep on in the murky darkness. But we manage somehow, with a good deal of bumping and boring, and our advance continues without any particular incident, except for intermittent shell fire and a certain amount of resistance from rifles and machine guns still holding out in enemy " pockets."

Then a note of excitement creeps in as the Brigadier comes through on the " blower." An enemy tank has been seen, slightly off our line of advance. Is anybody doing anything about it? The Colonel doesn't know, but he'll find out.

He does find out and nobody is doing anything about it. They're sorry, but they thought it was out of action. The Colonel tells off two tanks to go and investigate They are about to shoot it up from close range and take no chances. Then the Brigadier comes on again. He's worried about this tank. He's been up to have a look at it himself. He is told it is being taken care of. And so it is. Two subalterns are stalking it with the greatest care and hugely enjoying the task. They get close up and let fly. The tank doesn't answer. It seems to have been knocked out. But they're not going to be caught by the old dodge of the occupants lying low until the last moment and then opening up. So they creep up cautiously, machine guns trained and ready to fire at a moment's notice. Closer and closer they approach, one tank each side of the stricken foe. A figure moves behind the stricken tank. Fingers tremble on triggers. A startled word of command rings out. Hold hard! For God's sake! It's the Brigadier!! A near thing! It *was* an uninhabited tank and the Brigadier *had* found out for himself. Brave brigadiers should not be allowed in a battle. They make it so much more dangerous for everybody else!

After this incident, nothing of exceptional interest happens for hours. As we move slowly along, in fits and starts, the terrific din of battle merges into the background and we are hardly conscious of hearing it. Like the incidental music which goes on incessantly throughout a film, we should notice if it stopped, but otherwise are scarcely aware of it.

Then, at about half past three, we meet our first setback. We run into a minefield. Fortunately, the sappers have located it before it was able to do us any damage and, strangely enough, it turns out to be one of our own. They are Hawkins mines! It does sometimes happen that our own minefields are lost sight of— everything it so hectic in modern warfare. It is quite possible to lay mines and then lose the plan. The very idea sounds fantastic, but war itself is fantastic. At this moment, however, the presence of this minefield is maddening. Every minute's delay is dangerous. It is absolutely vital that we should be on the infantry's final objective by five forty-five, and a minefield is not an obstacle to be dealt with in a hurry! But the sappers go to it with a will, although it is perilous work, even without the mines, for the place is under fire from enemy posts in many directions and the shelling is fairly heavy.

Very soon there are casualties amongst the mine-sweepers, and this is not surprising. One sapper major has lost patience with the orthodox but tedious method of clearing and has adopted a system of his own. He has a theory that three ton lorries, being fairly high off the ground, are comparatively safe as far as land mines are concerned. By that he means that, although a mine will surely destroy such a vehicle, the driver has quite a good chance of escaping. Putting his theory into practice he leads the tanks himself, perched up in a three tonner, with the inevitable result. Before long his mount is blown up and thus reveals a minefield. His sappers then get busy and clear away the obstructions whilst the gallant major sets off in another three tonner in search of pastures new. This experiment works like magic and saves a deal of precious time; but its most agreeable feature, to all those present, is the miraculous manner in which the major comes through unscathed.

So at last a lane is cleared and our column begins to trickle through as the enemy shelling increases. We, in our tanks, are not so much affected by this unaimed shell fire, although it is hitting the Sherwood Foresters behind us pretty hard. ("Its not raining in here!" said Tweedledum, looking up into his umbrella!) We are sorry for those poor chaps out in the open! Anyhow, we ought to be there fairly soon now. A message comes through from Brigade to say that the 3rd Hussars have already arrived. " GRAFTON " is the code-word agreed upon to convey this —a compliment to the Master of the Grafton who is with the Regiment. So the ex-Master of the Whaddon Chase has just managed to get there first—in command of the 3rd Hussars ! That is good. But there is no news of the Warwickshire Yeomanry on our left. Wait a minute, though. The message continues. . . . Hell ! The artillery barrage has been put back half an hour. Five forty five plus thirty minutes . . . that makes it six fifteen. We shall only have half an hour's darkness to get to our objective, at that rate. We shall have to gallop now that the enemy minefields are behind us. A creepy feeling crawls up our spines and our hands are somehow clammy. That half-hour may make all the difference !

Five forty-eight ! We have arrived ! Three minutes behind time, but that's not bad under the circumstances. Anyhow we must wait for the barrage. Twenty-seven minutes. Not so very long, really. But, oh dear, we wish we could get going ! " One hour," said Professor Einstein, in an endeavour to explain his Theory of Relativity to the Press in simple language, " when you are sitting with your arm round a lovely girl, seems like five minutes. But five minutes, when you are sitting on a red hot stove, seems like an hour ! " We begin to understand his reasoning.

Meanwhile, as we wait impatiently, scraps of gossip are picked up on the wireless. The infantry attack has succeeded. It has been a bit sticky on the right, but on the left it went like a drill, both objectives being taken according to schedule. A very fine performance ! The Royal Dragoons have been ordered to " gate crash " through the enemy lines by the two southern routes. They should have good hunting amongst the Boche's soft-skinned supply vehicles if they get through all right. We subsequently hear that they do. It is described as a " grand party."

Time passes swiftly : It won't be long now !

* * * * * *

Coming up to six fifteen . . . six fifteen ! Now we are for it. So far we have only been in the wings, watching the infantry taking the leading part. But our call has come at last and the battle has become personal to us. We take a pull at ourselves and settle down to it. The Warwickshire Yeomanry have come up on our left and the 3rd Hussars are ready on our right. We are in good company . . . and here it comes ! With a roar the guns open up and the shells come hurtling overhead, forming a steel curtain to cover our advance.

The warning order is given but in most cases it is unnecessary. Nearly all the tanks are standing to ; but there are always a few stragglers, however good the discipline, and one or two drivers are feverishly completing some minor repair. But before long all are on the move and advancing into the unknown. The earnest work has begun.

Everything moves very slowly at first and, as they emerge from the minefield lanes, the tanks form one long line across the desert. Then they shake out and grope about in the darkness in order to take up that irregular pattern which, in cavalry days, used to be known as artillery formation. This somehow makes it all seem like a dream version of the old squadron drill at camp—only on a fantastic scale.

" B " Squadron goes first with its Crusaders. One troop is up in front, followed by the two Headquarter tanks ; the other two troops are staggered left and right in the rear. To begin with all are fairly close together, but they fan out as they move into the open.

The leading tanks move jerkily forward with their noses well up into the barrage which is playing hell with the enemy's infantry. Germans are scuttling about in all directions, running the gauntlet between the wrath of the oncoming metal monsters and the hail of missiles which pours from the skies. They bolt mostly, as the Besas rattle and drop many of them into the sand. Some fall in their panic and are crushed. Others get away in the difficult light of the dawn which is just breaking. Many try to give themselves up as the tanks approach close enough to see the uplifted arms. But there is no time to take prisoners. They are ordered, in dumb show, to make their way back to the British lines and there surrender. Some obey, but others go back to skulk in their slit trenches and snipe when the tanks have passed on.

Regimental Headquarters comes next and carries on in the centre, followed by the two heavy squadrons with their Shermans and Grants. Soon " C " Squadron shakes slowly out to the right and "A" to the left whilst the infantry take position, in open formation, about three hundred yards behind Regimental Headquarters. At last the whole Regimental Group is in formation and moving steadily into the night.

And so the advance continues, but it is hard to see what is going on. The moon is still well up, but the dust and that unearthly half-light which precedes the dawn distort and fog the Colonel's vision as he peers through his glasses from the turret of his tank. There seem to be shadows ahead where the enemy might be, but it is difficult to say for certain. Then a shell whines overhead from the British artillery. It bursts far forward. There is a quick flash and then a ball of smoke which soon grows bigger. There *are* tanks there. And enemy ones too! The flash fixes them in the eye and, as the smoke cloud grows, they stand out in shadowy silhouette. Quite a number of them. We are going to have opposition after all. We shall be hearing from them pretty soon no doubt! And so we shall. As yet we don't know the half of it!

The Colonel reports these tanks to the Brigadier. Then he tries to get a clearer picture. But there is so little to be seen and everything is so confused. Enemy infantry are scurrying in all directions and we seem to have over-run at least two of their headquarters in the darkness. It is a gruesome business, this crushing of men by tanks. Drivers, who in peace-time would risk their lives by swerving to avoid a dog, do not hesitate in the heat of battle. These Germans, flushed from their fox-holes, are run down by the score. They flee wildly before the British tanks, like rabbits trapped in the headlights of a car. But they do not run for long. Either they are dropped by machine guns, or they trip, fall and are over-run. Their screams go unheard in the uproar. Their mouths move like those of men on the silent screen. Their bodies are relentlessly mown down as the low hung masses of metal move over them. Then they are left in the sand, their heads between their legs and their arms outstretched behind them, like discarded dolls. The battle continues.

CHAPTER TWENTY

IN THE HEAT OF BATTLE

SHORTLY before dawn it becomes obvious that the Regiment are going to meet with a deal of opposition from anti-tank guns. " B " Squadron is already engaged and, as the darkness lifts and the outlines sharpen, a clearer picture of the situation can be gained. The result is not encouraging.

" B " Squadron cannot be far from the Regiment's objective but the dust and fog of battle make it difficult to see what is really happening. One thing is certain. They are embroiled in the devil's own scrap with a powerful array of anti-tank guns, if not with enemy tanks as well. There is no question at present of their being able to take up any covering position to protect the infantry from a counter-attack. They are obviously having their work cut out to deal with what is already on their plate.

Neither will it be possible for the other two squadrons to reach the objective in the face of this opposition. So the Colonel orders them both to halt and engage the anti-tank screen in support of " B." Then he tries to contact the troops under his command, but without avail. The Sherwood Foresters, as a matter of fact, have dismounted and have taken up a position some three hundred yards in rear of his Headquarters, together with the New Zealand anti-tank gun troop. But the Colonel does not know this. Their carriers have followed in the tail of " B " Squadron and are sharing in their fate. But they cannot stay there long. The pace is too hot, and they retire very soon to where the infantry company are dismounted.

Meanwhile " A " and " C " Squadrons continue to engage the enemy anti-tank guns. They are completely exposed because the desert is too flat for them to have found a hull-down position and the gravity of the situation begins to become apparent. In reply to their attack, the enemy anti-tank guns open up in a great semi-circle. From the north-west, west and south-west the shells come whining through the air. They are big shells too, and there is obviously no lack of weight behind the enemy's armament. They're getting the range of the two Royal Wilts heavy squadrons now and more than one of their Shermans has been silenced. The outlook for the rest of them is serious, but they fight back gamely.

For the moment, however, the Colonel is even more perturbed about what is happening in the " B " Squadron area. That is undoubtedly where the battle is hottest, but what it is all about is hard to discern ; nevertheless, the conversations which he hears on the air give him a fairly good idea.

"This is terrific," says one young officer to another, "we're having all kinds of fun." A cackle comes through and the voice continues, "they've got quite a nice little anti-tank screen dug-in here . . . or at least they *did* have, a little while ago!" The receiver of this message acknowledges it and expresses a hope that the situation will be coped with. "Oh, yes!" says the first voice, "We're coping." The Colonel grins. He knows that young man. *He* will cope with a vengeance. "By the way," continues the subaltern, "we've discovered a new game. Beetle-crushing. You must try it when you've got the time. Its fun. I've just scored a couple of eighty-eights and I'm on my way to a hat trick . . ." The voice breaks off abruptly. The Colonel looks worried. What *is* going on up there in the smoke, noise and confusion?

* * * * * *

In order to try and answer that question, let us go back to the start of the advance and imagine that we are with "B" Squadron. To begin with, we shall find that progress is much the same as with the rest of the Regiment. There is little opposition and the Crusaders, being faster than the Shermans and Grants, soon pull out ahead of the other two squadrons and take their appointed position in the lead. They are fairly close together, so as to keep touch in the darkness, and the Squadron Leader's driver casts many a glance at his compass in his anxiety to keep the squadron on its true course of 270 deg.—that is due West. Normally the Second-in Command and each Troop Leader would be provided with a compass, but on this occasion the tanks have been issued so late that there has been barely enough time to "swing" one compass and that is in the Squadron Leader's tank. It is therefore very precious. Leading a squadron straight under these conditions is a very different business from that which the Troop Leaders were taught in peace time. "Pick up two points in a line to march on and ride your horse dead straight . . ." Squadron drill seems very far away!

As in the case of the other two squadrons behind, a number of infantry positions are over-run and the Germans, their hands held high, are thumbed back to the British lines. Towards dawn, however, the resistance stiffens and there is a deal of opposition from slit trenches and dug-in tanks. Then the dreaded anti-tank guns begin to open up and it becomes obvious that the squadron is running into trouble.

That trouble soon develops, and the party starts in earnest just as dawn is breaking. It is opened by the arrival of a shell, which lands with a ringing "crang" against the side of the Squadron Leader's tank. This shakes the crew a bit but the only casualty is that last remaining compass.

The Squadron Leader curses to himself as he looks at the ruined instrument, but he needn't bother about it really. Although he doesn't know it, he isn't going to need that compass any more. In a very short time nobody in " B " Squadron will need a compass. Nobody in the whole Regiment will need one!

But time is pressing and he glances at his watch. Then he peers over the rim of his turret at the flashes in front of him which indicate the barrage being put down by the New Zealand gunners behind. If the squadron is going to reach its objective by the appointed time, it will have to get on faster than this! So he gives the signal to increase pace and the tanks motor steadily into and through their own supporting barrage. Risky? Of course: but risks just have to be taken. As a matter of fact driving through a barrage is not so unpleasant as might be expected. Some have a theory that the safest plan is to travel inside your own barrage, because it pins the enemy to the ground. Under the influence of a barrage he is not likely to bob up behind or in front of the tanks. Every now and again a shell splinter is bound to penetrate the open turret of a tank, no doubt, but the mathematical odds against this are very considerable. The men of " B " Squadron, however, are not mathematically minded at the moment, and, in any case, in the noise, smoke and excitement of the battle such things are taken in their stride. There is so much "stuff" flying about amidst the general concatenation of explosive sounds that a little extra is hardly noticed.

Soon after the tanks emerge from the barrage the Squadron finds itself approaching the Rahman Track. Then, as the silvered telephone posts which run along it become dimly visible and the daybreak sharpens their outlines, the trouble starts in earnest; when they mount the crest of a very slight rise they are in the midst of it. Below them the Boche is dug in. His position is formidable. His strength is terrific. This is the real thing.

The Squadron Leader thinks quickly. He must in a situation like this. A few moments hesitation may spell disaster. Summing up his chances he glances from left to right along the horizon where the dawn has brought the rim of the desert into shadowy view. Flash, flash, flash . . . in a great semi-circle the guns of the enemy wink viciously back at him as great balls of fire seem to leap out of the sand and hurtle towards the oncoming tanks. Some miss their mark and bounce on the sand, to die out gracefully like fireworks in the sky. Others land with a sickening metallic clang on the Crusaders and explosions add dull thuds to the pandemonium of sounds that fills the shattered air. This is not the sort of resistance that can be brushed aside. Those shells are fired by the dreaded "88 millimetres" and guns of even heavier calibre. "B" Squadron has bumped right into the middle of the enemy's main gun line !

It is neck or nothing now. That gun line must be smashed at all costs. The forward Troop Leader has also summed up the situation and has slewed his troop to the left. The Squadron Leader quickens the pace of his own tank and takes the lead in the old fashioned cavalry style. His mind is made up. There is only one way to deal with this situation. He gives the order—" Charge."

He should, of course, have used the expression "Over-run." He is now commanding tanks, not horses, but the slip is natural enough, although there is a deal of difference between a cavalry charge and its mechanical counterpart. The former is full of romantic associations and a man can do great deeds when his blood is up in good company with a stout horse between his knees. But, normally, there is little romance about a mechanised operation. These men are cooped up in steel prisons which are packed tight with high explosives. Each tank carries enough petrol to burn down a house and the air is thick with missiles. Nostrils are filled with the reek of engines and fumes of oil. Throats are choked with dust. It is a cold-blooded business, this grinding into the night in a mass of metal. Everything in a tank, like everything in a battlefield, is hard, hot or harmful . . . excepting human flesh ! There is iron to bruise, steel to cut and fire to burn. But no romance.

Nevertheless, a dash of the old cavalry spirit infuses the men of "B" Squadron as the order to charge comes over the air. A Crusader has a fair turn of speed and the lust of the chase is added to their excitement, for the hunt is on. Chaos ensues, therefore, as the squadron breaks formation and races recklessly into the German gun-line. Every man is keyed up to the highest pitch and every tank is extended to its limit. Wherever a flash is seen in the sand, there lies a gun-pit, and after those flashes go the Crusaders. With all weapons blazing they thresh about and mill around, flat out in circles, to crush the Boche guns out of action. The pace is terrific. It cannot and does not last long, with both sides losing so heavily in the dust and smoke-laden dawn.

Unbelievable things are happening if we could but see them. Already the enemy guns are badly mauled. That "nice little tank screen" is in reality very formidable. It is officially described, later on, as composed of "twenty to twenty-five '88 millimetres,'" supported by a vast number of smaller guns." Official reports are not given to exaggeration and understatement is usually one of their characteristics.

IN THE HEAT OF BATTLE

And guns are being literally over-run by tanks for the first time in history. Here, as just one example, is an impression of the sort of thing that is happening all round us.

A subaltern sees through his glasses that the crew of an " 88 millimetre," upon which he has set his heart, are busily engaged in firing point blank at another " B " Squadron tank. So he stalks them from a flank.

The British tank is blazing back gamely but its guns are hopelessly inaccurate on the move and the shells fly wide of the gun emplacement. Its machine guns, too are giving a lot of trouble. The German " 88 millimetre " is also shooting wild. The subaltern holds his fire. So far he has been unobserved whilst the Germans battle with the enemy to their front. Then the boches get a lucky hit. Flames spurt from the British tank. Its petrol is on fire. The crew leap out as the tank goes up in a bright flash of flame and is crowned with a great cloud of dove grey smoke. The German gunners rush for their machine guns, but, as they train them on the escaping British crew, the subaltern takes a hand. This is his opportunity. He is close enough to the gun pit now to fire right down into it and he lets fly with his Besas at the Boches. There are four of them, and, for a few moments, they cling, as though magnetised, to their machine guns. Then, realising that they can't possibly get back to their big gun, they flee in an access of terror. The Crusader races after them, its zipping bullets claiming first one and then another. The remaining two fling themselves on the ground and clutch cravenly at the sand. But their fate is sealed. The charging metal passes over them as the huge tank slews round and makes once more towards the now deserted gun.

Up till now this Crusader has been charging blind at German gun-pits, but this " 88 millimetre " is dug in eight feet deep. It is a formidable obstacle. So as the tank approaches the edge it checks and hesitates, as though measuring its distance. Then it advances more gingerly. Its nose hangs for a moment over the side of the emplacement—reaching towards the great breech of the German anti-tank gun. A few more inches. As it dips, it thud-jangles upon the " 88 millimetre." The engine races slightly. Metal grinds on metal. The stout steel from Krupp's crumples like cardboard beneath the massive weight of the British tank. Slowly . . . slowly . . . with great effort the tank struggles astride the wrecked gun. It grunts furiously and seems to look up towards the further side of the gun-pit. Then it gropes for a way out. It gets a purchase on the lip. Again it roars and snorts and makes a fearful noise. The earth gives. Cascades of dust fall into the pit. Gradually the tracks get a grip and the great beast seems to scramble up the side. Now it is out, a crumpled mass of steel behind it, where once was a deadly gun. The Crusader appears to shake itself after this encounter as though looking round with a snort. What's the next job? It moves off once more towards the centre of the battle.

* * * * * *

Meanwhile the Squadron Leader has lost control. It is every man for himself now, but he is worried about the petrol supply. His tanks have been running for fully twelve hours and they can't have much fuel left. They won't be able to keep this sort of thing up much longer. The Besas, too, are giving trouble. They keep jamming and, in the midst of all this hell, men have to keep getting out of the tanks and freeing them with ram-rods. This, and a thousand other dangers, add to the critical nature of the battle.

For twenty minutes or so this deadly racket is kept up, as the daylight grows . . . and with it the peril to the Regiment's tanks. Those that are left of the dug-in German guns can now see the Crusaders without being seen themselves and their advantage increases as the darkness recedes. But, so fierce has been the slogging match that, when full daylight has filled the scene, a complete lull sets in. Both sides have fought to a standstill!

The Squadron Leader now takes stock of the wreckage lying about beneath the pall of dust and smoke and then looks towards the enemy's lines. Everything moving has vanished and there seems to be nothing in front of him. All the mobile vehicles have been driven away by the Boche and nothing but smashed guns and equipment or dead and wounded bodies have been left behind.

But, as his gaze swings round the saucer-rim of the desert in the crisp dry morning air, he sees that there is also very little left of his own squadron. To his left front lie the remains of his leading troop. Nothing but burning machines there! Every tank has "brewed up." The same fate has been meted out to the troop on his right. He turns, as though in a dream, to look behind him. Then he sees one solitary tank intact . . . that of the troop leader. His own Crusader is the only other mobile unit. " B " Squadron is a smoking ruin in the centre of the enemy's equally shattered gun-line. He makes for the shelter of a deserted gun-pit.

Then, alongside the mangled remains of what once was a deadly anti-tank weapon he pauses as though for breath. This is his first opportunity of reporting progress to the Commanding Officer and he tries to raise Regimental Headquarters on his wireless. "Progress" may sound odd in view of what has happened . . . but progress it is, and progress bought very dearly. For " B " Squadron has played its part in bringing about that eerie lull which now hangs unnaturally over the German gun line, and until those guns were silenced General Montgomery's advance would have been held up.

Nothing but a sound like a " Bee's Wedding " comes from the Squadron Leader's ear-phones and he looks about him anxiously. Something must be wrong. He can't get a reply from anybody. Then, as he sees the remains of his shot away aerial, he grins and his eyes also take in the jagged metal upon which there once was mounted a Bren gun. That is missing too! He shrugs his shoulders slightly and sets to work to erect a new aerial. This time it works and he manages to get in touch with the troop leader on his left. Not much to be gathered from him, however, so he tries Regimental Headquarters again. Good. He's in touch. "We've had a hell of party," he says "and there doesn't seem to be much of the squadron left. Only a few wounded 'horses' lying about," then his expression brightens, "But we've done a devil of a lot of damage . . . can't see anyone in front of us at all."

The Colonel acknowledges the message and then the Squadron Leader continues. He can't stay where he is. Can he pick up as many chaps as possible and come back to R.H.Q. ?" "Yes," says the Colonel grimly, "you can if you like, but its none too healthy here!" He might almost have used Old Bill's classic words about a "better 'ole." For he has been having a very difficult time on his own account and although he has fully realised the desperate situation of " B " Squadron, all he has been able to do is to engage the enemy anti-tank guns in their support.

This, in itself, has been an unequal struggle for his two heavy squadrons halted out there on either side of him without a stitch of cover. Besides, so far there are no signs of either of the other two regiments in the Brigade. That makes him feel very naked and he wonders what has happened to them. He rakes the horizon with his glasses till his eyes are full of water. There *is* something there. He can just make out some specks, each at the narrow end of a plume of sand which carries high into the air. They are too heavy for supply vehicles. They must be tanks. They *are* tanks. They are about 1,800 yards away. He can see them clearly now, although the queer half light of dawn makes it impossible to distinguish what type they are. Anyhow, they are bound to be the Warwickshire Yeomanry because that is exactly where he would expect to find them. He suddenly feels less lonely. It is a comforting thing to have your flanks covered. They will take care of that end of the business and that helps a lot. A great deal happier, he turns towards his right to see whether he can make out where the 3rd Hussars are positioned. Anybody who happened to be close enough might hear him hum a snatch or two from song about a " Gambolier.', But of course, nobody *is* close enough.

He searches the desert with his glasses but cannot make out the 3rd Hussars. Probably that is because he expects them to be up level with him whereas, actually, they are over his right shoulder. They are there all right, and fighting furiously. But they have not come along as fast as the Royal Wilts. They have had a very sticky journey, even in the first advance, where they were heavily shelled and lost all their anti-tank guns. They are now also losing tanks fast and before long will have barely a dozen left all told. But they are doing deadly work upon that portion of the enemy's defences which lies before them. And that is what counts. That hole must be punched, no matter what the cost !

So the Colonel switches his attention back to the battle in front of him. The anti-tank gunfire is still very heavy from the flanks, each side of the section put out of action by " B " Squadron. It is taking toll of the squadrons right and left of him. He is also becoming worried about his supply of ammunition and increasing loss of tanks. He thinks he had better inform the Brigadier of his position. So he gets through to Brigade on the radio and is considerably cheered up. He is told that 10th Corps are very near and that he is to hold on at all costs. That is something definite, at any rate. There is still a chance that all may be well, in spite of his heavy losses. But how can he get a respite, even for a few minutes ? Smoke ? It is worth a trial. So he orders the two heavy squadrons, with whom he is still in touch, to fire smoke at maximum range. The result is highly successful. For ten blessed minutes a thick curtain hangs between the guns in front of him and the two harassed squadrons.

When the smoke has drifted away, the battle seems to have taken a strange turn. As far as he can make out, " B " Squadron, or what remains of them, are moving left-handed. A horrible suspicion enters his mind. Surely they can't have mistaken the Warwickshire Yeomanry for the enemy ! It looks, or rather sounds like it. He can tell from the noise of their guns that they are firing in that direction—and what is more the Warwicks are answering back. This is maddening. Has everybody gone crazy ? He tries frantically to get " B " Squadron Leader on the radio to warn him, as he probably doesn't realise where the Warwicks are supposed to be positioned. God, what a day this is turning out to be. He can do nothing about it, however ; there are no such things as runners or despatch riders available. He racks his brain to find a solution.

* * * * * *

But " B " Squadron Leader is quite right. He has spotted those tanks to his left rear as he emerges from the gun-pit in search of survivors. He is under no delusions about their being the Warwickshire Yeomanry. He knows them for what they are—Boches ! Rommel's 21st Panzer Division to be exact. So he and his only other surviving tank open up and take them on as best they can. It is a pathetic effort with nothing heavier than 2-pounders, and its result is foregone conclusion. It provokes a deadly counter-attack from the Panzers in which the Squadron Leader's tank is hit and set on fire. He himself is wounded in the legs and his wireless operator is killed. Then, as he feverishly drags the dead man's body from the burning tank, he is hit in the foot once more. After that the sole remaining tank picks him up and he manages to scramble onto its back. It is the only " runner " left in his squadron which, a few hours before, had gone into the battle with eleven new Crusaders !

Then his driver and a gunner clamber on the front and they make off half-right towards another smoking ruin. There they pick up two more survivors who also manage somehow to cling to the outside of the tank and the whole party is carried back towards the British lines.

In peace-time a person who has met with an accident dreads the journey to hospital in a modern luxurious ambulance. Every move of the well-sprung body jars him on his stretcher, as the careful driver goes smoothly over the macadam surface of the road. Imagine, then, the plight of these men, clinging wounded and exhausted to the merciless studded steel side of a Crusader. A lost grip means a lost life as the tank rattles, rocks and clanks across the rubbly desert at over thirty miles an hour, a moving target for the Boches to shoot at.

Only one of these passengers escapes being hit on the journey back. The Squadron Leader receives a third wound, this time in the arm, and a troop sergeant is killed. But the Crusader does manage to get back finally and it stops in the Gunners' lines. They are not even yet to be left in peace, however, for there is almost as much "stuff" flying about here as there was near the Rahman Track. But here, at least, there is a doctor!

* * * * * *

Meanwhile the Colonel's position is desperate. The Royal Wilts, after the pummeling it has received, is in no condition to take on a fresh Panzer regiment. There is only one thing to be done. The Colonel, realising now what has happened, engages the newcomers with both "A" and "C" Squadrons. The death struggle, has begun in earnest.

Both squadrons turn to engage, and Regimental Headquarters follows suit. But just as the tank marked "Trowbridge" slews round to meet this new enemy, there is an ominous "smack" ending in a sort of "ping." The Colonel has become accustomed to his tank being hit. For some time now there has been a monotonous "tuck . . . tuck . . . tuck" as bullets and shell splinters have bounced off its armour like harvest bugs against the windshield of a motor car. But this last was something different. It was clearly a heavier blow. Even so, it need not, of necessity, prove fatal. These tanks can take direct hits from heavy calibre guns and still carry on providing that nothing essential has been affected. The Colonel and his crew look serious. There is a strained atmosphere in that tiny enclosure within the heavy armour. They are waiting to see whether anything further will happen. They know they are severely hit. They can tell that much. But will there be complications?

And then, of a sudden, it happens. "Look out, Sir!" The Colonel reacts like lightning to the sergeant's warning. Instinctively the crew scramble out as fast as the awkward exits will allow. But only just in time! The flames which are licking round the fuel tank leap into a blaze. The tank goes up in a roar as the men fling themselves on the ground and crawl away as fast as their knees and arms will carry them. Then down come the machine guns. The Boches are on to them like a knife. The bullets flick up little puffs of sand around the fleeing men, like heavy rain drops. Then the two figures lie still, scarce out of range of the white hot metal which is spraying from the now exploding tank. The Colonel is only shamming dead, but the sergeant who once drove him is not.

For what seems a very long time the Colonel lies there, not daring to move lest the Boches should open up again. For the moment they seem to be satisfied that both the men are dead. Meanwhile a flow of thoughts rushes through the Colonel's brain. Just before his tank was hit he had noticed some Shermans moving from a westerly direction towards the north. Those he took to be the forward elements of 10th Corps—and he was right. But will they be in time to save what remains of his regiment? He doubts it and again he is right. "B" Squadron has fought itself to a standstill and the enemy is now settling down to the methodical destruction of the other two squadrons. Dealing, as always whenever possible, with one thing at a time he first of all takes on " C " Squadron. One by one he knocks them out. Then he " liquidates " what is left of Regimental Headquarters. Next, systematically, he turns to " A." The survivors, pinned out in the open, fight back for all they are worth. But it can only be a matter of time.

Sick at heart and weary from reaction, the Colonel decides to move. He has seen a radio truck which is stranded a few hundred yards behind him ; the sort that is generally known as a " gin palace." There might be a set still working in there ! So he decides to try and reach it. As he binds up his arm with his handkerchief (for a bullet has pierced his elbow), he takes a careful look around. It will be a difficult journey. Little pockets of the enemy are dotted all over the place and a number of miniature battles are still going on between them and his own Sherwood Foresters whom he now can make out, dug in about three hundred yards to the rear of his burnt out tank. Perhaps these men will see him and give him some help with covering fire. But it is so hard to spot anybody in all this confusion and they wouldn't know what he was up to, anyway. So he starts to crawl. Inch by inch he makes his dangerous way, noticing for the first time the handicap of his wound. He recalls his early days on his father's deer forest in Scotland. Thank heaven for the lore he learnt on the hill. He observes the tiniest rules of that lore now, as he has never done before. He is nearly there when . . . whoo-oo-sh ! ! ! thud ! ! ! A shell lands about thirty yards from the gin palace. Rotten shooting ! Too far over, my friends. Then again. Another shell lands. This time it is thirty yards short. That is not so funny. The Colonel realises that they are ranging and the next one will probably land smack in the centre and ruin his precious gin palace. He waits for it. Minute by minute. But somehow it doesn't come. The Boche seems to have lost interest. Perhaps he got a better target. Or perhaps he got knocked out himself. Anyhow it doesn't matter. The Colonel has made it. Carefully he creeps inside the radio truck.

A quick look round is encouraging. Doesn't seem to be much damage inside. But you never know with radio. Very delicate stuff, it is, and very soon put wrong. He fiddles with knobs, and crackly sparks confirm that there is current. He fits the headphones on and . . it works ! This is almost more than he has dared to hope for. He can now take charge of his Regiment once more.

But his joy is short-lived. He can only raise, besides the signals officer on the rear link, the Squadron Leader of "A" Squadron and three other tanks. For the second time in ten days, the Royal Wilts armour has been practically wiped out. He looks at his watch. It is a little after eight o'clock. There are no spare tanks or vehicles, and goodness knows how long it will be before he can find a mount. He'd better hand over. There is little else he can do. Calling back "A" Squadron Leader he tells him to take command of what is left of the Regiment and report to the Brigadier. Next he gives the signals officer a message for Brigade, telling them what he has done. Then, with a sigh of resignation, he puts down the radio headphones. So that is that. His task is over for the time being. His experience tells him that the Regiment, too, will be out of the hunt for a considerable time to come. Two hammerings like this in a fortnight will take some time to get over. He wonders just how long.

Meanwhile the battle has switched almost completely and now it is raging from north to south. A few immobilised tanks on either side are still firing in a desultory fashion from east to west, like dying gladiators exchanging feeble blows before the end. The Colonel, in his now useless gin-palace, is about midway between these two armoured forces and their shells fly overhead. There are still a considerable number of enemy infantry to be mopped up and a series of small battles is being waged between these and British infantry and crews whose tanks are knocked out.

For more and more " tank " men are on their feet now. They are faintly reminiscent of dishorsed riders in the Grand National, only *their* chief danger begins when they have lost their mounts whereas, with the jockeys, it works the other way round.

Then, for the next two weary hours, the Colonel makes his way back to the Headquarters of 1st Armoured Division. He walks a little, crawls a little and dodges a little as he trudges through acres of ploughed up desert. This is a bitter ending to so gruelling an experience. But, as the sound of the battle dies down over his shoulder, one thought keeps repeating in his brain, like a cracked gramophone record. Has 9th Armoured Brigade done its job ? Will the main armour be able to go through It is difficult to judge, although it is obvious that they have made a devil of a mess of the enemy's defences. Finally he arrives at the Headquarters about ten o'clock in the morning.

There he finds the G.S.O.3 of 9th Armoured Brigade, on whose radio he is able to report to the Brigadier. After that he can do little until the Regiment is ordered out at about four o'clock in the afternoon. They are to take no further part in the battle and to hand over what remains of their armour to the Warwickshire Yeomanry. They hand over four tanks !

THE DESERT AFTER THE BATTLE.
Below are two captured guns—(*left*) a German 88 mm. (*right*) an Italian 90/53.

MAP No. 11

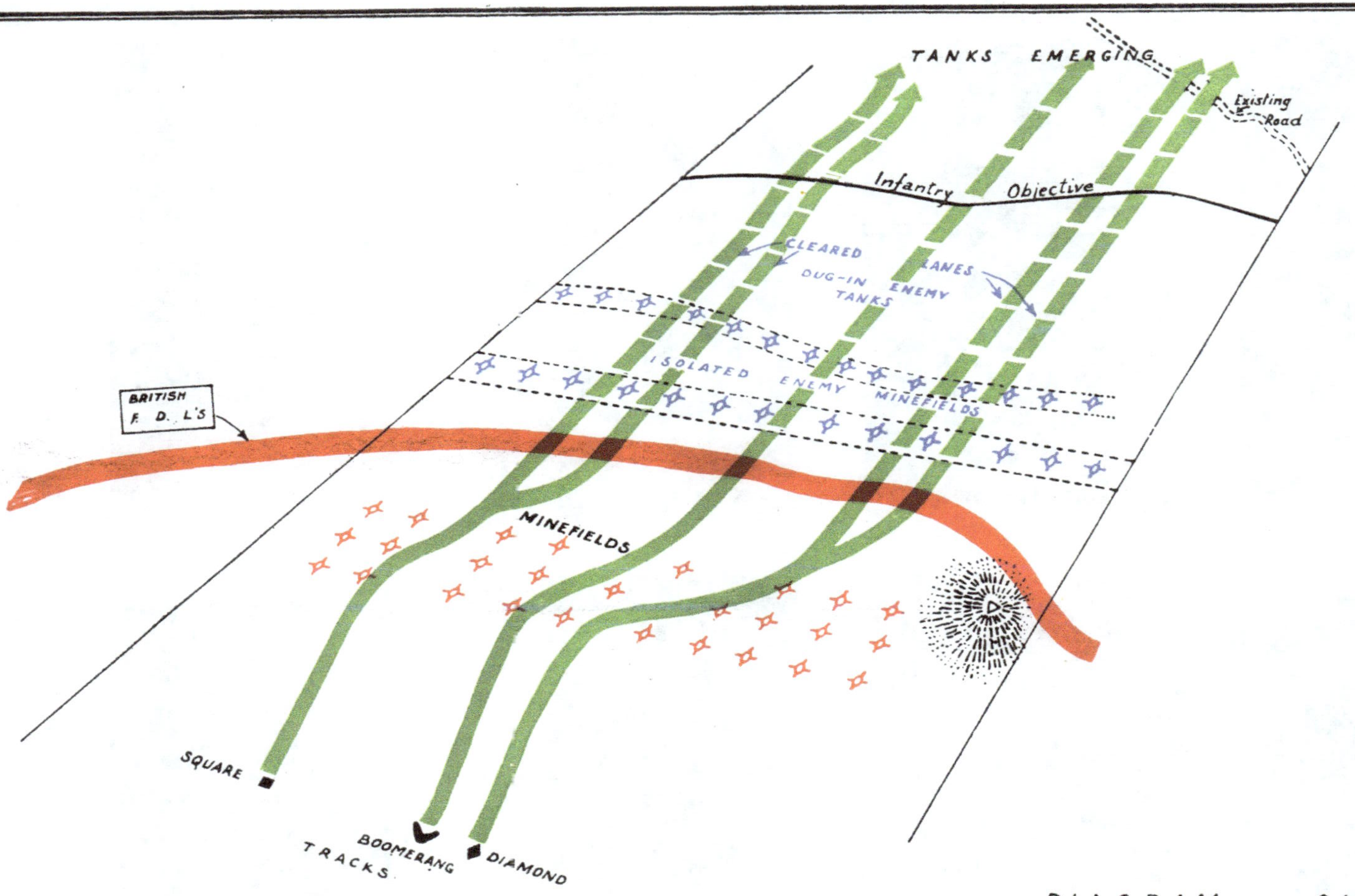

DIAGRAM SHOWING
2 NZ DIV ROUTES THROUGH MINEFIELDS
FOR OPERATION
SUPERCHARGE

Drawn by 2 NZ Division.   Reproduced by 512 Fd. Survey Coy. R.E., Dec. 1942.

Existing Road
TANKS EMERGING
Infantry Objective
CLEARED LANES
DUG-IN ENEMY TANKS
ISOLATED ENEMY MINEFIELDS
MINEFIELDS
BRITISH F.D.L'S
TRACKS
SQUARE
BOOMERANG
DIAMOND

M.D.R. Misc. 2141

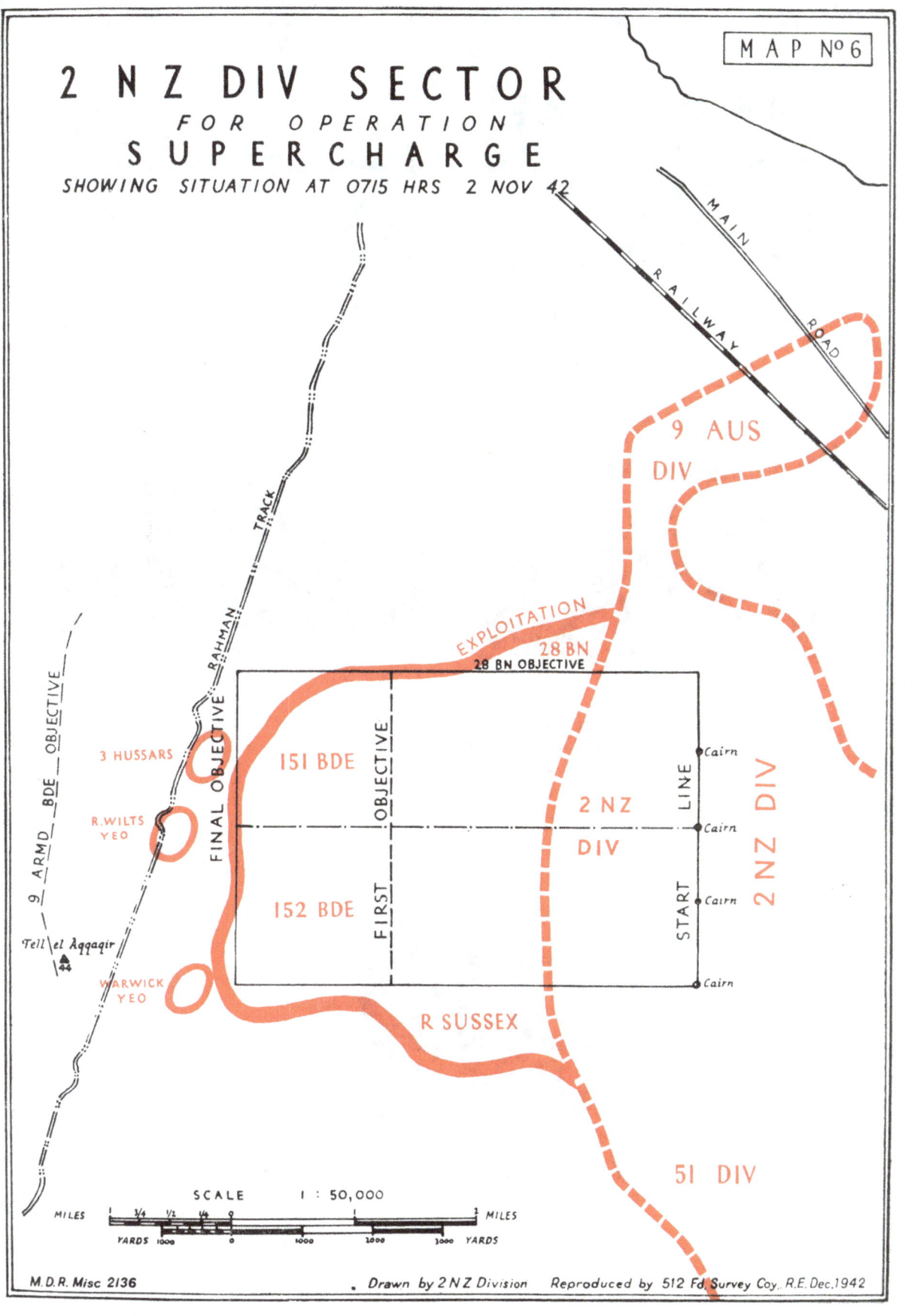

1.

2.

3.

4.

1. AN INFANTRY TRUCK BEING SHELLED WHILST CROSSING A MINEFIELD.
2. MOPPING UP, WITH A WARY EYE FOR SNIPERS.
3. "BREWING UP."
4. THE END OF A GERMAN "MARK IV SPECIAL."

THE REAL OBJECT OF HITLER'S "PEOPLE'S CAR."

CHAPTER TWENTY-ONE

" THE REST IS HISTORY . . ."

THAT is the story of the Royal Wilts in the Battle of El Alamein. Fate had cast them for an important role on that historic occasion and it is no exaggeration to say that they played it well. It was, however, only a part. El Alamein has been referred to as " the most decisive land battle of the war," and history may well confirm that description. Many units of the British forces were engaged and their individual stories will be told elsewhere. This book is, quite naturally, most nearly concerned with what happened to 9th Armoured Brigade.

That Brigade fought a terrible battle. Scenes such as those which have been described in the Royal Wilts sector were happening throughout the advance of the three armoured regiments. It is hard to realise those scenes, and no reporter could faithfully describe them. The mind soon became accustomed to reading about " heavy losses of tanks." Such headlines were taken very much for granted during the war. Even the men who were themselves in action became callous. " So-and-so's tank brewed up," they would say, and leave it at that. But what did it mean to the men inside that tank when it " brewed up " ? In order to try and gain just a faint impression of what it *did* mean, let the reader imagine that he or she is back again, for a few minutes, amidst the scenes which have just been described.

Up and down the whole El Alamein front the battle is raging furiously. Men are being killed, maimed, burned and mentally shattered for life. In one place two officers are earnestly discussing some important point whilst standing, for the moment, beside a tank. A shell screams past and one of them ducks. Then he looks round and finds that his companion's head has been blown clean off. His collar has fallen to the ground. That collar, with the tie still neatly tied inside it, will remain to bleach in the desert for years to come.

Everywhere the sand is littered with smashed and burning machinery. Wrecked German guns are lying in all directions. Some are the dreaded " eighty-eights " ; some, even, are big Russian anti-tank guns which the Boches have lugged all the way from the eastern front, so that with them they can fire upon the allies of the men who made them. Near one gun-pit, looking somehow slightly obscene with its under-belly exposed to view, lies a British tank on its side. It is hard to imagine how, even with a direct hit at twenty yards, it can thus have been bowled over. But there it is and there it will remain, a visible proof that such things can happen.

The whole of this strip of desert is a shambles. Men are being crushed between metal and sand, and others run screaming from blazing tanks, their very clothes on fire. They roll frantically in the sand as they tear the burning material from their bodies. Again, others pace pitifully up and down in charred uniforms, their hands swelled up with burns, their faces unrecognisable, their lips grotesquely puffed up. There are also swollen travesties of men lying, in fantastic attitudes, in burnt out tanks that reek of cooked flesh. Some of these will remain there for months and when, eventually, they are moved, their bodies will drop to pieces.

Some there are who, bodily unharmed, wander witless in the desert. These will live out their lives, but never again will they be as they were yesterday.

Over there a tank is hit broadside. A solid shell pierces the armour and smashes the driver's legs. His hands fly up. There is terror in his eyes. Not because he will never walk again. That thought has not yet occurred to him. But he knows that tanks catch fire when hit in certain places. He also knows that when this happens it is only a matter of seconds. This is the secret dread of all tank crews. In this tank, now, bits of metal, white hot from their passage through the armour plate, are flying around the tiny space behind the wounded driver. And that space is packed with shells. One is struck by a fragment. A tiny greenish flame appears. The driver instantaneously hauls himself out of the seat. He reaches the turret a moment after the rest of the crew have baled out. Gripping, pulling, levering himself up, he extricates himself, in spite of his useless legs, with the superhuman strength of a desperate man. Then he lands with a soft thud upon the sand as the tank goes up with a raucous " whoof." The heat singes his hair as he wriggles and scrambles away from it.

That is what happens when a tank " brews up."

Don't shudder, reader, and say, " How disgusting ! Why call attention to such unpleasant details ? " The author has already been asked to leave them out. Some have described them as " horrific." But others, who took part in the battle, have asked that they should be left in. These latter feel that you should know the truth and so the details have remained. This is not fiction. These are only a few specific and isolated instances of the horrors that took place on that battlefield of El Alamein. The men concerned were your relatives and friends. They would normally have been living at peace in England, and each one represents a family. Furthermore such scenes occurred, to a greater or lesser degree, on every battlefield throughout the world in this last appalling war.

You *should* know about such things because it is you who will have to prevent their recurrence in the future. Yes, you. Not the politicians. Not the man next door. But you, You, YOU ! Those men who fought have helped to wrest the torch of civilisation from the hands of the devil. They have paid with their lives, their limbs and their wits. All that they ask of you is that you should guard the flame.

If you do not guard it carefully, that flame will most surely die away. There will be more wars. Queen Victoria is credited with having said that, " The price of freedom is eternal vigilance." History has proved how right she was. Henceforth every man should make it a ceaseless mission to pursue that vigilance.

* * * * * *

1st Armoured Division did not, in fact, get forward before full light to take advantage of the gap. This was a great disappointment, but the gap was used later. Perhaps it were better to leave it to General Freyberg himself to describe the results of this battle. In his official report, which was published later on, when all aspects of the operation could be seen in their proper perspective, he said :

" Although the 9th Armoured Brigade did not reach its objective and had heavy casualties, the action was a success as the enemy gun line was smashed. It may be argued that it was a costly and incorrect method of using armour, but if one is to believe General von Thoma it may well prove to have been the deciding factor in breaking the German line, although advantage was not taken of the breach until later."

The 9th Armoured Brigade casualties had indeed been heavy. They went into battle with one hundred and thirty-three tanks. They came out with thirty-five. Not quite the one hundred per cent. casualties for which they had been warned to prepare, but getting on that way ! The comparison with Balaclava, with its intriguing contrast between the light and heavy brigades, is so obvious that any recorder of the battle has a constant struggle against the temptation to use it. The Whitehall " Official " account, published some eighteen months later, quite unblushingly yielded to this temptation. Let us leave it at that.

Meanwhile, beyond El Alamein, the pursuit was on. A London journalist wrote at the time, " No previous 5th of November has ever seen bonfires like those provided by Rommel's army, now blazing in the Western Desert." On that day Lieut.-Col. Gibb sat down and wrote a personal message to all ranks serving in the field at the time. This is what it said :—

" On the 2nd November, once more 9th Armoured Brigade were told to punch a hole in the enemy defences to enable the main armour of 10th Corps to pass through and finally destroy the enemy forces in North Africa. This was done, and at this juncture there is every indication that a big victory is in sight, the results of which must have a far reaching effect on the successful conclusion of the war.

Yesterday the Army Commander sent a personal message to Brigadier Currie in which he said that he appreciated the enormity of the task set to 9th Armoured Brigade, but congratulated him on its successful fulfilment. Further, that upon the success achieved by the Brigade had depended the success of the operation. This, he said, 9th Armoured Brigade had ensured.

Brigadier Currie sent a special personal message to me yesterday congratulating the Regiment upon the action which it fought. This is high praise.

The losses have been grievous but not irreparable and we must now all strive to build up again the Regiment to its former strength and efficiency. This action will be recorded in the annals of regimental history, and the epic of " B " Squadron will live for all time.

Once more I congratulate all ranks."

That message tells, as no other words could, the part played by the Regiment in the Battle of El Alamein. The rest is history.

CHAPTER TWENTY-TWO

IN EGYPT—AFTER THE STORM

AFTER these harrowing experiences at El Alamein the Regiment was sent to Alexandria to rest. There it frankly had a good time. " Alex " is a very pleasant place under any circumstances, and with their battle experiences as a background it was heaven to those men at that time.
They enjoyed the " seaside " atmosphere and all the peculiar attractions which go with it. Besides, for the time being they were heroes in the eyes of the local populace. As such they were fêted wherever they went. The ladies went to great pains to provide entertainment for the men in welfare centres, and " parties " were given for the officers. In fact, an enjoyable time was had by all. All, that is, who were still capable of enjoying themselves. There were others who were less fortunate and found themselves in the wards of the hospitals of Cairo and Alexandria.

It is not suggested that the Royal Wilts had done anything out of the ordinary at El Alamein. They had been given a job to do—an unpleasant one, admittedly—and they had done it to the best of their ability. So had all the others in the battle, and most of them were still carrying on out there in the desert at this time. But the people of Alexandria couldn't get hold of the others. They knew that Egypt—and their own town in particular—had been saved, and here were some of the men who helped to save it. So those men had to be treated as heroes. It must, in all fairness, be recorded that the Wiltshire Yeomen, together with a number of New Zealanders who were similarly placed, accepted the situation with becoming grace and considerable gusto. Incidentally, a bond was forged at El Alamein, between Wiltshire and New Zealand, which will last through many years.

And so the ancient city of Alexandria has many pleasant memories for the men of the Royal Wilts. Most of them, perhaps, were chiefly interested in the modernity of the present town with its cafés, cinemas and general French atmosphere of culture and mundane luxuries. But some of them dipped into its past and learnt that, had Nelson arrived three days earlier at that port in the year 1798, Napoleon's fleet would have been wiped out with all his expeditionary force and the French influence in Egypt would never have come into being. The town would be today, probably, much as it was when the great Cleopatra was carried about in it with all her Eastern splendour. When she was wont to summon thirteen neighbouring kings at a time to come and confer with her and when she would converse to each in his own particular language. That was a considerable feat, even in a country where, throughout the ages, the educated classes have always been at least tri-lingual.

It is interesting to note that, although these men of 9th Armoured Brigade were prepared to accept, for the time being, the role of conquering hero, they were characteristically modest about their recent participation in the battle. Some of them may have boasted a little, but the local inhabitants, even those who came into close contact with our troops, found it difficult to find out exactly what they had really done. As for the rest, even the great Nelson himself was human enough to yield, on occasion, to the hero worship which is inherent in the Mediterranean temperament.

Altogether, this brief visit to Alexandria was a very pleasant experience.

The next move was to a camp just outside Cairo. In Alexandria the Regiment had been on the crest of the wave, but for many the change was an anti-climax. Reaction, quite naturally, set in and somehow Cairo grated upon their sensibilities. To begin with it had remained, even during the greatest crisis, a predominantly peace-conditioned city. So had Alexandria, for the matter of that; but somehow the former seemed more blatant. It flaunted its failings whilst the latter was more successful in hiding them. Cairo, even at its best, was always a city of contrasts. The vast and arid desert against the rich luxuriance of nature along the fertile banks of the Nile. The squalor and poverty of the masses cheek by jowl with the great wealth of the few. The clamour, dust and heat of the busy city, by day, and the cool glint of the moon on peaceful water in the glamour of the Eastern night. The bustle of modernity and the serenity of the ancient monuments. Those who had leisure and money in happier times were wont to travel across the earth to see all this. But to the soldier at war its appeal had worn thin. It appeared almost sordid. For Romance was hiding her tear-stained eyes. Vulgarity had pushed her roughly aside.

To the man freshly back from battle, however, there was one great contrast which dwarfed all others. The contrast between Egypt and Britain in war time. Against the background of his recent experiences only a few miles away and his thoughts of those dear to him at home, working out the blood, toil, tears and sweat that was all Churchill had to offer when war began, he was shocked by the first impact of what he saw in Cairo. He was biased, of course, but to his war-conditioned mind the whole place would appear, at first, as a great vortex of corruption in which his own countrymen and their allies were swept up equally with the local inhabitants. Why did the members of the forces here fare better than the men in the firing line? The further you went from danger the more of everything there seemed to go round. Surely that could not be right! But it was so. Why should Egyptians of all classes make a good thing out of the war and contribute nothing to its effort? Why should they be paid whilst receiving the protection which others provided at such great sacrifice. But these things were happening.

And why not? What would you have the Egyptians do? They were a neutral nation. But it seemed that nobody should be allowed to remain neutral in this war. Everybody's existence was at stake! Yet that was one of the things for which the soldier was fighting: the right of small nations to do as they pleased—providing that they could get away with it! How difficult everything was, and how confusing.

There were, in reality, perfectly adequate answers to most of the questions which puzzled him, but you could not expect him to find them under those circumstances. He merely gained a confused impression of profiteers in the shops and restaurants and limpets holding soft jobs at G.H.Q. Such things were the subject of conversation all round him. The officers joked about them in the clubs and hotels. The other ranks good naturedly took them for granted and swopped rhymes about them in the cafés and barrack rooms.

This atmosphere was not, however, without its subversive effect upon morale. Many, by this time, were beginning to wonder what they were really fighting for. Cairo, and its obvious effect upon those whose duties kept them there, did much to increase their doubt. Those who were not over given to thinking were the most fortunate. They merely became annoyed at the unfairness of it all and put it down to war which never does make sense anyhow. The same things happened in the last war !

But many a less superficial man became considerably exercised in his mind. Civilisation ! That was what he was fighting for. Define it how you liked, we still used the word " civis," a Roman citizen, when we talked about it. Nobody had yet found a better way of describing it. Democracy was really the heritage of the Roman Empire conditioned by the " chivalry " handed down by the knights of the Middle Ages. A code of behaviour built up laboriously through centuries in defiance of the law of the jungle. And this is where it had all started ; Cairo was the birthplace of civilisation. These people were civilised 4,000 years before Christ was born. Their ideas were the foundation upon which the Romans built. And look at them now. Was this the ultimate result of the " civilisation " for which the world was fighting ? No wonder it was all so confusing.

Such moods did not persist as a rule, however. In most cases they slipped away, for human nature is full of resource. But nearly always they left an undefinable restlessness. Usually a soldier on leave would venture to the edge of this vortex and peer within. Then he would himself be sucked into it, to a greater or lesser degree according to his inclinations and powers of resistance. And why not ? He was there to enjoy himself ! All this nonsense would not stop just because he held aloof. And so he would sample the tinsel pleasures of this blatant modern edition of the once stately Memphis.

But always the restlessness would remain. A man with any imagination could not really enjoy himself in those surroundings at that time. He always had the feeling of wanting to get on with it all. It was difficult to relax. There was work to be done. So much to do and so little time in which to do it. Leave would seem somehow like enforced periods of idleness. Like a sea voyage when you are out of the swing of the world for a certain time and unable to do anything about it at all—but itching to get back to it. Even when he was enjoying his immediate surroundings for the moment the restlessness persisted. At a good film, for example, in a perfectly equipped theatre. He would somehow be wanting it to finish : to get on with something else. But what ? Besides, the people in the cinema annoyed him. To look at them you'd never believe there was a war on at all. They didn't even look interested. News would be read from the screen. Hot news. Exciting news. Rommel was on the run. Egypt, the fulcrum of the war at that crucial time, was being saved—and with it civilisation ! But these people didn't seem to care. Newsreels would come on, showing scenes of incredible bravery, hardship and suffering. The audience would settle itself more comfortably in its padded seat as though impatient to get on to the main film. All these news shots might as well have been the usual Hollywood heroics as far as they were concerned. Not men of flesh and blood making the supreme sacrifice that others might benefit. Looking around the theatre he would see people gossiping, flirting and eating over-sweetened ice-cream. Somehow he wanted to stand up and shout at them. To tell them what it was all about. To break into their complacency. To shatter their selfishness. But what was the use. They wouldn't understand. He'd leave the theatre in a disgruntled mood, which was in no way improved by having the dirty stump of an arm thrust in his face by a beggar child at the garish entrance—especially as he knew that its parents had probably mutilated the child on purpose to make money out of it.

Money, money, money. Baksheesh ! That was all these people seemed to think about. Time he got back to the desert to some honest fighting! This business here in Cairo disgusted him. It couldn't be allowed to last. Or could it? Again that doubt! Was he a poor fool who was to do all the fighting whilst people like this sat back and took the profits—and laughed at him. War just didn't make sense whatever way you looked at it. The flower of every nation was killed off. The weeds flourished. Standards were lowered all round. If you wanted proof, you only had to look around you here in Cairo. On every rung of the social ladder it was the same. At the top you could see people in high places behaving in a manner which would have scandalised their very selves a few years ago. At the bottom you could witness the dismal spectacle of normally decent citizens queueing up and paying good money for the privilege of a few degrading moments in the unhygienic company of ladies rejoicing in such names as "Tiger Lil." Apart from the horrors of the battlefield, war is a filthy business.

So no wonder your soldier returned from the battle feels restless as he wanders about Cairo, whatever his rank, providing that he has imagination. He may be attracted by the conviviality of the service clubs, the cabarets, the cafés, the barrel organs in the streets, but still he is haunted by the feeling that he is only filling in time until he gets on with the stern business of the war. But to what end? Not for the first time in British history many have lost sight of what they were fighting for. It happened in the dreary final years of the Napoleonic wars when Pitt, and a handful of others who had the ability to see into the future, found it so difficult to impress upon the British people that the foundations were being laid for a century of prosperity within their Empire.

Perhaps Mr. Churchill profited by his great knowledge of history when he expressed his own views on this subject. He did not try, too early in the struggle, to explain to the confused masses what the fruits of their difficult years of endeavour could be. He might have found, as Pitt did, that they were not yet ready to understand. He was therefore practical. Almost brutal. "We are fighting," he said, "in order that we may go on living. And when our ability to do so is more generally known throughout the world, we shall discuss our war aims!" How delightfully that is phrased! "That will be enough," the Prime Minister in his wisdom may have thought, "for the present and until the corner is turned. Later on, if, like Pitt, I am spared to see 'the prospect of victory,' I can explain to them more fully the destiny of their heritage."

Had we only listened in time to the warnings of that great man, the whole miserable business of the war might well have been avoided!

But Cairo wasn't really as bad as it had seemed to such unhappy soldiers. Perhaps they saw its faults more clearly because they themselves had moved on whilst Egypt had stood still. They were beginning to realise that all had not been quite so well with their pre-war world as their pre-war minds had imagined. Already there was stirring in many that uneasiness which was so well reflected, a few months later, in some verses of Sir Alan Herbert which appeared in the "Sunday Graphic."

THREE YEARS.

Three years! Three years! And it has scarce begun!
   Three years of waste and wretchedness and woe,
Since one man's lunacy put back the sun.
   Yet—were we happier three years ago?

Three years. Our swords were rusty—and our souls;
   And this old lion was despised of men.
Were we the people to defend the Poles?
   The very Wop was laughing at us then.

He is not laughing quite so much, we hope:
   We are not quite so comic as before.
Respected, feared, we struggle up the slope
   And march, if God commands, for three years more.

There was comfort in those lines. They pointed to something worth fighting for in addition to mere survival. For of what use is survival if the future holds no promise?

Fortunately for the Royal Wilts, however, they were not actually quartered in Cairo. They were camped in the desert outside, and somehow this seemed more fitting. Their tents were, in fact, pitched at the very foot of the Pyramids themselves. And there, in those surroundings, they were able to sift out their thoughts. But it must be admitted that, for many, these thoughts were sadly confused after all that had happened to them since they had left Palestine for Egypt such a short time previously.

And so during those months of the Egyptian winter, so unlike the winter to which they were normally accustomed, the yeomanry sat quietly in the desert in those romantic surroundings. Thus, at peace for the moment, with war so close along the desert track to Libya, those who were in the habit of thinking thought out a lot of things.

The previous three years seemed like some strange dream which had passed in the night and gone. What strange events had happened to these men who would, most of them, have normally lived out their lives in Wiltshire. The coming of the war with all its unreality. The chaos of those first few months. The horses and their sickness. Troops billeted on once pleasure-serving racecourses. The mud and cold of that first winter and then the move to warmer climes. The Mediterranean. The Jews and the Arabs. Boredom and "cleaning up" the horses. And then the change to armour. The Syrian desert in trucks. Sand and a first taste of real war. Fear and bombing. Heat and flies. Endless deserts, and always the sun. Syria, Iraq, Persia. The hum of the wheels of the trucks. Seven thousand miles across the deserts and then back to Syria again.

Then boredom once more until the greatest trial yet. The move to Egypt with all its excitement of the crucial days of the war.

Then the great climax. Their real test. The guns and the bombing. The clash of modern armour. The stench of the battlefield. That stench of rotting human flesh which never really leaves the nostrils once it has entered. The victory of El Alamein. A realisation of its great significance. Alexandria with its cobalt sea and modern buildings. The flush of coming out of battle to a grateful welcome. The vulgarity of wartime Cairo with its glamour worn thin. Pedlars, pimps, profiteers and pornography. The Nile by moonlight. Wealth and poverty. The Turf Club and Shepheard's Bar—those perennial menaces to security. Cafés, cabarets, blaring vulgar music. Flies, dust, dirt. And now this resting at the foot of the Pyramids.

The fruit of such speculation was comforting. Things were going better than the Allies had almost dared to hope. The corner seemed to have been turned at last. Just before Christmas the Prime Minister made a speech in which he said " November is usually a month of fog and gloom," but that year it was " a month in which our soldiers and sailors and airmen have been victorious, in which our gallant Russian allies have struck redoubtable blows against the common enemy, in which our American allies and our kith and kin far off in the Pacific have also seen their efforts crowned with a considerable measure of success. A great month, this last month of November."

The men of the Regiment were able to feel that they had played their part during that month of November. Mr. Churchill had fulfilled the promise made at Khatatba. He had given them the tools, and with those tools they had done the job that was demanded of them. It had not been an easy job but they had done it to the best of their ability.

They were also aware from the letters which they received from home that the autumn of 1942 had been one of the best that had been known for years as far as the weather was concerned. Being mostly interested in the land this pleased them, the more so when they thought of the desert around them at this time. So, by and large, Christmas found them in a mood which approached as nearly as possible to the cheer which is associated with that season.

The fleshpots of Egypt were combed to provide suitable fare, and the war did not seem to have any appreciable effect upon those proverbial fleshpots. The officers, following the usual custom, served the men with as good a Christmas dinner as they had tasted since they left Wiltshire.

Then, in the evening, there was a concert in the Sergeants' Mess which the officers, as usual, attended. There, within the same old tent, the atmosphere was exactly as it had been for the past twenty-five years. Those members of the mess who had been drafted into the Regiment since the war were now almost indistinguishable from the original Wiltshiremen. Indeed, those regular cavalry reservists who had joined just three years previously were loudly proclaiming themselves to be yeomen. And so they were, in spirit.

Precisely the same old show was given, run in the traditional way, with the usual surprising amount of talent. Now, who ever thought that " forty centuries would look down " upon a Royal Wilts Sergeants' Mess " Do " ?

Part Three

For the remainder of this book the author is indebted to those of his brother officers who contributed the end of the story, almost exactly as it stands. To them he offers his sincere thanks for their assistance.

CHAPTER TWENTY-THREE

INTERLUDE

WHILE General Alexander's forces were sweeping westwards and General Eisenhower's armies were advancing to the east, the Royal Wilts cursed the luck that had put them out of the hunt. Instead of fighting on with the Eighth Army, they had to content themselves with travelling back along that now well-known road across the Sinai Desert. Asluj, Tulkarem and Damascus were passed and finally a stop was made once more at Aleppo. Here their job was internal security and to prevent smuggling on the Turkish Frontier.

Unlike their previous stay, when they had encamped in the olive groves, this time they were slightly more fortunate in being stationed on an unfinished French aerodrome. The cold was intense, with biting winds sweeping straight down from the Taurus Mountains.

The first few weeks were spent settling in and waiting for the arrival of training tanks and reinforcements to replace the Alamein casualties. Towards the end of January a Squadron of the Royal Gloucester Hussars (which had been disbanded) arrived to make up the numbers, and also a few very old Crusaders, Grants and Shermans. The 2nd R.G.H., being a regiment of the adjoining county, very soon settled down and became complete 'moonrakers.'

A period of intensive training now commenced, and to show how intensive it was it is worthwhile repeating a favourite saying of the Brigadier's : " There are only twenty-four hours in a day and seven days in a week ; it is not enough." So the Royal Wilts got down to it in earnest, their days being full of troop training, squadron training, firing on the ranges, map reading, T.E.W.T.'s, etc. But, in spite of the unending hard work, a certain amount of levity crept into some of the orders and letters exchanged between Squadron Leaders and the adjutant. Here are two examples :—

" To R.H.Q.

From O.C. ' C ' Squadron.

Reference your letter 191 of 9th Jan., 1943. The maintenance of slit trenches has become extremely difficult owing to climatic conditions whereby all water from the roads seems to find its way into them. This situation is being aggravated by the organised sabotage of the natives, who are digging drains from the roads into the trenches. All the walls of the trenches have collapsed and are at the moment impassable. It is considered that, in the event of an air raid, more casualties will occur from drowning than by enemy action. Can any assistance be given to end such a deplorable situation ?

? ? ? ?
O.C. ' C ' Squadron."

" To O.C. ' C ' Squadron.
>Your dismal note of even date
>we feel has reached us somewhat late.
>Indeed it causes us much pain
>to know we cannot stop the rain.
>The damage which has now been done
>must wait until we get some sun,
>and so we hope that we shall see
>the grit that made you ' Fighting C '."

On the 19th March a march past of the whole division took place in Aleppo in honour of a visiting Turkish General. The regiment managed to scrape up twenty-six assorted tanks and, after a lot of spit and polish, these sallied forth to the rendezvous. The march past went smoothly until the Colonel's tank, on turning a corner just short of the saluting base, found the road almost blocked by two Crusaders (of another regiment) with broken tracks. Through the skill of the driver a further mishap was averted and the tanks passed with only inches to spare on either side.

The training continued in this vein until the 27th April when the whole of 10th Armoured Division moved out of Aleppo to a place called Dibsi, on the banks of the Euphrates, for Regimental, Brigade and Divisional training. This continued till 31st May, when the 7th Armoured Brigade took the 9th's place in the Division and the Royal Wilts moved south for special training.

At the end of the Divisional Training at Dibsi, three officers and fifty-three other ranks left the Regiment for special duty. This later transpired to be a Beach Maintenance Party which took part in the Salerno landing in Italy. There they did excellent work in clearing the beaches and unloading supplies under intense shell fire. Luckily the majority were able to rejoin the Regiment after their job was finished.

The old Crusaders were handed over to the 7th Hussars, and the few Shermans and Grants, creaking and groaning, set off under their own steam for Baalbeck. The journey south caused a certain amount of excitement for some of the crews, as the route rook them by way of Palmyra and El Qariateine, but, except for a few minor breakdowns, the trek was uneventful and all the tanks arrived safely at their destination.

On the 8th June, after two days at Baalbeck, the Regiment moved on to Tripoli (Syria) while the rest of the Brigade moved further south. At Tripoli the hardest work fell on " B " Squadron, who were busy converting themselves from Crusader to Sherman Tanks, while " A " and " C " Squadrons were experimenting at the School of Mountain Warfare which was situated next door. At the same time all the Echelon vehicles went through a course of what is known as " Dry Shod Training," which consisted of driving vehicles on and off sham landing craft made out of bits of tin and white tape. This amused the 'moonrakers' quite a lot and once, when a lorry backed through the side of the imaginary ship, the driver leaped out and, yelling " Watch oi doive," jumped over the side and started swimming in the sand.

At this time the 234th British Infantry Brigade were attached to the Regiment for training and future operations. This ' Brigade ' had only just arrived in the M.E.F., having spent several years fighting the Luftwaffe in Malta and, at first, they found the steep mountain slopes rather fatiguing, having been on short rations for so long. This training, which consisted of driving down the Lebanon mountain roads at night in the pitch dark with no lights, proved to be very useful to the Regiment in later operations in Italy.

Having completed their mountain schooling, the next stage was further " Dry Shod " training on a larger scale. On the 21st July the Regiment moved to Afula, in Palestine, for a fortnight, where full-scale landing operations were carried out thirty miles from the sea. The briny atmosphere created by the Army so far from the Mediterranean was remarkable, and the night schemes that the Regiment took part in gave all ranks a good impression of an actual landing—until first light showed that the water edge was only a bit of white tape !

On the 5th August they moved down with the Infantry Brigade to Kabrit, which is on the shores of the Great Bitter Lake in Egypt, for their first " Wet Shod Training " ; but unfortunately all the Tank Landing Craft (real this time !) had been removed for the Salerno Landing in Italy, so, once again, the Royal Wilts had to be content with make-believe. In the meantime the rest of the 9th Armoured Brigade had completed their combined operation training and were back in Palestine, now fully equipped with new tanks and waiting to embark. In fact the Warwickshire Yeomanry had already embarked, and it looked as if the Royal Wilts were going to be left behind. As it turned out it was to be several more months before the 9th Armoured Brigade were to fight the Huns again, and in the meanwhile a lot of tact and diplomacy was to be required of them in some delicate situations with our Allies.

The Royal Wilts rejoined the Brigade at Pardess Hanna, in Palestine, on 23rd August, and on 9th September the new Sherman tanks arrived. There followed several hectic weeks of shooting in the guns, running in the engines, and putting right a hundred and one small " teething troubles." All this was done amid a spate of rumours. The Warwicks were embarking ; no, they were not ; the 3rd Hussars were ; then it was the Wilts ; then the Warwicks again ; and so on. Finally the Infantry Brigade embarked minus their armour for that ill-fated operation in the Dodecanese Islands at Cos and Leros, which resulted in most of them being put in the bag.

It is worth while reflecting for a moment on what would have been the outcome of that operation if the ships had been available to transport the armour as well. In the first case the Island of Rhodes, with its airfields and bases, was to have been included in the islands to be seized, and it is quite possible that with a big island like that as a base, the rest of the Dodecanese Islands might have been captured one by one. As it was the 9th Armoured Brigade could only sympathise with the Infantry who for so long had been shut up in Malta and then, after such a short respite, were to be obliterated in their first land action.

On the 6th October, while the Regiment was still at Pardess Hanna, news was received of the Italian capitulation, which occasioned a certain amount of celebration. The officers were quietly having their dinner when a sudden crash and the noise of tearing canvas heralded the arrival of the Warwickshire Yeomanry, in a jeep, in the middle of the ante-room tent. It was not long before, amidst the bangs of practice grenades and showers of Verey lights, the 3rd Hussars, led by their Colonel, made a flank attack on the bar. Unfortunately, one of the practice grenades fell rather short and put the C.O. of the 3rd Hussars out of action, with bakelite splinters in his neck and legs. He also found it rather painful to sit down. By this time the 1st R.H.A. had also joined in and a general mêlée ensued, lasting till the early hours of the morning. The following day it was reported that the 3rd Hussars and 1st R.H.A., on their way back to bed, swept through Brigade H.Q. like a hurricane and left nothing standing. The firing of the Verey lights also caused a certain amount of excitement at Area H.Q. in Haifa, where they were taken to be a signal that enemy parachute troops were landing.

On Sunday, the 24th October, there was a Brigade Church Parade to commemorate the battle of El Alamein. Brigadier Roddick, D.S.O., received the following message from General Sir Bernard Freyberg, V.C., K.C.B., C.I.A.G., D.S.O. :—

"Personal for Commander from General Freyberg with memories of our happy association. All ranks 2 N.Z. Division send congratulations and best wishes on anniversary of Alamein. We shall never forget your magnificent and decisive attack which broke enemy's guns and line on 2nd November."

At the end of October, 1943, the Commanding Officers of the Royal Wiltshire Yeomanry and the 3rd King's Own Hussars were returning in a jeep from a Brigade Conference. It was dark, and just before dinner time. Their arrival at the 3rd Hussars Mess was heralded by an unprecedented and metallic crash as the jeep ran into the swill tubs outside the cookhouse. It was obvious that the occupants of the jeep were in a state of unusual elation. Anxious seconds-in-command hurried to their colonels to ask what the cause might be, to be told afterwards, as a great secret that the Brigade was on priority to go to Italy as soon as possible.

This was the gist of the talk given a few days later by the G.O.C. 3rd Corps, Lt.-Gen. Sir Desmond Anderson, when he addressed Squadron Leaders after the march past of the 9th Armoured Brigade with all its armoured vehicles and guns. But it was not yet to be. On the 15th November the Brigade, less 1 R.H.A. who had been removed from them and sent to 10th Armoured Division in Egypt, were suddenly moved to the Lebanon where the growing crisis between the French and the Lebanese Governments made the presence of a strong British force imperative to guard lines of communications and essential bases such as the Tripoli Pipe Line, the Beirut Docks, etc.

So once again the Regiment found itself at Tripoli (Syria) in the same camp as before, amongst the olive groves. But whereas last time the sun was almost unbearably hot, now the rain came down with monotonous regularity.

The moment the Lebanese trouble was over the Brigadier allowed the Regiment a slight amount of relaxation so as to compensate them for the disappointment they had suffered in being out of action for so long. Weekends were allowed and a number of men went away to Beirut from Saturday till Sunday. Also, excursions were arranged to the Cedars and to the Crak des Chevaliers, and, for the officers, expeditions to the lakes of Idlib and Homs for duck and snipe shooting. The following chapter, written by the author at the time, may give an impression of the atmosphere on such occasions.

At this time the 7th Battalion The Rifle Brigade, were attached as the motor battalion of the 9th Armoured and the Warwickshire Yeomanry were moved to Suez to train with them. The Royal Wilts and the 3rd King's Own Hussars remained in the Lebanon till the 1st March when they were ordered to concentrate at Burg-el-Arab, forty miles west of Alexandria. It was now obvious to all that the next move would entail a sea voyage. Alexandria being then the principal port of embarkation in the Middle East, troops and vehicles could be seen entering the dock gates daily. Many thought that this was the beginning of the journey back to England—"After all, the Regiment had been abroad for over four years; why not send them home, give all the men leave, and then let them have a crack at the second front?" But when they did embark, towards the end of April, there were very few who really thought that they were going home; it seemed very clear by then that Italy was the destination.

During our stay at Burg-el-Arab, conducted tours were organised to the Alamein battlefields; this proved of great interest to all those who had fought there. Tremendous arguments ensued as to where the start line was and where such and such a squadron was, but in the end, although this was a year and a half after the battle, the whole engagement could be visualised by the location of the spot where the

THE MAJESTY OF THE CRUSADERS' CRAK DES CHEVALIERS.

C.O.'s tank had been. This was done by the finding of the driver's greatcoat and the side door of the tank, which had been shot off its hinges at the time.

* * * * * *

Even while preparing to embark at Alexandria, the Royal Wilts had one further job to do in the Middle East. A political disturbance occurred in the Greek Brigade at Burg-el-Arab, which was due to embark for Italy before the 9th Armoured Brigade. This necessitated a considerable reorganisation. The Greeks forfeited their chance of going to Italy, and their place was taken by 9th Brigade, which not only had to put forward their own move but were called in to help restore order at the same time.

CHAPTER TWENTY-FOUR

BOXING DAY IN THE LEBANON *

HAVING been separated from my regiment for a long time as a Staff Officer I was lucky enough, on one occasion, to be able to spend my Christmas with them. They were camped in the Lebanon at the time, and we had heard that woodcock had been seen in the pine forests below the snow belt on the mountains. So, having the whole of Boxing Day to ourselves, we set out to see whether or not the report was true. Of the four of us, I was the only one who showed any outward visible signs of warlike intent because, although as a visitor I had borrowed a very fine tweed coat and a shot-gun, I was unable to find a cap and had, in consequence, to wear my Army " headdress." As for the others, they might have been out for a day's rough shooting anywhere at home.

To begin with, our journey took us along the coast road which so resembles that one in the South of France which many of us used to visit in peace-time. The sea was dead calm in the sunshine, and the reflection of the clear sky gave it that deeper shade of Mediterranean blue which turns almost to a cobalt on the coast of the Lebanon. It had turned out to be a glorious day and, as our eyes took in the country from the sea to the snow-capped peaks of the neatly terraced and cultivated mountains inland, we reflected that, in peace-time, the lucky few who could afford it would have paid much good money to come and visit such glorious scenery. Yet we were here against our will, because there was a war on, and longing to get home and away from it all as soon as possible.

But this was Christmas time and, for the moment, we were at peace and prepared to enjoy whatever sport the gods might send, with the proper and seasonable good-will. We were, in fact, full of good-will as we drove along that coast road, and it should be added that this good-will had largely to do with the festivities which had taken place the night before. It would be unfair to call it a hangover, but . . . well, we were in good spirits.

The first sample of sport which the gods had in store for us turned out, in actual fact, to be a little fishing. We did not fish ourselves, but we were able to watch other people fishing and a very pleasant occupation it was, as we stopped to look on

---

* This chapter was written by the author at the time. It is included in the hope that it may give some idea of the Lebanese countryside.

in the warm sunshine of the beach. Fishing is always a leisurely pursuit, and the Arab fishermen who ply their nets on these shores have reduced that aspect of it to a fine art. Over the centuries they have evolved a technique which requires the ultimate minimum of exertion to pull in the net from the sea and to land the catch on the beach. Quite possibly, this particular technique had already been perfected before the Roman Empire was thought of, and is still in use without having changed at all. What happens, quite briefly, is this. The net is put out from the boat and, when time has allowed for the fish to congregate within its orbit, it is gently brought inshore, and a long rope from each end is passed to the men whose job it is to pull it out of the sea. Each of those men is provided with a piece of rope which is looped round his waist, with about three foot to spare and a good stout knot on the loose end. When the rope from the net has been put ashore, they line up tug-o'-war fashion and each man attaches himself by means of the rope round his waist.

This attachment of each man's original rope to the main landing rope is very neat. It is done in one motion by hitching the knot round the main rope, in a single turn, so that the individual rope presses on the knot, gives it a grip, and prevents it from slipping along the wet rope which pulls in the net. But this is where the labour saving comes in. They all " take the strain " against the net as it tends gently to be washed away from the shore. Then, having " held it " by leaning on the ropes round their waists, they walk back a pace or two as the next wave reverses the motion of the net and washes it towards the shore. Then they " hold it " again as the wave goes out once more, and so gain a few paces with each successive wave Thus, by the simple expedient of leaning on the rope, they let their own weight and the sea do all the work that is necessary. As it is brought in, the main rope is coiled up and each time the rear man reaches the coil he unhitches, leap-frogs up to the front of the line and hitches on again.

So it goes on until somebody is required to go into the sea, guide the net on to the beach and unload the catch. On this particular occasion the two fishermen of the most authoritative appearance took on this job. Stripping off their clothes, and bashfully attempting to cover their nakedness with the palms of their hands, they dashed into the sea as the nets neared the shore, and an atmosphere of excited expectancy became apparent. This must always be a big moment for men who fish with nets, and we ourselves were filled with interested speculation. What would the catch be? Many or few? Would there be a lot of big fish—or even, possibly, a relic of the war? For, in spite of these peaceful surroundings and pursuits, battles were still raging just across the horizon! Enemy submarines might even now be quite close at hand.

The catch, in fact, was quite a good one and distinctly varied. A few " loups de mer," some soles, crabs, hefty-looking prawns that were almost big enough to be baby lobsters, hundreds of small fish, and quite a lot of weird looking squids, of the small octopus type, the latter being obviously infuriated at being removed from their native element. They puffed, blew, and made rude noises, until one of them, in its indignation, was delivered orally of a fish, nearly as big as itself, which it had recently swallowed. I suppose the chief value of their catch lay in the small fish which looked like an assortment of different types of sardines and were probably for local consumption. Just possibly, the small number of bigger fish and prawns would bring the highest profit from the market in Beirut, however. Judging by the price of the latter in the French officers' club in that city, one prawn would have been worth the whole of the rest of the catch put together. But doubtless the actual fishermen see little of the final amount for which these delicious " crustacés " are sold.

The sea-fishing episode being over, we struck inland up one of those typical Lebanese roads through the foothills, on our way to the pine forests which showed as a dark green band below the snow on the distant ridge. The scenery from these roads, as they wind through tiny villages with prosperous looking inhabitants, is unbelievably beautiful. The scores of turns and hairpin bends, as they climb slowly up, show innumerable different facets of the contrast between the Alpine effect of the snow-capped mountains and the Mediterranean scene along the blue fringed coast below.

Originally such roads were nothing much more than tracks to feed the tiny villages, but the Turks improved many of them for strategic purposes and the villages grew proportionately. Now you will find quite a handsome church in most of them (because a very large number of their inhabitants are Christian), to say nothing of some quite sizeable houses. Since the war our troops have also improved many of these roads and we learnt afterwards that the one along which we drove on that occasion had recently been repaired, at very great expense, in order to bring down timber from the forest. Very costly timber, no doubt, but then money seems to mean nothing in war-time, although the villagers must be very grateful for the stroke of luck which has befallen them.

So on we drove, negotiating the most hair-raising corners and ravines, as we gradually rose towards the range of mountains with its brilliant white ridge, which gradually gave place to a powdery effect as the snow thinned out on the lower slopes, like sprinkled sugar below the icing on a rich reddy-brown chocolate cake. Below, in the valleys, was a patchwork of tiny fields of all shapes and sizes, like a jig-saw puzzle. Each of those fields was levelled off and encircled with a small stone wall, so that the general effect was one of terraced neatness, stretching from the fairly wide bottoms of valleys, right up the sides of the foothills until they became too steep to cultivate, even with the aid of terraces. It is very hard, at times, to tell which of these terraces has been caused by the outcrop of natural rock strata and which has been built by the hand of man. In some cases man has even taken advantage of the natural formation and improved upon it. Whatever their origin, these terraces add considerably to the charm of the scenery. We thought, also, what fun it would be to have a gallop right down one of those " vales," leaping a succession of stone walls, with a considerable drop on the far side of each. In an ambitious mood one might even have attempted it the other way on!

Soon, as we neared the top, we realised from the lie of the country, that we were likely to have a distant view of the Crak des Chevaliers—that magnificent specimen of a Crusader castle, which still stands in a quite extraordinary state of preservation, on a bluff about 2,000 feet high, giving the impression of a rugged but still very powerful sentinel, posted to guard the broad plain of Homs which lies below it. It remained hidden from us, however, till we had nearly reached the fir trees where we hoped to find a woodcock.

And so we climbed on until, at about 5,000 feet, we reached a small plateau which commanded a splendid view. Here we sat down for quite a while and contemplated the country spread out below. What a marvellous site for a house it would make! Slightly behind us and over our right shoulders, the ridge of snow gleamed almost incandescent in the sunshine in colourful contrast to the pastel blue of the Lake of Homs, which lay below it about twenty miles away. Our thoughts turned to the wonderful duck shooting to be had in that large stretch of water, as our gaze swept slowly to the left and took in the distant hills away on the other side of the plain. Behind their smoky purple silhouette lay Turkey and it is said that, on very clear days, Cassius, near Antioch, can be seen from the spot upon which we were sitting.

Closer to us, and a little more to our left, a ridge of hills ran out from the distant range to form a peninsula in the plain. There, on a dominiating spur of these hills, lay the great mass of the Crak des Chevaliers. From where we sat it appeared as a grey speck upon the side of the basin of hills, like a pearl in the colourful shell of a vast oyster. Viewed thus, it was easy to realise why this fortress came into being on such a spot. The lush pastures and rich land to this fertile plain must have well repaid those men of old for the fifty odd years of toil they spent in piling up its magnificence. In their heyday the lot of the Crusaders must have been a very pleasant one in this prosperous country, with its abundance of native labour and rich natural resources. Their lives must have contrasted strongly with those of their compatriots left behind in Europe, especially during the winter!

As we gazed at this distant castle, I formed a mental picture of those gallant knights of ancient times, clanking down the zig-zag path to go about their business in the plain. Lords of all they surveyed, they were, their armour flashing messages of defiance in the sunlight and well-bred Arab horse-flesh between their knees. There were ladies in their train as well, the fine silks of Damascus flowing from their high-pointed hats. It is possible that some of those Christian gentlemen, in possession of all that this country had to offer, may, at any rate upon occasion, have lost sight of the original object of their Crusade, the wresting of the Holy Grail from the hands of the unbelievers!

To finish off this panorama, on our extreme left, as far as the eye could see, the broad sweep of the Mediterranean drew from the sky a wealth of that shade of blue to which it has given its name. For many minutes we sat and contemplated this very pleasant country. Then we had lunch.

After lunch the question of woodcock arose. For, after all, that had been the real object of our visit! So we decided to follow the road up a little further to where it seemed to lead into the belt of fir trees below the snow line. This we did until, topping a rise, we found ourselves in a veritable enchanted glade.

At first this place quite took away our breath. Apart from its beauty, it was so very different from anything else we had come across in the Middle East. Its shape was that of a flat-bottomed bowl with fir trees round the sides and grass growing in the centre, where cattle quietly grazed. It looked, as a matter of fact, exactly like a piece of Scotland. We had *seen* other places with almost the same similarity—on parts of Mount Carmel, in Palestine, for instance. But usually, when the Middle East looks like home, it somehow doesn't *feel* the same. But this place was different. It did feel like Scotland. The air happened to be absolutely calm and you could hear many familiar noises from the hushed woods. The flutter of a bird disturbed, the echoing call of another, and the crunching of dried twigs on moss as one of our party ventured under the trees. There was a nip in the air, too, and a film of ice across the puddles. No hunting tomorrow, we thought. Still too much "bone" in the ground!

Looking more closely beneath the silver firs and occasional walnut trees, we discovered lots of old friends. Primroses were there and violets, but not just yet in bloom. We also found wild sage and cyclamen and anemones, the last in great profusion. At some time of the year, we were not quite certain which, this place must be a blaze of colour. Juniper bushes also suggested vaguely the possibilities of local gin! But the woodcock must not be forgotten and there was work to be done, so we lined up and began to walk the woods. Lovely going, it was, soft and spongy, with all those fascinating things which drop off fir trees. There were places where a man might lie upon his stomach and find all sort of treasures in a single square foot of ground beneath his nose.

Instinctively we began to make all those well remembered noises which are the language of men beating birds out of woods. Our "ho, ho, ho's" and the tapping of trees with sticks echoed hollowly as we slowly made our way, the now unfamiliar feel of a gun in our hands calling up a host of happy memories. Then "woodcock over" rang out, bang went a gun, and a voice said "I think I got him." Silence for a few moments as we all held hard, and then the snapping of twigs as the lucky gun went to pick up his bird. He *had* got him, too, but although we put up a dozen or so more nobody else managed to bring one down.

So, as we made our way once more down the long winding road to the sea, we did not talk so much as we had done on the way going up. Each one had his thoughts and there seemed, somehow, to be less appeal in the showy beauty of the Mediterranean scene. It was as though part of each of us had been left amidst those fir trees up on the mountain where, for a little while, we had recaptured many of the intangible things which were once so very dear to us.

It had, indeed, been a very pleasant Boxing Day.

Part Four

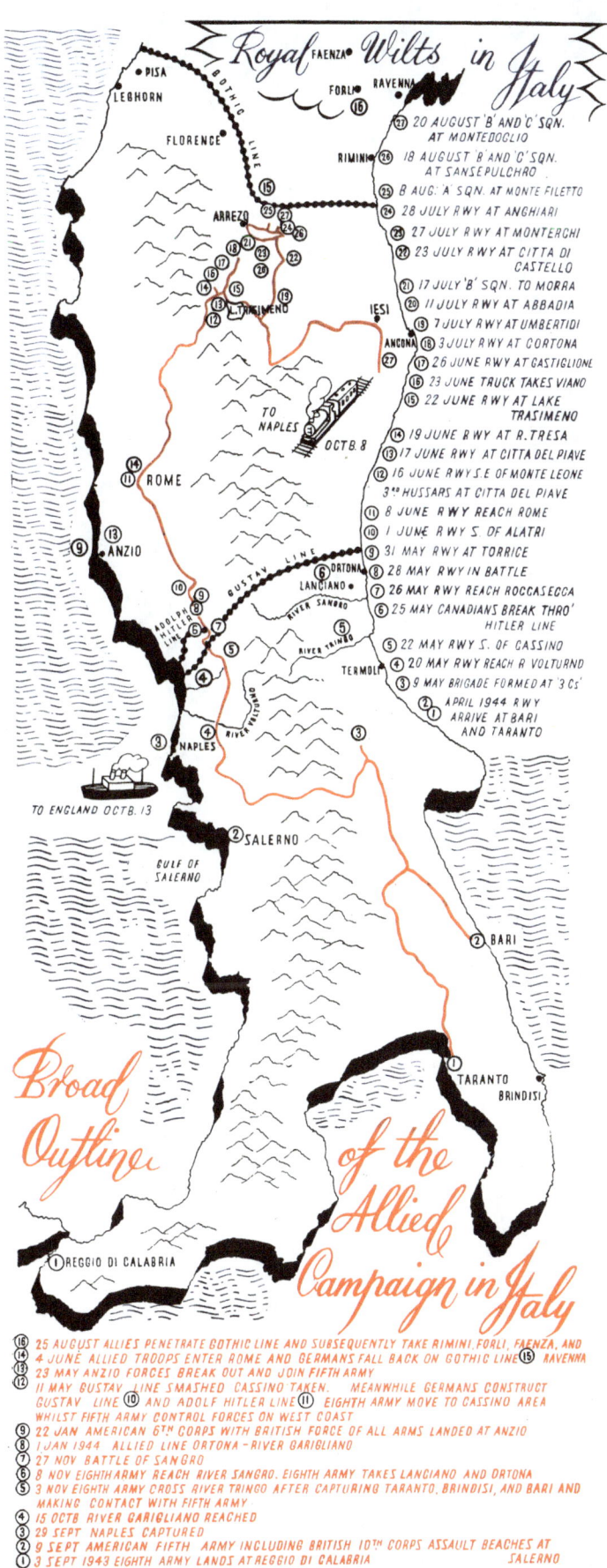

CHAPTER TWENTY-FIVE

ARRIVAL IN ITALY

WHEN, at long last, the Regiment really knew that they were off on another campaign, their feelings could be compared to those of any regiment which had been training all the war in England, but with one big difference. Practically every man in the Royal Wilts knew what campaigning was like and knew what they were in for. After so many months of waiting and disappointments, here at last was their opportunity. They were trained to as near perfection as possible and, besides, they had had their tanks long enough to know their character. A tank, when you get to know it, acquires a sort of soul of its own, very much like a horse, and it is true to say that the crews become genuinely fond of their own vehicles.

Thus it was that, with a spirit of adventure and feelings of anticipation, the tanks, lorries, scout cars, trucks and jeeps streamed into Alexandria Docks to be loaded on to their respective ships. The usual secrecy was exercised, no cap badges, all vehicle signs covered over, and no word of the impending move allowed to be uttered. With a carelessness typical of the Middle East the names of the tanks were ordered to be left uncovered. Therefore, any observer standing by the dock gates could see familiar names such as Trowbridge, Salisbury, Devizes, Swindon, etc., rumbling past and advertising to all the world that an armoured regiment from Wiltshire was embarking along with the rest of its Brigade. It would not require much intelligence to spot that the 9th Armoured Brigade was leaving the Middle East, and, as no other destination was then open other than Italy, the picture was complete.

The Regiment, when it sailed for Italy, was officered as follows:—

Commanding Officer	Lieutenant-Colonel A. M. Gibb
Second-in-Command	Major The Earl Cadogan, M.C.
Adjutant	Captain C. R. Thursfield.
Technical Adjutant	Captain R. S. Walker.
Headquarters Squadron	Major C. E. Awdry.
"A" *Squadron*	Major H. G. Awdry.
"B" *Squadron*	Major S. V. Christie-Miller.
"C" *Squadron*	Major Hon. A. E. G. Herbert

The journey was without incident. The various convoys sailed for their respective destinations, all arriving safely except one ship which was late owing to engine trouble and which came on afterwards. Most of the tanks went to Bari on the east coast of Italy, while the remainder, with the men and the " B " vehicles, went to Taranto in the very south.

Here perhaps is the moment to give a brief outline of what was happening in Italy at the time, and to describe something of the country. The date of arrival was the last week in April, 1944. All the winter the armies in Italy had been more or less static, on a line running across the country, with Cassino as its centre.

The Italian winter is a beastly thing, keeping all traffic to the main roads, and therefore confining all attacks to the neighbourhood of those same roads. All rivers, of which there are a great many, are flooded and cross country going is virtually impossible.

The bridgehead which had been captured at Anzio was being hard pressed, and, instead of making Kesselring pull back behind Rome, had not even succeeded in cutting Route 6.

Thus it was, with the coming of spring, a big offensive was being prepared to continue the advance up the leg of Italy, and to contain as many German troops as possible, thereby drawing them off the Russian Front and the proposed invasion Front in Northern Europe.

To describe the country and the people, imagine an old stocking which has been in wear for many weeks without a wash. The foot is completely rotten and useless, the leg is bespattered with filth, while the top is reasonably sound. This was how Italy was in April, 1944. It came as a great shock to discover that the Italians, living in one of the most fertile of countries, were so many years behind the rest of Europe in standards of prosperity.

The towns and ports, such as the two at which the Regiment landed, were unbelievably squalid. All normal amenities had ceased to function and the morale of the people themselves was so low that they appeared quite unable to do anything to help themselves.

In the villages which, in a great many instances, had escaped the war, conditions were so primitive that you realised at once why they were built on hills. Sanitation was non-existent and hygiene depended entirely on the rain storms to wash all the refuse down the hills into the valleys below.

Providing you keep away from the towns, the scenery in Southern Italy is very picturesque, being undulating country with pretty little farms, villages and vineyards everywhere. The vines grow on wires stretched between poles six to eight feet high, while underneath crops were just beginning to show. The picture from a distance was one of orderly husbandry, but on closer inspection of the inhabitants and their homes it is an apt description to say, as the troops did, that they were " worse than the Wogs." So much for a brief sketch of Italy as the Royal Wilts found it on arrival.

To return to the narrative. The regiment found itself divided between Bari and Taranto by a distance of seventy miles. These two ports are very much alike in that they resemble miniature and rather more revolting editions of Marseilles. The only life in either place, as in all other Italian towns at that time, was the odd cinemas and the Opera which the army had got going.

The only commodity in plentiful supply was " Vino." Long ago any good wine had been drunk by the Germans, and later by the British and Americans. " Vino," as a name, covers a multitude of sins. It varies from a dirty greenish colour, through all shades of yellow to golden brown, from the deepest red to the palest insipid pink, and is a raw beverage bound to give the consumer an acid stomach and a head the next day.

While the unloading process went on, and the senior officers dashed backwards and forwards between the two places, everyone learnt, if nothing else, that " Vino " is not a thing to be trifled with and that only the very best is fit for human consumption.

The next job was to marry up the two parts of the Brigade. For this the rendezvous was a place known as the ' Three C's ' not far from the important air bases at Foggia and Lucera. The ' Three C's ' derived its name from three nearby villages all commencing with the letter C. Thither an advance party was despatched and found their area to be in an oak wood with a stream running through it and surrounded by green fields. The only other inhabitants were the nightingales, who sang beautifully at night. When the rest of the regiment arrived by train, transporters and by road, they continued to sing each night as though they welcomed the intrusion and were doing their bit towards everyone's entertainment.

By the 9th May the whole Brigade had arrived, and every moment was spent cleaning up the tanks and preparing them for the battles to come. Even so, everyone had time for an occasional walk in the surrounding country, and of an evening little parties of Yeomen could be seen discussing the crops and methods of farming in Italy. Somehow the atmosphere here was slightly unreal. All that had been seen of war was a certain amount of damage in the towns, caused by our bombing, and the bridges blown by the retreating Germans.

The ' Three C's ' were in a little pocket, from which the Germans had withdrawn in the early stages of the campaign with hardly any fighting. It was well off any main road, so there were no signs of the endless supply dumps which follow up an advancing army. Here the Royal Wilts remained for a matter of ten days, enjoying weather like that of a perfect English June.

Some of the officers went up to the Sangro to be shown where the 4th Armoured Brigade had fought their way across this river, and to get a view of how other Brigades were operating. It was a curious feeling to be warned once again not to walk about on the skyline in case it attracted shelling. It made one realise that there really was a war being fought in Italy after all.

On 10th May the Brigadier called all officers to a conference at his H.Q. and informed them that General Sir Harold Alexander was launching his offensive at 23.00 hours the following night. He also read out the General's order of the day, the gist of which was that the honour of striking the first blow in the liberation of Europe had been bestowed upon the Armies under his command and that he intended to destroy the German Forces in Italy.

On the evening of the 19th May the tanks were loaded on to transporters and the whole party moved off to an area by the Volturno River. This was the first real stepping stone towards the battle. It took two days, and as they progressed more and more signs of war were to be seen.

Everyone seemed keyed up and the inevitable last minute rush was on. Equipment, ordered days before, as usual had not arrived. Ammunition had to be stowed and a hundred and one final preparations to be made.

The Brigadier called all officers and senior N.C.O.'s to a conference and outlined the position. Maps were issued and everyone was " put in the picture," with daily alterations to be marked up.

The exact task of the 9th Armoured Brigade was not yet absolutely cut and dried but it would, for the first phase, be in reserve, and was to be used for the pursuit when the line had been broken.

The front chosen for the attack was about thirty miles wide and can be divided into three sectors. On the right was Cassino, with Monastery Hill towering above it; in the centre was the five mile wide valley of the River Liri, through which passed Route 6 leading to Rome; and on the left flank was another mountain range, the Aurunci Mountains, sloping down to the sea.

The enemy had, in addition to controlling the heights on both flanks, built the Gustav Line on the Rapido River, and about seven miles further back another line, known as the Adolf Hitler Line.

The enemy forces in Italy at this time were estimated at about 25 divisions; ten, under Von Veitinghoff, were on the main front; nine, under Von Mackensen, were employed round the Anzio Beach Head; while a further six were in reserve in the north.

The allied assault, besides the primary aims as already stated in General Alexander's "Order of the Day," had two secondary tasks; the first was to break through the enemy's Liri Valley defences and advance up Route 6 to Frosinone and the second was to link up with our troops in the Anzio Beach Head.

In spite of heavy gunfire, a bridgehead was established across the Rapido and Garigliano rivers. Soon afterwards Polish troops, in an epic action, captured Monte Cassino on the right flank, while the British occupied the town itself. The Poles then took Monte Cairo (5,500 feet), which was the northern bastion of the Adolf Hitler Line. The capture of this dominant feature turned the strong frontal defences of Piedmontone and also resulted in the capture of the enemy's gun positions covering the Liri Valley from the East.

Meanwhile on the left flank French Moroccan Troops (the Goums), attacking in the Aurunci Mountains, captured Monte Majo, and, pressing gallantly on, worked their way right through the mountain range to the approximate line from Pontecorvo to Pico.

By May 25th the Canadians had burst through the Adolf Hitler Line north of Pontecorvo and had reached the line of the Melfa River, where they established a bridgehead at Ceprano.

The Royal Wilts' stay by the Volturno went in a flash. On the 22nd May they climbed on to their transporters for the last time and moved right up behind Cassino. There by the village of San Vittore the Brigade "toed the line," waiting for the "off."

It was particularly noticeable how a change had come over everyone. Grim determination had taken the place of the usual lightheartedness now that the sound of guns was our constant companion, and at night we were awakened by occasional air raids. Here once again was the real thing.

The Regiment sat on the flat plain in view of Cassino and Monastery Hill, which had been such a stumbling block, costing so many lives during the preceding months. Orders arrived almost at once. The Brigade was to support 78 Infantry Division, who had been fighting ever since the landings of the First Army in North Africa with hardly a rest. It would take over from the Canadians when the River Melfa was reached. Routes up through the almost completely obliterated village of San Angelo were reconnoitred, and then, on the afternoon of the 26th May, the Brigade moved forward to the Roccasecca cross-roads, which had only been taken that morning. Here the Guards Brigade could be seen fighting in the hills on the right and here was the "sharp end of the battle," for which everyone had been waiting for so many weary months.

CHAPTER TWENTY-SIX

78TH DIVISION—RIVER MELFA TO CORTONA

ALL was now set for a big push, for the crumbling process along the whole front was complete. The Germans were being hustled back. It was appreciated that if they could be kept on the run, and if the British could keep their supplies moving up fast enough, then the Germans' days in Italy were numbered.

The plan for the 78th Division and the 9th Armoured Brigade was briefly as follows :—The 78th Division would cross the Melfa River on the night of the 27th-28th May, with two Brigades up. Each Brigade would have an Armoured Regiment in support. 1st R.H.A. would be split up to form the usual Regimental groups; that is to say, the Royal Wiltshire Yeomanry would have E Battery, with whom they had always trained. The remainder of the Artillery would be under the Divisional Commander's control.

Their objectives were to drive north up Route 6, make contact with the Anzio Beach Head, and press onwards past Rome. It must be remembered that this northward drive was taking place along the whole breadth of Italy. Only the part played by the 9th Armoured Brigade, and those who worked with them, is included in this narrative.

All day was spent getting to know the Infantry. 36th Infantry Brigade, consisting of the 8th Argyll and Sutherland Highlanders, the 6th Royal West Kents and the 5th Buffs, were to be supported by the Royal Wilts. Therefore a squadron was married to each Battalion. Speed was considered vital, so the Armour would lead the Infantry throughout.

By studying the map the country to be traversed could be seen to be very bad for the tanks—vineyards and cultivation everywhere interspersed by woods. All villages and towns were, as usual, on top of hills, making them difficult to approach, and although Route 6 ran through a plain, it was far from flat. The Germans had mined all the roads and blown up all the bridges and culverts, thus forcing the Armour to keep, for the most part, to cross-country going.

The text-books would describe this as enclosed country in which Infantry should lead, but, as so often happens in battle, the text-book maxims were to be reversed. There was another reason for this reversal of policy besides the question of speed. 78th Division was a very tired division; they had suffered enormous casualties in the past and had recently received a large number of moderately trained reinforcements.

If it appears, as the campaign progresses, that the 9th Armoured Brigade did most of the work, then the reader must realise that it was the speed of the advance that kept the Armour in the lead. The Infantry had to take over the ground gained and overcome resistance in country which was impassable to tanks.

The 3rd Hussars with their Infantry Brigade moved across the river to the right of the road during the day. That night the Royal Wilts kicked off up the main road. They were to go through the Canadians' Bridgehead at Ceprano, with C Squadron in the lead. This proved very difficult; the Canadians were pulling westwards to get out of the way and the muddle in the outskirts of the town was terrific. However, this sorted itself out by the early hours of the 28th May, and in went the Yeomanry.

Progress was slow, the chief enemy being the bad going. The Infantry Brigadier pushed up his other Battalions and the whole party had fanned out beyond Ceprano by the afternoon. For the Royal Wilts this was a nightmare drive; tanks were getting bogged or going up on mines right and left. Troop Leaders were reporting enemy self-propelled guns and tanks, which they could not engage as their own guns were buried in a tangled mass of vines and wire. So blind was the country that one tank even drove over the edge into a quarry, while several others were lying on their sides.

In the late afternoon the Infantry, with tanks in support, managed to seize a small hill; this annoyed the Germans considerably, for it was not long before hell was let loose and it seemed that every enemy gun and mortar in Italy was directed against this small place. It went on for almost an hour, but, when the dust of exploding shells had blown away, it was found that the casualties were very small and that the Infantry and Tanks were still in possession of the hill.

As night fell about half the Regiment was collected together north of Ceprano and the rest remained in their forward positions while the Infantry consolidated. The next four days saw the same thing continuing, with one big difference—the whole Regiment was up all the time. Sleep was almost unknown. The technical Adjutant and the Light Aid Detachment were working like demons, recovering and mending tanks, which rushed on to catch their squadrons. Ammunition and fuel could only be got up in the Honeys of the Reconnaissance troop at night, and at times even these necessities could not reach them.

It was a very battered and tired Regiment which reached Torrice on the morning of the 31st May, when the Infantry entered the town. On the next ridge resistance had stiffened somewhat; the 1st German Paratroop Division were trying to hold up the advance. They fought in little groups with fanatical determination until completely surrounded, depending on the darkness to get back to their next position. As dusk fell on the night of the 31st May the Regiment, such as it was, was scattered round Torrice. If it didn't get a breathing space soon it was in danger of becoming completely exhausted!

However, the orders were to push on, so first light on Thursday, the 1st of June, saw the Royal Wiltshire Yeomanry through Torrice heading North-East. The Warwicks, who had been in reserve until now, came up to take over, and visions of a slight rest hove in sight. This respite was still not to be. Frosinone, on the main line of advance, had been taken by the Canadians: 36th Brigade were to push on to Alatri with their reserve Battalion and, of course, they must have some Armour to help them.

At mid-day a conference was held at the Torrice Cross-Roads, and it was discovered that all that the Royal Wilts could raise was a composite Squadron. At ten minutes' notice this Squadron was formed, tank crews from different Squadrons being thrown together to form Troops under other Troop Leaders. The Brigadier even lent his own Honey to this strange conglomeration.

The infantry were supposed to have already started from beyond Frosinone, so off the Composite Squadron dashed, netting its sets and sorting out its maps as it went. On arriving at the rendezvous it was discovered that the Infantry, luckily, were not moving for an hour or two; the Yeomen therefore had a rest and a " brew up," one of the first proper meals it had had since leaving the Melfa River. At 16.00 hours they moved off, all going well until two fighters of the R.A.F. chose to strafe them by mistake. This caused some disorganisation of the Infantry.

The Germans were definitely trying to pull out. This was proved by the leading Troop, which, having passed through the German rearguard, came round a corner to find a huge German lorry being loaded up at a cross-road—no doubt some German Quarter-Master trying to get away with what equipment he could. The gunner in the leading tank didn't wait for any command; he just trod on the switch of his 75 mm., scoring a direct hit in the back of the lorry, and that was that. By this time it was getting dark and the tanks were two miles forward on their own; it was too late for the Infantry to come up to them, so the Divisional Commander ordered the Squadron back. It was nearly midnight before they got into leaguer, so from then until dawn had to be spent in refilling with fuel and ammunition.

By first light a half Squadron was on the move again, and by ten o'clock the remainder were under way. A conference was held, and, as the opposition was firm, the Infantry was ordered to by-pass Alatri, while the Armour was to try to dash through the town itself. To the meanest intellect this was not a good plan for the Armour, but it was the only way.

Alatri was on top of a particularly steep hill; the bridges approaching it were known to be blown and the going on either flank was impassable to tanks. When the Squadron reached the foot of the hill they were greeted by a veritable shower of mortar bombs, the enemy having got the road absolutely taped. The leading tank tried to get over a dried-up river bed, but lost a track on the bank. The third tank received a direct hit in the turret with a mortar bomb, as did a Honey belonging to the Sappers; both burst into flames. It was some time before the confusion could be sorted out and suitable positions found from which supporting fire could be directed. By the afternoon a way had been dug across the river bed and the Squadron started to climb up the zig-zag road into Alatri itself. Two more tanks were lost before the Squadron was recalled from the far side of the town, from which the enemy had retreated, leaving behind them the usual complement of booby traps and snipers.

That night the Regiment was collected together South of Alatri, in a completely exhausted condition, and were told to stay where they were for at least three days. Italy was the worst possible place for offensive war—Tank Column, Royal Wiltshire Yeomanry, began to realise this in time.

Now a dreadful shock awaited the Wiltshire Yeomen. That night it was learnt that the Colonel, Lt.-Colonel A. M. Gibb, had to return home to England. Lt.-Colonel Gibb had commanded the Regiment since taking it over at Alamein; he had built it up and made it what it was. There was not a single man who was not deeply disappointed that he should have to leave at this juncture. On Saturday, the 3rd June, Lt.-Colonel S. L. Lloyd, who had been second-in-command of the 3rd Hussars, took over; he was no stranger, and most people in the Regiment knew him well.

The battle now had switched back to Route 6, the Germans really were on the run, and the Royal Wilts looked like being left behind. By the 4th June the Americans had joined up with the Anzio Beach Head and Rome was evacuated by the Germans. The early hours of the 8th June found the Royal Wilts passing through the outskirts of the capital hard on the heels of the 3rd Hussars and Warwicks, who were fighting their way northwards.

The country here was rather more open and progress was speeded up. Prisoners were being taken in ever-increasing numbers and stragglers were constantly being picked up. Castlenuovo, Fabrica di Roma, Viterbo and Ficulle were halting places. Each day the Regiment expected to go into the lead again, but the pace was so hot that it was not until 16th June that they saw another action.

" B " Squadron was sent to support 11th Brigade, which was attacking a village on a hill South-East of Monteleone, and the rest of the Regiment was to take over from the 3rd Hussars. " B " Squadron had a successful battle in difficult country, knocking out several enemy guns. By the afternoon the head of the Regiment was at Monteleone with " A " Squadron in the valley on the left. " B " Squadron's objective was behind and to the East of Monteleone. " C " Squadron was to take over the lead at Citta della Pieve, which the 3rd Hussars were attacking.

At this juncture " B " Squadron reported an enemy tank pulling out from a village along a road running parallel with the highway to Monteleone, and " C " Squadron were ordered to send a troop off to the right to cut it off. As the three tanks in the troop, backed up by a fourth tank from Squadron Headquarters, turned down the side road there was a feeling of tense excitement. Would they catch that German tank or not? The enemy usually tried to avoid tank *versus* tank battles because, although their armament was bigger and better than the British, they only liked to fight when their numbers were vastly superior. The silence, except for the roar of engines, made the seconds seem like hours. Suddenly there was a noise like half-a-dozen express trains going through a tunnel, and yellow streaks of light from the tracers flew in all directions. This was no single German tank, but obviously quite a large number of big Anti-Tank Guns. The leading tank was enveloped in flames in the first second. An enemy bazooka, hidden in the ditch, got the second tank from about twenty yards range and it plunged off the road out of control. Above the din the officer in the H.Q. tank was heard on the wireless exhorting the third tank to get under cover; alas, he was too late. For a moment it sat where it was with its gun traversing round, apparently trying to get a shot off at the spot from which it had seen one of the flashes; with a colossal crash an enemy armour-piercing shell hit it. The gun stopped traversing and smoke started to curl upwards out of the turret. Three of the Royal Wilts tanks were gone in less time than it takes to tell.

This was a job for a larger force. While the crews of the knocked-out tanks were crawling away to safety, two more troops were brought up. These were cautiously manœuvred into position under the directions of the Squadron H.Q. tank, which was itself completely pinned in a hollow. Then the battle commenced in earnest.

It was soon discovered that the enemy had in this pocket quite a considerable force of Infantry and Anti-Tank guns, together with large ammunition dumps in a wood farther back. They looked like trying to hold on. However, the Yeomen were out for revenge. Their 75 mm. were firing away at the enemy gun flashes, while the A.P. bounced and roared over their heads. Gradually the Germans began to give ground. Four of their guns were knocked out for the loss of only one more tank, the crew of which suffered several casualties while they were evacuating their wounded. By now the ammunition dumps were burning nicely. Just before dark the Germans decided that they had had enough and their casualties in men must have been very great as they fled into the cover of the wood. Long after sunset the Royal Wilts kept up their fire until they had the whole wood blazing. Some of the tanks got right up to the wood itself, but it would have been folly to have pressed on any farther, so they were recalled. The question now arose, would the enemy counter-attack?

If the Germans did counter-attack and recaptured Monteleone, then the 3rd Hussars would be cut off. It was therefore vital that this cross-road should be held. By midnight, with the help of an Anti-Tank Troop which volunteered its assistance, some sort of position was formed. What would have happened if the counter-attack had materialised does not bear thinking about. The fact remains that it did not.

Ammunition was practically exhausted, but in spite of the shelling on the road the Echelon did come up.

The muddle at Monteleone cross-roads that night, and the worry it caused, makes one shudder still. Yet dawn broke and the enemy were gone. Everyone sighed with relief and turned their minds to the job of taking Citta della Pieve.

Here we must hark back for a moment and see how the 3rd Hussars had been faring the day before ; Citta della Pieve was an important battle and requires careful explanation.

The town itself is on the North edge of a ridge running North and South overlooking a plain on the left. The line of the road winds along the ridge and round the lower half of the town. You cannot see Citta della Pieve till you are on top of it, the only approach being from Monteleone, which is about five miles south on the same ridge. It was an ideal place to defend and here the Germans decided to make a stand. On the 16th June the 3rd Hussars' leading Squadron reached the town and at once set about getting through it. After suffering considerable casualties and finding that it was a job for which Infantry were essential, they asked for a battalion to come up. The Armour had got some way in front of their Battalion and it took till evening before the Infantry arrived. As reconnaissances had to be done, this attack did not go in until first light on the 17th June, when one company got into the edge of the town, but were pinned down amongst the houses. The 3rd Hussars gave all the support they could, but there were very few positions from which tanks could help. This, therefore, was the situation when the Royal Wilts were ordered to take over.

They moved into almost the same positions that the 3rd Hussars had been in and the only place from which R.H.Q. could see what was happening, and control the battle, was a corner on the very edge of the town itself. This meant that R.H.Q. was in front of its Squadrons, and here it had to remain, being heavily mortared and sniped at most of the time, for two days. It afterwards transpired that R.H.Q. had been occupying the somewhat glorious, if extremely uncomfortable, honour of being the leading tanks in the whole 8th Army.

The first day was spent in trying to get round Citta della Pieve, while the Artillery tried everything they could think of to silence the mortars. Meanwhile a big infantry attack, on a Brigade basis, was being laid on. The second day a bit of progress was made round the right flank with " B " Squadron, while the other two Squadrons knocked hell out of the front of the town.

There were a number of towers in this town, and, when it was realised that the Germans were using these for Observation Posts, the Royal Wilts, suppressing their natural disinclination to destroy churches and ancient buildings, engaged these with their 75 mms. The most successful shoot was performed by a Troop Leader of " C " Squadron, who knocked the ladder away from under an Observation Post with the first round, leaving two Germans isolated up in the belfry. The Officer Commanding " C " Squadron earned the title of " Chief Campanologist, 9th Armoured Brigade," for the number of bells he subsequently rang.

Thus the battle progressed very slowly, with the Armour edging its way round yard by yard until the morning of the 19th June, when the Infantry went in to attack.

The Germans, with their usual skill, managed to avoid the issue, slipping away during the night, to everyone's intense annoyance.

Two interesting and conflicting reports reached the Brigade from Army Headquarters. One stated: Had Citta della Pieve not held out for four days, and had the speed of the advance been maintained, the enemy would never have had time to make a stand in the Gothic Line. The second report was that, had Citta della Pieve fallen on the first day, our supplies would never have been able to catch up and the whole advance would have had to wait for the " Q " services. The most galling, but probably the most true report, was that Citta della Pieve was held by only one hundred of the German " Para " Division. This goes to show what a determined and fanatical defence can achieve given suitable positions and sufficient mortar and artillery support from behind.

As for the weather, it had been fine and hot except for a few very heavy showers, though rain fell in earnest during the fighting at Citta della Pieve. As it was fairly high ground this did not matter much, except for the discomfort. Some of the Echelons got bogged, but with super-human efforts, as always, managed to unbog themselves.

The praises of the Echelon of an Armoured Regiment are seldom sung; as it is their pride to keep their Regiment constantly supplied, their efforts are apt to be taken for granted. All too easily do the tank crews forget that lorries are " thin skinned," and that they must come up into the front line travelling night after night on dangerous and badly damaged roads.

For the next few weeks the weather was most unkind, the Italian summer breaking with little warning into torrential thunderstorms, turning the whole countryside into a bog and keeping all tracked and wheeled vehicles to the roads. Although the hot sun dries it all up fairly quickly, those who had to fight all day, and every day, were apt to take a jaundiced view of a country which, in an hour or so, can turn into a flood that would have launched the Ark. There are few Wiltshire Yeomen who will ever believe the travel posters!

During the day of the 19th June, with the fall of Citta della Pieve, there was another surge onwards. " B " Squadron, which was already on the right, got well forward with their Infantry Battalion and crossed the Tresa river. " C " Squadron, who were progressing up the road, met considerable opposition and suffered a number of casualties. They got to the river by 15.00 hours and found themselves in a most unenviable position, being overlooked from the opposite bank by steep, wooded slopes.

The Germans were determined that no one should cross the river and the shell-fire and sniping were terrific. Before long there were casualties. First an armoured car of the Artillery was knocked out, and disappeared in smoke and flame. Then one of the tanks received a direct hit on the driver's compartment, killing the lap gunner and wounding the driver. In spite of this they grimly held on to the river crossing till late evening, when the Infantry, supported by " A " Squadron, managed to get across.

Next day, with " B " Squadron in the lead, Strada was captured. A valiant attempt to get into Viano proved abortive, a whole troop being knocked out in the effort.

It was here that we suddenly heard a noise like hundreds of corks being screwed round in the necks of giant bottles. A loud moaning could be heard roaring towards us, with an ever-increasing crescendo, to end abruptly with a series of shattering explosions. We had met our first Moaning Minnies. These were the German " Nebblewaffers "—rockets fired six or nine together, at one second intervals.

Resistance had stiffened so much that it was decided to bring through the 4th British Infantry Division, supported by the Canadian Armoured Brigade, and pull 78th Division right-handed towards the shores of Lake Trasimeno to increase the number of troops in this part of the line. This manœuvre was completed by nightfall on the 22nd June, and the Regiment was collected together at Paciano for a day's rest.

A most interesting incident took place on the next day. One of the Regimental water trucks came up the road towards Strada on its own, in the early morning. As the driver could not see any Wiltshire Yeomanry tanks, he drove straight through the infantry positions and on into Viano. Here he discovered his mistake and also that Viano was clear of the enemy. As soon as he found the Regiment at Paciano he reported his discovery. The information was at once passed on to 4th Division, who hotly denied it. However, they sent a patrol out which confirmed the water truck driver's story. Thus, to the great amusement of everyone, not in 4th Division, Viano was captured by a Royal Wilts Water Truck.

Meanwhile Brigade Headquarters had established themselves in the town of Panicale. This town is worthy of mention because it stands on the Northern edge of the hills overlooking the whole western side of Lake Trasimeno, right up to Cortona. From here a most perfect grandstand view of the battle could be obtained. Here also, having found some reasonably good " Vino," Brigade Headquarters gave an impromptu party. All the available senior officers turned up and sat sipping their wine, watching the battle progressing below—a curious mixture of peace and war.

Next day fighting began again in earnest for the Regiment. Refreshed and re-organised, the Royal Wilts and the whole of the 36th Infantry Brigade sallied forth to try and get over the Pescia river. This was not an easy objective, because, apart from the difficulty of crossing the river, the approaches were heavily wooded and filled with snipers. By the time the main attack was organised it was nearly 1800 hours, and, to make matters worse, the father of all thunderstorms had started, the river being turned into a raging torrent. However, the tanks fought their way to the banks and here they were forced to remain, stuck. The Infantry could not get across either, as by now it was getting dark. The situation began to look most unpleasant. R.H.Q. was at Pucciarelli, on the ridge overlooking the river, while all the three Squadrons were milling around in the mud below.

Some Tank Destroyers, which had been attached to the Regiment that morning, were in equal difficulties, with two of their self-propelled guns knocked out by enemy fire. Through the rain and the flash of the exploding shells you could make out the cumbersome outline of three Scissor Bridges and a Troop of Sherman Dozers floundering about, trying to get out of the way of the snipers' bullets. It took nearly all night to collect about a Squadron together, but, in spite of unhealthy conditions, the only casualty was a large white goose, which was blown inside out when a mortar bomb landed just behind it.

During the night the Infantry got a bridgehead over the river, down by the shore of the lake, and at 0725 hours a long written order arrived from the Infantry Brigade, requiring three Squadrons over the river by 0730 hours. This was an impossible request, but even the explanation that all he had left was one Squadron which, at that very moment was getting bogged down in its attempts to meet his wishes, would not satisfy the Infantry Brigadier.

It was mid-day before " A " Squadron could be got down to the Bailey Bridge, and here they met with a most hostile reception from the enemy. The bridge was in full view of the German Observation Posts in Castiglione, and, apart from making every effort to destroy it with heavy calibre guns, the presence of tanks made them bring every weapon they had to bear on this one spot. " A " Squadron managed to slip tanks across one at a time. In doing this one was pierced by an 88 mm., which passed through the turret and fell on to the floor, but hurting no one. Another tank was not so lucky, and its crew and commander were killed. However, the Squadron succeeded in getting across and joined the Infantry in the bridgehead.

The remainder of the Regiment were salvaged as soon as possible and rather rudely told that, as they were late, they were not now required. For the next three days very little happened. About half the Regiment was employed, as the bridge-head over the Pescia river gradually expanded.

On the morning of the 29th June " C " Squadron were attached to 56th Reconnaissance Regiment in order to probe forward and destroy the pockets of enemy resistance which were holding up the general advance. They passed through Castiglione del Lago at about 0900 hours in perfect peace and quiet; the sun was shining on the old castle, which stood out in vivid relief against the azure blue of the lake, and the purple mountains beyond. About three miles north of the town this pleasant atmosphere was rudely shattered by " Moaning Minnies," mortar bombs and shells which came crashing down amongst the tanks. Everyone was quickly jerked back to the realities of war.

The country here was thickly wooded and mined, so it was impossible to find out where the fire was coming from.

Meanwhile " B " Squadron, who on the 28th June had taken over from the Warwickshire Yeomanry at Frattavecchia, were forcing their way steadily forward with their Infantry through an almost impenetrable forest. Several German Self-Propelled Guns were engaged and driven back. As always the Germans put forward their stiffest resistance just before they intended to take another bound backward.

This they did on the 3rd July, when " C " Squadron and 56th Reconnaisance Regiment had a most successful run of at least ten miles before breakfast, capturing the town of Cortona and taking a lot of prisoners.

That same evening 6th Armoured Division came through. 78th Division was going to be pulled out and sent back to Egypt for a rest. 9th Armoured Brigade could not have a break, but had to go across to the East of Lake Trasimeno to support the 4th and the 10th Indian Divisions.

So here ends the first phase of two months' fighting, when the Royal Wilts said good-bye to the 78th Division.

CHAPTER TWENTY-SEVEN

10th AND 4th INDIAN DIVISIONS

THE 9th Armoured Brigade now found itself in the mountain range which runs up the centre of Italy. For three days the Regiment rested and maintained its vehicles at a village called Magnano.

Looking North you could see ridge after ridge of hills gradually rising higher and higher, and, in the far distance, the line of mountains which subsequently formed the Gothic Line. In describing this as the backbone of Italy, you get a very accurate picture of how the consecutive ridges can be likened to vertebræ. As fast as one was captured there is always another just ahead.

Between the ridges lateral roads run in the valleys ; thus, when you are fighting up some main road running North and South, there are secondary roads running East and West every few miles.

The going for tanks is extremely difficult and the skill of the drivers is tested to the utmost. It is also a great strain on the tank itself, as Shermans were never designed to emulate mountain goats.

But in these mountains the Royal Wilts were to learn during the following weeks that, with determination, the ubiquitous Bulldozer and Indian Sappers, there are very few places a Sherman cannot get to.

The three days at Magnano will be well remembered by those lucky enough to find time to visit the beautiful city of Perugia and the lovely town of Assisi. The latter, with its tranquility and restfulness, as though a spell had been cast upon it by Saint Francis, was a wonderful tonic for the battle weary soldier. Even the Germans had respected the memory of Saint Francis, declaring Assisi an open city and leaving this charming oasis untouched by the horrors of war.

The Royal Wilts were proud and happy to find themselves with the Indians, remembering well their efficiency when they met them once before in Persia.

On the 7th July they moved up, through battle-scarred villages, to the south of Umbertide, where four days were spent waiting to be employed. Only " A " Squadron was used and even they were in reserve. It was not until the 11th July that the Regiment moved up through Umbertide to Abbadia and came under command of the 10th Indian Division.

This day was remarkable for a reconnaissance done by two Honeys and a troop of tanks. This deserves detailed description, more for the audacity with which it was carried out by the Reconnaissance Officer than the valuable information it gained.

Owing to the craters in the main road running up the Tiber valley, a route over the ridge north of Abbadia had to be found before the attack on Monte San Maria could be launched. 10th Indian Division were on the ridge, but had to wait there until wheels and tracks could be brought forward. The orders given to the Reconnaissance Officer were: to find a way over this ridge to the next lateral road and then, turning left, to try and get as near Monte San Maria as possible to see what sort of force was holding it.

It was appreciated that he would have to fight for this information, so his force was composed of two Honeys and a Troop of Shermans. This little party set off shortly after midday, crossed the ridge through the Indian forward defended localities, and started to descend into the valley below. Here they met with a certain amount of shelling and sniping, but they pushed on down to the bottom and found a bridge over a river. It was impossible to examine this bridge carefully to see if it was prepared for demolition as, at this juncture, heavy mortar fire was being brought down on them. However they all got safely over and reached the road beyond.

This road ran along under the next ridge: the enemy naturally had its range taped for their mortars, so the exploding shells followed them every yard. To add to their troubles the enemy could be seen moving along the ridge about 200 yards away, firing down on them. The tanks were unable to help much, as they could not elevate their Brownings sufficiently to reach the Germans above them. However, the two Honeys, by using their .5 A.A. Brownings, managed to hit back a bit. Thus the party progressed, under heavy shell fire all of the time.

It is quite remarkable that the crews of the Honeys managed to survive, sitting, as they were, in turretless vehicles, completely open to the hail of bullets.

When they reached a point from which they could see Monte San Maria, having reported back all the information they had gained, they still had to return several miles to the bridge. All the time they would be running the gauntlet as before. Somehow the whole party turned round and, except for one man who had been wounded earlier on, reached the bridge without further casualties. Here the Honeys passed over first, calling the tanks over one by one. The Germans were ready for them and, having let the Honeys call one tank across, waited until the second was in the middle of the bridge and then blew it up by an electric remote control. There was a shattering explosion which completely demolished the bridge, and the tank dived twenty feet into the river bed below, its turret blown right off. Thus there were two Honeys and one tank on our side of the river and one tank cut off on the enemy bank.

Completely unruffled, the Officer ordered one tank to keep the enemy off, while the other tank was to try and find a way across the river. Meanwhile he and his crews went down into the river and rescued the injured tank crew. By some miracle no-one was actually killed, and the last tank managed to flounder across the river. The Reconnaissance returned in the dark to where the Regiment awaited them at Abbadia.

It was an astounding achievement thus to have progressed so far down the road against such very heavy odds and to have returned almost without casualties. This fact was recognised by both the Corps and Divisional Commanders.

Before embarking upon an account of the fighting in support of the Indians, a general description of how it was normally carried out must be given.

By the beginning of July the enemy, having definitely decided to try and stand at the Gothic Line, were making desperate efforts to hold up the Allies' advance. Every available man was pushed into the defence and the artillery was greatly reinforced. On the other end of the scales it must be remembered that the Allies had been considerably depleted by the invasion of the South of France, while almost all reinforcements were being sent to Northern Europe.

This was real infantry country, speed being impossible, and the armour's job was to support them. Every ridge and hill had to be taken by a separate infantry attack, while tanks clambered up behind them, often having to have a track built before they could reach their objective. Undoubtedly the fantastically improbable places to which tanks were got to not only helped the morale of the troops they were supporting but also flabbergasted the German defence.

Great use was made of the 75 mm. high explosive shell, with which Shermans are armed. This gun is extremely accurate and, once on a ridge, the day would be spent engaging pin-pointed enemy positions, while the divisional artillery harassed the enemy on the reverse slopes. Thousands of rounds were fired off in this way, and with great effect judging by the reports from prisoners.

When the Indians were planning an attack it was laid on as a purely infantry and artillery operation, with a plan for the armour superimposed. If the tanks were held up by bad going the attack could succeed without them. The Royal Wilts can pride themselves on the fact that it was very seldom that they failed. Even when it took a long time to get up with the Indian forward troops they always had some proportion of their tanks in a position nearby, from which they could give support.

There was one other task evolved for the armour. This was called an "armoured swan" and requires a brief description.

It consisted of an independent armoured attack, usually carried out on the flanks, when half a squadron, or sometimes more, would go forward on its own to probe the enemy positions, draw their defensive fire and return, having done as much damage as possible.

The day after the reconnaissance 10th Indian Division attacked all along its front, " A " Squadron supporting the attack towards Monte San Maria. By that night " A " Squadron had got a good position south of the town, which stands on the top of a very sharp pinnacle dominating the whole of the surrounding country. It was not a spot at which to dwell for longer than necessary, so the Indians pushed on all night, taking Monte San Maria by the next morning. By doing this they captured a most useful salient in the German positions.

" A " Squadron sent forward a half squadron to try and get on beyond the town but were held up by craters in the road. However, they found a useful place from which they were able to shell the enemy positions, on their flanks and in front of them. Here " A " Squadron remained for several days doing most useful work, being, as they were, well forward of the rest of the line.

To the East of Monte San Maria there was a feature called Cedrone. It was expected that, with the fall of Monte San Maria, the Germans would fall back to straighten their line. However, this they did not do ; in fact they reinforced Cedrone and hung on there for four days.

Each night the Indians attacked, and each morning, having got on to the feature, they were counter-attacked off as their reserve ammunition could not be brought up. By the 18th July half " C " Squadron got on to Cedrone, with a battalion of Indians. These the enemy failed to dislodge. That day " A " and " C " Squadrons had some successful shoots and estimated that they had killed quite a number of Germans. The only trouble was that when the tanks started firing they drew rather a lot of mortar and shell fire which, while it was only unpleasant for the tanks, caused a lot of casualties to the Indians.

Meanwhile, on the 17th July, " B " Squadron had been transferred to the 4th Indian Division and came under command of 7th Indian Brigade at Morra, with whom they stayed till the 29th July. They were operating further over to the west, their objective being the Alpi Di Poti feature north of Arezzo. To get there from Morra was no easy task, as sappers had to make a track up a precipice before the operation could really get going.

This they did, naming it "Jacob's Ladder," which aptly describes how steep it was.

The Brigadier commanding 7th Indian Infantry Brigade used the armour with such skill that everyone in "B" Squadron voted this the happiest time of the whole campaign.

Their tasks, apart from the normal ones, were very varied. They carried Ghurkas on their tanks up onto the Alpi di Poti. They joined the King's Dragoon Guards on reconnaissances. They fired a barrage in support of an infantry attack, using 450 rounds of high explosive and 25,000 rounds of .30 Browning—and they even fired twenty-five rounds of high explosive per gun one night on a defensive fire task.

These, and other ingenious uses of tanks, were most successful, and valuable lessons were learnt.

The Corps Commander, General Sir R. L. McCreery, said that the operations which "B" Squadron undertook with this Brigade were a model of good co-operation between infantry and armour. They only lost two tanks, both of which fell over a 100 foot precipice. Luckily, in both cases, the complete crews managed to bail out just in time.

To return to the rest of the Regiment with 10th Indian Division. After Cedrone was captured the Division pushed steadily on. On the 21st July "C" Squadron supported the 3rd Hussars in an attack they were doing east of the River Tiber. They caught a large party of Germans in a gully and had a very good shoot. The next day, with "A" Squadron in the lead, the Regiment pushed on up the Tiber Valley, while the Indians worked their way forward in the hills on the left.

During the next two days "A" Squadron destroyed a number of enemy posts in houses, driving the Germans back past Citta Di Castello on to the high ground north of La Colle.

From now onwards the enemy had blown up every bridge and culvert right up to the Gothic Line. This served a double purpose because, although it slowed up the advance, it also meant that the Germans could not counter attack in any great strength. Because of this the Army Commander allowed the line on the east of the Tiber to be held thinly by a force of armoured cars, and pushed on to the west of the river. This meant that our right flank from now on became more and more open and enabled the Germans to shell our lines of communication along the Tiber Valley, making life very uncomfortable for the Echelon.

The next three days were spent fighting in support of the infantry as they attacked ridge after ridge; the Indian troops were adept at leap frogging their troops quickly from one objective to another, never giving the enemy any respite. Sometimes these changes took place so quickly that it was hard to know who one was supporting, but by now everyone knew the Indians so well that this did not really matter. On the 27th July the Regiment reached Monterchi, while the Indians were consolidating for the next drive to Anghiari.

At 0530 hours on the 28th July "A" and "C" Squadrons left Monterchi and proceeded north along the road to Anghiari. "A" Squadron were to support the infantry on the high ground overlooking the Tiber valley, while "C" Squadron, on the right flank, was to pass through Fighille and create a diversion at St. Leo crossroads. If possible they were to get astride the road north of Anghiari and cut the enemy off. The whole area was overlooked by the high mountains in which the Germans had built the "Gothic Line"; in fact, the Royal Wilts were now attacking the outposts of it.

 1.

 2.

 3.

 4.

 5.

1. THE END OF A TIGER NEAR FICULLE.
2 AND 3. THE PEACE AND QUIET OF ASSISI.
4. ROYAL WILTS PASS THROUGH CASTIGLIONE DEL LAGO.
5. PUCCIARELLI. BATTLE FOR THE PESCIA RIVER.

1.

2.

3.

4.

1. LOOKING TOWARDS SAN SEPOLCHRO FROM ANGHIARI.
2. IN SUPPORT OF 3RD HUSSARS. CITTA DI CASTELLO.
3. A ROYAL WILTS TANK IN "BATTLE DRESS."
4. THE UMBERTIDE PLAIN WITH THE GOTHIC LINE IN THE BACKGROUND.

It was not long before both squadrons came under heavy shell fire from enemy long-range guns, this happening as they negotiated a dried up river bed where the bridge had been blown. " A " Squadron then turned off the road and started a tortuous climb up the steep slope, giving what support they could to the infantry and driving the enemy back yard by yard. Suddenly over the wireless came the report, " Three enemy tanks in the wood to your front, and three self-propelled guns guarding the St. Leo crossroads." They had been spotted by our own aircraft, which had dropped a message on the rear half of " C " Squadron. Every tank commander and gunner strained his eyes to try and get a view of these enemy tanks, but without success. All this time " A " Squadron were being subjected to a considerable amount of attention from the German gunners, with shells and mortar bombs exploding all round them. " C " Squadron were progressing fairly rapidly along the valley and, having passed under an embankment, discovered a " time bomb " ticking away under the bridge. The time was now 0700 hours, and when the sappers arrived five minutes later to remove the bomb they discovered it had been set for 0715 hours. So the road was saved from being blocked with only ten minutes to spare.

They reached a small knoll about half a mile south of St. Leo without any further incident, but from now on things started warming up. There were Germans all round them ; they were being heavily machine gunned from the wooded slopes on the left, shelled from their front and mortared from the right. Owing to the vines, visibility was very limited, and it was impossible to see where the enemy fire was coming from. Luckily " A " Squadron, through being on high ground, had a bird's eye view of the whole situation and were able to direct the " C " Squadron guns on to an enemy self-propelled gun with great success.

The right hand troop had managed to spot a nest of enemy mortars about 200 yards away and knock them out at point blank range. There were also a number of German infantry moving about in some high maize ; these were bowled over like shooting rabbits in a cornfield.

After knocking out the self-propelled gun and the nest of mortars, and having plastered the crossroads with shell fire, both squadrons and the infantry had a slight respite from the attentions of the enemy. This enabled " C " Squadron to proceed to St. Leo and mop up a few more Germans who were running about amongst the houses.

Finding the country beyond even more enclosed and being completely on their own, " C " Squadron were ordered to withdraw. They then moved round to the left flank to help the 8th Battalion Manchesters, who were held up by machine gun fire.

Everyone thought, on returning under the embankment, how lucky it was that the time bomb had been removed. If not, the whole Squadron would have been cut off on the enemy's side. This battle cost the Germans two self-propelled guns destroyed, four mortars knocked out, and between thirty and forty casualties.

The whole of the time " A " Squadron were slowly fighting their way forward till, by nightfall, Anghiari had fallen and the prospect of the next lateral road to Arezzo being opened loomed ahead. The best way to describe this road is to liken it to the Cheddar Gorge. The next few days were occupied in driving the enemy off the northern slopes, so it was not until the 1st August that the road was opened to soft-skinned vehicles.

The Royal Wilts were now getting into really high country, while mountain gunners and mule trains were to be seen daily making their way forward. Also at this time the higher command were preparing for their big offensive on the Adriatic coast, leaving the 10th Indian Division to hold what had previously been a two Divisional front. In consequence, the Royal Wiltshire Yeomanry found themselves split up, with " C " Squadron on the right flank working with the Armoured Car Force, sometimes on the east bank of the Tiber ; " B " Squadron at Anghiari ; and

"A" Squadron on the extreme left in the area north of Arezzo, a distance of approximately twenty-five miles.

On the 1st August all three squadrons were being employed with their respective Brigades; although it was a busy day of mountaineering not much advance was achieved. R.H.Q. moved to the strangest spot it ever occupied. This was west of Anghiari, in a river valley by Souara and in full view of the Gothic Line. The Intelligence Officer chose the place and, when remonstrated with, explained why he had done so. In the farmhouse round which R.H.Q. was grouped he had discovered a peroxided blond Italian slut, called Josephine. She had in her possession a photograph of a German gunner officer named Rudolph. From other inhabitants of the farm he learnt that, not only had Rudolph been Josephine's boy friend, but also that he was Adjutant of some Artillery Regiment which had moved back into the Gothic Line a day or so previously.

The Intelligence Officer appreciated that if he put R.H.Q. close to the farm it would probably be perfectly safe. He was dead right. The Germans plastered the whole area day after day, but never a shell fell within 300 yards of Rudolph's Josephine.

A few days before "B" Squadron had done an "armoured swan" to Viaio, north-east of Saint Leo, where they had surprised and killed a number of Germans. On the 3rd August they repeated the experiment and met with particularly heavy shelling. Although this Swan did not appear to achieve much it, and subsequent ones of the same sort, did a great deal of good by keeping the enemy from creeping forward into the Tiber Valley.

Meanwhile "A" Squadron were preparing for a feat of mountaineering hitherto unrivalled. 20th Brigade were forming up to attack Monte Filetto, which is over 4,000 feet high. If possible they wanted half a squadron of tanks on top of this mountain to shoot up the Germans on the feature beyond. This was a formidable task, but by the 6th August half "A" Squadron were on top of Monte Filetto, up above jeep head and mule head, amongst the Indian Forward Defended Localities which had to be supplied by man pack. Actually jeeps did get there shortly afterwards, or they would never have been able to get their ammunition up.

They made an attempt to sally forward from the top of Filetto a few days later, but one tank got stuck. This tank was never recovered and will probably remain for ever as a monument to the Royal Wiltshire Yeomanry's mountaineering achievements.

This half squadron had to stay where they were until the Royal Wilts were withdrawn at the end of the month. Before leaving Monte Filetto there are two stories to tell, one about the Ghurkas, and the other about "E" Battery I R.H.A., stories, typical of both, and, as they happened on Filetto, should be recounted here.

"E" Battery were armed with 'Priests' (150 mm. self-propelled guns on Grant chassis). As they were supporting the Royal Wilts they were independent of the Divisional Artillery and could go where they liked. Throughout the whole campaign they were always in action, further forward than any other battery. One day at a conference the Divisional Commander warmly congratulated the Mountain Regiment Royal Artillery for getting into action so far up Monte Filetto. "E" Battery Commander smiled quietly to himself and remarked in an undertone to those sitting next to him, "That's absolutely nothing. We're hundreds of feet higher up Filetto."

This was perfectly true, for "E" Battery would have had a shot at climbing Mount Everest to give closer support to their Regiment and to keep their noses ahead of any other gunners.

The Ghurkas, as everyone knows, are famous for the deadly use they make of their "kukris" whenever an opportunity arises for hand-to-hand fighting. The

Germans were shy of battle at close quarters with any Indian troops for this very reason. Therefore, when they counter-attacked, they usually tried to take on the sector held by the British battalion in each Indian Brigade. They knew that, if they failed, however hot the reception they received, they would avoid the Indians' knives.

Having managed to identify a British battalion on top of Monte Filetto, they planned a counter attack the next day just before dawn. What they did not know was that the Ghurkas were taking over during the night. It so happened that the reserve company of the Ghurkas battalion got too far forward in the darkness and, finding itself in front of its own Forward Defenced Localities, turned back parallel to the front line to get out of the way.

By now it was just first light and, on rounding a spur, the company found a whole German battalion moving up a gulley below them. Screaming their battle cry, and grinning with lust for blood, they drew their kukris and rushed down upon the surprised Germans. For a moment the enemy stood stunned with horror, then turned and fled. They were too late. The Ghurkas jumped upon them, chopping off heads, arms and legs—left, right and centre. The whole action was over in a matter of minutes and the German battalion were legging it back from whence they had come, leaving seventy mutilated bodies behind them.

10th Indian Division were now " leaning on the Gothic Line " from Anghiari to Subbiano, with their right flank, running sharply back down the Tiber valley, practically unguarded. For this reason " B " Squadron were still left at Fighille while " C " Squadron were at Monterchi, from which bases armoured swans could be undertaken.

Hitherto no mention has been made of an organisation existing within the Regiment, known to all as " the Post." It was evolved and organised by that Scottish Moonraker, the Technical Adjutant, and consisted of the recovery vehicles and Regimental fitters, reinforced by the Light Aid Detachment (a R.E.M.E. formation attached to every Armoured Regiment).

Normally " the Post " positioned itself close up behind R.H.Q., near the " A " Echelon, where it undertook the recovery and repair of damaged tanks. It was usually to be found in the most comfortable house in the vicinity and also where the best " Vino " was obtainable. This in no way detracted from the truly valuable work done by " the Post," but it left its mark on the Regiment in that the fitters, whose correct title is " Vehicle Mechanics," are known even now as " Vino Mechanics."

Round about the beginning of August " the Post " was in a comfortable farm to the east flank of the spot where " B " Squadron had their H.Q. When told that they were unwittingly doing right flank protection to the whole Division the Technical Adjutant merely laughed, thinking that he was having his leg pulled and that " B " Squadron wanted to evict him from his nice H.Q.

However, on the night of the 11th August, an excited little Wop on a bicycle arrived at " the Post " in a fearful state of agitation. " Fifty Germans," he cried, " have crossed the Tiber at San Sepolchro and are advancing towards this very farm." The Technical Adjutant, in great haste, stood his men to. Pulling their weapons out from the bottoms of the lorries in which they normally reposed, they prepared to defend themselves to the last man and the last round. Then, rushing over to " B " Squadron, the Technical Adjutant awoke the the Squadron Leader, demanding that the whole Squadron come over immediately to his aid. The Officer Commanding " B " Squadron told him in no mean terms, that " God helps those who help themselves," and, having warned his guard that an enemy patrol might be about, went to sleep again. This did not satisfy our Scotsman, who kept nagging until " B " Squadron sent an officer over to R.H.Q. to find out what he was to do.

This officer very apologetically woke the duty officer at R.H.Q. and described his mission. Having examined the map and found that San Sepolchro was at least four miles away from " the Post," and since all Italians are known to exaggerate, the betting was that it was only a small party of Germans anyhow. Therefore a message was sent back to the Technical Adjutant that he was not to worry and if he really was attacked by a large number of Germans to retreat behind " B " Squadron.

Needless to say nothing did happen, and the fifty Germans turned out to have been an Indian fighting patrol who had been across the Tiber to probe the German defences round San Sepolchro.

To this day that gallant Scotsman, who incidently has become a complete moonraker and settled down in Wiltshire, has never quite forgiven R.H.Q. for not sending out the entire Regiment to his aid.

The Reservists, who had been abroad before joining the Royal Wiltshire Yeomanry, had almost completed their five years overseas service. Therefore on the 11th August an order arrived for them to be sent down to Naples and there to embark for home.

Naturally this was a great shock to the Regiment, for not only did it mean the loss of seventy-two most highly tried and trusted friends, but the loss of twenty-five per cent. of the senior N.C.O.'s. There were very few reinforcements to make up the numbers but, by promoting a lot of Yeomen, the Regiment managed to carry on as though nothing had happened. Here once again was proof of how the Yeomanry can rise to any occasion.

The next week was occupied with several armoured swans to keep the enemy busy, while the Indians remained almost static. On the 18th August " B " and " C " Squadrons put in an attack across the Tiber through San Sepolchro, but heavy rain stopped play. About fifteen Germans were killed.

The last big battle took place on the 20th August when " C " Squadron crossed the Tiber to attack the Monte Doglio feature, supported by " B " Squadron and " E " Battery from the Anghiari heights. Monte Doglio was known to be strongly held, but it was hoped that the tanks might be able to inflict heavy casualties on the enemy. This they succeeded in doing but, owing to the fact that the feature was thickly wooded, they could not clear it. Having remained there for an hour they were ordered to return. They had killed forty Germans, and one self-propelled gun was known to have been destroyed. The whole operation was very hazardous owing to enemy snipers and bazookas, who got all round the squadron. Two tanks were knock out by the bazookas, in one of which the officer was killed, the remainder of his crew being taken prisoner.

The sands of time were running low, for, on the 25th August, just as an offensive was being planned north of Subbiano, orders came through to say that all men with four and a half years' service were to be withdrawn from battle. This wiped out any chance of carrying on, as it affected all original Yeomen, who were by now holding eighty per cent. of the senior ranks.

It was on the 26th that the whole Regiment was withdrawn to Villa Guillichini, just north of Arezzo, where they remained for three weeks packing up.

A holiday camp was organised on the shores of Lake Trasimeno, and bathing in a nearby river. Here the Yeomen rested on their laurels and discussed what it would feel like to be home after all these years, and wondered if they would have to see battle again.

CHAPTER TWENTY-EIGHT

HOME AGAIN

ON the 9th September the Brigadier addressed the whole Regiment and told them that, owing to heavy casualties sustained by the Armour on the Adriatic coast, only those officers and men who had completed four and a half years' overseas service would return home with the Regiment. This was heartbreaking, as it meant that twenty-eight officers and 353 other ranks would have to stay behind.

On the 17th and 18th the tanks were loaded on transporters and sent away to the East Coast for handing over, while the personnel who were going home left for Iesi, just west of Ancona. The remainder, amidst a lot of handshaking and goodbyes, went to the 1st Reinforcement Regiment and were there split up amongst various other units.

Once again, owing to the appalling weather, the Regiment had to move from Iesi to some billets in the small town of Macerata. Here they stayed until the 8th October, when they entrained for Naples and embarked on the "Monarch of Bermuda," sailing on Friday, 13th October, for England.

They disembarked at Liverpool on the 24th October, four years and nine months after they had set sail from these island shores. They then entrained for Bury St. Edmunds, Suffolk, where they found the first party of men who had left them in Italy waiting to welcome them. This was a more than pleasant surprise, and a great reunion took place.

On the 19th December twelve officers and 100 other ranks paraded at Salisbury, where the Mayor, accompanied by the members of the Council, presented to the Regiment the Title Deeds of the Freedom of the City.

The Royal Wilts were destined to see no more fighting; instead they were to impart their knowledge to others.

On the 27th July all those who had been awarded decorations went to Buckingham Palace for an Investiture, where they received their medals from their King.

Appendices

LIST OF PRE-WAR CAMPS.

1921	Embodiment in Defence Force, Tidworth.	
C.O.	Lt.-Col. W. F. Fuller, D.S.O., T.D.	
2 i/c	Lt.-Col. The Earl of Pembroke and Montgomery, M.V.O.	
Adj.	Major M. F. Radclyffe, M.C., 4th H.	
Q.M.	Capt. W. R. M. Barrett, M.C.	
A.	Major S. Herbert.	
B.	Major R. W. Awdry, T.D.	
C.	Major W. H. Mann, M.C., T.D.	
R.S.M.	R.S.M. Barnard.	

1922	WEYMOUTH.
C.O.	Lt.-Col. W. F. Fuller, D.S.O., T.D.
2 i/c.	Major R. W. Awdry, T.D.
Q.M.	Capt. W. R. M. Barrett, M.C.
A.	Major S. Herbert.
B.	Capt. E. P. Awdry, M.C.
C.	Major W. H. Mann, M.C., T.D.
R.S.M.	R.S.M. Gill, D.C.M.

1923	WILTON PARK, SALISBURY.
C.O.	Lt.-Col. W. F. Fuller, D.S.O., T.D.
2 i/c.	Major R. W. Awdry, T.D.
Adj.	Capt. R. A. Radclyffe, 4/7 D.G.
Q.M.	Capt. W. R. M. Barrett, M.C.
A.	Major S. Herbert.
B.	Major E. P. Awdry, M.C.
C.	Major W. H. Mann, M.C., T.D.
R.S.M.	R.S.M. Barker.

1924	MARLBOROUGH
C.O.	Lt.-Col. R. W. Awdry, T.D.
2 i/c.	Major W. H. Mann, M.C., T.D.
Adj.	Capt. R. A. Radclyffe, 4/7 D.G.
Q.M.	Capt. W. R. M. Barrett, M.C.
A.	Capt. C. Lestock Reid.
B.	Major The Hon. R. E. O. Long, T.D.
C.	Major E. P. Awdry, M.C.
R.S.M.	R.S.M. Barker.

1925	LANSDOWNE.
C.O.	Lt.-Col. R. W. Awdry, T.D.
2 i/c.	Major W. H. Mann, M.C., T.D.
Adj.	Capt. S. R. F. Spicer, 12th Lancers.
Q.M.	Capt. W. R. M. Barrett, M.C.
A.	Major S. Herbert.
B.	Major E. P. Awdry, M.C.
C.	Major The Hon. R. E. O. Long, T.D.
R.S.M.	R.S.M. Barker.

1926	COUNTY TREK.
C.O.	Lt.-Col. R. W. Awdry, T.D.
2 i/c.	Major W. H. Mann, M.C., T.D.
Adj.	Capt. S. R. F. Spicer, 12th Lancers.
Q.M.	Capt. R. E. Vine.
A.	Major S. Herbert.
B.	Major The Hon. R. E. O. Long, T.D.
C.	Major E. P. Awdry, M.C., T.D.
R.S.M.	R.S.M. Barker.

1927	WINDMILL HILL.
C.O.	Lt.-Col. R. W. Awdry, T.D.
2 i/c	Major W. H. Mann, M.C., T.D.
Adj.	Capt. S. R. F. Spicer, 12th Lancers.
Q.M.	Capt. R. E. Vine.
A.	Major S. Herbert.
B.	Major E. P. Awdry, M.C.
C.	Major The Hon. R. E. O. Long, T.D.
R.S.M.	R.S.M. Barker.

1928	MARLBOROUGH.
C.O.	Lt.-Col. W. H. Mann, M.C., T.D.
2 i/c	Major E. P. Awdry, M.C.
Adj.	Capt. P. Vincent, M.C., 3rd D.G.
Q.M.	Capt. R. E. Vine.
A.	Capt. C. Lestock Reid.
B.	Major The Hon. R. E. O. Long, T.D.
C.	Major A. A. Bankier.
R.S.M.	R.S.M. Haines, D.C.M.

1929	WIMBORNE ST. GILES.
C.O.	Major E. P. Awdry, M.C., T.D.
Adj.	Capt. P. Vincent, M.C., 3rd D.G.
Q.M.	Capt. R. E. Vine.
A.	Major C. Lestock Reid.
B.	Major The Hon. R. E. O. Long, T.D. and 2 i/c.
C.	Major A. A. Bankier.
R.S.M.	R.S.M. Haines, D.C.M.

1930	WINDMILL HILL.
C.O.	Major E. P. Awdry, M.C., T.D.
Adj.	Capt. P. Vincent, M.C., 3rd D.G.
Q.M.	Major R. E. Vine.
A.	Major C. Lestock Reid.
B.	Major The Hon. R. E. O. Long, T.D. and 2 i/c.
C.	Capt. H. J. Nicholson, M.C.
R.S.M.	R.S.M. Haines, D.C.M.

1931	MINEHEAD.
C.O.	Lt.-Col. W. H. Mann, M.C., T.D.
2 i/c.	Major E. P. Awdry, M.C., T.D.
Adj.	Capt. P. Vincent, M.C., 3rd D.G.
Q.M.	Major R. E. Vine.
A.	Major C. Lestock Reid.
B.	Capt. P. W. Pitt.
C.	Major A. A. Bankier.
R.S.M.	R.S.M. Haines, D.C.M.

1932	COUNTY TREK.
C.O.	Lt.-Col. E. P. Awdry, M.C., T.D.
Adj.	Capt. G. L. Welstead, 13/18 H.
Q.M.	Major R. E. Vine.
A.	Capt. O. St. M. Thynne.
B.	Major The Hon. R. E. O. Long, T.D.
C.	Major A. A. Bankier.
R.S.M.	R.S.M. Haines, D.C.M.

1933	SPARSHOLT, HANTS.		1937	WIMBORNE ST. GILES.
C.O.	Lt.-Col. E. P. Awdry, M.C., T.D.		C.O.	Col. E. P. Awdry, M.C., T D.
2 i/c	Major The Hon. R. E. O. Long, T.D.		2 i/c	Major H. J. Nicholson M.C.
Adj.	Capt. G. L. Welstead, 13/18 H.		Adj.	Capt. F. F. B. St. George, Life Guards.
Q.M.	Major R. E. Vine.		Q.M.	Lieut. F. A. Riddeford.
A.	Capt. O. St. M. Thynne.		A.	Major O. St. M. Thynne.
B.	Major H. J. Nicholson, M.C.		B.	Major P. W. Pitt.
C.	Major A. A. Bankier.		C.	Major D. G. Williams.
R.S.M.	R.S.M. Haines, D.C.M.		R.S.M.	R.S.M. Frost.

1934	MUNTHAM COURT, SUSSEX.		1938	MUNTHAM COURT, SUSSEX.
C.O.	Lt.-Col. E. P. Awdry, M.C., T.D.		C.O.	Lt.-Col. H. J. Nicholson, M.C., T.D.
2 i/c	Major A. A. Bankier.		2 i/c	Major D. G. Williams.
Adj.	Capt. G. L. Welstead, 13/18 H.		Adj.	Lieut. H. B. Blount.
Q.M.	Major R. E. Vine.		Q.M.	Lieut. F. A. Riddeford.
A.	Major C. Lestock Reid.		A.	Major O. St. M. Thynne.
B.	Major H. J. Nicholson, M.C.		B.	Major P. W. Pitt.
C.	Major D. G. Williams.		C.	Capt. The Lord Ashley.
R.S.M.	R.S.M. Frost.		R.S.M.	R.S.M. Frost.

1935	WILTON.		1939	CORFE CASTLE.
C.O.	Lt.-Col. E. P. Awdry, M.C., T.D.		C.O.	Lt.-Col. H. J. Nicholson, M.C., T.D.
2 i/c	Major A. A. Bankier.		2 i/c	Major D. G. Williams.
Adj.	Capt. G. L. Welstead, 13/18 H.		A/Adj.	Lieut. H. B. Blount.
Q.M.	Major R. E. Vine.		Q.M.	Lieut. F. A. Riddeford.
A.	Major C. Lestock Reid.		A.	Major O. St. M. Thynne.
B.	Major H. J. Nicholson, M.C.		B.	Major P. W. Pitt.
C.	Major D. G. Williams.		C.	The Lord Ashley.
R.S.M.	R.S.M. Frost.		R.S.M.	R.S.M. Frost.

1936	CHILCOMBE, WINCHESTER.
C.O.	Col. E. P. Awdry, M.C., T.D.
2 i/c	Major H. J. Nicholson, M.C.
Adj.	Capt. F. F. B. St. George, Life Guards.
Q.M.	Lieut. F. A. Riddiford.
A.	Major C. Lestock Reid.
B.	Capt. O. St. M. Thynne.
C.	Major D. G. Williams.
R.S.M.	R.S.M. Frost.

PERSONNEL EMBODIED IN AUGUST AND SEPTEMBER, 1939.

(1). KEY PARTY CALLED UP ON 25 AUGUST, 1939.

"A" SQUADRON.

550388	L/Sgt.	Arnold, N. A. H.	2651902	L/Cpl.	Baragwanath, H. W.
550214	Sgt.	Coates, F. W.	556409	Tpr.	Culverhouse, C.
556424	Tpr.	Davis, A. D. N.	557837	,,	Day, C. W.
552256	Cpl.	Harraway, J.	557406	,,	Oakley, H. C.
552254	Tpr.	Pickford, H. W.	553352	Cpl.	Pickford, H. S.
546127	Sgt.	Pike, R. E. J.	381435	Tpr.	Siminson, L. H.
322936	Tpr.	Thorne, J.	540993	S.Q.M.S.	Webster, J. J. S.
553357	Cpl.	Watts, R.			

"B" SQUADRON.

554337	L/Sgt.	Adams, P. E.	555435	Tpr.	Blackbeard, W. J.
324476	Tpr.	Davis, H. J.	556665	,,	Fay, C. F.
322900	,,	George, T. E.	322287	,,	Harding, E. J.
329477	,,	Lawrence, M. H. J.	551317	L/Sgt.	Marsh, F. W. J.
558096	,,	Mortimer, B. B.	555436	Tpr.	Smith, E. A.
551660	,,	Vaughan, W. F.	558112	,,	Taylor, G. C.
557675	,,	Warman, R. J. N.	556884	L/Cpl.	Wenham, R. S.
547798	S.Q.M.S.	Wheeler, L. C.	544527	Tpr.	Wordley, H. W.
556954	Tpr.	Yates, D. A.	325553	,,	Allan, A. G. G.

"C" SQUADRON.

556880	Tpr.	Cull, R. E.	556863	Cpl.	Greer, F.
324542	,,	Myers, W. W.	776241	L/Sgt.	Thorn, A.
556879	Cpl.	Wickenden, R.	556150	Tpr.	Woodward, D. G.

"H.Q." SQUADRON.

323852	Tpr.	Andrews, M. H. J.	558299	Tpr.	Alley, A. N. C.
324454	,,	Angell, R. J.	552701	Bdsmn.	Baker, K. G.
344498	,,	Bellamy, D. F.	553746	L/Cpl.	Coleman, R. R.
558110	,,	Hill, W. A.	324455	Tpr.	Holmes, S. J.
324498	,,	Molloy, B.	322748	,,	Miles, W. L.
324506	,,	Newman, C. E.	544929	S.Q.M.S.	Osmond, R. H.
324065	,,	Perkins, E. E.	779031	Sgt.	Pollard, H. D.
324051	,,	Perry, E. H.	558213	Cpl.	Reed, V.
324505	,,	Randall, J. G.	534795	S.Q.M.S.	Slatford, H.
322779	,,	Spender, A. W. J.	558089	Tpr.	Simons, E. E.
542317	Sgt.	Tulk, F. S.	760775	S.Q.M.S.	Willett, L. I. A.

OFFICERS.

Lt. (Q.M.) F. A. Riddiford.   Lt. F. A. G. Blackwood.
Lt. The Hon. A. E. G. Herbert.   2nd Lt. M. St. J. V. Gibbs.

PERMANENT STAFF.

Capt. F. St. George, Adjutant (Life Guards).

7816266	R.S.M.	Frost, E. T.	398377	S.S.M.	Allenden, M. C.
529647	Sgt.	Barker, E. J.	394888	Sgt.	Hitch, B. J.
311862	,,	Prime, G.			

(2). THE FOLLOWING OFFICERS AND OTHER RANKS WERE CALLED OUT AND REPORTED FOR DUTY ON 30 AUGUST, 1939.

"A" SQUADRON.

Lt. H. G. Awdry.

558171	Tpr.	Brown, S. F.	555353	Cpl.	Brake, E. J.
318469	,,	Bond, R. H.	556483	Tpr.	Bond, R.
557673	,,	Burt, W. H.	556611	,,	Button, V. G.
557594	,,	Blake, P.	556461	,,	Cox, H. L.
555856	,,	Coggan, D. T.	322004	,,	Creese, H. G.
555940	Cpl.	Dufosee, A.	322765	,,	Egremont, D. S.
557830	Tpr.	Foord, W. M.	557593	Farr.	Ford, A. H.
557955	,,	Golding, W. J.	549708	Sgt.	Golden, C. W.

556598	Tpr.	Gatehouse, R. P.		555939	Tpr.	Goddard, E.
558141	,,	Hinton, E. G.		555938	,,	Hoare, R. H.
534269	Cpl.	Horne, F. C.		5566856	,,	Hervin, H. F.
322005	Tpr.	Hibberd, H. G.		557856	,,	Jeans, E. J.
556359	L/Cpl.	Jeffries, C. H.		557591	,,	Light, D.
556343	Tpr.	Luff, M. G.		552323	Cpl.	Locke, W. C.
557522	Tpr.	Miles, A. E.		556481	Tpr.	Mason, J. E.
557055	,,	Merritt, L. M.		557596	,,	Miller, H. J.
556663	,,	Newbury, G.		555857	,,	Noyce, H.
318470	,,	Pearce, A. G.		558142	,,	Philpott, J. W.
551506	L/Sgt.	Pike, E. A. G.		322003	,,	Pearce, F. E.
555354	Tpr.	Read, E. G.		557405	,,	Rolls, R. W.
558143	,,	Reason, H. L.		554434	Cpl.	Smith, J.
556423	,,	Simonson, J. R. W.		555352	Tpr.	Scott, M. W. A.
557592	,,	Tongs, M.		323465	,,	Thomas, W. E.
322764	,,	Trethowan, M.		555413	Cpl.	Waters, H. E.
556862	,,	Williams, L.		323466	Tpr.	Wilson, A. J.
557402	,,	Wheble, L. de la F.		557401	,,	Wheble, M. de la F.
556226	,,	Wardle, D. C.		316616	,,	Woods, A. H.
557674	,,	Williams, A. D.		815759	L/Cpl.	Woodruff-Minett, R. W.
322766	,,	Weir, S. V.		324067	Tpr.	Winter, E. R.
858383	,,	Yeates, G. J.		557345	,,	Hughes, A. W.

(3). THE FOLLOWING OFFICERS AND OTHER RANKS JOINED ON EMBODIMENT, 2 SEPTEMBER, 1939.

Lt.-Col. H. J. Nicholson, M.C., T.D.
Major O. St. M. Thynne.
Major The Lord Ashley.
Capt. C. E. Awdry.
Lt. J. G. Morrison.
Lt. J. F. Brown.
Lt. H. P. Hunloke, M.P.
2nd Lt. J. E. Gibb.
2nd Lt. C. R. C. Thursfield.
2nd Lt. The Marquis of Lansdowne.
2nd Lt. W. J. Ewart.
Lt. F. N. Rogers.
Captain P. G. Ormrod.
Captain M. H. Evans, R.A.M.C.

Major D. G. Williams.
Major P. W. Pitt.
Captain The Viscount Weymouth.
Captain C. H. F. Fuller.
Lt. E. F. Spicer.
Lt. H. Blount.
2nd Lt. The Earl Cadogan.
2nd Lt. Sir J. E. L. Clarke, Bt.
2nd Lt. G. A. Best.
2nd Lt. J. C. Bartholomew.
2nd Lt. S. V. Christie-Miller.
Lt. Smith-Piggott.
Captain C. L. Broomhead, R.A.M.C.
Captain M. Bridgman, R.A.V.C.

"A" SQUADRON.

326983	Tpr.	Bourne, C. P.		326935	Tpr.	Burt, B. J.
548105	Sgt.	Burton, C.		323455	,,	Bennett, H. R.
747216	Cpl.	Bartlett, R. E.		547171	Sgt.	Bracher, F. D. S.
324523	Tpr.	Burt, J.		326873	Tpr.	Baker, E. R.
326872	,,	Brain, N. W.		323001	,,	Baker, P. D.
326843	,,	Bishop, S. H.		326929	,,	Checketts, C.
552324	Cpl.	Clifford, R.		556480	,,	Collins, C. A.
324459	Tpr.	Carpenter, R. J.		324522	,,	Coward, J. T.
324591	,,	Dampney, T. D.		326875	,,	Doggrell, R. D.
326876	,,	Douglas, H. O. A.		324063	,,	Elgar, D.
324596	,,	Edwards, F. N.		555330	L/Cpl.	Forward, G.
324518	,,	Furnall, A. N.		324592	Tpr.	Garrett, E. S.
324516	,,	Gregory, F. J.		6596013	,,	Hunt, C.
324069	,,	Hughes, J. C.		326877	,,	Harris, J.
324457	,,	Holloway, H. D.		556483	,,	Hooper, E. A.
324593	,,	Hoddinott, J. L.		326845	,,	Hoddinott, R. R.
323076	,,	Hoskins, E. C.		550387	,,	Haines, C. J.
324517	,,	Hawkins, W. H.		324458	,,	Jeffries, R. D.
326910	,,	Jesse, E. F.		325266	,,	Light, R.
326879	,,	Lodge, P. W.		323462	,,	Lugg, C. H.
323002	,,	Lawes, A. H.		326911	,,	Legg, A. J.
326878	,,	Lodge, H. H. F.		538433	S.S.M.	Luxton, A. T. P.
5244459	Farr./Sgt.	Matthews, A. W.		556661	Tpr.	Newbury, C. L.

324519	Tpr.	Pickford, H. J.	324070	Tpr.	Payne, R. W.
324061	,,	Patience, M. C. W.	324062	,,	Palmer, R. B.
326912	,,	Pickford, A. H.	1012068	Sadd./Cpl.	Rickard, R. G.
326844	,,	Rendell, E. W. A.	323464	Tpr.	Rudkin.
324590	,,	Roberts, P.	557400	,,	Ricketts, H. C.
556600	L/Cpl.	Simmonds, P. J.	555335	,,	Scott, A. J.
324521	Tpr.	Stockley, R.	324456	,,	Soule, M. L.
324068	,,	Smith, G. A.	551381	Cpl.	Salisbury, E. F.
323175	,,	Stilwell, R. H.	324524	Tpr.	Silcox, G. T.
324460	,,	Saunderson, R. A.	324520	,,	Trimby, H. A.
324060	,,	Thacker.	556612	Cpl.	Woods, H. J.
326881	,,	Woodward, C. E.	324059	Tpr.	Worvell, F. T. B.
324595	,,	Webb, G. H.	323851	,,	Whitmarsh, H. E.
326880	,,	Woolford, R. F. S.	323006	,,	Webb, F. W.
324064	,,	Waters, E. C. M.			

"B" SQUADRON.

318532	Tpr.	Aslett, W. C. E.	557799	Tpr.	Arkell, G.
555974	,,	Ayres, E. A.	326936	,,	Budd, T.
323854	,,	Berry, L. H.	326900	,,	Bidler, H. D.
554757	Cpl.	Baker, A.	322781	,,	Bryant, D. A.
556019	Tpr.	Boscombe, L. H.	324487	,,	Bewley, D. H. T.
552087	Cpl.	Burry, D. G.	326889	,,	Beedell, L. H.
556358	Tpr.	Budds, F. G.	324489	,,	Bletsoe, F. S.
556885	,,	Brown, A. H.	322097	,,	Black, E.
323855	,,	Bull, J.	326888	,,	Beaven, E. T. G.
555388	,,	Cox, C. L.	324478	,,	Carter, K. G.
324484	,,	Coleman, R. S.	558113	,,	Carter, T.
326890	,,	Chilcott, I. J.	555801	,,	Cole, E.
322288	,,	Curtis, G.	555401	Cpl.	Clothier, C. E. E.
326891	,,	Chisling, H. A.	326923	Tpr.	Blewett, B. L.
557404	,,	Cabble, W. R.	324485	,,	Cleverley, C. R.
324479	,,	Creswick, R. J.	555975	,,	Dixon, W. J.
554754	,,	Dixon, W.	551542	,,	Draper, A. L.
553889	Cpl.	Davis, J. H.	558170	,,	Draper, C. A.
322782	Tpr.	Davis, R. E.	552353	,,	Escott, L.
556250	,,	Fido, H. S.	552787	Sgt.	Fielding, P. C.
556996	L/Cpl.	Green, F. G.	6395867	Tpr.	Giddings, J. W.
354756	,,	Goldsworthy, F. W. J.	324465	,,	Gray, R.
556418	Tpr.	Giddings, F. A.	555861	,,	Hale, C.
558122	,,	Harris, E. W.	556664	,,	Huntley, A. G.
323172	,,	Hobbs, C. S.	558169	,,	Hardy, A. E.
556610	,,	Hiscock, C. A.	548763	,,	Howse, R.
324482	,,	Hibberd, R. S.	558168	,,	Holborn, W. T.
554451	,,	Hayter, A. J.	556614	,,	Hiscocke, R.
326924	,,	Haines, A. J. B.	326894	,,	Halliday, B. A.
326895	,,	Hewer, T. W.	324471	,,	Harris, L. E.
324468	,,	Head, E.	324483	,,	Hawkins, P. E. T.
326893	,,	Hornblow, K. A. G.	326895	,,	Jessett, D. W. E.
556419	Cpl.	Lye, J. H. E.	557460	Cpl.	Little, A. G.
324474	Tpr.	Lampard, E. H. T.	324480	Tpr.	Lloyd, W. J. C.
555802	,,	Mees, J.	548904	Cpl.	Manning, F. J.
558237	,,	Martin, F.	324466	Tpr.	Monday, L. G.
556006	,,	Morris, D. H.	326896	,,	Mason, A. A.
556148	Cpl.	Mitchell, J. S.	550080	Sgt.	McLoughlin, J.
322780	Tpr.	Ley, P. G.	556886	Tpr.	Nutley, W. F.
557399	,,	Norman, L. F.	323173	,,	Nurdin, J.
550069	,,	Powell, V. J.	5568814	Cpl.	Palmer, F. C.
556883	,,	Park, R. J.	324462	Tpr.	Perry, J. T.
557397	,,	Paget, A. L.	556147	L/Cpl.	Pearce, E. W.
326937	,,	Pile, W. A.	547997	Farr./Sgt.	Platt, C. L.
325554	,,	Pitman, A. J.	555336	Cpl.	Pictor, D. J.
556952	,,	Perrott, E. B.	324463	Tpr.	Perry, A. F. G.
324475	,,	Rawlings, H. C. L.	556613	,,	Razey, G.
324470	,,	Russ, N.	324464	,,	Rudman, A. C.
557428	,,	Rickard, R. G.	556995	,,	Rickard, S. R.
326897	,,	Rowland, J. L.	323174	,,	Reynolds, S. R. A.

550086	Sgt.	Smith, W. T. A.		322908	Tpr.	Sawyer, L. G.
528361	S.S.M.	Stiles, H. R.		322546	,,	Spackman, C.
326898	Tpr.	Sims, R. T.		555947	,,	Sweetman, F. G.
554653	Cpl.	Selby, A. G.		554450	Cpl.	Smith, T. W.
324486	Tpr.	Smith, T. E.		557953	Tpr.	Smith, H. T.
325522	,,	Slacke, D. O. D.		554837	L/Cpl.	Tucker, R. I.
557444	,,	Timbrell, G. A.		553417	Cpl.	Teagle, A. E.
327120	,,	Underdown, C. E.		556887	Tpr.	Wiltshire, W. D.
557568	,,	Whittle, S. T.		324469	,,	Watts, E. E.
324473	,,	Woolley, R. F.		553418	Cpl.	Worsdell, R. D.
325551	,,	Welch, A. E.		557465	Tpr.	Wood, A. B.
553781	,,	White, T.		557463	,,	Woods, R. L.
324467	,,	Wadman, R.		322778	,,	Wordsell, A. E.
326899	,,	Whatley, L. F. C.		327121	,,	Clarke, C. T. A. C.

"C" SQUADRON.

535541	Tpr.	Archard, S.		324536	Tpr.	Armon, D.
324550	,,	Barnes, S. A.		545600	Sgt.	Alexander, W. F.
552195	,,	Banks, J.		318698	Tpr.	Bateman, B. E.
540136	,,	Baker, B. R. H.		557681	,,	Bleaken, R.
326839	,,	Baker, E. S.		324551	,,	Batt, K. G.
318712	,,	Baker, E. G.		326852	,,	Browning, N. C.
318700	,,	Collett, S. W.		550509	,,	Clifford, A. J.
556533	,,	Chedd, P.		324533	,,	Carter, S.
324125	,,	Crump, M.		323073	,,	Cross, R. C.
551332	Cpl.	Comely, W.		545599	S.S.M.	Carter, N.
324549	Tpr.	Clarke, E.		556585	Tpr.	Clothier, R. E.
556881	,,	Carvey, W. E.		545378	,,	Carter, T. W.
324525	,,	Caple, G.		324528	,,	Christopher, R. F.
555438	,,	Collingbourne, E. C.		327014	,,	Cooper, R.
553381	,,	Deacon, F. G.		324594	,,	Davies, W. E.
324541	,,	Denton, A.		555544	,,	Davies, J.
558215	,,	Daw, H.		557429	,,	Davies, K. A. W.
553512	Sgt.	Drury, D. C.		324531	,,	Dash, D. B.
326944	Tpr.	Frost, A. C.		556814	,,	Ferris, C.
557931	L/Cpl.	Ferrar, M. E.		326851	,,	Frayling, D.
326850	Tpr.	Gardner, J. R.		556815	Cpl.	Godsell, L.
324526	,,	Goddard, P.		324547	Tpr.	Gunter, F.
555420	L/Cpl.	Greenhill, F. R.		553151	,,	Guest, G. F.
324530	Tpr.	Garne, W.		322619	,,	Gazzard, D. H.
324546	,,	Hill, E. A.		557825	,,	George, A.
324539	,,	Hancock, E. A.		324548	,,	Haines, J. H. F.
553426	Cpl.	Honeybone, O.		556149	,,	Haynes, A.
557680	Tpr.	Hatherell, W. T.		322545	,,	Huggins, A. E.
775733	Cpl.	Heath, A. F.		546237	Sgt.	Harding, V. S.
323074	Tpr.	Heath, K. E.		324125	Tpr.	Hacker, H. S.
550559	Sgt.	Harding, A. D.		558271	,,	Hunter, A.
556130	Tpr.	Jarman, P.		554226	Cpl.	Hedges, J. E.
326846	,,	Jones, A. G. P.		748144	Tpr.	Johns, W.
557052	,,	Jeffries, F. J.		555196	,,	Kennedy, J.
553833	L/Sgt.	Knapp, M. H.		553130	Cpl.	Knight, C. H. E.
557518	L/Cpl.	Lovelle, A. J.		326943	Tpr.	Lawry, F. J.
326838	Tpr.	Mason, G.		318696	,,	Mundy, R. L.
556131	,,	McNally, L.		324543	,,	Miles, D. W. J.
322618	,,	Norris, C. R.		556813	Cpl.	Nash, L.
557677	,,	Pound, J.		324540	Tpr.	Ockwell, E.
522620	,,	Potter, W. P.		549579	Cpl.	Powell, R.
556192	,,	Ponting, D. A.		324534	Tpr.	Perry, S. O.
322799	,,	Payne, F. J.		522617	,,	Clayfield, R. E. J.
557679	,,	Parker, A. J. D.		551522	,,	Powell, H.
556581	,,	Punter, J.		326964	,,	Pike, H. J.
318699	,,	Rendell, V.		326841	,,	Potter, L. R.
3245350	,,	Sturmey, K. A.		557428	,,	Ricketts, P.
557654	,,	Shipton, A.		324532	,,	Smith, D.
326842	,,	Smith, A. E.		318695	,,	Smart, L. C.
326975	,,	Simpkins, L. V.		324126	,,	Soper, L.

326849	Tpr.	Shinwell, G. H.		318758	Tpr.	Strachan, D. C.
324527	,,	Spruels, H. R.		548632	Cpl.	Stanton, J. H.
324537	,,	Thorne, C. R. T.		552331	Cpl.	Smith, T. H.
318766	,,	Taylor, J. M.		556884	Tpr.	Tanner, A.
5566226	Cpl.	Truckle, J. R. C.		5431637	,,	Timms, F.
554538	Tpr.	Thompson, D. A.		556583	,,	Tidy, H.
557610	,,	Webb, J.		324538	,,	Williams, D.
318173	,,	Webb, E. G.		326853	,,	Willis, N.
327080	,,	Withers, J.		322002	,,	Walcroft, J.
555472	,,	Wilkins, S.		817489	L/Cpl.	Wade, D.
555437	,,	White, W.		326913	Tpr.	Walker, K. E. P.
557461	,,	Williams, S. R.		324552	,,	Westmacott, G.
324072	,,	Wheeler, V. A.		322006	,,	Wilks, T.
324073	,,	Webb, W. J.		324071	,,	Woodman, E.
324545	,,	Wilcox, N.		324544	,,	Westmacott, M. R.
548015	Sgt.	Witchell, H. G.		545549	,,	Willoughby, W.

"H.Q. SQUADRON.

324495	Tpr.	Burchell, H. J.		324490	Tpr.	Antell, W. J.
326963	,,	Betteridge, E. A.		323005	,,	Brunt, W. H.
556457	Bdsmn.	Berrett, V. E.		558109	,,	Bray, L. H.
323456	Tpr.	Boon, R. K.		324503	,,	Button, A. H.
557462	,,	Brown, W. J.		324132	,,	Butcher, R. W.
558114	Tptr.	Barton, D. V.		557404	,,	Bull, K. T.
552720	Bdsmn.	Bond, A. E.		556859	L/Cpl.	Brain, C. G.
324515	Tpr.	Bath, E. L.		324053	Tpr.	Baker, R. L.
324514	,,	Bale, R. J.		324066	,,	Byers, L.
318471	,,	Bradnam, H. L.		5566819	,,	Brown, J. W. E.
5563271	Bdsmn.	Cleverley, A. F.		324493	,,	Bridle, P. T. M.
555726	Tpr.	Cave, A. H.		324494	,,	Charmbury, L. R.
327119	,,	Cave, R. P.		555976	,,	Connor, G. S.
324492	,,	Collis, H. N.		558214	,,	Carrier, L. S.
322902	,,	Channon, M. F. H.		554317	Cpl.	Chivers, F. R.
554318	,,	Cogsbill, T. F.		553749	Tpr.	Clothier, D. P.
552786	L/Sgt.	Cleverley, H. C.		321886	,,	Coole, N. W. H.
553094	Bdsmn.	Dunning, A. J.		324507	,,	Cox, A. B.
324057	Tpr.	Eyres, C. K.		556068	,,	Draper, W. S.
555810	,,	Ford, R. G.		323171	,,	Escott, E. R.
324512	,,	Francis, L. H.		324058	,,	Ferris, D.
6340432	,,	Fayers, A. F.		552239	L/Cpl.	Ferris, H. M.
557676	,,	Farmer, R. G. F.		323457	Tpr.	Fielding, L.
557858	,,	Fryer, W. G.		558098	,,	Francis, H.
324454	,,	Goodman, A. C.		326976	,,	Gerrish, A. A.
558088	,,	Green, J.		324497	,,	Gadd, A.
548123	F.Q.M.S.	Gurd, A. H.		556428	,,	Giddings, E. W.
322763	Tpr.	Gilbert, D. H. J.		322098	,,	Goodman, K. G.
318767	,,	Hodgson, C. J.		551507	,,	Goddard, I. G. J.
269460	,,	Henley, J. T.		323458	,,	Hands, B. B.
548108	Sgt.	Hayter, W. H.		556861	,,	Harris, P. V.
324127	Tpr.	Hillman, H. G.		324501	,,	Hillman, A. E.
5567059	,,	Hood, S. G.		323459	,,	Hanney, N. F.
556548	Bdsmn.	Harris, F. C.		322901	,,	Hancock, F. B. S.
552761	Tpr.	Ingram, D. E.		324502	,,	Hoare, H. F.
323460	,,	James, G.		556458	,,	Ingram, O.
5567067	,,	Johnson, R. G.		557441	L/Cpl.	Johnson, F.
556445	Bdsmn.	Jeffrey, F.		5566772	Tpr.	Johnson, H.
318759	Tpr.	Knight, G. R.		5562060	Bdsmn.	Jones, A. S.
322542	,,	Keates, W. A. C.		323853	Tpr.	King, C.
324055	,,	Lintern, E. K.		324511	,,	Lawrence, H. J.
324509	,,	Lawrence, K. E. P		554331	Cpl.	Lakey, G. E.
326887	,,	Mitchell, E. H.		529953	S.S.M.	Mead, E. F.
322543	,,	Mattick, W. W.		558097	Tpr.	Marston, C. V.
555687	,,	MacMillan, F. R.		557442	,,	Muspratt, R. G.
324491	,,	Maidment, R. J.		4448780	,,	Marshall, T. W.
5565579	,,	Norris, J. V.		524129	,,	Neathy, D. J.
5610898	Bdsmn.	Parkin, A. G.		324499	,,	Oakley, L. W. T.

322504	Tpr.	Powell, W. H. C.		552762	Tpr.	Pratten, S. J.
324496	,,	Poole, T. G.		324128	,,	Papps, J. D.
557341	,,	Perrott, J. E.		553420	Band. Sgt.	Price, D. J.
324508	,,	Pike, K. D.		323463	Tpr.	Parfitt, C. I.
555688	,,	Pink, A. P.		323075	,,	Puddy, W. D.
558243	,,	Redsull, S. W.		318701	,,	Reynolds, R. C. W.
323004	,,	Rose, A. T.		318523	,,	Randall, F. J.
553819	Tptr./Maj.	Slade, F. G.		541795	Bdsmn.	Reynolds, T. J.
558066	Tpr.	Sheppard, A. J.		556993	Sgt.	Shipp, D. W.
552700	Bdsmn.	Stevens, H. R.		556992	Sig. Sgt.	Sturge, R. L.
326854	Tpr.	Sumbler, A. W.		324052	Tpr.	Smart, E. P.
318615	L/Cpl.	Shears, M. W.		552542	Bdsmn.	Sims, C. W.
324500	Tpr.	Smith, I. W.		322903	Tpr.	Smith, R. A. P.
326977	,,	Smale, C. G.		528373	R.Q.M.S.	Sutcliffe, R. J. M.
557926	Cpl.	Townsend, L. E.		1019765	Sadd.S/Sgt	Stagg, L. G.
557053	,,	Udy, W. J.		5562172	Cpl.	Tippetts, F.
558002	Tpr.	Vennell, D. W.		326927	Tpr.	Uncles, D. S.
324510	,,	White, S. J.		558239	,,	Winfield, W. H.
557521	,,	Ward, F.		556744	,,	Webb, E. S. G.
322621	,,	Wilkins, H. H.		322632	,,	White, J. D.
558217	,,	Warburton, J. J.		326925	,,	Wilkins, R. G. E.
318524	,,	Warburton, G. F.		324513	,,	Wake, E. G. L.
556994	L/Cpl.	White, W. F.		552721	Bdsmn.	Weston, C. G.
323176	Tpr.	Walke, A. W.		557520	Tpr.	Witts, L. M.
323461	,,	Legge, L. H. J.		552784	Bdsmn.	Weston, A. K. G.
5565850	,,	Payne, G. E.		324504	Tpr.	Vowles, W. E.

THE FOLLOWING OFFICERS AND OTHER RANKS WERE EMBODIED ON THE DATES SHOWN.

OFFICERS.

2nd September.

2nd Lt. G. S. Wills (Reserve of Officers).

10th September.

Capt. A. M. Gibb (from Kenya).

11th September.

Capt. The Rev. L. A. Fereday.

OTHER RANKS.

1st September.

"C" SQUADRON.

326954	Tpr.	Cordoff, G.

2nd September.

"B" SQUADRON.

324472	Tpr.	Barton, H. R.		326892	Tpr.	Fay, P. C.
556339	,,	Ford, W. H.		548726	,,	Marshall, D.
558067	,,	Nurdin, F.		324461	,,	Ritchens, E. W.
555310	,,	Spreadbury, G. F.		324488	,,	Way, R. A.

3rd September.

"A" SQUADRON.

556251	Tpr.	Symonds, R. M.

4th September.

"C" SQUADRON.

556768	Tpr.	Bannister, D.		324529	Tpr.	Clarke, S.
559519	,,	Clifford, G.		326840	,,	Hunt, P. A.
557829	,,	Mudie, M. C.		326848	,,	Newcombe, G.
326948	,,	Steel, T. H. G.		557653	,,	Wilkins, M. G.

7th September.

326847	Tpr.	Young, P. R. G.		538641	S.Q.M.S.	Rhodes, C.

NOMINAL ROLL OF RESERVISTS ABSORBED IN DECEMBER, 1939, AND JANUARY, 1940.

"H.Q." SQUADRON.

548516	Sgt.	Aucott, C.	553662	L/Cpl.	Appleby, W. E.
405003	Tpr.	Ambrose, J. F.	405018	Tpr.	Ainsley, J. W.
552283	Cpl.	Beal, A.	403653	L/Cpl.	Bush, J.
316281	Tpr.	Beech, A.	1034643	Tpr.	Burtenshaw, G.
405831	,,	Bowen, C.	543603	,,	Baveillot, L.
551848	L/Cpl.	Boyden, J. T.	404455	Cpl.	Calvert, D.
314651	Cpl.	Cawkwell, W. S.	3905395	Farr.	Clifford, T.
4970507	Tpr.	Edwards, G. F.	554880	Tpr.	Elliott, W.
325996	,,	Ferguson, P.	404022	,,	Felton, J.
5667384	,,	Franklin, C. E.	402618	,,	Gadsby, J. T.
405408	,,	Gambles, H. J.	4609986	,,	Gibbs, D.
3706262	,,	Gallagher, T. C.	409535	L/Cpl.	Heaton, J.
547783	L/Cpl.	Hasdell, A.	316729	,,	Hardy, F.
405687	Farr.	Hinton, A. G. L.	405153	Tpr.	Hayward, W.
398403	Tpr.	Hill, J.	480427	,,	Jones, D. J.
402022	,,	Jones, G.	4912167	,,	Jerromes, A.
811030	,,	Jackson, W.	315540	,,	Kirby, H.
406115	Cpl.	Kendrick, A.	405893	,,	Kurlew, A. H
7539218	Tpr.	Le Vallois.	6198142	,,	Lines, G. H.
407225	,,	Lamb, J.	393281	,,	Munroe, S.
404062	,,	Mullis, J.	549770	,,	Monney, M.
533390	,,	Marshall, J.	540538	,,	Mawson, J. W.
534447	T.S.M.	McGough, W. M.	3053313	L/Cpl.	Mitchell, D.
551193	Tpr.	Millburn, J.	407133	Tpr.	Marsden, J. H.
402687	,,	Newman, H. W.	324506	,,	Newman, C. P.
398761	,,	Nixon.	550389	,,	Otter, M.
544121	Cpl.	Pearce, A.	406463	,,	Pinnock P. G.
404389	Tpr.	Parry, E. J.	316438	,,	Pearson, W.
318538	,,	Poole, E.	399049	,,	Pilling, L.
402356	Farr.	Powell, J.	406321	,,	Pert, J.
316515	Tpr.	Roberts, W. G.	404682	,,	Rowell, F.
558232	,,	Richardson, C. A.	317209	L/Cpl.	Rees, M.
405212	,,	Rosevear, O.	403972	Cpl.	Richards, G
599553	L/Cpl.	Smith, J. D.	549827	Sgt.	Spence, J.
3242961	Tpr.	Sally, J.	406651	Tpr.	Thomas, H. J.
544102	,,	Taylor, B.	104959	,,	Thornbury, C.
548745	,,	Thrall, J. E.	549691	,,	Thompson, A.
544096	,,	Tingey, W.	4060908	,,	Ward, J.
404935	,,	Whalley, H.	544843	,,	Wheeler, A.
803701	,,	White, S.	316387	,,	Wilson, E. E.
4448298	,,	Wilkinson, G.	405872	,,	Whooton, W. J.
3958314	,,	Williams, H. L. G.			

"A" SQUADRON.

549771	Tpr.	Arch, S. J. C.	4188241	Tpr.	Bowler, A.
550182	,,	Brown, H.	3049629	Sgt.	Burnett, T.
4970065	Cpl.	Beniston, J.	405864	Tpr.	Brown, J.
405463	Tpr.	Brook, J.	405492	,,	Bradford, G. W. H.
405047	Cpl.	Curtis, L. H.	404769	,,	Connochie, F.
405921	Tpr.	Coleman, J. S.	4912587	,,	Cooper, W. F.
548774	Sgt.	Dunn, J. A.	556283	L/Cpl.	Dunscombe, A.
404423	Tpr.	Davis, J. L.	406242	,,	Dixon, W.
405466	,,	Evans, R.	552541	Tpr.	Finthan, T.
780434	,,	Finnis, A. H.	535877	,,	Goodridge, H.
5782987	,,	Gale, S. V.	543920	Sgt.	Hampshire, D.
404738	,,	Highton, G.	351782	L/Cpl.	Heaton, A.
405810	,,	Harrison, J. E.	407223	Tpr.	Halfpenny, G. S.
551101	,,	Jayes, A.	405661	,,	Jones, F.
398193	,,	Kelly, T.	552809	,,	Kendrick, E.
398823	Cpl.	Logan, R.	6198641	,,	Leaven, A.
550568	,,	Lilley, D.	548738	,,	Luck, B. E. J.
550153	Tpr.	Lynn, W. J.	406564	,,	Lee, R.
551591	L/Cpl.	Lunn, W.	2563842	,,	Marshall, R. W.
2566508	Tpr.	Moore, A.	552803	,,	McPike, J.

549773	Bdsmn.	McPherson.		546189	Bdsmn.	Marsham.
547090	,,	Mount, A.		3708008	Farr.	Ousby, W.
400233	,,	Orsett, A.		4263786	Tpr.	Pollard, S. W.
405983	Tpr.	Powell, J.		549660	,,	Penny, P.
553137	,,	Parton, A. G.		546788	,,	Potter, R.
549732	,,	Ransom, F.		398935	,,	Reeves, F.
402263	Farr.	Rippon, M.		397508	,,	Reader, J.
547691	Tpr.	Rothery, J.		552789	,,	Reeves, W. G.
553569	,,	Snell, W.		407237	,,	Stack, J.
546825	,,	Savin, C. H.		398770	,,	Shelton, F.
310735	,,	Thorncroft, H.		6200853	,,	Tibble, H.
548993	,,	Taylor, G.		823158	Cpl.	Thornton, L.
553578	,,	Thorley, H.		551814	Tpr.	Thomas, R. F.
552864	,,	Vaughan, J.		548519	,,	Walker, A.
401955	,,	Williams, R.		403094	,,	Williams, A.
5494701	,,	Withers, A.		549846	,,	Young, J.

"B" SQUADRON.

398397	Tpr.	Allen, W.		553554	L/Cpl.	Baines, W.
405382	L/Cpl.	Berrell, J.		405152	Tpr.	Burnham, J. W.
551673	Tpr.	Boult, F.		405479	,,	Bridges, A. J.
404700	,,	Best, P. J.		551909	,,	Bryne, G.
405052	,,	Ball, L.		547659	Sgt.	Durbar, D.
804412	,,	Elsom, A.		4911387	Tpr.	Fellows, J.
398896	,,	Fletcher, T. W.		404710	,,	Faithfull, H. W.
4799053	,,	Francis, A. W.		549174	,,	Genter, E.
550792	,,	Griffiths, A.		549762	,,	Gross, W.
552621	,,	Givnan, J.		402292	,,	Green, A.
550421	,,	Garnett, J.		550617	Sgt.	Hyde, A. F.
398400	,,	Hasdell, T.		403401	Tpr.	Hare, F.
405811	L/Cpl.	Hutton, A.		551828	,,	Jones, H.
1661877	Tpr.	Jenkins, A.		552069	,,	Jones, S. T.
406499	,,	Kermath, E.		549149	Cpl.	Kendrick, F.
551962	,,	King, C. F.		404752	Tpr.	Kingswell, H.
769317	Cpl.	Lowe, D.		402811	,,	Linfield, S.
405338	Tpr.	Lee, J. R.		550448	,,	Lester, J.
404743	Cpl.	Mannell, A. M.		551616	,,	Martland, F.
403407	Tpr.	Morris, J.		402006	,,	Mayo.
775659	,,	Machin, G.		550577	Sgt.	Parkes, G.
548892	,,	Parslow, E.		552857	Cpl.	Parker, G. H.
543049	Farr.	Pettitt.		549833	Tpr.	Pope, G. W.
554392	Tpr.	Read, P.		405028	,,	Sutcliffe, A.
553687	,,	Stark.		543214	Cpl.	Smith, E.
552804	,,	Stocks, R.		722456	Tpr.	Smedhurst, A.
552060	,,	Simpson, A.		404688	,,	Stewart, D. L.
316583	,,	Thurlow, R.		551043	,,	Turner, A. E.
549799	,,	Talbot, A.		550738	Farr.	Wingfield, J.
398926	,,	Waterhouse, A.		549507	Tpr.	Walker, T.
398878	,,	Whittaker, M.		550589	,,	Wood, J.
352611	,,	Webb, F.				

"C" SQUADRON.

404679	Tpr.	Allen, H.		402242	Tpr.	Armitage.
404445	,,	Arnold, C.		403410	,,	Asborne.
768780	,,	Brogan, D.		403509	,,	Baxter, L.
406075	Cpl.	Bumford, D.		398881	,,	Berry.
803340	Tpr.	Buckley, R.		404786	,,	Bonehill.
405472	,,	Barham, A. W.		405402	,,	Bayliss, T.
404732	,,	Boushear, T.		404775	,,	Baggott, A. E.
405437	,,	Cooper, A.		399144	L/Cpl.	Cook, J. L.
402445	,,	Calcutt, N.		405351	Tpr.	Clayden, W.
403405	,,	Clarke, E.		550628	,,	Davis, W.
4607719	,,	Dawson.		552102	,,	Giles.
4768612	,,	Dunthorne, A.		317107	,,	Harding, T.
405482	,,	Harrison.		402047	,,	Harrison, T.
398897	,,	Jeffery, T. T.		7812129	,,	Jones, H.
405049	,,	Jackson, H.		404756	,,	Kelly, A.

310931	Cpl.	Linfield, H.	549863	Tpr.	May, H.
405991	,,	MacDonald, E.	406698	,,	McNair, H.
2211347	Tpr.	MacDonald, D. G.	407506	,,	Moore, J. W.
6978342	,,	Murphy, H. S.	405063	,,	Monk, J. W.
402890	,,	Newman, C.	552610	,,	Nelson, J. C.
547755	Sgt.	Peppiatt, S. H.	549312	Cpl.	Palmer, L.
316646	Cpl.	Peterkin, J.	543221	Sgt.	Pearson, H.
405263	Tpr.	Parkin, W.	405491	Tpr.	Pressley.
402276	,,	Potter, I.	405001	,,	Pritchard.
405427	,,	Pattinson, J.	542973	,,	Repton, H.
316782	,,	Redman, C.	318155	,,	Robertson, H. A.
406595	,,	Redwood, H.	550653	Cpl.	Randall, H. J.
403458	Cpl.	Reeves, E.	4535678	Tpr.	Simpson, A.
811213	Tpr.	Smith, H.	405024	,,	Scott.
549505	L/Cpl.	Toll, R.	407096	,,	Turner, G. F.
317015	Tpr.	Thorpe, J.	552926	,,	Tarlton, R.
402650	L/Cpl.	Thompson.	4744651	,,	Thickett.
552019	Tpr.	Thompson, F.	553025	,,	Vincent, A.
404664	,,	Ward, C.	550392	,,	Warrington.
404511	,,	Webb, J.	5723784	,,	White, G.
5674804	,,	Wilkins, S.	548708	,,	Wilson, T.
405107	,,	Wilson, C.	398239	,,	Yates.

THE FOLLOWING OFFICERS AND OTHER RANKS EMBARKED FOR PALESTINE IN FEBRUARY, 1940.

ADVANCE PARTY.

Capt. H. Blount.

528373	R.Q.M.S.	Sutcliffe, R. J. N.	542317	T.S.M.	Tulk, F. S.
322748	Cpl.	Miles, W. L.	556469	Tpr.	Culverhouse, C. F.
551673	Tpr.	Boult, F.			

MAIN PARTY.

Lt.-Col. D. G. Williams.
Major The Viscount Weymouth.
Capt. F. St. George. Adjutant.
Capt. F. N. Rogers.
Lt. (Q.M.) F. A. Riddiford.
Lt. F. A. G. Blackwood.
Lt. H. G. Awdry.
2nd Lt. J. E. Gibb.
2nd Lt. Sir J. E. L. Clerke, Bt.
2nd Lt. The Marquis of Lansdowne.
2nd Lt. S. V. Christie-Miller.
Capt. M. H. Evans, R.A.M.C.
Capt. The Rev. L. A. Fereday. R.A.C.D.

Major A. M. Gibb.
Major C. E. Awdry.
Capt. C. H. F. Fuller.
Capt. J. G. Morrison.
Lt. The Hon. A. E. G. Herbert.
Lt. E. F. Spicer.
2nd Lt. M. St. J. V. Gibbs.
2nd Lt. The Earl Cadogan.
2nd Lt. G. A. Best.
2nd Lt. J. C. Bartholomew.
2nd Lt. G. S. Wills,
Capt. M. Bridgman, R.A.V.C.

"H.Q." SQUADRON.

323852	L/Cpl.	Andrews, M.	324454	Tpr.	Angell, R. J.
558299	Tpr.	Alley, A. N. C.	405003	,,	Ambrose, J.
405018	,,	Ainsley, J. W.	402242	,,	Armitage.
398987	,,	Allen, W.	553662	L/Cpl.	Appleby, A.
548516	Sgt.	Aucott, C.	323005	,,	Brunt, W. H.
552701	Tpr.	Baker, K. G.	316281	Tpr.	Beech, A.
556457	,,	Berrett, V.	104643	,,	Burtenshaw, G.
557462	,,	Brown, W. J.	324515	,,	Bath, E. L.
324066	,,	Byers, L.	318471	,,	Bradnam, H. L.
326963	,,	Betteridge, E. A.	324132	,,	Butcher, R. W.
323456	,,	Boon, R. K.	326843	,,	Bishop, S.
324503	,,	Button, A. H.	552720	L/Cpl.	Bond, A. E.
551842	L/Cpl.	Boyden, J.	324498	Tpr.	Bellamy, D. F.
543603	Tpr.	Bavoillot, L.	557404	,,	Bull, K. T.
326929	,,	Checketts, C.	548105	S.Q.M.S.	Burton, C.
324522	,,	Coward, J.	405831	Tpr.	Bowen, C.
557346	L/Cpl.	Coleman, R.	552853	Cpl.	Beel, A.
324492	Tpr.	Collis, H. N.	5563271	Tpr.	Cleverley, A. F.
404455	Cpl.	Calvert, D.	554317	Sgt.	Chivers, F. R.

322004	Tpr.	Creese, G.		324529	Tpr.	Clarke, S. J.
323171	,,	Escott, R.		326886	,,	Coole, N. W. H.
325996	,,	Ferguson, P.		552324	Cpl.	Clifford, R.
552237	Cpl.	Ferris, M. H.		405921	Tpr.	Coleman.
404022	Tpr.	Felton, A.		4979507	,,	Edwards, G. F.
551507	,,	Goddard, I. G.		7816266	R.S.M.	Frost, E. T.
548123	F.Q.M.S.	Gurd, A. H.		554880	Tpr.	Elliott, W.
324054	Tpr.	Goodman, A. H. G.		5667384	,,	Franklin, C.
4509986	,,	Gibbs, D.		326976	,,	Gerrish, R. A.
405408	,,	Gambles, H. J.		322098	,,	Goodman, K.
409535	L/Cpl.	Heaton, A.		322763	,,	Gilbert, R. H. J.
323459	Tpr.	Hanney, N. F.		558088	,,	Green, J.
6596013	,,	Hunt, C.		402618	,,	Gadsby, T.
556861	,,	Harris, P. V.		3706260	,,	Gallagher, T.
555938	,,	Hoare, R. H.		550559	Sgt.	Harding, A. D.
405687	Farr.	Hinton, L.		324501	Tpr.	Hillman, A. E.
547783	L/Cpl.	Hazell, A.		323458	,,	Hands, B. B.
5567059	Tpr.	Hood, S. G.		548108	Sgt.	Hayter, W. H.
323460	,,	James, G.		324455	Tpr.	Holmes, J. S.
5180427	,,	Jones, D. J.		316729	L/Cpl.	Hardy, F.
323853	,,	King, C.		398403	Tpr.	Hill, J.
405893	,,	Kirlew, A. H.		550387	,,	Haines, E. C. W.
406115	Cpl.	Kendrick, A.		557441	L/Cpl.	Johnson, F.
323461	Tpr.	Legge, L.		402022	Tpr.	Jones, G.
324509	,,	Laurence, K. E. P.		1661877	,,	Jenkins, A.
407225	,,	Lamb, J.		322542	L/Cpl.	Keates, W. A. C.
324491	,,	Maidment, R. J.		315540	Tpr.	Kirby, H.
324130	,,	Molloy, B.		324511	,,	Lawrence, H. J.
404062	,,	Mullis, J.		554331	Cpl.	Lakey, G. E.
555687	,,	MacMillan, F.		326943	Tpr.	Lawry, F. J.
522543	,,	Mattick, W. M.		6198642	,,	Lines, G. H.
328481	,,	Morey, W. W. P.		558997	,,	Marston, C. V.
407133	,,	Marsden, D.		393281	,,	Munroe, S.
549770	,,	Mooney, M.		533390	,,	Marshall, J.
543038	,,	Mawson, J. W.		4448780	,,	Marshall, T. W.
324506	,,	Newman, C. P.		326887	,,	Mitchell, E. H.
402687	,,	Newman, W. H.		3053313	L/Cpl.	Mitchell, D.
324499	,,	Oakley, L. W. T.		551193	Tpr.	Milburn, J.
779031	Cook Sgt.	Pollard, H. D.		557829	,,	Mudie, A. C.
5565850	Tpr.	Payne, G. E.		398761	,,	Nixon.
1055577	Farr.	Plummer, H. C.		5565579	,,	Norris, J. V.
5610898	L/Cpl.	Parkins, A. G.		544929	S.Q.M.S.	Osmond, R. H.
557341	Tpr.	Perrott, J. E.		5503519	Tpr.	Otter, H.
323075	,,	Puddy, W. D.		324065	Cpl.	Perkins, E. E.
406321	,,	Pert, J.		324051	Tpr.	Perry, E. H.
404389	,,	Parry, F. J.		553420	Sgt.	Price, D.
399049	,,	Pilling, L.		324128	Tpr.	Papps, J. D.
558213	Cpl.	Reed, V.		324508	,,	Pike, K. D.
327443	Tpr.	Roberts, L. J.		316438	,,	Pearson, W.
317209	L/Cpl.	Rees, N.		544121	Cpl.	Pearce, A.
323464	Tpr.	Rudkin, G. R.		402356	Farr.	Powell, J.
316515	,,	Roberts, W. G.		406463	Tpr.	Pinnock, P.
405212	,,	Rosevear, O.		318523	,,	Randall, F. J.
553819	T.M.	Slade, F. G.		323004	,,	Rose, A. P.
558066	Tpr.	Sheppard, A. J.		406682	,,	Rowell, F.
322779	,,	Spender, A. W. J.		403972	Cpl.	Richards, S. G.
1019765	S.S.S.	Stagg, L. G.		548532	Tpr.	Richardson, C.
324052	L/Cpl.	Smart, E. P.		556992	Sgt.	Sturge, R. L.
552700	Tpr.	Stevens, H. R.		326977	L/Cpl.	Smale, C.
3249261	,,	Sally, J.		552752	Tpr.	Sims, C. W.
547926	P. Sgt.	Townsend, L. E.		326854	,,	Sumbler, A. W.
5562172	Cpl.	Tippett, F.		556993	Sgt.	Shipp, D.
5432637	Tpr.	Timms, F. C. W.		558089	Tpr.	Simons, E. E.
404959	,,	Thornbury, G.		324527	,,	Spruels, H.
548745	Cpl.	Thrall, J. E.		549582	,,	Smith, J. B.
326927	Tpr.	Uncles, D.		544096	,,	Tingey, W.
558002	,,	Vennell, D.		3127428	,,	Thompson, C.

557521	L/Cpl.	Ward, F.		544102	Tpr.	Taylor, D.
318524	Tpr.	Warburton, G. F.		406657	,,	Thomas, H. J.
556994	L/Cpl.	White, W. F.		557053	Cpl.	Udy, W. J.
558212	Tpr.	Warburton, J. J.		324504	Tpr.	Vowles, W. E.
322621	,,	Wilkins, H. H.		547798	T.S.M.	Wheeler, L. C.
4448298	,,	Wilkinson, G.		323176	Tpr.	Walke, W. A.
326925	,,	Wilkins, R. G. E.		324510	,,	White, S. J.
405872	,,	Wootton, W. J.		324513	,,	Wake, E. G. L.
316387	,,	Wilcox, E. C.		5567440	,,	Webb, E. S. G.
550392	,,	Warrington, P.		803781	,,	White, S.
324545	,,	Wilcox, R. J.		358239	,,	Winfield, W. F.
404664	,,	Ward, C.		326913	,,	Walker, K. E. P.
				3958314	,,	Williams, H. L.
				324059	,,	Worvell, F.
				557520	,,	Witts, L. N.
				404935	,,	Whalley, H

"A" SQUADRON.

550388	Sgt.	Arnold, N. A. H.		324490	Tpr.	Antill, W. J.
549771	Tpr.	Arch, S. J. C.		529647	S.S.M.	Barker, E. J.
747216	Cpl.	Bartlett, R. E.		555353	Cpl.	Brake, E. F.
323001	Tpr.	Baker, P. D.		557594	Tpr.	Blake, P.
318469	,,	Bond, R. H.		557673	,,	Burt, W. J.
326874	,,	Baker, E. R.		323453	,,	Bennett, H. R.
550255	Farr.	Bishop, J.		556482	,,	Bond, R.
326872	Tpr.	Brain, N. W.		326935	,,	Burt, B. J.
405063	,,	Brook, J.		4970065	Cpl.	Beniston, J.
405492	,,	Bradford, G. W. H.		550182	Tpr.	Brown, H.
326985	,,	Bourne, C.		4188241	,,	Bowler.
550545	Cpl.	Chambers, R. G.		404769	,,	Connochie, F.
555856	Tpr.	Coggan, D. T.		556480	,,	Collins, C. A.
550388	Sgt.	Coates, F.		556461	,,	Cox, H. L.
405047	Tpr.	Curtis, L. H.		4912587	,,	Cooper, N.
555940	Cpl.	Dufosee, A.		326875	,,	Doggrell, R. D.
556424	Tpr.	Davis, A. D. N.		556068	Tptr.	Draper, W. S.
406242	L/Cpl.	Dickson, W.		404423	Tpr.	Davis, L. J.
656283	,,	Dunscombe, A.		326875	,,	Douglas.
405466	Tpr	Evans, R.		324063	,,	Elgar, D.
322765	,,	Egremont, D. S.		555330	Cpl.	Forward, G.
557830	,,	Foord, W. M.		557593	F/Cpl.	Ford, A. H.
540709	Sgt.	Golden, C. W.		324592	Tpr.	Garrett, E. S.
556398	Tpr.	Gatehouse, R. P.		557595	,,	Golding, W.
782987	,,	Gale, S.		324516	,,	Gregory, F. J.
535877	,,	Gradidge, M.		534269	Cpl.	Horne, F. C.
543920	Sgt.	Hampshire, D.		553356	,,	Harraway, J. R.
554451	Tpr.	Hayter, A.		326877	Tpr.	Harris, J.
324517	,,	Hawkins, W.		324127	,,	Hillman, H..G.
407223	,,	Halfpenny, G.		558141	,,	Hinton, G. E.
324593	,,	Hoddinott, J. R.		557345	,,	Hughes, A. W.
316729	,,	Hardy.		404738	,,	Highton, G.
551782	,,	Heaton.		405661	,,	Jones, F.
405153	,,	Haywood.		324458	L/Cpl.	Jefferies, R. D.
551101	,,	Jayes.		556359	Tpr.	Jefferys, C. H.
552809	,,	Kendrick, E.		398193	,,	Kelly, T.
552323	L/Sgt.	Locke, W.		550568	Cpl.	Lilley, F.
548728	Tpr.	Luck, E.		326911	Tpr.	Legg, A. J.
551391	L/Cpl.	Lunn, W.		323002	,,	Lawes, A. J
326879	Tpr.	Lodge, P. W.		406564	,,	Lee, R.
550152	,,	Lynn, N.		6198641	,,	Leaven, A.
323462	,,	Lugg, C. H.		556343	,,	Luff, M. G
389823	Cpl.	Logan, J.		325266	,,	Light, R.
5244459	Farr. Sgt.	Matthews, A.		326878	,,	Lodge, H. H. F.
557596	Tpr.	Miller, H. J.		557055	,,	Merrett, L. M.
557522	,,	Miles, A. E.		1039371	Farr.	Morris, R. A.
316504	Farr.	Macey, W. A.		2563842	,,	Marshall, R. W.
547090	Tpr.	Mount, A.		546189	Bdsmn.	Marsham, D.
	,,	Marks, D. L.		2566508	Tpr.	Moore, A.

223

552803	Tpr.	McPike, J.		556481	Tpr.	Mason, J. E.
555857	L/Cpl.	Noyce, H.		549773	Bdsmn.	MacPherson.
400233	Bdsmn.	Orsett, A.		556663	Tpr.	Newbury, G.
546127	S.Q.M.S.	Pike, R. E. J.		553354	Cpl.	Pickford, H. W.
553352	Cpl.	Pickford, H. S.		551506	L/Sgt.	Pike, E. A. C.
4263786	Tpr.	Pollard, S. W.		326841	Tpr.	Potter, L. R.
324519	,,	Pickford, H. J.		318470	,,	Pearce, A. G.
324070	,,	Payne, R. W.		553137	,,	Parton, A. G.
549660	,,	Penny, J.		326912	,,	Pickford, A. H.
1012069	S/Sgt.	Rickard, R. G.		405983	,,	Powell, J.
547691	Tpr.	Rothery, J.		549732	,,	Ransome, F.
326844	,,	Rendell, R.		399508	,,	Reader, J.
552798	,,	Reeve, W. G.		557405	,,	Rolls, R. W.
557408	,,	Ricketts, H. C.		398935	,,	Reeves, F.
324590	,,	Roberts, P.		555354	,,	Read, E. G.
553569	,,	Snell, W.		556600	L/Cpl.	Simmonds, P.
555335	,,	Scott, K.		554434	,,	Smith, J.
323175	,,	Stilwell, R. H.		324524	Tpr.	Silcox, G. T.
398770	,,	Shelton, F.		546025	,,	Savin, C. F.
555354	,,	Scott, M. W. A.		556251	L/Cpl.	Symonds, R. N.
407237	,,	Stack, J.		324068	Tpr.	Smith, G. A.
324460	,,	Saunderson, R.		324521	,,	Stockley, R.
323465	L/Cpl.	Thomas, W. E.		310737	,,	Thorncroft, H.
548993	Tpr.	Taylor, G.		823158	Cpl.	Thonton, L.
324520	,,	Trimby, H. A.		324068	Tpr.	Thacker, A.
557592	,,	Tongs, M.		322956	,,	Thorne, J.
551814	,,	Thomas, R. S.		549691	,,	Thompson, A.
322764	,,	Trethowan, M.		553578	,,	Thorley, H.
552864	,,	Vaughan, J.		6200853	,,	Tibble, H.
548513	,,	Walker, A.		815759	L/Cpl.	Woodruff-Minett, R.
324064	,,	Waters, E. C. M.		318616	Tpr.	Woods, A. H.
323466	,,	Wilson, W. J.		557401	,,	Wheble, M. de la F.
556226	,,	Wardle, D.		326881	,,	Woodward, C. E.
323851	,,	Whitmarsh, H. E.		322766	,,	Weare, S. V.
556612	Cpl.	Woods, H. T.		324067	,,	Winter, E. R.
553357	,,	Watts, A. R.		553413	Cpl.	Waters, H. E.
402955	Tpr.	Williams, R.		403094	Tpr.	Williams, A.
556862	,,	Williams, L.		326880	,,	Woolford, R.
				858383	,,	Yeates, E. J.

"B" SQUADRON.

554337	L/Sgt.	Adams, P. E.		545600	S.Q.M.S.	Alexander, W. F.
325553	Tpr.	Allen, A. G.		555974	Tpr.	Ayres, E. A.
557799	,,	Arkell, G.		324472	,,	Barton, H. R.
3766959	,,	Bartlett, H.		553554	L/Cpl.	Baines, W.
405052	,,	Ball, L.		326889	Tpr.	Beedell, L. H.
405382	,,	Berrell, J.		404700	,,	Best, T. J.
324489	,,	Bletso, F.		326923	,,	Blewett, B. L.
555435	,,	Blackbeard, W.		322097	,,	Black, E.
556019	,,	Boscombe, L. H.		551909	,,	Boyne, G. W.
553885	,,	Brown, A. H.		322781	,,	Bryant, D. A.
326936	,,	Budd, J.		323855	,,	Bull, J.
552097	L/Sgt.	Burry, D. G.		405479	,,	Bridges, A.
405152	Tpr.	Burnham, J. W.		324481	,,	Butler, R. B.
558113	,,	Carter, T.		557403	,,	Cabble, W. R.
324485	,,	Cleverley, C. R.		555726	,,	Cave, A. H.
553749	Tptr.	Clothier, D. P.		555401	Cpl.	Clothier, C. E.
553889	Cpl.	Davis, J.		555388	Tpr.	Cox, C. L.
554754	Tpr.	Dixon, W.		324476	,,	Davis, H. J.
558170	,,	Draper, C. A. E.		551542	,,	Draper, A. L.
547659	Sgt.	Durbar, D.		408057	,,	Duncan, J. L.
326892	Tpr.	Fay, P. G.		804412	,,	Elsom, A.
398896	,,	Fletcher, T. W.		404710	,,	Faithfull, H. W.
4799053	,,	Francis, A. W.		491130	,,	Fellows, J.
556250	,,	Fido, H. S.		324512	,,	Francis, L. H.
322920	,,	George, T. E.		550421	,,	Garnett, J.
552621	,,	Givnan, J.		549174	,,	Genter, E.

324465	Tpr.	Gray, R.		554756	L/Cpl.	Goldsworthy, F.
402292	,,	Green, A.		556996	,,	Green, F. G.
550792	,,	Griffiths, A.		549762	Tpr.	Gross, W.
398400	,,	Hasdell, T.		555861	,,	Hale, C.
558122	,,	Harris, E. W.		558169	,,	Hardie, A. E.
403401	,,	Hare, F. T.		324483	,,	Hawkins, P. E.
323173	,,	Hobbs, C. S.		324483	,,	Hibberd, R. S.
326893	,,	Hornblow, K. A. G.		558168	,,	Holborn, W. J.
405811	L/Cpl.	Hutton, A.		548743	,,	Howse, R. E.
326895	Tpr.	Jessett, D. W.		550617	Sgt.	Hyde, A. F.
551828	,,	Jones, H.		552069	Tpr.	Jones.
551962	,,	King, C. F.		549149	Cpl.	Kendrick, F.
324474	,,	Lampard, E. H.		404752	Tpr.	Kingswell, H.
324477	,,	Lawrence, M. H.		406499	,,	Kermath, E.
550445	,,	Lester, J.		322780	,,	Lay, P. G.
324480	,,	Lloyd, W. J.		405338	,,	Lee, J. R.
402811	,,	Linfield, S.		557460	Cpl.	Little, A. G.
402006	,,	Mayo.		556419	,,	Lye, J.
548904	Cpl.	Manning, F. J.		769317	,,	Lowe, D.
551317	Sgt.	Marsh, F W J.		775659	Tpr.	Machin, G.
403407	Tpr.	Morris, J.		404743	Cpl.	Mannell, A.
558237	,,	Martin, F.		551616	Tpr.	Martland, F.
555802	,,	Mees, J.		556006	,,	Morris, D. H.
316836	Farr.	Nicola, G. F.		550080	Sgt	McLoughlin, J.
311862	Sgt.	Prime, G.		556148	Cpl.	Mitchell, I. S.
3568814	Cpl.	Palmer, F. C.		556886	Tpr.	Nutley, W. F.
556883	Tpr.	Park, R. J.		550577	Sgt.	Parkes, G.
548892	,,	Parslow.		557397	Tpr.	Paget, A. L.
556147	L/Cpl.	Pearce, E. W.		552857	Cpl.	Parker, G. H.
324462	Tpr.	Perry, J. T.		543049	Farr.	Pettit, R.
325554	,,	Pitman, A. J.		556952	Tpr.	Perrett, C. V.
556609	,,	Powell, V. J.		555336	Cpl.	Pictor, D. J.
556192	,,	Ponting, D. H.		547997	Farr./Sgt.	Platt, C. L.
323174	,,	Reynolds, S. R.		549833	Tpr.	Pope, G. W.
556613	,,	Razey, G.		554392	,,	Read, T.
324461	,,	Ritchens, E. W.		324475	,,	Rawlings, H. G.
324464	,,	Rudman, A. C.		556995	,,	Rickard, S.
3522456	,,	Smethurst, G.		362897	,,	Rowland, J. L.
543214	Cpl.	Smith, C.		324470	,,	Russ, N.
554653	,,	Selby, A. G.		552804	,,	Stocks, R.
552060	Tpr.	Simson, A.		322908	,,	Sawyer, L. R.
558436	,,	Smith, E. A.		326898	,,	Sims, R. G.
557953	,,	Smith, H. J.		1030029	Farr.	Skinner, A. L.
550085	Sgt.	Smith, W. T.		324486	Tpr.	Smith, D. E.
555310	Tpr.	Spreadbury, G.		554450	Cpl.	Smith, T. W.
553687	,,	Stark, T.		322546	Tpr.	Spackman, C.
555947	,,	Sweatman, F. C.		404688	,,	Stewart, D. L.
316583	,,	Thurlow, R.		405028	,,	Sutcliffe, J.
551042	,,	Turner, A. E.		553417	Cpl.	Teagle, A. E.
324467	,,	Wadman, R.		554837	L/Cpl.	Tucker, R. L.
549507	,,	Walker, T.		326900	Tpr.	Vidler, A. D.
324488	,,	Wey, R. A.		324469	,,	Watts, E. E.
553781	,,	White, T.		556884	Cpl.	Wenham, R. S.
556887	,,	Wiltshire, L.		398926	Tpr.	Waterhouse, A.
544527	,,	Wordley, H. W.		557568	,,	Whittle, S. T.
553418	Cpl.	Worsdell, L. V.		324473	,,	Woolley, R. F.
557465	Tpr.	Wood, A. B.		322778	,,	Worsdell, A. E.
352611	,,	Webb, F.		557463	,,	Woods, R. L.
				550588	,,	Woods, J.

"C" SQUADRON.

553541	Tpr.	Archard, S.		404445	Tpr.	Arnold, C.
404679	,,	Allen, H.		406075	Cpl.	Bumford, D.
403653	L/Cpl.	Bush, J.		540136	Tpr.	Baker, B. R. H.
326839	Tpr.	Baker, E. S.		326852	,,	Browning, N.
324551	,,	Batt, K.		324550	,,	Barnes, S. A.
552195	,,	Banks, J.		557678	,,	Bannister, D.

557681	Tpr.	Bleaken, R.	324493	Tpr.	Bridle, P. T. M.
803340	,,	Buckley, R.	404775	,,	Baggott, A. E.
404786	,,	Bonehill, J.	405472	,,	Barham, A. W.
405402	,,	Bayliss, T.	768780	,,	Brogan, D.
403509	,,	Baxter, L.	318712	,,	Baker, G.
398881	,,	Berry, T.	405437	,,	Cooper, A.
545599	S.S.M.	Carter, N. K.	392064	F/Sgt.	Coots, D.
556880	Tpr.	Cull, K.	556581	Tpr.	Carvey, W. E.
399144	L/Cpl.	Cook, J. L.	324553	,,	Carter, S.
324549	Tpr.	Clarke, E.	324528	,,	Christopher, R. F.
522617	,,	Clayfield, R. E. J.	318700	,,	Collett, A.
324125	,,	Crump, M.	323073	,,	Cross, R.
545738	,,	Carter, T. W.	556585	,,	Clothier, R. E.
324525	,,	Caple, G.	327014	,,	Cooper, R.
555976	Tptr.	Connor, G. S.	403405	,,	Clarke, E.
403445	Tpr.	Calcutt, N.	405351	,,	Clayden, W.
3905395	Farr.	Clifford.	553152	Sgt.	Drury, D.
324594	Tpr.	Davies, W. E.	324531	Tpr.	Dash, D.
553381	,,	Deacon, F. G.	558215	,,	Daw, H.
607719	,,	Dawson.	768612	,,	Dunthorne, A.
550628	,,	Davies, W.	324057	Tptr.	Eyres.
556814	,,	Ferris, C.	326851	,,	Frayling, J.
6340432	,,	Fayers, A.	555420	Cpl.	Greenhill, F.
556860	Cpl.	Greer, F.	556815	,,	Godsell, L.
322619	Tpr.	Gazzard, D.	324526	Tpr.	Goddard, P.
324530	,,	Garne, W.	324547	,,	Gunter, F.
553151	,,	Guest, G. F.	552012	,,	Giles.
546257	Sgt.	Harding, V. S.	553426	Cpl.	Honeybone, O.
554226	Tpr.	Hedges, J.	326840	Tpr.	Hunt, P. A.
556149	,,	Haynes, J.	557680	,,	Hatherell, W. T.
310715	Farr.	Horton.	421384	Farr.	Hall, S. T.
323076	Tpr.	Hoskins, E. C.	402047	Tpr.	Harrison, T.
317107	,,	Harding, T.	748144	,,	Johns, W.
405049	,,	Jackson, H.	553833	L/Sgt.	Knapp, M.
553150	Cpl.	Knight, C. H. E.	404756	Tpr.	Kelly, A.
557518	Tpr.	Lovelle, A.	406698	,,	McNair, H.
310931	Cpl.	Linfield, H. F.	407506	,,	Moore, J.
6978342	Tpr.	Murphy, H.	534447	T.S.M.	McGough, W.
405991	Cpl.	MacDonald, E.	324542	Tpr.	Myers, W. W.
556131	Tpr.	McNally, L.	405063	,,	Monk, J. W.
2211347	,,	MacDonald, D.	326843	,,	Newcombe.
556831	,,	Nash, L.	552621	,,	Nelson, J. C.
463410	,,	Osborne.	324540	,,	Ockwell, E.
557406	,,	Oakley, H.	316646	Cpl.	Peterkin, J.
549312	Cpl.	Palmer, L.	522620	Tpr.	Potter, W. P.
557677	Tpr.	Pound, J.	557679	,,	Parker, A. J. D.
551522	,,	Powell, H.	556581	,,	Punter, J.
326964	,,	Pike, H.	405491	,,	Pressley.
402276	,,	Potter, I.	405001	,,	Pritchard.
405427	,,	Pattinson, J.	405263	,,	Parkin, W.
547755	Sgt.	Peppiatt, S.	543221	Sgt.	Pearson, H.
549759	Cpl.	Powell, R.	550653	Cpl.	Randall, H. J.
550641	S.Q.M.S.	Rhodes, J.	403458	,,	Reeves, E. R.
557428	Tpr.	Ricketts, P. R.	406595	Tpr.	Redwood.
542973	,,	Repton, H.	318699	,,	Rendell, V.
316782	,,	Redman, C.	776241	Sgt.	Thorn, A.
324126	,,	Soper, L.	549505	L/Cpl.	Toll, R.
4535672	,,	Simpson.	324537	Tpr.	Thorne, C.
318758	,,	Strachan, D.	744651	,,	Thickett, C.
557654	,,	Shipton, A.	407096	,,	Turner, G. F.
548632	Cpl.	Stanton, J.	556584	,,	Tanner, A.
5566226	Cpl.	Truckle, J.	318766	,,	Taylor, J. M.
402650	L/Cpl.	Thompson.	318695	,,	Smart, L.
1037567	Farr.	Tilley, H.	324535	,,	Sturmey, K.
552019	Tpr.	Thompson, F.	326948	,,	Steel, T. H. G.
552926	,,	Tarlton, J.	324532	,,	Smith, D.
317015	,,	Thorpe, J.	405024	,,	Scott, W.

554838	Tpr.	Thompson, D.		552331	Cpl.	Smith, T.
322120	Sgt.	Underdown, C. E.		553025	Tpr.	Vincent, A. A.
555472	Sadd./Cpl.	Wilkins, S.		760775	Cpl.	Willett, L. I. A.
326853	Tpr.	Willis, N.		556879	Tpr.	Wickenden, E. K.
556150	,,	Woodward, D.		322002	,,	Walcroft, E. J.
324554	,,	Westmacott, M.		324071	,,	Woodman, E.
324073	,,	Webb, W.		324072	,,	Wheeler, V.
322006	,,	Wilks, T.		318713	,,	Webb, E. G.
555437	,,	White, W.		545549	,,	Willoughby, W.
557461	,,	Williams, S. R.		557653	,,	Wilkins, M.
817489	,,	Wade, D.		405107	,,	Wilson, C.
548708	,,	Wilson, T.		404511	,,	Webb, J.
5674804	,,	Wilkins, S. P. G.		723784	,,	White.
398239	,,	Yates.				

REAR PARTY.

Major O. St. M. Thynne.   Lt. C. R. C. Thursfield.
2nd Lt. W. J. Ewart.

"H.Q." SQUADRON.

324053	Tpr.	Baker, R. L.		558098	Tpr.	Francis, H.
557442	L/Cpl.	Muspratt, R. G.		558243	,,	Redsull, S. W.
544843	Tpr.	Wheeler, A.				

"A" SQUADRON.

405864	Tpr.	Brown, J.		3049629	Sgt.	Burnett, T.
552541	,,	Fantham, T.		780434	Tpr.	Finnis, A. H.
555939	,,	Goddard, E.		415810	,,	Harrison, J. E.
546788	,,	Potter, R.		402623	Farr.	Rippon, N.
5494701	,,	Withers, A.		549846	Tpr.	Young, J.

"B" SQUADRON.

556358	Tpr.	Budds, F. G.		554757	Cpl.	Baker, A.
324487	,,	Bewley, D.		326892	Tpr.	Fay, P. G.
6395867	,,	Giddings, J. W.		326896	,,	Mason, A. A.
557399	,,	Norman, L. F.		398878	,,	Whittaker, M.
325551	,,	Welch, A. E.		550738	Farr.	Wingfield.

"C" SQUADRON.

404732	Tpr.	Boushear, T.		775733	Cpl.	Heath, A. E.
324548	,,	Haines, J. H. F.		405482	Tpr.	Harrison.
7812139	,,	Jones, H.		402890	,,	Newman, C.
326975	,,	Simpkins, L. V.		811213	,,	Smith, H.
314884	Cpl.	Upson.				

NOMINAL ROLL OF REINFORCEMENTS RECEIVED, AUTUMN, 1940.

327934	Tpr.	Ahern, M. F.		328591	Tpr.	Attwell, P.
328029	,,	Burns, J.		328209	,,	Bolton, C. E.
328703	,,	Bunday, F.		328997	,,	Bendon, J. W.
378007	,,	Brown, C. J.		328167	,,	Brown, L.
327547	,,	Bayes, F.		327811	,,	Bowman, F.
552332	,,	Comely, W. J.		6802864	,,	Carlisle, L. A.
328053	,,	Dawson, W. W.		328048	,,	Collins, R.
327480	..	Davis, A.		388112	,,	Coyne, S.
328061	,,	Evans, R.		327629	,,	Domoney, C.
326944	,,	Frost, A. E.		327824	,,	Davies, D.
398230	Cpl.	Follows, T. A.		328230	,,	Dunn, W. A.
328245	Tpr.	Gray, K. T.		328765	,,	Fagan, D. G.
328260	,,	Harding, T. S.		327508	,,	Flocton, E.
328253	,,	Ham, H.		327506	,,	Gilpin, L.
327748	,,	Jesson, A.		327974	,,	Green, E. W.
328034	,,	Laycock, J. C.		410383	,,	Henderson, W.
327484	,,	Mead, D.		327991	,,	Heywood, D.
328092	,,	Messham, J.		327183	,,	Littlewood, J.

328827	Tpr.	McGaw, H. S.		328275	Tpr.	Lovelle, E. M.
558067	,,	Nurdin, F.		555239	,,	Metcalfe, T.
327988	,,	Newton, L.		328090	,,	Moloney, M.
551914	Sgt.	Paviour, J.		327936	,,	Morrison, J.
328909	Tpr.	Parker, J. C.		406785	,,	McLaggan, J.
410427	,,	Robertson, G. E.		328416	,,	Prince, C.
840466	,,	Ruane, J.		328707	,,	Petts, J. V.
437965	,,	Stafford, A. R.		329305	,,	Pooley, S. A.
328803	,,	Stephenson, K.		328605	,,	Royce, A. E.
328104	,,	Sweeting, J. W.		327990	,,	Smart, C. R.
327986	,,	Strong, J.		328721	,,	Stanton, M. C.
327895	,,	Sedgewick, H.		7341193	,,	Stewart, J.
328139	,,	Templeton, G.		328317	L/Cpl.	Stockley, E. R.
328445	,,	Wilson, C. W.		327472	Tpr.	Smith, R. F.
327994	,,	Walsh, G.		328441	,,	Turner, E. F.
328109	,,	Weekes, J. J.		327516	,,	Winfield, S. E.
410068	Farr.	Winks, J. A.		328116	,,	Walls, L. T.
				328458	L/Cpl.	Waud, H.
				2758940	Tpr.	White, O. L.

HONOURS AND AWARDS.

D.S.O.

Major M. St. J. V. Gibbs	Alamein.
Major The Hon. A. E. G. Herbert	Italy.
Lt.-Col. S. L. Lloyd	Italy.

M.C.

Major H. Blount	Alamein.
Capt. The Earl Cadogan	Alamein.
Lt. W. J. Ewart	Alamein.
Lt. A. B. W. Pennell	Alamein.

M.B.E.

546127 R.S.M. Pike, R. E. J.

B.E.M.

7585541 S/Sgt. Eastlake, G. B., R.E.M.E. (Armourer).

M.M.

324515	Tpr. Bath, E. L.	Syria.
322765	Cpl. Egremont, D. S.	Syria.
557680	Tpr. Hatherell, W. T.	Syria.
547090	L/Cpl. Mount, A.	Alamein.
547755	S.S.M. Peppiatt, S. H.	Alamein.
403972	Sgt. Richards, S. G.	Alamein.
811213	L/Cpl. Smith, H.	Alamein.
324071	Sgt. Woodman, E.	Italy.

MENTIONED IN DESPATCHES.

	Lt. H. G. Awdry	Syria.
	Capt. G. S. Wills	Italy.
	Capt. D. W. P. Bluett	Italy.
	Lt. P. Brittlebank	Italy.
557429	Cpl. Davies, K. A. W.	Mersah Matruh.
	Lt. M. St. J. V. Gibbs	Syria.
405402	Tpr. Bayliss, T.	Syria.
405437	L/Cpl. Cooper, A.	Syria.
310930	Cpl. Linfield, H.	Syria.
811213	Tpr. Smith, H.	Syria.
553105	Sgt. Knight, C. H. E.	Italy.
326911	Sgt. Legg, A.	Italy.
324052	Sgt. Smart, E. P.	Italy.
547703	Cpl. Hazell, A.	Italy.

G.O.C.-IN-C. CERTIFICATE, EASTERN COMMAND.

	Major R. S. Walker.	
	Capt. G. S. Wills.	
405472	Sgt. Barham, A. W.	
555352	Sgt. Scott, M. W. A.	

Honours and Awards to members of the Royal Wiltshire Yeomanry whilst employed on extra-regimental duties.*

Lt.-Col. Morgan Evans	M.B.E.
Major The Viscount Weymouth, T.D.	American Bronze and Silver Star.
Lt. F. Wetherley	M.C.
Tpr. Cave	M.M.
Tpr. Worsdell	M.M.
Lt.-Col. P. W. Pitt, T.D.	Mentioned in Despatches (twice). Commendation Card.
Lt.-Col. O. St. M. Thynne, T.D.	Mentioned in Despatches.
Lt.-Col. H. Hunloke	Mentioned in Despatches (twice) Commendation Card.
Lt.-Col. Morgan Evans	Mentioned in Depatches.
Major Maurice Knapp	Mentioned in Despatches.
R.Q.M.S. Golden	Mentioned in Despatches.
S.S.M. (Late Bandmaster) D. Price	Mentioned in Despatches.
Tpr. Cave	Mentioned in Despatches.

* This list is not complete.

(1). TOBRUK AND SYRIA.

KILLED IN ACTION.

Tobruk.

407133	Tpr.	Marsden, J. R. G.	... ...	30.5.41

Syria.

324455	Tpr.	Holmes, J. S.	... ...	21.6.41
540538	,,	Mawson, J.	... ...	22.6.41
324593	,,	Hoddinott, J. L.	... ...	30.6.41
557595	,,	Golding, W.	... ...	1.7.41
398935	,,	Reeves, W. F.	... ...	30.6.41
555353	Cpl.	Brake, E. J.	... ...	30.6.41

DIED OF WOUNDS.

Syria.

3958314	Tpr.	Williams, H. L.	... ...	25.6.41
324515	,,	Bath, E. L.	... ...	26.6.41
415810	,,	Harrison, J. E.	... ...	4.7.41

(2). WESTERN DESERT.

KILLED IN ACTION.

322781	Cpl.	Brown, T. A.	... ...	24.10.42
7892014	Tpr.	Garlick, R. F.	... ...	20.10.42
556359	L/Sgt.	Jeffries, C. H.	... ...	20.10.42
557460	Sgt.	Little, A. G.	... ...	20.10.42
326975	Tpr.	Simpkins, L. V.	... ...	20.10.42
7938183	,,	Greenway, H.	... ...	20.10.42
4611897	,,	Sedgewick, H.	... ...	20.10.42
4799053	L/Cpl.	Francis, A. W.	... ...	20.10.42
556861	Tpr.	Harris, P. V.	... ...	20.10.42
328109	,,	Weekes, J. J.	... ...	20.10.42
85579	Lt.	J. R. H. Hornby	... ...	2.11.42
189033	2nd Lt.	T. H. Elsom	... ...	2.11.42
200636	,,	R. C. Boyd-Smith	... ...	2.11.42
557673	L/Cpl.	Burt, W. H.	... ...	2.11.42
327480	Tpr.	Davis, A.	... ...	2.11.42
556250	,,	Fido, H. S.	... ...	2.11.42
557340	,,	Hughes, A. W.	... ...	2.11.42
311780	,,	Lay, P. G.	... ...	2.11.42
326879	,,	Lodge, P. W. W.	... ...	2.11.42
553352	Sgt.	Pickford, H. S.	... ...	2.11.42
3242961	Tpr.	Sally, J.	... ...	2.11.42
7951524	,,	Shipman, R. E.	... ...	2.11.42
553413	Sgt.	Waters, H. E.	... ...	2.11.42
327994	Tpr.	Walsh, G.	... ...	2.11.42
556884	L/Sgt.	Wenham, R. S.	... ...	2.11.42

DIED OF WOUNDS.

5723784	L/Cpl.	White, G.	... ...	7.11.42
546788	Tpr.	Potter, R.	... ...	21.11.42
324460	,,	Saunderson, R.	... ...	11.12.42
327484	L/Cpl.	Mead, D.	... ...	11.12.42
322956	Tpr.	Thorne, J.	... ...	11.12.42
557592	,,	Jones, M.		

DIED WHILE P.O.W.

556434	L/Sgt.	Luff, M. G.	

(3). ITALY.

KILLED IN ACTION.

7932904	Tpr.	Wales, M. W.	31.5.44
554331	Cpl.	Lakey, D. E.	2.6.44
5779549	Tpr.	Chittock, W. J.	16.6.44
547090	L/Cpl.	Mount, A. T.	17.6.44
4752660	Tpr.	Titmuss, W. L.	19.6.44
555221	,,	Cottrell, P.	20.6.44
3458675	,,	Hodson, T.	20.6.44
558141	Cpl.	Hinton, G. E.	25.6.44
555310	Tpr.	Spreadbury, G. F.	27.6.44
169940	Lt.	D. F. Gilliat	1.8.44
72231	Capt.	The Marquis of Lansdowne	20.8.44
7901837	Tpr.	Gray, T.	

DIED WHILE P.O.W.

7949648	Tpr.	Long, R.

DIED OF WOUNDS.

279304	Lt.	F. B. Buckle	26.7.44
326877	L/Cpl.	Harris, J.	18.6.44

MIDDLE EAST.

DIED FROM NATURAL CAUSES.

	Lt.	N. K. Carter	1941
	Lt.	S. D. James	1941
550545	Sgt.	Chambers, R. G.	1941
405153	Tpr.	Haywood	1940
553819	,,	Slade, F.	1943
318712	,,	Baker, E. G.	1943
420241	,,	Lindsay, T.	1943
556461	,,	Mason, J. E.	1941
553762	,,	Pratten, S. J.	1939 (England)
	,,	Stephens	
	,,	Morris, L.	

CONGRATULATORY MESSAGES.

The following documents are included as a Regimental record :—

SPECIAL ORDER OF THE DAY.
by
Brigadier J. C. CURRIE, D.S.O., M.C.

On leaving 9th Armoured Brigade, my chief regret is that I have been ordered to do so at such short notice that I am unable to come round and say good-bye and good luck to all my friends.

It has been a great honour, of which I have been extremely proud, to have commanded this Brigade ; we have been through stirring times together, and more lie ahead of you. You have made a name for yourselves which is second to none in the M.E.F., and I know that when you are called upon again you will produce the same form, and lucky indeed will be the man who commands you when that time comes. But you must work now and think only of the day when you go into action and of what will be asked of you then. From wherever I may be I shall watch the future of the 9th Armoured Brigade with affection and with the keenest interest.

From the bottom of my heart I want to say Thank You, every one of you, for the loyal support that you have given me, for your great courage which enabled us to break the line at Alamein, and for your cheerful spirits.

I hope that we shall meet again some day. Good luck, and God bless you all.

(Signed) J. C. CURRIE, Brigadier.
Commanding 9th Armoured Brigade Group.

20th February, 1943.

SPECIAL ORDER OF THE DAY.

3rd June, 1944.

On June 4th, 1794, one hundred and fifty years ago, the Regiment was formed at Devizes. It is fitting that an anniversary such as this should come at a time when the name and reputation of the regiment has never stood higher. You have fought these last five days a hard and difficult action, the results of which have been outstanding. You have been the spearhead of the Eighth Army attack, and I have been congratulated on the magnificent performance you have put up. It is a sad day for me, as I am leaving you. We have had many good scraps together, and I look forward to the day, which I hope is not far distant, when we shall have a reunion in England. I thank you for the help and support which you have never failed to give, and I wish you, until we meet again, the best of luck and a speedy return to your homes.

A. M. GIBB, Lieut.-Colonel.
Commanding Royal Wiltshire Yeomanry.

EXTRACT TAKEN FROM REGIMENTAL ORDERS DATED 8th SEPTEMBER, 1944.

2. Appreciation.

The following message has been received by the Commanding Officer from Lieut.-General Sir Richard L. McCreery, K.C.B., D.S.O., M.B.E., M.C., Commander 10 Corps.

" Now that the time has come when you will be no longer operating as a complete unit, I want to take the opportunity of congratulating All Ranks on the first-class show everyone has put up whilst in 10 Corps.

All have shown enterprise, determination and initiative, and have done their utmost to give whole-hearted support to the infantry in the most difficult country.

A good finish to a fine record of service overseas in this war. If the Germans survive till then, I know that the regiment will play a prominent part in the final phase.

All good wishes and the very best of good luck to All Ranks.

(Signed) R. L. McCREERY."

Confidential and Secret.

10 CORPS.
SPECIAL MESSAGE FROM THE CORPS COMMANDER.
To All Ranks, 9th Armoured Brigade.

I take this opportunity, when 9th Armoured Brigade is leaving 10 Corps, to congratulate All Ranks on their good work. In most difficult enclosed or mountainous country, you have always done your utmost to support the infantry, with most successful results.

All Ranks have shown determination, skill, and a willing spirit of co-operation.

We all remember the gallant and decisive part which 9th Armoured Brigade played on 2nd November, 1942, in the great victory of Alamein, when the smashing of the strong German anti-tank gun screen that morning enabled the irresistible advance of the Armoured Divisions of 10 Corps to start.

To-day, under vastly different conditions in Italy, you have shown the same fine fighting spirit.

All good luck and success in the future.

(Signed) R. L. McCREERY,
Commander, 10 Corps.

18*th September*, 1944.

Confidential and Secret.

TOPSEC(.) Personal to Colonel Lloyd, Commanding Wiltshire Yeomanry from Leese(.) On the return of the Wiltshire Yeomanry to England I send my thanks and best wishes to all ranks on their leaving the Eighth Army(.) I well remember your great fight with the New Zealanders at Alamein in 1942(.) In this campaign you have done valuable work in the fighting round Lake Trasimene and in your advance in the Upper Tiber Valley(.) I wish the Regiment every success in the future.

20*th September*, 1944.

Headquarters,
2 N.Z. Division,
2 N.Z.E.F., C.M.F.
22*nd November,* 1944.

Lieut.-Col. Ian Lloyd, D.S.O.,
Royal Wiltshire Yeomanry,
Trowbridge,
Wilts,
England.

My Dear Lloyd,

Your charming letter of 30th September, written on the eve of your departure from Italy, has been left unanswered for a long time; not because we were in any doubts but because I have been away from the Division after being injured in an aeroplane smash.

Yesterday I sent you and the Warwickshire Yeomanry a messages answering your question. Needless to say, we will be very proud to know you are continuing to wear the fernleaf as a reminder of Alamein days together. We have served with many formations and units during this war. No association was happier than that between the Officers and men of the 9th Armoured Brigade and ours in the difficult days at Miteiriya Ridge and in the battle to break out. Those of us who saw your magnificent attack at dawn on the morning of the 2nd November will never forget it. Your gallant advance that morning, though at great cost, broke the gun line and was the turning point in one of the most decisive battles of the war. We are all very proud of the " honorary New Zealanders " of the 9th Armoured Brigade who were members of the 2nd New Zealand Division, and on behalf of all ranks I send the Royal Wiltshire Yeomanry our best wishes.

With every good wish to you all for the future.

Yours sincerely,

B. C. FREYBERG.

27th November, 1944.

MEMORANDUM FOR:
THE COMMANDING OFFICER,
ROYAL WILTSHIRE YEOMANRY,
MALMESBURY,
WILTS.

The following message has been received for you from Lieut.-General Sir B. C. Freyberg, V.C. :—

" We will be delighted if you wear the Fernleaf as reminder of our happy association and your gallant exploits at Alamein. Kindest regards and best wishes from us all. Writing."

SPECIAL ORDER OF THE DAY.

LIEUT.-COLONEL S. L. LLOYD, D.S.O., COMMANDING ROYAL WILTSHIRE YEOMANRY.

8th May, 1945.

At the close of the war with Germany, I send all ranks of R.W.Y. my very best wishes. They can be well satisfied with the part each one of them has played to help bring about this successful conclusion. I am sure that the Regiment will not wish to forget the relatives and friends of those of our comrades who have laid down their lives, and I have sent to all next-of-kin a letter in the following terms :—

" Now that the war against Germany is over and while the Allied victory is being celebrated, I write to you on behalf of the Royal Wiltshire Yeomanry to tell you how much at this time our thoughts turn to the relations and friends of those men who gave their lives for their country while serving with the Regiment.

" We join with you in proud and grateful remembrance."

(Signed) S. L. LLOYD, Lieut.-Colonel,
Commanding Royal Wiltshire Yeomanry.

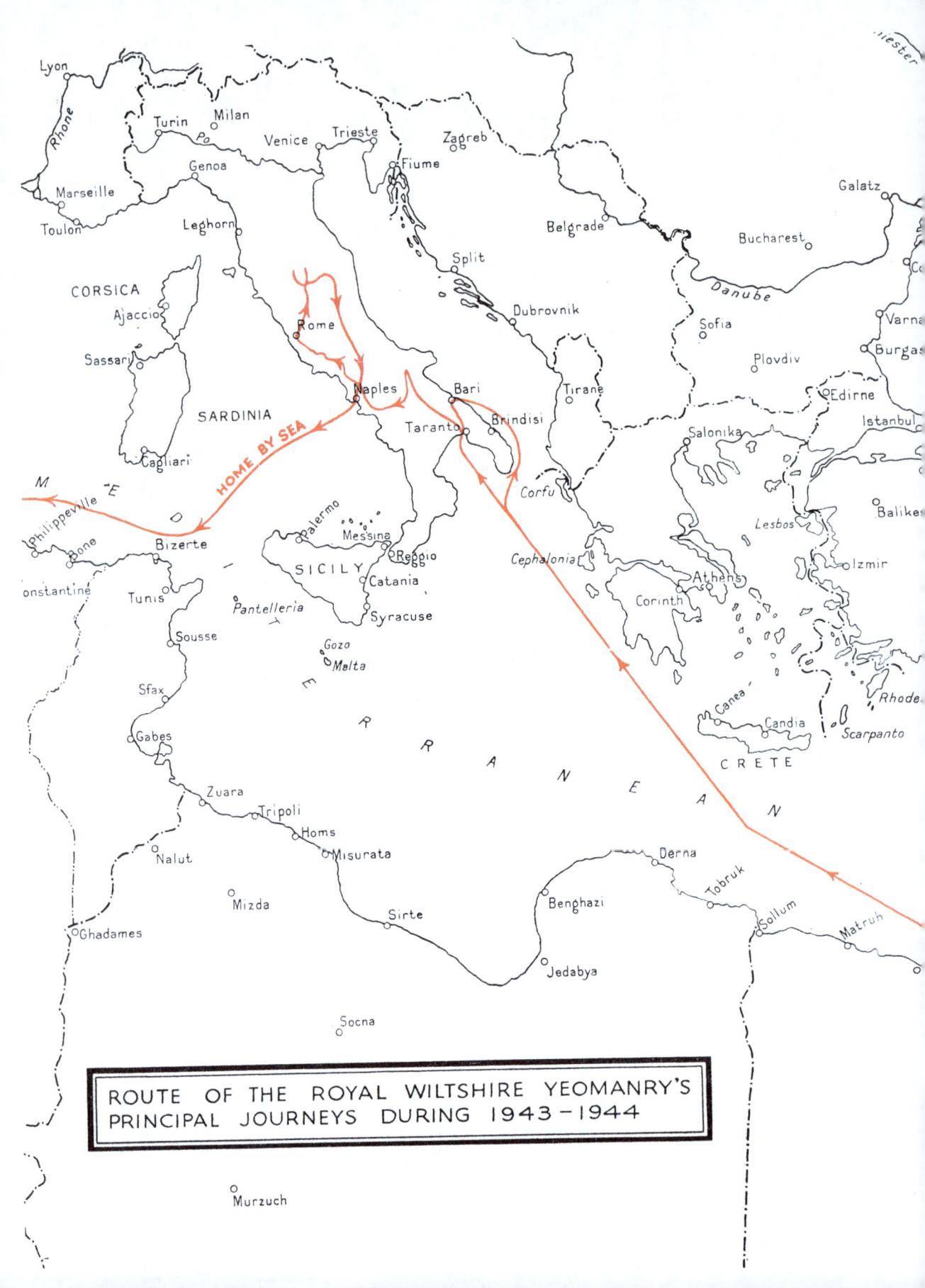

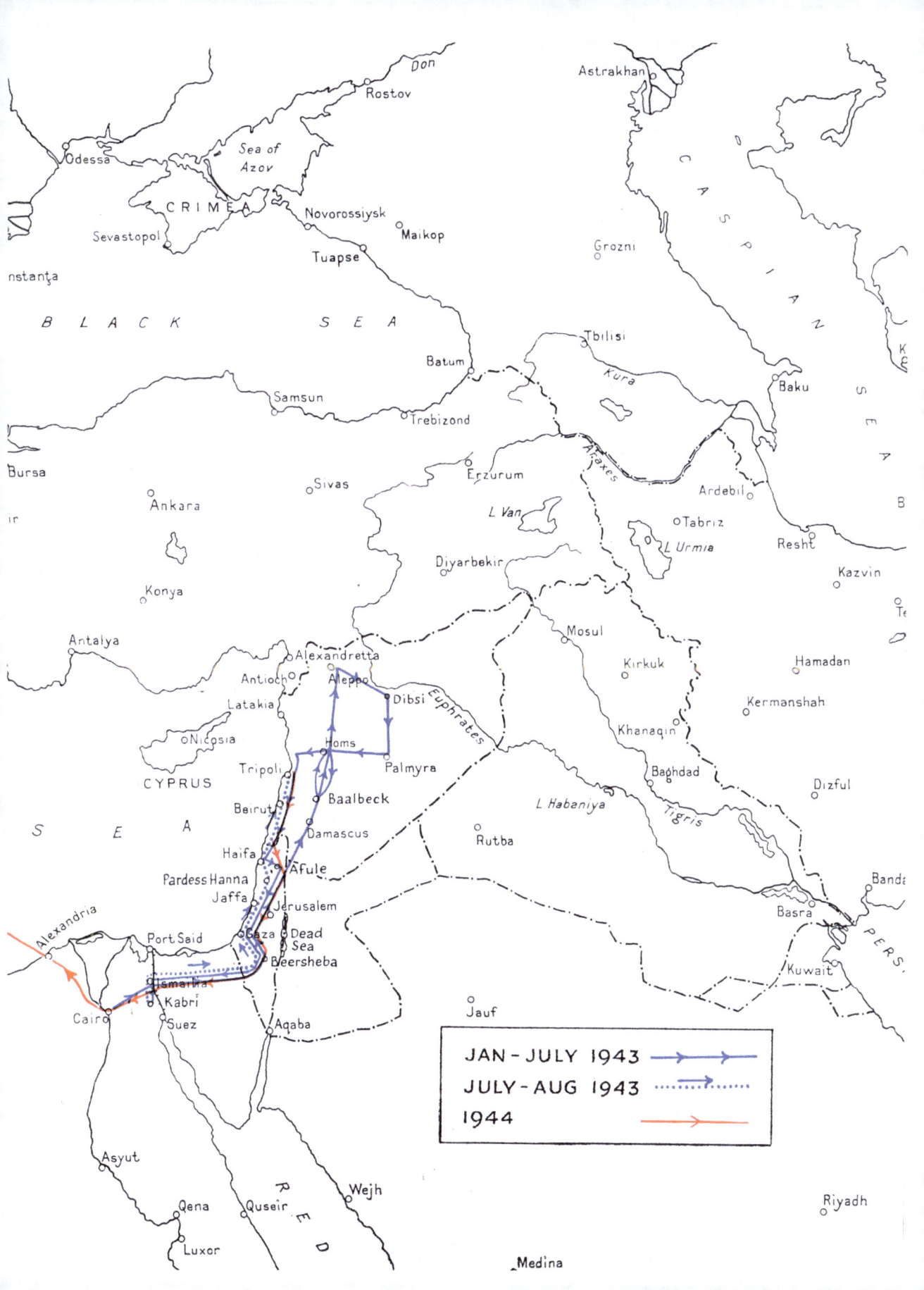

www.ingramcontent.com/pod-product-compliance
Lightning Source LLC
Chambersburg PA
CBHW060337010526
44117CB00017B/2867